T0391658

A FORTIFIED FAR RIGHT?

Petho-Kiss and Gunaratna understand the nature of the threat posed by the far right because of their findings and they propose effective provisions and mechanisms for detecting and countering it.

The book undertakes a consistent procession and empirical examination of available information to arrive at the recognition that in order to dissolve the complexity of the associated threat, we need to scrutinize the functioning of far-right threat groups. In-depth and consistent analysis on their mode of operation and mindset enables us to identify ways to detect and counter their malicious efforts and activities. The theoretical framework for the analysis lies upon the concept of wave theory. The main question that this book examines is whether far-right terrorism constitutes a new wave of global terrorism. One question emerges from this statement that requires further elaboration. Is far right terrorism a novel wave of terrorism? If yes, how is it novel and what are the novelties or developments in it?

This book is for scholars as well as practitioners in the counter-terrorism (CT) and the prevention/countering violent extremism (PCVE) field. Through specific case studies students studying CT and/or PCVE could gain insight into the operational functionalities of far-right threat groups. This may help them to get a more accurate understanding of the threat posed by these entities. Examining the recruitment, funding, communication practices, and modus operandi of worrisome threat actors equips us to design the most effective countermeasures and identify the hiatuses in applicable legislative regimes.

Katalin Petho-Kiss is a senior fellow at the Global Peace Institute and Senior Security Policy Analyst at the Counter Terrorism Information and Criminal

Analysis Centre in Hungary. As a recipient of an Endeavour Scholarship, she holds a Master of Research Studies in Policing, Intelligence, and Countering Terrorism at Macquarie University, Australia.

Rohan Gunaratna is Professor of Security Studies at the S. Rajaratnam School of International Studies, Nanyang Technology University, Singapore. He is the author of 30 books including *Inside al Qaeda: Global Network of Terror* (University of Columbia Press) and most recently, *Sri Lanka's Easter Sunday Massacre – Lessons for the International Community* (Penguin-Random House).

A FORTIFIED FAR RIGHT?

Scrutinizing the Threat

Katalin Petho-Kiss and Rohan Gunaratna

LONDON AND NEW YORK

Designed cover image: © Getty Images/Images_By_Kenny

First published 2024
by Routledge
4 Park Square, Milton Park, Abingdon, Oxon OX14 4RN

and by Routledge
605 Third Avenue, New York, NY 10158

Routledge is an imprint of the Taylor & Francis Group, an informa business

British Library Cataloguing-in-Publication Data
A catalogue record for this book is available from the British Library

ISBN: 9781032708034 (hbk)
ISBN: 9781032708058 (pbk)
ISBN: 9781032708041 (ebk)

DOI: 10.4324/9781032708041

Typeset in Galliard
by Newgen Publishing UK

CONTENTS

FIGURES

TABLES

1

FAR-RIGHT VIOLENCE

A new wave of global terrorism?

Far-right-inspired political violence is increasingly seen as a growing transnational threat. In its 2020 Global Terrorism Index Report the Institute of Economics and Peace[1] claimed that right-wing extremist violence tends to be not as lethal as Islamist terrorism in the West. Even though between 2002 and 2014, the far right accounted for not more than 14% of annual terror attacks in Western countries, this had risen to 46% in 2018.[2]

The absolute number of far-right attacks remains lower when compared with other forms of terrorism. Nevertheless, in North America, Western Europe, and Oceania the occurrence of far-right incidents has risen by 250% since 2014, with death increasing by 709% in the same period. In 2019, in total, 89 of the 108 deaths from terrorism in the West were perpetrated by far-right extremists.[3] In February 2020, FBI director testified, that "racially/ethnically motivated violence is the top threat we face from domestic violent extremists".[4] After the Hanau attack, German interior minister warned that right-wing extremism is "the greatest threat to security in Germany".[5]

In contrast to these reports, according to the Right-Wing Terrorism and Violence (RTV) dataset (C-REX), 2020 was "among the five years with least fatal attacks since 1990".[6] This is in line with the declining trend in the number of fatal attacks occurred in Western Europe. It is also notable that "since 2001, the number of fatal attacks per year was relatively stable with an average of five fatal attacks per year, thereby placing 2020 below average".[7] Reportedly, 2021 was "the third least violent year since 2015 [...]it was among the three least violent years since 1990".[8]

DOI: 10.4324/9781032708041-1

It has been established that right-wing extremism and terrorism are mostly dominant in the Western world, more specifically in North America, Europe, Australia, and New Zealand. Nonetheless, there are initial indications that far-right ideologies are not limited to the West. In Singapore, a 16-year-old boy was the first detainee on 27 January 2021 inspired by far-right extremist ideology. He was arrested for planning to attack Muslims with a knife in two nearby mosques on the Christchurch attacks' anniversary. Inspired by Brenton Tarrant, the detained boy intended to livestream his offending.[9] Another noteworthy instance is India, where Hindu nationalists see Islamist extremism as an existential threat to the nation.[10] They have been using the internet to spread their ideology and support for Prime Minister Narendra Modi, who is regarded as one of "the mainstream faces of the global far right".[11] In the referred Western countries, the threat posed by the far right seems to supplant Muslim extremism. This does not mean, however, that Islamist violent extremists do not require special attention. Notably, Islamist attackers were held accountable for both the murder of French teacher Samuel Paty[12] and the Vienna shooting[13] in 2020.

Numerous driving factors may shape this current threat landscape in the future. First, although the long-term impact of the COVID-19 is yet to be seen, the crisis has been capitalized by far-right groups worldwide.[14] Novel circumstances created by the pandemic were crucial in establishing a fertile ground for an elevated level of radicalization. At the same time, right-wing extremist participants in lockdown protests were resorting to more aggressive behavior. According to the Global Terrorism Index 2020, in the past decade the number of politically motivated attacks increased, whereas the incidents of religious background declined.[15] This trend may be further accelerated due to the severe economic consequences the pandemic resulted in.

Second, the Russian-Ukrainian conflict may also have a relevant impact on far-right movements. Historically, the rebel forces during the Syrian civil war attracted thousands of foreign jihadists.[16] Getting to the conflict area was considered as the "fourth wave" of jihadist travelling.[17] These volunteer fighters "increase the intensity, duration, and complexity of conflicts and may constitute a serious danger to their States of origin, transit, destination, as well as neighboring zones of armed conflict in which they are active".[18] The resurgence of violent extremists in conflict zones "poses regional and global national security threats".[19] At the same time, joining Syrian jihadist groups was an essential part of radical agendas disseminated among potential recruits.[20] Terrorist and violent extremist groups around the world have uttered about the Russian-Ukrainian war in their propaganda, some of them also participated in the conflict as combatants. There are persistent uncertainties regarding the ongoing war's complex mid- and long-term consequences on a future international violent extremist threat.

Third, incidents suggest that supporters of the far right are ready to resort to violence. Considering that far-right extremists stormed the US Capitolium and some months earlier the German,[21] the threat can be regarded as global. Additionally, events of other far-right actions or future jihadist attacks could inspire new waves of right-wing violence. As we have seen several copycat attacks after the Christchurch shootings,[22] anti-Muslim incidents swept across the United Kingdom in the aftermath of the murder of Lee Rigby.[23]

Trends in far-right violence were also in the focus of scholarly research. To begin with, Ravndal and Bjørgo's (2018) analysis investigated "how research on terrorism and violence from the extreme right has evolved over the past two decades".[24] The mediatory role of social media was a primary subject of academic research projects. In line with this, Crosset et al. (2019) through qualitative indicators recontextualized Twitter users' profiles and analyzed "how digital traces participate in providing far right ideas with a wider representation".[25] Likewise, Miller's work (2019) scrutinizes whether social media plays a crucial role in establishing a blurred line between domestic and international terrorism.[26] Similarly, Carter and Kondor (2020) examined "how traditional quantitative and qualitative measures can be applied and extended to the online, and used to access hard-to-reach participants and communities"[27] of the far right. Steinek and Zetinigg (2020) critically examined "the mechanisms and impact of extremist propaganda on the Internet". They delineated the frames and identity concepts available online "as they occur in radicalization processes among individuals who are in some way engaged in Islamist and right-wing extremist scenes".[28]

In parallel, the complexity of the far-right-related threat was addressed by scholarly works. Ashe's (2021) research provides an in-depth "discussion about the methodological, ethical, political, personal, practical and professional issues and challenges that arise when researching far-right parties, their electoral support, and far right protest movements".[29] Meanwhile Doering and Davies (2021) investigated the applicability of indicators established by macro-level criminological theories to the study of right-wing terrorism. More specifically these indexes are related to immigration, economic conditions, and social demographic composition.[30] The aim of Holbrook and Macklin's (2022) work was to offer a guide on the complexity of elements that constitute right-wing extremism.[31]

Novel concepts were introduced and applied to better understand the phenomenon of extreme right-wing violence. For instance, Allchorn and Dafnos (2020) studied the actions of the British far-right "through the presentation of a new "Far-right mobilisations in Great Britain" (FRGB) protest events dataset that has mapped protest actions during this heightened period of far-right street activism (2009–2019)".[32] Meanwhile Scrivens et al. (2020) applied a "sentiment analysis-based algorithm that adapts criminal career measures, as well as semi-parametric group-based modeling, to evaluate how users' anti-Semitic, anti-Black, and anti-LGBTQ posting behaviors develop on a sub-forum of the most conspicuous white supremacy forum".[33] Some years later Martini and da Silva (2022) provided critical reflections on far-right terrorism and extremism.[34]

Is this a new wave of global terrorism?: A critical review

It has been argued that far-right extremism is a new wave of global terrorism.[35] Two questions emerge from this statement that require further elaboration. First, is far-right terrorism a novel wave of terrorism? If yes, how is it novel and what are the novelties or development in it? Second, is far-right extremism and violence a global phenomenon? To answer these questions, relevant scholarly points in these discussions are presented in the upcoming text/chapters.

First, terrorism is a dynamic phenomenon, which transforms and takes shape in accordance with prevailing social and political circumstances in a duly manner. Considering the question of the phenomenon's novelty, it is indispensable to mention here,[36] David S. Rapoport and his theory of terrorism.[37] Rapoport contends that there have been four waves of modern terrorism, which began in the late nineteenth century. He further argues for the emergence of a new one after this latest so-called religious wave which has been present since 1979. Rapoport, however, has not provided his reflections on the nature of the fifth wave of terrorism. Meanwhile D.K. Gupta claims that a new wave of modern terrorism "should exhibit a collective consciousness based on ethno-nationalism, religious identity, or economic class. In all probability, it would contain elements of all three".[38] Jeffrey Kaplan infers that the new wave would include "ethnic utopians trying to remake their societies, following the example of Cambodia's Khmer Rouge".[39] He envisions that the aim of these fifth-wave groups will be "to create a new ethnicity or tribal society, reconstructed from a lost model or by establishing an entirely new world order".[40] Jeffrey D. Simon suggested that instead of a principal ideology, a "Technological Wave will emerge with lone operators using the internet, cyber tools and weapons of mass destruction".[41] Honig and Yahel see the next wave with "terrorist semi-states that control territory but continue to launch terrorist attacks internationally".[42] Florian Hartleb asserts that the four previous waves of terrorism were followed by a fifth one, which can be characterized by "lone wolf terrorism of different ideological inspiration but with new opportunities through the internet in the USA and Europe".[43] Meanwhile Amber Hart contends that "the cusp of the next wave is upon us, with the global coronavirus pandemic a likely catalyst".[44]

Interestingly, a lot of the characteristics associated with the far-right-related threat have been listed by the aforementioned scholars. Accordingly, ethnic nationalists and their utopian ideologies, the prevalence of lone actors as well as the relevance of digital solutions all can be traced in our times' far-right extremism and violence. To conclude, we dare to state that far-right terrorism should be classed as a novel wave of terrorism.

Second, researchers and practitioners have both argued for the transnational nature of far-right extremism and violence. It has been a reoccurring assertion that seemingly disparate offenders are connected via a global network through ideologically analogous acts of terror. Seeking to substantiate the argument for the global nature of the far-right terrorism-related threat, we have decided to take the following approach. Later in the text, we have attempted to take stock of all factors and circumstances that are important elements in the interactivity and transnational collaboration of far-right extremists.

To begin with, the transnational nature of far-right violence can be best captured through the examination of the geographical distribution of far-right-inspired terrorist attacks. Without aiming to give an exhaustive list, some of the most significant incidents include the following:

- Norwegian Anders Behring Breivik killed eight people by detonating an explosive-laden van in Oslo and then shot dead 69 participants of a summer camp on the island of Utøya.[45]
- A 21-year-old white supremacist, Dylann Roof, was charged with Charleston church shooting. Nine African Americans were killed on 17 June 2015 in Charleston, South Carolina, during a Bible study at the Emanuel African Methodist Episcopal Church.[46]
- British Labor Party Member of Parliament Jo Cox was murdered by 53-year-old white supremacist Thomas Alexander Mair on 16 June 2016.[47]
- Alexandre Bissonnette (27 years old) pleaded guilty for the Quebec City Mosque shooting. On 29 January 2017, Bissonnette opened fire after the evening prayer and killed six worshippers and seriously injured five others.[48]
- Lone actor, 46-year-old Robert Gregory Bowers, was held liable for the Pittsburgh synagogue shooting, which has been the deadliest attack on the Jewish community in the United States. In the white supremacist terrorist mass shooting that took place on 27 October 2018, the attacker killed 11 people and wounded 6 others.[49]
- More far-right-inspired terrorist attacks were recorded in 2019. A 29-year-old white supremacist Australian national, Brenton Tarrant, admitted the murder of 51 people at 2 mosques in Christchurch, New Zealand, on 15 March 2019. He livestreamed the entire incident via a head camera he was wearing.[50]
- Some weeks later, on 27 April 2019 a gunman fired a shot inside the Chabad of Poway synagogue in Poway, California, United States. The attacker, John Timothy Earnest, killed a woman and injured three others.[51]
- On 2 June 2019, German regional Governor Walter Lübcke was killed in the garden of his home near Kassel. The offender, Hessian right-wing

extremist Stephan Ernst, confessed and was formally charged with the criminal act.[52]

- Another 21-year-old white nationalist, Patrick Wood Crusius, was arrested and charged with the deadliest attack on Latinos in modern American history. Crusius shot and killed 23 people and injured 23 others at a Walmart store in El Paso, Texas, United States, on 3 August 2019.[53]
- Some months later, 27-year-old Stephan Balliet fatally shot two people and injured two others during the Jewish holiday of Yom Kippur outside the Halle synagogue on 9 October 2019.[54]
- Next year, 11 people died and 5 others were wounded when 43-year-old German far-right extremist Tobias Rathjen fired shots at two shisha bars in Hanau, near Frankfurt, Germany. After the attacks, the gunman returned to his home, where he killed his mother and then committed suicide.[55]

Moving on to the next factor, international alliances have long been existing among far-right threat groups, although their main targets remained their home nations.[56] With the spreading of livestreaming, preferring to use English and not only national languages, as well as social media platforms the globalization of right-wing extremism have also emerged.[57] Certain operational patterns obviously reemerge such as targeting Muslims, migrants, and Jewish people together with drafting manifestos. All assume a connected network via online forums and gaming platforms which function as a sort of guidebook for a next offender.[58]

In this vein, the internet has been devoted a significant role in the globalization of far-right extremism. The worldwide network of computer systems enables the creation of a global community and is an "invaluable tool for recruitment and the sharing of tactics and tradecraft for the purpose of committing violence".[59] Livestreaming their acts and spreading their messages through manifestos alike are seemingly instruments that aim to help offenders reach out to their like-minded fellows regardless of geographical boundaries.[60]

Another interesting observation is that while white supremacists were fighting for their own home country in the past, recently they have been defending the whole "white race".[61] The example of US-based neo-Nazi demands special attention here. As the group's founder Rinaldo Nazzaro claimed the formation was established as "an umbrella group for right-wing extremists who are interested in a more global perspective. [...] The Base was neither a neo-Nazi nor a terrorist organization but a social networking platform for individuals who are interested in survivalism and self-defense".[62] The group's objective is to "unify militant white supremacists around the globe and provide them with paramilitary training in preparation for a 'race war' ".[63]

Taking stock of all the examined circumstances, we can safely say, the transnational nature of far-right terrorism is traceable. It is important to stress straight away that the novel features together with the network's global coverage make the threat posed by the extreme right a particular concern. This has driven us to examine the phenomenon through an operational perspective and draw the lessons of this research to enrich our existing understanding of far-right extremism and terrorism.

Conceptualizing the far right: The definition of problem

To fulfill the ultimate goal of this research and provide a more nuanced understanding of the threat associated with so-called far-right extremism and terrorism, it is crucial to set what we exactly mean by these terms. Accordingly, this section focuses on clarifying the most important conceptual issues for the discussion.

One of the most frequently reoccurring expressions in the book is the "extreme right". To explain this term, we have turned to ADL's concept, which claims that the extreme right refers to "right-wing political, social and religious movements that exist outside of and are more radical than mainstream conservatism".[64] In accordance with their interpretation, the "extreme right" essentially incorporates two hubs, however, their borderlines are particularly blurred. One of these is the white supremacist movement which embraces several "submovements,[65] namely the neo-Nazis, racist skinheads, and the alt-right".[66] The other one incorporates anti-government (also known as) Patriot extremists who are promoting the militia movement. Besides them, there are various "single-issue"[67] movements, "which each tend to be the extreme wing of a more mainstream conservative movement; these include anti-abortion extremists, anti-immigrant extremists, anti-Muslim extremists, and anti-public lands extremists, among others".[68]

Considering that this research attempts to better understand the threat posed by right-wing extremism and violence, these concepts should also be clarified. When examining right-wing extremism, Tore Bjørgo and Jacob Aasland Ravndal identify three "families"[69] of far-right political movements (cultural nationalists, ethnic nationalists, and racial nationalists). Daniel Koehler shares this assertion and claims that right-wing extremism should be viewed as a "family of ideologies",[70] which is "an overlapping web of groups and ideologies based on racially, ethnically or culturally defined superiority of one group and inferiority of all others".[71] In the meantime, Jackson apostrophizes right-wing extremism as an activity that "in reaction to perceptions of negative change, aims to revert fundamental features of the political system to some imagined (though not necessarily imaginary) past state".[72] Elisabeth Carter has proposed a "minimal definition for right-wing extremism"[73] and conceptualized it as "an ideology that encompasses authoritarianism, anti-democracy and exclusionary and/or holistic nationalism".[74]

Right-wing terrorism generally refers to "the use or threat of violence by sub-national or non-state entities whose goals may include racial, ethnic, or religious supremacy; opposition to government authority; and the end of practices like abortion".[75] Daniel Byman adds that "right-wing terrorism should be seen as a label of convenience that lumps together various causes".[76] Koehler, however, asserts that

> the term right-wing extremism covers a broad range of ideologies that essentially see violence as a legitimate tool to combat a political and ethnic "enemy" (including individuals with different culture, religion, nationality or sexual orientation) seen as a threat to the (sic) own race or nation.[77]

For our research, Richard English's terrorism definition will be applied:

> Terrorism involves heterogeneous violence used or threatened with a political aim; it can involve a variety of acts, of targets, and of actors; it possesses an important psychological dimension, producing terror or fear among a directly threatened group and also a wider implied audience in the hope of maximizing political communication and achievement; it embodies the exerting and implementing of power, and the attempted redressing of power-relations; it represents a subspecies of warfare, and as such it can form part of a wider campaign of violent and nonviolent attempts at political leverage.[78]

An extensive ideological as well as organizational heterogeneity characterizes the so-called far right. It can be defined as "an overlapping web of groups and ideologies based on racially, ethnically, or culturally defined superiority of one group and inferiority of all others (e.g., white supremacism, neo-Nazism, fascism)".[79] The following core themes have been identified with regard to the far-right movement. First, Jamin suggested "the valorizing of inequality and hierarchy, especially along racial/ethnic lines, ethnic nationalism linked to a mono-racial community and racial means to achieve aims and defend the imagined community".[80] Perliger added another core elements, namely "nationalism, xenophobia, racism, exclusionism, traditional values and anti-democratic ideologies".[81] Meanwhile Lauder would include "race/ethnicity as the foundation of social solidarity/nationalism, xenophobia, racism, especially anti-Semitism, illegitimacy of established regime of power".[82] Similarly, the Institute for Economics and Peace provides a particularly extensive definition for the far right. Due to the authors' intention to cover all emerging right-wing extremist ideologies, there are obvious overlaps in this comprehensive approach.

> Far right refers to a political ideology that is centered on one or more of the following elements: strident nationalism (usually racial or exclusivist in some

fashion), fascism, racism, anti-Semitism, anti-immigration, chauvinism, nativism, and xenophobia.[83]

Additionally, the Global Terrorism Index classified the following ideological groupings as far right:

- Anti-feminist extremists
- Anti-Muslim extremists
- Neo-fascists
- Anti-immigrant extremists
- Anti-Semitic extremists
- Neo-Nazi extremists
- Anti-Islam extremist
- Right-wing extremists
- Anti-LGBT extremists
- Incel extremists
- White nationalists/separatists
- Anti-liberal extremists[84]

Researcher Cynthia Miller-Idriss argues that the far right should be viewed as a "spectrum of groups and individuals who are often at odds with one another but hold in common some combination of four elements: exclusionary and dehumanizing beliefs, antigovernment and antidemocratic practices and ideals, existential threats and conspiracy theories, and apocalyptic fantasies".[85] She added that "exclusionary and dehumanizing beliefs are at the core of far right ideologies through ideas about superiority and inferiority according to race, ethnicity, nationality, gender, religion, or sexuality".[86] Another common feature of far-right ideas is the fact that they are generally opposed to democratic norms and values and rather promote authoritarianism.[87] They also embrace white supremacist ideologies and espouse "ethnic cleansing or ethnic migration, and the establishment of separate ethno-states or enclaves along racial and ethnic lines".[88] Additionally, an "existential threat"[89] orchestrated through a conspiracy theory is also attested to far-right ideologies. They also believe in "an inevitable violent apocalypse, which will be followed by a period of restoration and re-birth for white civilization".[90] As researcher Cas Mudde argues, "far right parties and groups can be either radical or extremist",[91] although some are "situated on the borders between radicalism and extremism".[92]

With all this in mind, we have built our concept on the far right upon this "composite and fluid movement".[93] For the purpose of this research, far-right terrorism refers to the use of terrorist violence by right-wing extremists.[94] Their core concept entails supremacism or the idea that a certain group of people sharing a common element is superior to all others. Numerous variants of far-right extremism exist, such as neo-Nazism, neo-fascism, and ultra-nationalist formations. Racist behavior, authoritarianism, xenophobia, misogyny, and hostility to lesbian, gay, bisexual, transgender, and queer (LGBTQ+) communities and immigration are common attitudes among far-right extremists.[95]

We have gone further and set the ambitious goal to exploit this ideological and organizational heterogeneity that characterizes the phenomenon. Considering the security threat associated with its unpredictability, we strive to shed light on the operational similarities within this extensive diversity.

There is an ongoing conceptual debate whether right-wing terrorism should be classified as an act of terrorism or as a hate crime. Despite the similarities between these two concepts,[96] our analysis specifically focuses on far-right extremism and terrorism, in which violence or the threat of violence occurs. Accordingly, hate crimes, which may also include non-violent incidents have not been a subject of this research.

Research design

A lot has been lamented about the ascending threat of far-right extremism and violence. Still, numerous blurred concepts, interchangeable terms, and reoccurring alerts on a detected increase in far-right-related terrorism characterize recent discussions on this topic. With all this in mind, we have decided to undertake a consistent procession and empirical examination of available information on this matter. We have arrived at the recognition that open-source information presents great opportunities to better understand the functioning of far-right threat groups. An in-depth and consistent analysis of their mode of operation and mindset enables us to identify ways to detect and counter their malicious efforts and activities. The ultimate goal of this research was to better understand the nature of the threat posed by the far right and as a result of its findings to propose effective provisions and mechanisms for detecting and countering it.

Quantitatively, a database containing 35 profiles of far-right threat groups operating in 10 countries was compiled. Where we use the term *threat group*, we refer to Law Insider's concept of a *security threat group*. Accordingly, we examined entities that "mean a group of individuals which threatens, intimidates, coerces or harasses others or which engages in any activity which violates or encourages the violation of statutes, administrative rules or department policy".[97] As an additional criterion, we selected those threat groups that engaged with any of the aforementioned far-right ideologies. This knowledgebase served as the basis for our research.

Our ambition in this project was to substantiate the transnational nature of the threat associated with the far right. In line with this, first, we attempted to validate that far-right threat groups operating in various geographical locations use very similar functionalities. To make the research feasible and focused, we set very clear and measurable factors (funding, recruitment, structure, modus operandi, communication, targeting, weaponry, ideology/mindset, and international connections) with regard to all the 35 threat groups. We conducted the analyses of selected threat groups' practices precisely and exclusively along these factors. We firmly believe that this research methodology ensured that the geographical breadth of the project has not undermined the depth and insightfulness of the work. Second, we were eager to better understand how to effectively counter the threat posed by the far right. To do that, we attempted to represent the diversity of national counter strategy approaches. This heterogeneity turned out to be a very instructive analysis that helped us identify the most relevant hiatuses in counter-terrorism strategies.

It has been widely argued that lone actors and the so-called leaderless resistance are of the greatest security concern. The reason why our research focused on threat groups and not on worrisome individuals is the following. We believe that it would be extremely challenging to obtain open source information about currently active extremists' mode of operation without the risk to disrupt ongoing intelligence operations. Meanwhile, most of the examined worrisome threat groups are still operating, tracking their online activities offers invaluable insights into the details of their functionalities. From a practitioner perspective, we assume that concerning individuals used to be or are still members of far-right-ideology-driven entities. Thus, we presume that based upon their own experience, their mode of operation will likely be very similar to the group(s)' functionalities. With this in mind, elaborating group-level mode of operation could be highly informative to understand the operational details of lone actors.

In accordance with all that has been said, examined formations are listed as under per country in alphabetical order.

Australia
- Antipodean Resistance
- Australian Defence League
- Lads Society
- National Socialist Network
- Reclaim Australia

Canada
- Atalante
- Blood and Honour
- La Meute
- Northern Guard
- Soldiers of Odin
- Storm Alliance

France
- Generation Identity (Génération Identitaire)

New Zealand
- Action Zealandia
- Dominion Movement
- Wargus Christi

Germany
- Gruppe S
- Identitarian Movement
- National Socialist Underground

Norway
- Nordic Resistance Movement
- Stop the Islamisation of Norway

PEGIDA
Reichsbürger

Ukraine
AZOV Battalion

United Kingdom
Britain First
English Defence League
Feuerkrieg Division
National Action
Sonnenkrieg Division

Sweden
Swedish Resistance Movement

United States
Atomwaffen Division
Oath Keepers
The Base
The Boogaloos
The Proud Boys
Three Percenters

To analyze selected threat groups' operational functionalities, nine factors have been set to organize available information. Factual knowledge was collected across their funding, recruitment, structure, modus operandi, communication, targeting, weaponry, ideology/mindset, and international connections. These underlying elements have formed the backbone for the research and have determined the manuscript's key pillars.

Limitations

First, there are obvious limits to how far research like this can go into the operational details of the threat environment. Importantly, respecting the work of intelligence agencies and to avoid the risk of interrogating ongoing surveillance operations or investigations, the authors relied only on openly available information.

Second, examined far-right threat groups were selected based on the fact that how extensive available open-source information on their mode of operation is available. We were determined to draw upon case studies in which detailed and substantial analysis is possible.

Book structure

This research aims to promote a better understanding of the threat posed by far-right extremism and terrorism. Essentially, this objective has determined the backbone of this manuscript. The chapters in this book proceed by *first* introducing the current far-right-related threat landscape. Later, those driving factors are elaborated which may shape this in the future. Afterward, a critical literature review is presented addressing the burning question of whether far-right terrorism counts as a new wave of global terrorism. Additionally, definitions and terminologies applied in this book have been clarified.

Chapter 2 provides a detailed analysis of the threat landscape in the most concerning countries. Accordingly, we present relevant circumstances, counter-policy strategies, and case studies in Canada, the United States, the United Kingdom, France, Germany, Norway, Sweden, Ukraine, Australia, and New Zealand. Based upon this information, preliminary projections on threat levels have been provided. With the intention to identify the key trends in the threat associated with far-right terrorism, nuances in distinctive terrorism patterns have been detailed. To do so, incidents that occurred between 2010 and 2020 in the aforementioned countries are examined.

Chapter 3 aims to better understand the nature of the threat posed by far-right extremism and terrorism. This can be achieved by scrutinizing the operationalities of selected far-right threat groups. To ensure the most comprehensive insight into these functionalities, their ideology and mindset, fundraising methods, structure, communication channels, mode of operation, targeting, and weaponry together with their transnational network are elaborated.

We have been thrilled to explore not only the complexity of the far-right threat but also to examine how national regimes conceptualize their responses to the challenges of the existing threat environment. Therefore, Chapter 4 focuses on national counter-strategies combating the complex threat of far-right extremism and violence. We have been deliberate to explore the heterogeneity as well as the similarities in national counter-policy approaches. In line with this, the most relevant pillars of selected countries' counter-strategies are examined in this section.

Chapter 5 attempts to scrutinize the novelties in far-right threat groups' modus operandi and functionalities of their fundraising, recruitment, and communication with the intention to put forward implications on future counter-terrorism policies. With this in mind, we try to identify legislative and operational gaps in counter-policies and accordingly design the most effective countermeasures to fill in these hiatuses.

Notes

1 Institute for Economic and Peace, "Global terrorism index 2020". www.visionofhumanity.org/wp-content/uploads/2020/11/GTI-2020-web-1.pdf
2 Ibid.
3 Institute for Economic and Peace, "Global terrorism index 2020".
4 "FBI oversight", FBI News, 5 February 2020. www.fbi.gov/news/testimony/fbi-oversight-020520
5 Oliver Towfigh Nia, "Far right terrorism biggest threat to German security", AA, 9 July 2020. www.aa.com.tr/en/europe/far right-terrorism-biggest-threat-to-german-security/1905114
6 Jacob Aasland Ravndal, Madeleine Thorstensen, Anders Ravik Jupskås, and Graham Macklin, "RTV trend report 2021 right-wing terrorism and violence in Western Europe, 1990–2020". www.sv.uio.no/c-rex/english/publications/c-rex-reports/2021/rtv-trend-report/c-rex-rtv-trend-report-2021.pdf
7 Ibid.

8 Jacob Aasland Ravndal, Charlotte Tandberg, Anders Ravik Jupskås, and Madeleine Thorstensen, "RTV trend report 2022 right-wing terrorism and violence in Western Europe, 1990–2021". www.sv.uio.no/c-rex/english/publications/c-rex-reports/2022/rtv_trend_report_2022.pdf
9 Aquil Haziq Mahmud, "16-year-old Singaporean detained under ISA after planning to attack Muslims at 2 mosques", CNA, 27 January 2021. www.channelnewsasia.com/news/singapore/16-year-old-singaporean-detained-isa-planned-attack-2-mosques-14052400
10 Eviane Leidig, "The far right is going global", *Foreign Policy*, 21 January 2021. https://foreignpolicy.com/2020/01/21/india-kashmir-modi-eu-hindu-nationalists-rss-the-far right-is-going-global/
11 Hüseyin Pusat Kildis, "The far right is not limited to the west: The case of India", Ankasam, 11 February 2021. www.ankasam.org/en/the-far right-is-not-limited-to-the-west-the-case-of-india/
12 "France teacher attack: Four pupils held over beheading", BBC, 19 October 2020. www.bbc.com/news/world-europe-54598546
13 "Vienna shooting: What we know about 'Islamist terror' attack", BBC, 4 November 2020. www.bbc.com/news/world-europe-54798508
14 Joe Mulhall and Safya Khan Ruf, "State of hate far right extremism in Europe 2021". www.hopenothate.org.uk/wp-content/uploads/2021/02/ESOH-LOCKED-FINAL-1.pdf
15 Institute for Economics and Peace, "Global terrorism index 2020".
16 B. M. Jenkins, "The role of terrorism and terror in Syria's civil war", Testimony presented before the House Foreign Affairs Committee, Subcommittee on Terrorism, Nonproliferation, and Trade on 20 November 2013. www.rand.org/pubs/testimonies/CT402.html
17 R. Coolsaet, "Facing the Fourth Foreign Fighter Wave. What Drives Europeans to Syria, and the Islamic State? Insights from the Belgian Case". Brussels: Egmont – The Royal Institute of International Relations, 2016.
18 United Nations Security Council Counter-Terrorism Committee Executive Directorate (UN CTED), "Foreign terrorist fighters", 2018. www.un.org/securitycouncil/ctc/sites/www.un.org.securitycouncil.ctc/files/ctc_cted_factsheet_ftfs_november_2021_0.pdf
19 R. Broadbent, "Syria redux: Preventing the spread of violent extremism through weaponized populations and mobile safehavens", Belfer Center Paper, May 2020. www.belfercenter.org/publication/syria-redux-preventing-spread-violent-extremism-through-weaponized-populations-and#footnote-061
20 D. Weggemans, E. Bakker, and P. Grol, "Who are they and why do they go? The radicalization and preparatory processes of Dutch Jihadist foreign fighters". *Perspectives on Terrorism*, 8(4), 100–110, 2014.
21 "'Anti-corona' extremists try to storm German parliament", *The Guardian*, 29 August 2020. www.theguardian.com/world/2020/aug/29/berlin-braces-for-anti-coronavirus-protest-against-covid-19-restrictions
22 "Christchurch shootings: Brenton Tarrant pleads guilty to 51 murders", BBC, 26 March 2020. www.bbc.com/news/world-asia-52044013
23 Raffello Pantucci, "How Lee Rigby's murder changed the face of terror", 15 April 2018. www.theguardian.com/commentisfree/2018/apr/15/day-new-terror-unleashed-lee-rigby-murder-woolwich

24 Jacob Aasland Ravndal and Tore Bjørgo, "Investigating terrorism from the extreme right: A review of past and present research". *Perspectives on Terrorism*, 12(6), 5–22, 2018. www.jstor.org/stable/26544640
25 Valentine Crosset, Samuel Tanner, and Aurélie Campana, "Researching far right groups on Twitter: Methodological challenges 2.0". *New Media & Society*, 21(4), 939–961, 2019. DOI: https://doi.org/10.1177/1461444818817306
26 Gregory D. Miller, "Blurred lines: The new 'domestic' terrorism". *Perspectives on Terrorism*, 13(3), 66–78, 2019. www.universiteitleiden.nl/binaries/content/assets/customsites/perspectives-on-terrorism/2019/issue-3/05---miller.pdf
27 Pelham Carter and Katherine Kondor, "Researching the radical right: Making use of the digital space and its challenges", in: Mark Littler, Benjamin Lee (Eds.). *Digital Extremisms: Readings in Violence, Radicalisation and Extremism in the Online Space*. Palgrave Studies in Cybercrime and Cybersecurity. Cham: Palgrave Macmillan/Springer Nature, 223–252, 2020. DOI: https://doi.org/10.1007/978-3-030-30138-5_11
28 Victoria Steinek and Birgit Zetinigg, "Islamist and right-wing extremist propaganda: A literary analysis on the mechanisms and impact of violent extremist narratives online". *SIAK-Journal – Zeitschrift für Polizeiwissenschaft und polizeiliche Praxis*, 1/2020, 68–78, 2020. DOI: https://doi.org/10.7396/2020_1_F
29 Stephen D. Ashe, et al. (Eds.), *Researching the Far Right: Theory, Method and Practice*. Routledge Studies in Fascism and the Far Right. Abingdon: Routledge, 2021. www.universiteitleiden.nl/binaries/content/assets/customsites/perspectives-on-terrorism/2022/issue-5/tinnes1.pdf
30 Sara Doering and Garth Davies, "The contextual nature of right-wing terrorism across nations". *Terrorism and Political Violence*, 33(5), 1071–1093, 2021. DOI: https://doi.org/10.1080/09546553.2019.1598390
31 Donald Holbrook and Graham Macklin, "Deconstructing rightwing extremism: Conceptual variance and attitudes towards Islam", RESOLVE Network Research Report, June 2022. DOI: https://doi.org/10.37805/remve2022.3
32 William Allchorn and Andreas Dafnos, "Far-Right Mobilisations in Great Britain, 2009–2019". London: Centre for Analysis of the Radical Right, October 2020. www.radicalrightanalysis.com/2020/11/19/carr-report-far-right-mobilisations-in-great-britain-frgb-dataset-2009-2019
33 Ryan Scrivens, Garth Davies, and Richard Frank, "Measuring the evolution of radical right-wing posting behaviors online". *Deviant Behavior*, 41(2), 216–232, 2020. DOI: https://doi.org/10.1080/01639625.2018.1556994
34 Alice Martini and Raquel da Silva, "Critical approaches to extreme right wing terrorism and counter-terrorism special issue". *Critical Studies on Terrorism*, 15(1), 2022. DOI: https://doi.org/10.1080/17539153.2022.2032549
35 Jonathan Collins, "A new wave of terrorism? A comparative analysis of the rise of far-right terrorism". *Perspectives on Terrorism*, 6(15), 2021. www.universiteitleiden.nl/binaries/content/assets/customsites/perspectives-on-terrorism/2021/issue-6/collins.pdf
36 Vincent A. Auger, "Right-wing terror: A fifth global wave?". *Perspectives on Terrorism*, 14(3), 2020. www.jstor.org/stable/26918302?seq=1#metadata_info_tab_contents
37 David C. Rapoport, *Waves of Global Terrorism: From 1879 to the Present*. New York: Columbia University Press, 2022. https://doi.org/10.7312/rapo13302

38 D. K. Gupta, "Waves of international terrorism: An explanation of the process by which ideas flood the world", in: Jean E. Rosenfeld, (Ed.). *Terrorism, Identity and Legitimacy: The Four Waves Theory and Political Violence.* New York: Routledge, 40, 2011.
39 Jeffrey Kaplan, "Terrorism's fifth wave: A theory, a conundrum and a dilemma". *Perspectives on Terrorism*, 2(2), 12–24, January 2008.
40 Ibid.
41 Jeffrey D. Simon, "Technological and lone operator terrorism: Prospects for a fifth wave of global terrorism", in: Jean E. Rosenfeld (Ed.). *Terrorism, Identity and Legitimacy: The Four Waves Theory and Political Violence.* New York: Routledge, 44–65, 2011.
42 Or Honig and Ido Yahel, "A fifth wave of terrorism? The emergence of terrorist semi-states". *Terrorism and Political Violence*, 31(6), 1210–1228, 2019. https://doi.org/10.1080/09546553.2017.1330201
43 Florian Hartleb, *Lone Wolves: The New Terrorism of Right-Wing Single Actors.* Switzerland: Springer Nature, 2020.
44 Amber Hart, "Right-wing waves: Applying the four waves theory to transnational and transhistorical right-wing threat trends". *Terrorism and Political Violence*, 2021. https://doi.org/10.1080/09546553.2020.1856818
45 Heather Ashby, "Far right extremism is a global problem", Foreign Policy, 15 January 2021. https://foreignpolicy.com/2021/01/15/far right-extremism-global-problem-worldwide-solutions/
46 Harriet McLeod, "Charleston church shooter pleads guilty to state murder counts", Reuters, 10 April 2017. www.reuters.com/article/us-south-carolina-shooting-roof-idUSKBN17C15W
47 "Jo Cox: Man jailed for 'terrorist' murder of MP", BBC, 23 November 2016. www.bbc.com/news/uk-38079594
48 "Quebec: Alexandre Bissonnette charged with six murders", Al Jazeera, 31 January 2017. www.aljazeera.com/news/2017/1/31/quebec-alexandre-bissonnette-charged-with-six-murders
49 Dakin Andone, Jason Hanna, Joe Sterling, and Paul P. Murphy, "Hate crime charges filed in Pittsburgh synagogue shooting that left 11 dead", CNN, 29 October 2018. https://edition.cnn.com/2018/10/27/us/pittsburgh-synagogue-active-shooter/index.html
50 "Christchurch mosque attack: Brenton Tarrant sentenced to life without parole", BBC, 27 August 2020. www.bbc.com/news/world-asia-53919624
51 Spencer Kimball, "'It was a hate crime': One dead, three injured in synagogue shooting in San Diego area", CNBC, 27 April 2019. www.cnbc.com/2019/04/27/police-respond-to-reports-of-shooting-at-synagogue-in-san-diego-area.html
52 Ben Knight, "Neo-Nazi convicted of German politician's murder", DW, 28 January 2021. www.dw.com/en/neo-nazi-convicted-of-german-politicians-murder/a-56366905
53 "Death toll in El Paso shooting rises to 22 as investigators put together timeline of accused shooter's movements", CBS News, 5 August 2019. www.cbsnews.com/news/el-paso-shooting-death-toll-rises-today-2019-08-05-timeline-suspected-shooter-patrick-crusius/
54 Lizzie Dearden, "Germany synagogue shooting: Gunman kills multiple people in Halle attack", *Independent*, 9 October 2019. www.independent.co.uk/news/world/europe/germany-shooting-synagogue-attack-latest-halle-today-shooter-death-toll-grenade-a9148791.html

55 David McHugh, David Rising, and Frank Jordans, "German gunman calling for genocide kills 9 people", AP News, 20 February 2020. https://apnews.com/article/shootings-turkey-germany-international-news-cultures-b5736c3dba1d677e89ef947bcf5ab213
56 Daniel Koehler, *Right-Wing Terrorism in the 21st Century*. United Kingdom: Routledge, 2016.
57 Mattia Caniglia, Linda Winkler, and Solène Métais, "The rise of the right-wing violent extremism threat in Germany and its transnational character", European Strategic Intelligence and Security Center, 27 February 2020. www.esisc.org/upload/publications/analyses/the-rise-of-the-right-wing-violent-extremism-threat-in-germany-and-its-transnational-character/The%20Rise%20of%20the%20Right-Wing%20Violent%20Extremism%20Threat%20in%20Germany%20and%20its%20Transnational%20Character_ESISC.pdf
58 Ibid.
59 J. O. Ellis and R. B. Parent, "Working paper series: The future of right-wing terrorism in Canada". Canadian Network for Research on Terrorism, Security and Society, 16(12), 2016. www.tsas.ca/wp-content/uploads/2018/03/TSASWP16-12_Parent-Ellis.pdf
60 Vincent A. Auger, "Right-wing terror: A fifth global wave". *Perspectives on Terrorism*, 14(3), 87–97, June 2020.
61 "White supremacy extremism: The transnational rise of the violent white supremacist movement". New York: Soufan Center, 2019.
62 Yassin Musharbash, "The globalization of far right extremism: An investigative report", CTC Sentinel, July, August 2021.
63 Christopher Miller, "An international neo-Nazi group thought to have been dissolved is recruiting again in the US", Buzzfeed, 9 June 2021.
64 ADL, "Extreme right/radical right/far right". www.adl.org/resources/glossary-terms/extreme-right-radical-right-far right
65 Ibid.
66 Ibid.
67 Ibid.
68 Ibid.
69 Tore Bjørgo and Jacob Aasland Ravndal, "Extreme-right violence and terrorism: Concepts, patterns, and responses", ICCT Policy Brief, September 2019. https://icct.nl/wp-content/uploads/2019/09/Extreme-Right-Violence-and-TerrorismConcepts-Patterns-and-Responses.pdf
70 Daniel Koehler, "German right-wing terrorism in historical perspective. A first quantitative overview of the 'database on terrorism in Germany (right-wing extremism)', DTG Project". *Perspectives on Terrorism*, 8(5), 48–58, October 2014.
71 Daniel Koehler, "Violence and terrorism from the far right: Policy options to counter an elusive threat", ICCT Policy Brief, February 2019. https://doi.org/10.19165/2019.2.02
72 Sam Jackson, "A schema of right-wing extremism in the United State", ICCT Policy Brief, October 2019. https://doi.org/10.19165/2019.2.06
73 Hart, "Right-wing waves: Applying the four waves theory to transnational and transhistorical right-wing threat trends".
74 Elisabeth Carter, "Right-wing extremism/radicalism: Reconstructing the concept". *Journal of Political Ideologies*, 23(2), 4 May 2018. https://doi.org/10.1080/13569317.2018.1451227

75 The Definition of Right-Wing Extremism in National Consortium for the Study of Terrorism and Responses to Terrorism (START), Ideological Motivations of Terrorism in the United States, 1970–2016. College Park, MD: START, 6 November 2017. www.start.umd.edu/pubs/START_IdeologicalMotivationsOfTerrorismInUS_Nov2017.pdf
76 Daniel Byman, “Is right-wing terrorism rising?”, The National Interest, 13 August 2019. https://nationalinterest.org/print/feature/right-wing-terrorism-rising-73241
77 Koehler, “German right-wing terrorism in historical perspective. A first quantitative overview of the ‘Database on Terrorism in Germany (Right-Wing Extremism)”.
78 Richard English, “The future study of terrorism”. *European Journal of International Security*, 1(2), 2016. https://doi.org/10.1017/eis.2016.6
79 A. MacKenzie and C. Kaunert, “Radicalisation, foreign fighters and the Ukraine conflict: A playground for the far right?”. *Social Sciences*, 10, 116, 2021. https://doi.org/10.3390/socsci10040116
80 J. Jamin, “Two different realities: Notes of populism and the extreme right”, in: A. Mammone, E. Godin, & B. Jenkins (Eds.). *Varieties of Right-Wing Extremism in Europe*, 38–52. Abingdon: Routledge, 2013.
81 Arie Perliger, “Challengers from the sidelines understanding America’s violent far right”, Combatting Terrorism Center, November 2012. https://apps.dtic.mil/sti/pdfs/ADA576380.pdf
82 Matthew A. Lauder, “The far rightwing movement in Southwest Ontario: An exploration of issues, themes, and variations”. Guelph, Ontario: The Guelph and District Multicultural Centre, 2002.
83 Institute for Economics & Peace, Global Terrorism Index 2019: Measuring the Impact of Terrorism, Sydney, November 2019. http://visionofhumanity.org/app/uploads/2019/11/GTI-2019web.pdf
84 Ibid.
85 Cynthia Miller-Idriss, “White supremacist extremism and the far right in the U.S.”, The Gale. www.gale.com/intl/essays/cynthia-miller-idriss-white-supremacist-extremism-far right-us#_edn1
86 Ibid.
87 Ibid.
88 Ibid.
89 Ibid.
90 Ibid.
91 Cas Mudde, “The populist radical right: A pathological normalcy”. *West European Politics*, 33(6), 1167–1186, 2010.
92 Jens Rydgren, “The radical right: An introduction”, in: Jens Rydgren (Ed.). *The Oxford Handbook of the Radical Right*. Oxford: Oxford University Press, 1–16, 2018.
93 Aurélie Campana and Samuel Tanner, “Meanwhile in Canada: Anti-Muslim ordinary racism and the banalization of the far right ideology”, TSAS Research Paper, 2019. www.tsas.ca/wp-content/uploads/2019/04/RR2019_01_Campana_Tanner.pdf
94 EUROPOL, “Terrorist situation and trend report 2021”. www.europol.europa.eu/activities-services/main-reports/european-union-terrorism-situation-and-trend-report-2021-tesat

95 Ibid.
96 Daniel Koehler, "Right-wing extremism and terrorism in Europe current developments and issues for the future", PRISM, 6(2). https://cco.ndu.edu/Portals/96/Documents/prism/prism_6-2/Koehler.pdf?ver=2016-07-05-104619-213
97 Law Insider, "Security threat group definition". www.lawinsider.com/dictionary/security-threat-group

2

THE ASCENDING THREAT OF FAR-RIGHT TERRORISM

By delving into the most relevant circumstances, this preliminary projection aims to better understand the threat posed by far-right terrorism. It has been argued that the Western world is heavily affected by far-right political violence. With this in mind, this research focuses on the most concerning countries, namely Canada, the United States, the United Kingdom, France, Germany, Norway, Sweden, Ukraine, Australia, and New Zealand. The outcome of this threat assessment on each country was evaluated on a five-grade threat level scale, specifically, *low*, *moderate*, *substantial*, *severe*, and *critical*.

Canada: Threat level: Moderate

With a lower level of organization and lethality compared with the United States or Europe, white supremacist and/or Islamophobic and anti-immigrant right-wing groups have been steadily present in Canada since 2001.[1] A yearly 3.3 violent attacks committed by white supremacist movements have been recorded since 2001.[2] Between 2010 and 2019, most of far-right activities occurred after 2016 (18 in 2017, 34 in 2018, and 40 in 2019). Property crimes, protests, and rallies were the most frequent extremist actions.[3] Reportedly, in 2015 there were somewhere between 80 and 100 hate groups, and by 2019 already 300 entities operating in Canada.[4] The Canadian Security Intelligence Service asserted that these "fragmented right-wing extremist circles pose threat to public order and not to national security".[5]

According to the Canadian Incident Database, "supremacist extremist incidents" since 2001 have occurred predominantly in the province of Alberta, less frequently in Ontario, British Columbia, and Québec. Most of these cases

DOI: 10.4324/9781032708041-2

are spontaneous and isolated violent acts on individuals of special racial or religious identities. The only recorded coordinated attack happened on 22 May 2008 when 20 supremacists raided Kurdish individuals in an Edmonton café.[6] Still, it is of serious concern that Canadian far-right terrorism is closely connected with the European and – even stronger – with the American counterparts and events.[7] More severe security concerns exist with regard to lone actors, who may not necessarily affiliate with specific extremist groups or movements. Such individuals were responsible for the deadliest violent extremist incidents in Canada. In 2014, Justin Bourque shot five RCMP officers, and in 2017 Alexandre Bissonnette was charged with killing six Muslim men at prayer in a mosque in Quebec City.[8]

In 2020, about 6,660 right-wing extremist channels, pages, groups, and accounts were identified across seven social media platforms in Canada. The most frequent topics of these virtual discussions are anti-Muslim sentiments and anti-Trudeau rhetoric.[9] The Institute for Strategic Dialogue's report claimed that in 2020 Canadians were more active than their US- or UK-based counterparts.[10] The far-right extremist threat environment has been particularly "diverse and fragmented"[11] with numerous overlaps between far-right groups, biker gangs, and other organized criminal entities.[12] Regardless of the small number of right-wing extremist movements and organizations, with the smart adaptation and exploitation of innovative solutions offered by social media, a strong virtual collective identity could be created within this digital subculture.[13]

United States: Threat level: Severe

The Anti-Defamation League reported that right-wing domestic extremists were responsible for 75% of 435 violent terrorist attacks that occurred in the United States between 2010 and 2019. Since the Oklahoma bombing in 1995, the deadliest year for right-wing extremist violence was 2019.[14] An internal 2009 DHS report warned the administration that the economic recession together with the election of the first Black President "could create a fertile recruiting environment for right-wing extremists".[15] According to the Southern Poverty Law Center, the number of home-grown extremist groups increased by 250% in the first year of Barack Obama's presidency and there has been a steady growth in the far-right-related threat. Hate groups operating across the United States increased to a record high 1,020 in 2018,[16] which then stagnated at 838 in 2020. It is also informative that 50% of these entities were made up of white nationalist groups.[17] In 2019, right-wing extremists were liable for two-thirds of the attacks on US soil. Between January 1 and 8 May 2020 this ratio increased to 90%.[18] The number of hate groups as well as extremist propaganda remains considerable. Circulated hateful online content nearly doubled in 2020 (from 2,724 in 2019 to over 4,500 incidents in 2020).[19] This information originates though not from one single far-right entity but from a number of white supremacist and neo-Nazi groups.[20]

US militia groups are considered "an increasing and serious threat across the US".[21] These armed groups have been more involved in demonstrations and amplified their training and recruitment activities. Militia membership is loose and flexible, people can float from group to group without changing any of their beliefs. Allegiance to the ideology is more important than a pledge to a specific organization.[22] Far-right online propaganda and the militia subculture ideology have been thriving since the COVID-19 lockdowns. By mid-April 2020, at least 125 boogaloo-promoting groups were identified on Facebook, 60% of them were founded within three months with an online membership of 73,000.[23] The YouTube video titled "Top 5 Boogaloo Guns" was watched 340,000 times.[24] According to the Anti-Defamation League's Center on Extremism, in 2020 white supremacist propaganda efforts doubled (2,724 incidents were reported in 2019 and 5,125 cases in 2020).[25] Timothy Wilson died in a shooting with FBI agents in a COVID-19-related thwarted attack. He was suspected to attack a hospital with an explosive-loaded vehicle in its parking lot. Previously Wilson was also considering a nuclear plant, Islamic centers, and the Walmart headquarters as potential targets.[26]

Another worrisome circumstance is the white supremacist infiltration of law enforcement. Violent extremist groups not only recruit from law enforcement communities but officers in ranks volunteer their professional resources for white supremacist purposes.[27] Reportedly, active-duty police officers and military officials make up 6–10% of Oath Keepers' members. Even more followers are veterans or retired officers.[28] Likewise, ranks of police and the army have joined the Three Percenters.[29] There is a concerning number of military service members, veterans, and former or current police officers among the demonstrators of 2020 and 2021. While in 2018 no active-duty personnel was involved in domestic terrorist incidents, this ratio increased to 1.5% in 2019 and then to 6.4% in 2020.[30] It is also noteworthy that domestic extremists themselves strive to join the military forces to obtain combat and tactical experience. To further enhance the effectiveness of existing military accessions and personnel security processes the FBI's symbols library and tattoo database could improve recruiters in identifying typical white nationalist tattoos. Social media postings are also deemed to be excellent indicators of involvement in domestic extremist activities. Therefore, during the vetting process, applicants' social networking should be given particular attention.[31]

Far-right incidents were striving in 2020. Activists capitalized on lockdowns in the spring, racial demonstrations during the summer, and the presidential elections in fall.[32] Extremists exploited the pandemic to "expand their mobilization efforts around anti-government conspiracy myths criticizing the current restrictions".[33] They amplified their misinformation campaigns through encrypted messaging apps[34] and social media posts.[35] The far right capitalized on the uncertainty and fear in the crisis situation to "radicalize, recruit, and inspire plots and attacks".[36] Besides their elevated intensity in digital operations, anti-lockdown protests hosted extremist meetups.[37] After the lifting of pandemic restrictions in July 2020, nationwide demonstrations of racial injustice became the primary targets of US armed far-right militias.[38] The online hub of misinformation and conspiracy theories around COVID-19 has fortified far-right groups into an audience of more than a million.[39] Besides local protesters, reports suggest an ensemble of lone anarchists, radical opportunists, and extremist groups who exploited these demonstrations to spread their propaganda and incite violence.[40] According to Armed Conflict Location and Event Data Project (ACLED), far-right groups were involved in demonstrations against the election results. Protests more likely turned into violent outbursts if militia members were presented. It is also important to see that these – mostly anti-government – groups not only attended demonstrations but also ramped up training and recruitment events (Figure 2.1).[41]

The Capitolium siege on 6 January 2021 proved the proximity of the threat posed by violent extremists. Rioters could successfully attack one of the world's most secure buildings. The Capitolium Police that are "one of the largest, best-funded and most single-focus police departments"[42] in the United States could not stop the crowds to surge into the building. In the unrest, 5 individuals were killed and over 100 people were injured.[43] Federal authorities arrested almost 300 individuals[44] who participated in the 6th January riot. Members of various extremist groups throughout the country coalesced in the storm of the US Capitol. They are allegedly affiliated with organizations such as The Three Percenters, The Oath Keepers, Proud Boys, and Texas Freedom Force.[45] Several followers of the QAnon online conspiracy theory were also arrested.[46] QAnon supporters believe that "a group of Satan-worshiping elites who run a child sex ring is trying to control our politics and media".[47] Charged persons arrived at the siege from over 180 counties throughout the United States.[48] It was an unprecedented event where previously concurring and disparate extremist groups mobilized themselves together. It is of great concern whether these violent extremists have established links with each other and will mobilize themselves together in the future.[49] In the aftermath of the Capitolium siege, certain members have left extremist groups and only those remain who are more likely to be prone to political violence.[50] The Capitolium Insurrection marks a transition in far-right communities from "traditional organizational structures towards diffuse systems of decentralized radicalization".[51] The situation is further exacerbated by the fact that "online connection to extremist culture and ideology could be equally important for inspiring violence as connections to on-the-ground groups".[52]

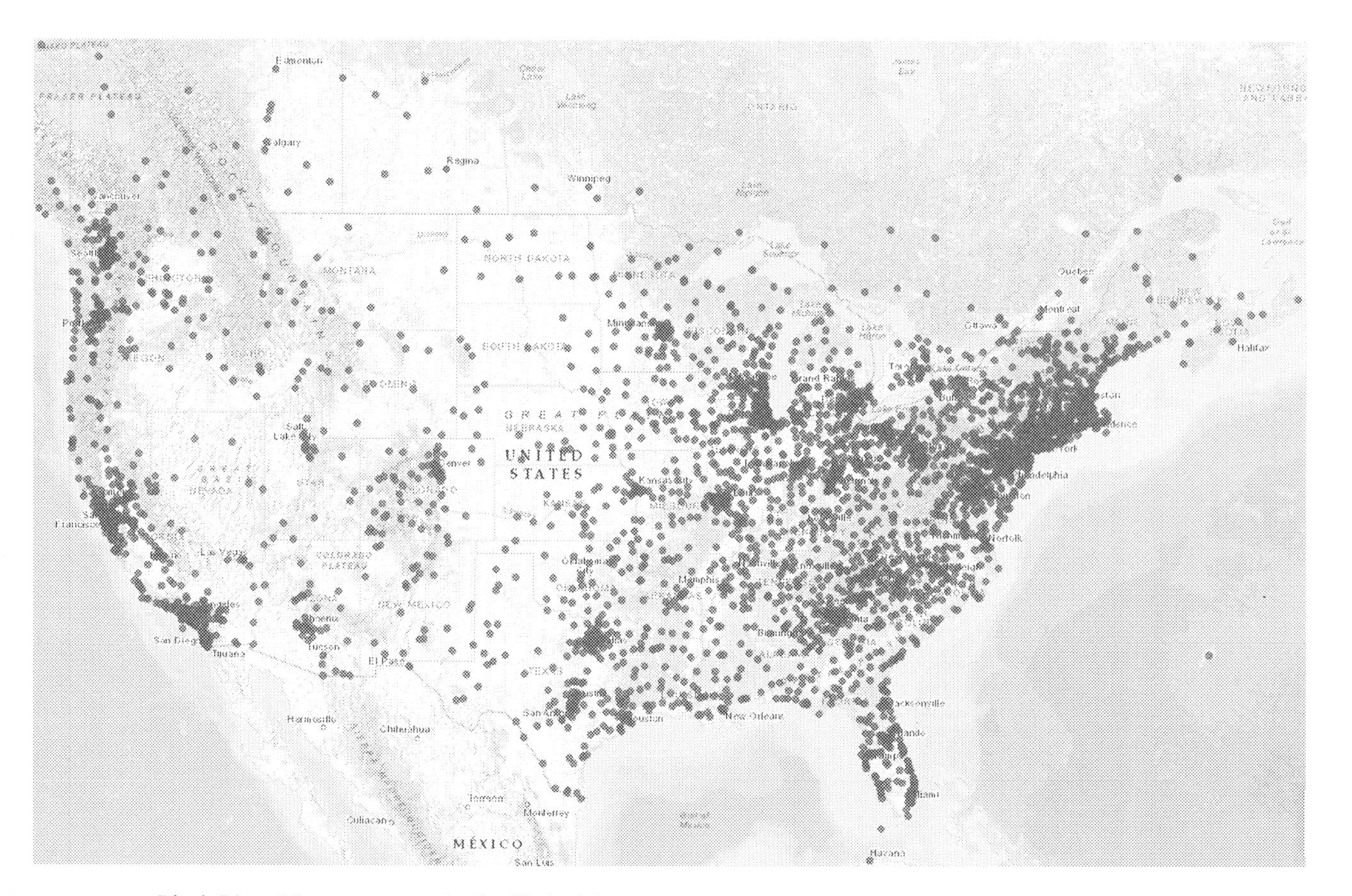

FIGURE 2.1 Black Lives Matter protests in the United States.

Source: Creosotemaps.

According to the Department of Homeland Security's threat assessment for 2021, white supremacists remain the most "persistent and lethal threat"[53] in the United States. Right-wing extremist attacks and plots greatly outnumbered far left incidents and resulted in more casualties.[54]

Since 2015, right-wing extremists have been involved in 267 plots or attacks and 91 fatalities. At the same time, attacks and plots ascribed to far left views accounted for 66 incidents leading to 19 deaths.[55] More than a quarter of right-wing incidents and just under half of the deaths in those incidents were caused by people who showed support for white supremacy or claimed to belong to groups espousing that ideology.[56]

United Kingdom: Threat level: Substantial

Islamist terrorism has remained the most concerning security threat to the United Kingdom's domestic security in 2021. Roughly three-quarters of terrorist detainees in British prisoners are categorized as Islamist extremists. They were responsible for 19 of the 27 terrorist plots thwarted between 2018 and 2021. Far-right extremists were held accountable for the nine remaining incidents, making the associated security threat as a runner-up. Nonetheless, there is a steady increase in the ratio of extreme-right activists in custody for terrorism-related offences. While this number was only 13% in 2019, more than double, 29%, of individuals in custody for terror-related offences adhered to extremist right-wing ideologies in 2020.[57] Data emerging from the UK Home Office asserted that the number of far-right prisoners is record high with 44 people serving their sentence for terror offences.[58] MI5 head, Ken McCallum, highlighted that "bitty, but meaningful international connectivity has begun to emerge, in a way that was not present a few years ago".[59] In its "The State of Hate 2021" report UK anti-racist and anti-fascist advocacy group, HOPE not Hate, warned for the alarming rise of hate groups, the proliferation of the QAnon conspiracy, and green nationalists.[60]

According to a Jane's analysis, the far-right movement in the United Kingdom is "diverse, adaptable and in many cases committed to violence".[61] Besides a persistent British nationalist sentiment, by seeking transnational connections, there is a remarkable tendency towards internationalization. The European migration crisis amplified the anti-immigration sentiment, which culminated in the so-called Great Replacement narrative. A three-tiered pyramid serves to better understand the operational activity of "ideologically and demographically heterogenous" right-wing extremism. The broadest first tier encompasses individuals who support mainstream far-right ideologies and organize rallies to speak out for their causes. These supporters do not necessarily constitute a direct threat of violence but are worrisome as functioning as the support base for far-right views and as a pool of new recruits. The second tier with lone actors and small groups are, however, ready to perpetrate hate crimes targeting people and property. In the third tier, small far-right groups (Sonnenkrieg Division and Feuerkrieg Division) espousing extreme worldviews operate mainly in a secretive manner. Members of this tier are more likely to have ideological or operational links to transnational extremist groups (Figure 2.2).[62]

In 2018, "right-wing extremist referrals to the UK's deradicalization program climbed by 36% and now accounted for one in five notifications to the scheme".[63]

The most pressing statistic concerns the rising influence of far right ideology on the young. 'The number of under-18s associated with right-wing extremism has been rising since 2015 and is now roughly equal to the number of referrals for Islamist radicalization.'[64] Around a quarter of the most concerning cases are taken into the Channel process, of which the largest group now is far right extremists (making up 43% of referrals, compared to Islamist extremists at 30%). Worryingly, 10 out of the 12 under 18s who were convicted on terrorism charges in 2020 were linked to the far right. The rapidity of the ideology's growth amongst the youth will mean far right extremism will

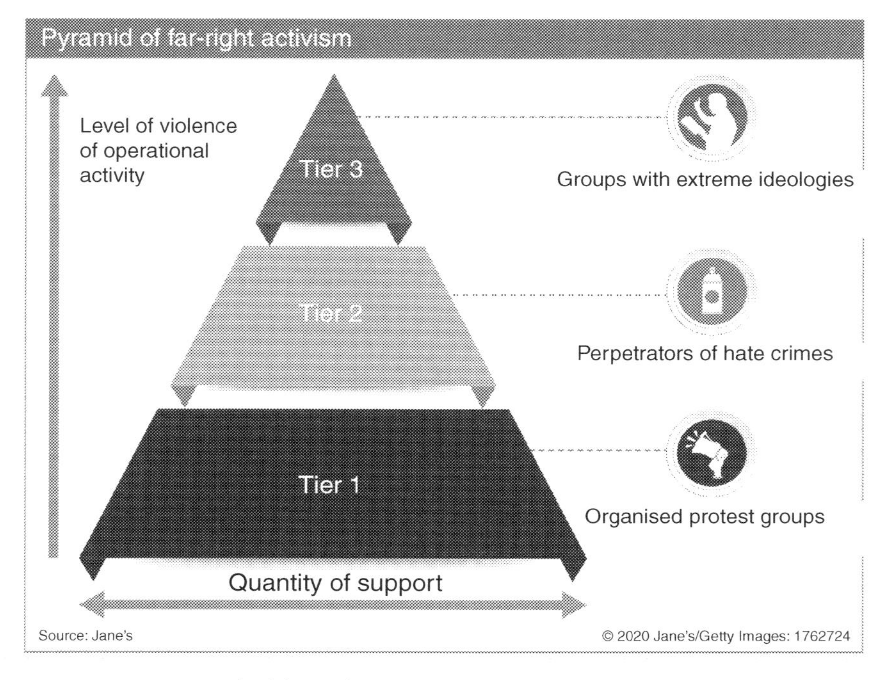

FIGURE 2.2 Pyramid of far-right activism.
Source: Jane's.

relatively soon outstrip Islamist extremism to emerge as the major domestic security threat to the UK.[65]

The British far-right movement reacted to world events in a timely manner. At the time of the Black Lives Matter protests, the far right capitalized on the uncertainty and intensified its anti-immigrant narratives.[66] The Brexit campaign together with the elections resulted in the rise of racist and xenophobic incidents. The number of reported hate crime cases increased five times in the direct aftermath of the announcement of the Brexit vote.[67] MP Jo Cox was stabbed 15 times and shot 3 times during the EU referendum campaign. Fifty-three-year-old Thomas Mair was held accountable for killing the woman for political and/or ideological reasons. According to the investigation, the perpetrator researched far-right material prior to the attack.[68] The number of subscribers to Britain First's Twitter account increased by over 700 in 5 days following Jo Cox's murder.[69] The most prominent far-right groups – British Unity, the English Defence League, the British National Party, and Britain First – all amplified their online presence during the Brexit campaign.[70]

The far right has used conspiracy theories about COVID-19 for recruiting purposes. These fallacies are particularly engaging for the younger British audience.[71] The pandemic has also brought novel, environmentalist narratives to be circulated by right-wing extremists. Activist group, Extinction Rebellion's poster declared "Corona is the cure, humans are the disease". Such racist posts seemingly aim to make temporary travel restrictions towards unwelcomed people permanent even in the post-pandemic times.[72] At the same time, due to lockdowns, the threat posed by the British far right went through a transformation and was consistently decentralized. It is now "digitally led and reflective of online culture [...] plotted in a leaderless, peer-to-peer bubble, with link-minded individuals sharing materials, plans and hate, eventually acting independently". Supporters of the far right aim to "live in an isolationist, parallel white supremacist society, and its relatively younger leadership have adapted to lockdown by recruiting and inculcating via online gaming tournaments, livestreams and home schooling".[73] The post-pandemic economic downturn, high employment, and poor prospects for the future may generate an elevated level of resentment which extremists may strive to exploit.

France: Threat level: Substantial

France has suffered serious losses from Islamist terrorism. Since 2012, nearly 300 people have been killed and over 1,000 wounded in Islamist terrorist incidents.[74] Samuel Paty, 47, was beheaded close to his school in October 2020 after showing cartoons of the Prophet Muhammad to his students.[75] In April 2021, a Tunisian assailant stepped to death a 49-year-old French police employee at a police station in Rambouillet, south-west of Paris. The 36-year-old assailant was unknown to security services. He arrived in France illegally in 2009 but had since obtained residency papers.[76] French terrorist attacks of Islamist background[77] provided fertile grounds for National Rally's anti-immigration narratives.

The number of ultra-right groups targeting Muslims has neither increased nor decreased since the 2015/16 Islamist plots.[78] A 23-year-old man in 2017[79] and six people in 2018[80] were charged with planning to murder French President Emmanuel Macron. Anti-terror police thwarted a far-right plot on mosques and migrants in 2017.[81] Two French women were arrested after stabbing another two, unveiled Muslims in Paris in 2020.[82] Later that year, an alleged member of the French Identarian Movement attacked a passerby in Avignon.[83]

Far-right politics headed by Marine Le Pen has achieved a huge breakthrough in France. Le Pen has been the second most popular political leader in the country. According to a 2020 opinion poll, one-third of French citizens are eager that Le Pen "play an important role in the country's future". Her party's – National Rally (Rassemblement National) – program promotes a patriotic pathway for the future. With strengthened security forces, it suggests massive cuts on immigration.[84] Despite the harsh critics of Macron's pandemic management, the far right was not successful in developing a more coherent counterstrategy to manage the crisis situation. The number of supporters also seems to decline, considering the results of the municipal elections in 2020. While in 2014 the party won 1,498 town council positions, in 2020 they got only 827.

High rates of youth unemployment clearly pushed this generation to the far right. Patriotism and identitarianism are the driving ideologies for the French far right. These nationalists frequently protest to express their oppression of French values.[85] They claim to protect French people from globalization, unemployment, and mass immigration.[86] Another important factor is the increased popularity of conspiracy theories in the digital sphere. One of the most notable is the so-called Great Replacement theory which was set in Renaud Camus' book. This asserts that "white and Christian European culture is being replaced by waves of Muslim non-European immigrants in order to achieve the destruction of French civilization".[87] Both Christchurch attacker, Brenton Tarrant, and El Paso shooter, Patrick Crusius, referenced the theory in their online manifestos.[88]

Germany: Threat level: Severe

German police recorded 23,064 far-right crimes in 2020 which is a rise of 6% from the previous year and the highest number accounted since 2001.[89] Criminal activities ranged from "displaying Nazi symbols and anti-Semitic remarks to physical attacks and murder".[90] Acts targeted "mainly immigrants, refugees and black Germans, but also included a rise in anti-Asian violence, linked to the pandemic".[91] The number of anti-Semitic harassment increased by almost 15% and occurred mainly online.[92] In 2020, the country recorded a 72.4% rise in anti-immigrant crimes, up to 5,298 cases.[93] The number of far-right incidents in 2020 is 49 more compared with the previous record during the refugee crisis in 2016.[94] The Federal Office for the Protection of the Constitution (BfV) reported in 2020 that the number of right-wing extremists operating in Germany "has increased to 33,300 of whom 13,300 are thought to be willing to commit violence".[95] Politically motivated violent crimes increased by 20% to 3,365 including 11 murders and 13 attempted murders.[96] German parliament's commissioner for military announced that the number of recorded cases of far-right crimes in the Bundeswehr increased to 477 in 2020 from 363 in 2019. According to official estimations, 15,000 people residing in Germany are prepared to carry out violent acts of racism. Nationally, 1,200 people are registered as suspected right-wing extremists who legally possess weapons. Compared with the end of 2019, this shows a 35% increase.[97] In 2018, altogether 1,091 firearms were confiscated from right-wing extremists, which shows a 61% increase compared with the previous year.[98]

Preceding right-wing extremist attacks raise concerns over the evolving threat posed by the far right. A week before the Hanau incident, German police raided a neo-Nazi cell, who were planning to carry out attacks on mosques, politicians, and asylum-seekers.[99] In Halle in October 2019, Stephan Balliet shot two people and wounded two others. He livestreamed his acts as trying to storm a synagogue. Walter Lübcke, a pro-migrant politician, was shot and found dead in his garden in June 2019. The attacker was linked with far-right connections. A 38-year-old right-wing extremist was arrested in Neuhausen, Munich, on 15 October 2019 for an anti-Semitic attack on teenagers. A wheelchair-bound Libyan migrant was assaulted by a group of people in Chemnitz on 14 September 2019. One of the attackers yelled anti-immigrant slogans at him. A 26-year-old Eritrean man was shot on 22 July 2019 in a small town near Frankfurt in an alleged racist attack. A 27-year-old man stabbed a 16-year-old traveler in a tram in Bremen after shouting anti-Muslim narratives.[100] A 53-year-old man was arrested in May 2021 and accused of threatening and sending hate messages to leftist politicians over 3 years.[101] In his letters, he referenced the National Socialist Underground which was suspected to be responsible for the killings of eight Turks, a Greek, and a German police officer between 2000 and 2007.[102]

Nearly 3,560 politically motivated crimes – including 500 violent acts – are directly related to the pandemic.[103] Protests have brought together demonstrators of a wide range, including conspiracy theorists and those who oppose vaccinations, masks, or deny the existence of the virus.[104] Far-right movements were striving to capitalize on lockdown critics and coronavirus deniers.[105] Anti-Semitic and racist conspiracy theories were spread,[106] attributing the source of the crisis to Jews[107] and blaming migrants for bringing in the coronavirus.[108] Pandemic restrictions set up a new anti-governmental voice in German society. "Querdenken 711" is a Stuttgart-based organization that attempts to bridge German far right.[109] They "share a distrust of representative democracy and a belief in conspiracy theories".[110] Their anti-lockdown protests turned increasingly violent during the second wave of COVID-19. In November 2020, more than 50 violent acts committed by the protesters were recorded.[111] During the August 2020 Querdenken protest, neo-Nazis and members of the so-called Reichsbürger movement attempted to storm the Bundestag.[112] Supporters of the movement do not accept the legality of the Federal Republic of Germany and its governing authorities. They do not pay taxes and use passports and driving licenses printed for their own supposed states. Their affinity for firearms and stockpiling weapons is concerning for German security authorities.[113]

German nationalist and right-wing populist Alternative for Germany (AfD) has been the country's most successful far-right political party[114] and the first far-right group which got into the Bundestag since World War II.[115] The 2015 European migration crisis turned the anti-immigrant party into the largest opposition force in the German parliament. Close ties exist between AfD and right-wing extremist street movements. Anti-Muslim protesters of far-right political movement PEGIDA voted for AfD in the 2017 general elections. At the same time, PEGIDA provided security for AfD events during the 2017 campaign.[116] Besides AfD's affinity towards Russia, the extent of German far-right groups' transnational contacts resulted in the development of "a leaderless, transnational and apocalyptic violent extreme right-wing movement".[117]

Another concerning factor has been uncovered by a Bundestag report from November 2020. The document draws attention to the presence of far-right extremists within federal and regional security agencies.[118] German police arrested 10 suspects aged between 24 and 55 years in a mega-operation targeting right-wing groups allegedly involved in drug- and arms-trafficking and money-laundering in early March 2021. Police officers from Thuringia, Hessen, and Saxony-Anhalt took part in the operation.[119] As Thuringia's interior minister said the case can draw attention to the intersection of right-wing extremism and organized crime. A German soldier and a relative were arrested on 1 March 2021 on suspicion of illegally possessing weapons and expressing far-right ideologies.[120] In Hesse, between 2015 and 2020 at least 38 internal cases were elaborated on far-right police officers. At the same time, four police officers from Hamburg and Berlin retrieved personal data from police computers on a journalist and a cabaret artist. Another police officer is a suspect in the bombing of the Fatih Mosque in the city of Dresden.[121]

While previous instances were regarded as isolated cases, far-right networks of serving and former members of Germany's military and police have been investigated. As a consequence, a series of reforms have been implemented. In line with these measures, military control over the handling of weapons and ammunition has been enhanced and the screening of the personnel has been increased.[122]

Norway: Threat level: Moderate

Until 2021, Norway has not experienced any terrorist attack perpetrated by individuals of Muslim background.[123] Right-wing extremists were held liable for both large-scale terrorist plots between 2011 and 2019. Norway suffered its most devastating terrorist attack on 22 July 2011, when far-right extremist Anders Behring Breivik killed 77 people and injured over 300 in two sequential domestic terrorist attacks.[124] The first explosion was plotted inside a van in the government quarter of Oslo. The blast killed 8 and injured at least 209 people.[125] The second attack occurred in less than two hours later at a summer camp organized by the youth division of the ruling Norwegian Labor Party. In a homemade police uniform, Breivik took a ferry to the island and opened fire at the participants, killing 69 and injuring at least 110 people.[126] He was meticulously preparing for the attacks, mastered his shooting skills, and used the Call of Duty video game as a training aid.[127] In his 1,518-page compendium, he expressed his militant far-right ideology and xenophobic worldview.[128] According to court documents, Breivik was diagnosed criminally insane with paranoid schizophrenia and was psychotic at the time of offending.[129] He claimed to be a modern-day Templar Knight, a Christian crusader fighting to chase Islam from Europe and rid the world of "Marxists".[130] In his manifesto, he argued that he had operated as an online ideological guide for others in forum discussions. He also established contact with online communities, which "had a considerable influence on him".[131] He used the internet not only for ideological but also for operational purposes. He obtained weapons, purchased chemicals, and tools and raised money for his actions online. Before the attack, Breivik was placed on Norway's intelligence watchlist as buying chemical fertilizer from a Polish company which was under scrutiny. The transaction was regarded as legal, therefore there was no reason for further investigation.[132] His manifesto titled "2083 – A European Declaration of Independence" was cited by right-wing blogs as valuable reading material. His assertions were shared extensively on right-wing forums. Moreover, Russian far-right entities chanted "Glory to Anders Breivik" in the national movement's annual march in Moscow.[133] Admiration for Breivik was on the rise until early 2015. Important contacts of Breivik's circles were detected via about 4,000 letters sent and received during his detainment. After the first 12 months in detention, the Norwegian Ministry of Justice ordered to isolate Breivik and started to censor his incoming and outgoing letters. This was a milestone in losing sympathizers, and subsequently Breivik fans shut down their forums and turned to other national heroes.[134]

Breivik had a substantial influence on future attackers. In 2012, Czech and Polish authorities foiled two Breivik copycat attacks. Vojtěch Mlýnek was stockpiling weapons and manufacturing a remotely operated explosive device when police arrested him.[135] Meanwhile, Brunon Kwiecień, a 45-year-old lecturer in chemical engineering at the Agricultural University of Cracow, was preparing a similar attack against the lower house of the Polish parliament.[136] With charges to carry out Breivik-inspired violent extremist attacks, four people were arrested in the United Kingdom between January 2013 and June 2015.[137] Meanwhile in Newtown, Connecticut, 20-year-old Adam Lanza – allegedly obsessed with Breivik – opened fire at an elementary school on 14 December 2012. He shot and killed 26 people before shooting himself.[138]

Since 2010 the Annual Open Threat Assessment of Norwegian Police Security Services deemed terrorist attacks perpetrated by "radical Islamists to constitute the pre-eminent terrorist threat against Norway".[139] Still, the 2019 National Threat Assessment declared the threat of a right-wing terrorist attack "very unlikely".[140] In the aftermath of the Christchurch attacks in New Zealand, hate crimes and incidents of anti-immigrant hatred have reportedly been on the rise in Norway.[141] Reportedly, 60–70 neo-Nazis marched in 2019 in an anti-Muslim rally in Kristiansand. At the event, the leader of Stop Islamisation of Norway attempted to set fire to a copy of the *Holy Quran*.[142] Twenty-one-year-old Philip Manshaus opened fire at the Al Noor Mosque in Bærum outside of Oslo on 10 August 2019. Interestingly, the shooting was thwarted by two elderly Norwegian-Pakistani members of the mosque congregation.[143] Earlier on the same day, Manshaus shot to death his stepsister, who was adopted from China as a 2-year-old.[144] The attack was widely condemned in Norway, and provided the impetus for the Norwegian government's acceptance of the need for a state action plan against anti-Muslim hatred, which was presented in 2020.[145]

Prior to the 2019 Norway attacks, Europol had noticed an elevated level of sophistication and a surge in far-right propaganda. Even though the threat of a large-scale attack was considered to be on the decline. As the 2010 Europol report concluded, there is a "lack of cohesion, a lower degree of overall coordination of right-wing terrorist and extremist groups, little public support and effective law enforcement operations [...] had gone a long way towards accounting for the diminished impact of right-wing terrorism".[146] In parallel with this, European interior ministers agreed to revisit the threat posed by far-right extremists. Subsequently, the EU Radicalization Awareness Network was established to operate in September 2011.[147] Breivik's case drew authorities' attention to the fact that right-wing extremists substantially differ from those neo-Nazi fanatics who carried out violent acts in 1980s' Europe. This new far right has a more considerable support base.[148]

Capitalizing on the economic recession and immigration, there has been an increasing support base of nationalist political parties in Europe. For instance, the National Front in France, the Dutch Freedom Party together with the Norwegian Progress Party all entered the national political mainstream. Populist right-wing Progress Party of which Breivik was a member got into the Norwegian parliament in 2013 in alliance with the Conservative Party. While the Conservative Party gained control over economic policies, Progress settled down the principles for the national immigration and integration policy. There are only estimations of how many Europeans are involved in far-right parties. According to German intelligence sources, the number of ultra-rightists is around 25,000 including those 5,000 who are of great security concern. The Swedish far-right internet forum Nordisk.nu has 22,000 followers.[149] A 2008 report of collaboration among Dutch organizations claimed that "right-wing terrorism is not always labeled as such because right-wing movements use the local traditions, values, and characteristics to define their own identity".[150] The report argued, that "many non-rightist citizens recognize and even sympathize with some of the organization's political opinions, a formulation which will be familiar to Indians, where communal violence is rarely referred to as a form of mass terrorism".[151] The European Union Security Commissioner Sir Julian King asserted, "I'm not aware of a single EU member state that is not affected in some way by right-wing violent extremism. I think we also need to keep in mind the growing menace of right-wing violent extremism".[152] He cited the Breivik massacre in Oslo, the assassination of British MP Jo Cox, and attacks on asylum centers in Sweden. On the ninth anniversary of the Oslo attack, the threat posed by the far right remained persistent.

Anders Behring Breivik decided to target "Cultural Marxists – the alleged traitors responsible for multiculturalist policies which facilitated the Muslim invasion".[153] In the aftermath of the 2011 attacks, "partly cooperating and partly competing"[154] right-wing and anti-Islam movements are present in Norway. Seemingly these nationalist movements are highly transnational. Stop Islamisation of Norway was inspired by other European "Stop Islamisation of" organizations, the Norwegian Defence League is associated with the English Defence League, and Pegida Norway originates from Germany.[155] Rivalry and internal conflicts characterize the co-existence of these entities. They are mostly active in the digital sphere through their social media accounts.[156] To better understand Norwegian far-right extremists' reluctance to resort to political violence, Bjørgo and Gjelsvik took account of all factors kicking in. Mostly due to the Nazi occupation of the country during World War II, right-wing extremism is regarded as highly stigmatized. Simultaneously, with one of the lowest homicide rates in Europe, violence is not prominent in Norway.[157] Except for the Nordic Resistance Movement, right-wing extremism in Norway is characterized by "unorganized and loosely connected networks".[158] The anti-immigration Progress Party established a novel narrative as a response to COVID-19. To avoid "import infection",[159] it demanded stricter control of borders, migrants, and migrant labor. The pandemic elicited an increase in inequality between rural areas and the wealthier urban zones. The centrist, populist, anti-EU, nationalist Senterpartiet aims to benefit from this situation and may provide a new home for far-right Norwegian voters.[160] Researcher Anders Ravik Jupskås noted a shift in far-right operations and claimed that prior to 2011 right-wing activists accommodated the internet from the streets. Another turning point is happening in 2020, when they started to return to demonstrations.[161]

Sweden: Threat level: Moderate

The most remarkable factors that contributed to the rise of the far right in Sweden can be summarized as follows. First, the European migration crisis of 2015 resulted in an unprecedented wave of irregular migration into Sweden. These circumstances were highly beneficial for the far-right Swedish party Sweden Democrats to gain popularity.[162] The previously "marginal movement of militant skinheads in black uniforms, holds nearly 18% of seats in the Riksdag, Sweden's Parliament by 2021".[163] With accepted 163,000 refugees in 2015 alone, "the number of foreign-born Swedish residents rose to 17%, making the Scandinavian country the largest per capita recipient of refugees in Europe".[164]

Second, the influx of migrants from North Africa and the Middle East has made employment and housing opportunities particularly competitive. At the same time, considering the Nordic standards, the unemployment rate has settled at a particularly high rate.[165] This increased economic inequality, and insecurity has spurred both employed and unemployed Swedish citizens.[166]

Third, an upsurge in violent gang activities has been reported in Swedish immigrant neighborhoods. An estimated 50% of Swedish gang members are foreign-born and 85% of them have an immigrant background.[167] Police reports on the "heavily armed and ruthless criminal underclass"[168] in the socially most deprived suburbs. Although the overall homicide rate remained at a globally low level, deadly shootings reached a record level in 2018, when more than 300 shootings resulted in 45 deaths and 135 injuries in the country.[169] This rising crime rate warns Swedish authorities to address these integration problems in a duly manner.[170] On top of that, the catastrophic COVID-19-related mortality rates in the country have made the far-right voices even louder. Sweden Democrats have been blaming "the country's health crisis on immigrants and Swedish multiculturalism".[171] Despite the relatively small number – estimated at around 100 – of Swedish far-right extremists, their considerable media coverage raises further grave concerns.[172]

Ukraine: Threat level: Critical

Extreme nationalist views have been on the rise in Ukraine since the 2014 Euromaidan Revolution, which was followed by Russian aggression.[173] In the armed conflict in eastern Ukraine starting in 2014, the Ukrainian armed forces turned out to be unable to halt pro-Russian separatists. This led to the emergence of more than 40 pro-government volunteer paramilitary battalions.[174] Economic recession, low living standards, high rates of unemployment, and lingering corruption[175] have added "a socioeconomic dimension to ultra-nationalist agendas".[176] After Kyiv's signing of the Minsk I and Minsk II peace accords, efforts strive to cease the independence of volunteer battalions operating across the country. By 2015, most of them were disbanded or incorporated into Ukraine's state army.[177] In November 2014, Azov was officially registered as a regiment within the Ukrainian National Guard.[178] The number of ultra-nationalists is estimated to be about 10,000. This includes mostly motivated and active young teenage members who have already undergone "organizational, military and ideological training".[179] Statistics by the Organization for Security and Cooperation in Europe (OSCE) indicate that "the number of hate-motivated incidents in Ukraine has grown steadily in recent years, with 178 incidents recorded by the police in 2018 alone".[180]

It raises serious security concerns that army veterans of the Donbas War participate in the activities of Ukrainian far-right groups.[181] Besides their real-life combat experience, they also have access to arms. According to reasonable assessments, far-right extremists' street activities have severe consequences on the societal development in Ukraine.[182] Besides disrupting public events through street patrols, they aim to restore "order" in the country. They storm Jews and Roma people, LGBT communities, and women's rights groups. To facilitate assassinations, the personal data of thousands of journalists were made public in 2016.[183] Another worrisome factor is that these radical right groups exercise a strong attraction over Ukrainian youth. Their promotional materials pursue a common goal, moreover, they operate a considerable infrastructure of sporting clubs and regular training camps.[184] Since the outbreak of the war in the eastern part of the country, far-right groups have been growing in prominence and sophistication.[185]

Ukraine has been considered an emerging hub in a transnational extreme-right network.[186] The Azov movement, with its own National Guard regiment and links to the leadership of the Interior Ministry, poses the most remarkable threat. Outside Ukraine, Azov occupies a central role in a network of extremist groups. Through social media it

> has fueled a global ideology of hate that [...] is a growing threat throughout the Western world. In the context of the white-supremacist movement

> globally, Azov has no rivals on two important fronts: its access to weapons and its recruiting power.[187]

The regiment maintains close ties with like-minded groups abroad.[188] Allies from Western Europe gather at its annual "Paneuropa" event, while counterparts in central and eastern Europe meet at the "Intermarium" conference.[189] Christchurch shooter Brenton Tarrant also mentioned a visit to Ukraine in his manifesto.[190] A report of the Centre for Countering Digital Hate claimed "the sales of the merchandise fund two neo-Nazi extreme movements operating from Ukraine".[191] It organizes regular children's training camps and provides joining opportunities for members of the state-operated army.[192] As Alberto Testa, an expert on far-right radicalization at the University of West London, said "Eastern Ukraine had become a critical staging ground for the international white jihad struggle of the far right, where extremists could train for what some would call racial holy war".[193] Researchers warn that Ukraine is radicalizing far-right foreign fighters in the same way Syria does with jihadist – albeit on a smaller scale – creating a global network of combat-tested extremists who pose a security threat that is now beginning to manifest itself.[194] Alex MacKenzie and Christian Kaunert, however, argue against Ukraine becoming a hub for the far right. First, they claim that those far-right activists who travel to Ukraine have "little in common and likely maintain only loose ties, therefore there is only little chance of an imminent coordinated threat developing from events to date".[195]

Australia: Threat level: Moderate

Although the scene of the Christchurch massacre was not in Australia, the shooter was made in the country.[196] After going underground in the aftermath of the Christchurch shootings, since the beginning of 2020, the workload of Victoria Police Counter Terrorism Command reportedly doubled.[197] While before 2016 far-right extremism cases took up between 10% and 15% of the Australian Security Intelligence Organization's (ASIO) caseload, in 2020 the ratio for investigations of right-wing extremism increased to about 30–40%.[198] As the ASIO director general said in 2020, the threat of right-wing terrorism was real and growing and the number of terror-related investigations doubled compared with the previous year.[199] In its 2017–2018 annual report, ASIO noted "While the threat of terrorist attacks conducted by lone actors continues, these threats are not isolated to Islamic extremists. Individuals motivated by other ideologies – such as extreme left or right-wing ideology – may consider conducting an act of terrorism".[200] There was only one closely preceded far-right incident recorded by ASIO. In December 2019, Phillip Galea was charged with preparations for an alleged terrorist attack on Victorian Trades Hall.[201] According to the prosecution, Galea intended to overcome "the perceived

Islamisation of Australia".[202] He allegedly had affiliations with the UK Combat 18 and the United Patriots Front in Australia. He was a member of both far-right Reclaim Australia and the True Blue Crew.[203]

In 2021 far-right groups were more visible in Australia. A white supremacist group's 30 members reportedly burnt a cross and performed Nazi salutes in the Grampians in Western Victoria in January.[204] A few weeks later, Victoria Police charged Thomas Sewell, the leader of the neo-Nazi National Socialist Network with assault. In a video footage, Sewell was attacking a TV channel security guard.[205] Mike Burgess, the head of ASIO, claimed that right-wing groups accounted for 40% of terror-related investigations in the past 12 months.[206] In April 2021, South Australia Police carried out a series of raids on Adelaide-based members of the far right. During their operation, an Adelaide man was charged for possessing an improvised explosive device and a second person was charged with the possession of extremist material.[207] In 2020, a shop in Melbourne's north-west was closed down after it had merchandized Nazi memorabilia.[208] In a Western Victorian national park, a group of 30 men practiced Nazi salutes and chanted Nazi slogans. Local residents stated that the participants posted stickers with emblems of the National Socialist Network.[209]

The pandemic offered excellent opportunities for the far right to recruit new members and resulted in the rise of anti-lockdown groups. Capitalizing on the anger against COVID-19 restrictions, these gatherings include not only right-wing extremists but also anti-vaccination and anti-government entities. The heterogenic nature of these loud voices makes the identification of these violent non-state actors' motives extremely difficult.[210] In parallel, the pandemic has also raised discrimination against Australia's minorities. It has reinforced anti-Chinese and anti-Asian agitation in far-right circles.[211] One in five Chinese Australians experienced physical threats or been attacked since the pandemic outbreak.[212] The Executive Council of Australian Jewry reported an increase in anti-Semitic incidents in Australia. The recession during and after the COVID-19 pandemic may further accelerate the threat posed by violent extremists. The highest official Australian unemployment rate since 2001 was recorded in May 2020 (7.1%).[213] This economic hardship mostly affected young Australians further diminishing their economic confidence.[214] This together with the declining trust in government may increase the number of disillusioned people prone to turn to extremist ideologies.

Experts learned that the Australian right-wing extremist environment considerably differs from its counterparts either in the USA or in Europe. It is a more fluid and less structured movement, which has limited capabilities and is less prone to engage in violence. In addition, it is not a "homogenous network"[215] but rather consists of numerous very different entities. These groups are positioned at a wide ideological spectrum and do not adhere to any particular ideology. They embrace extremist beliefs from anti-government, "conservative anti-immigration, anti-Islam groups to far right neo-Nazi, anti-Semitic, generally racist, white supremacy groups".[216] There are fragmented individuals who attempt to galvanize into groups. The extreme-right encourages "opportunistic attacks on ethnic minorities, immigrants, Muslims, Jews, leftists and the LGBT community".[217] By 2019, groups organized online have begun to intimidate street activity.[218] Compared with the situation in Europe and in the United States, the Jewish diaspora is less frequently attacked in Australia. Nevertheless, the Executive Council of Australian Jewry reported a year-by-year 30% increase in the number of verbal harassment and intimidation towards Jews.[219] According to a 2019 national survey, 82% of Asian Australians, 81% of Australian of Middle East descent, and 71% of Indigenous Australians had experienced forms of discrimination.[220] Australian right-wing extremist movements have never "formed in isolation of the global RWE community".[221] Active international exchange and relations may refer to their intentions for creating a "global white community".[222] Leaked audio recordings reveal interviews with Australian applicants who attempted to join the militant American neo-Nazi terror group, The Base.[223]

Anti-immigrant rhetoric is a "strategic tool"[224] for far-right entities. They strive to capitalize on the ambiguity and fear associated with immigration. These narratives lack factual bases. "The overwhelmingly productive and law-abiding 2% of the Australian nation is blamed for the country's economic and social problems".[225] The ASIO 2019–2020 Annual Report asserted "right-wing extremists are more organized, sophisticated, ideological and active than previous years [...] these individuals compromised around one-third of our counter-terrorism investigative subjects".[226] The document went on to say that these groups and individuals promptly seized on the COVID-19 pandemic and see it "as proof of the failure of globalization, multiculturalism and democracy, and confirmation that societal collapse and a 'race war' are inevitable".[227] Considering the elevated level of isolation among young people due to the epidemiological restrictions, the Parliamentary Joint Committee on Intelligence and Security inquired into extremism and radicalization in Australia.[228] ASIO Director General Mike Burgess added that the number of terrorist cases leads under investigation doubled in 2019. "While we expect any right-wing extremist-inspired attack in Australia to be low capability, i.e. a knife, gun or vehicle attack, more sophisticated attacks are possible".[229]

Australian security agencies closely monitor the operation of extremist activists and react in a timely manner. While countermeasures target both the Islamic terrorism-related and the right-wing extremist domains, since the Christchurch shootings, Australian law enforcement and intelligence agencies have devoted considerable resources to building knowledge on the newly emerged right-wing threat landscape.[230] Neo-Nazi Sonnenkrieg Division was formally listed in Australia in March 2021. This UK-based terrorist organization is the first right-wing entity to be banned on the Australian continent. Consequently, it became an offence to be a member of the group, fund, or in any other ways associate with its members.[231]

New Zealand: Threat level: Severe

Australian national Brenton Tarrant shot and killed 51 people and wounded 40 others during Friday prayer on 15 March 2019.[232] A 28-year-old gunman entered two mosques, first the Al Noor and 12 minutes later drove to the Linwood Islamic Centre.[233] White supremacist attacker livestreamed the first shooting on Facebook[234] and prior to the attack posted an online manifesto.[235] He meticulously prepared for the attack, visited the Al Noor mosque several times,[236] and practiced shooting in the range of a South Otago gun club.[237] He was a frequent member of right-wing discussions on 4chan and 8chan[238] and got into contact with far-right organizations during his trips to Europe[239]. In his manifesto, titled "The Great Replacement", he claimed to have been inspired by Anders Breivik and white supremacist Dylan Roof, who killed nine African Americans at a church in Charleston, South Carolina.[240] Tarrant inspired several copycat incidents, for instance Poway,[241] El Paso,[242] and Bærum[243] attackers all praised the Christchurch shooting.

Before the Christchurch attack, both Australia and New Zealand reported that their main security risk was from Islamist terrorism. The 2018 annual report of New Zealand's Security Intelligence Service made no reference to right-wing extremism.[244] Meanwhile, the New Zealand Human Right Commission reported about 100 race- and religion-related hate crimes during the period of 2004–2012. These collected media reports included incidents ranging from murder, kidnapping, serious assault, abuse, deliberate damage to property, and desecration of sacred sites.[245] According to the ASIO's 2017 report, the country experienced "low levels of communal violence [...] one person was charged with far right terrorism in 2016".[246] The document did not dismiss the possibility of a far-right attack but claimed that "far right extremist attacks would probably target the Muslim and left-wing community, be low-capability, and be more likely to be perpetrated by a lone actor or small group on the periphery of organized groups".[247] Two days prior to the Christchurch attack, Tarrant tweeted images about the weapons he was about to use. About 30 minutes before the shootings, he detailed his plans in an online forum. A few minutes earlier he emailed a manifesto explaining why. The fact that Tarrant had no close friends and was financially independent considerably diminished the chances for warning signs.[248]

Prior to the Christchurch shootings, the Global Peace Index recorded New Zealand as the second most peaceful country on the planet. The terror rating was "low" (meaning attacks were believed to be unlikely) and the national homicide rate by firearms (about 10 a year for the whole country) was insignificant according to international standards. Two important factors should be considered when assessing the right-wing threat in New Zealand. First, far-right followers of a couple of hundred were nurtured online. Tutorials and guides teach people how to obtain, manufacture, and use weapons. At the same time, these virtual communities reinforce individual extremist ideologies.[249] Second, weapons are easily accessible in New Zealand. "Its rate of gun ownership is one of the highest in the world and civilians are able to legally obtain semiautomatic guns".[250] According to 2020 statistics, 4.6 million New Zealanders own 1.5 million guns.[251] Only six days after the Christchurch attack, the New Zealand Parliament passed the gun reform bill and banned the sale of all military-style, semi-automatic and assault rifles.[252] In a second set of gun reforms, a new firearms registry was introduced. Consequently, license holders will be required to update this repository as they buy or sell guns.[253]

Considering the copycat attacks of the Christchurch shooting, Brenton Tarrant has further internationalized right-wing terrorism. Right-wing formations historically had widespread international connections with like-minded groups, but their target audience was the nation of their origin. With his manifesto and the livestreaming of his acts, Tarrant has designed the far right's weapons.[254] Posting these outlets in English facilitates reaching out to followers on a global scale. This elevated level of publicity about an attack is also a novelty. Previously, publicity was considered as a risky potential to be detected by authorities.[255]

A year after the Christchurch attack, an estimated 60–70 far-right groups and between 150 and 300 right-wing extremists operate in New Zealand.[256] Regardless of their low numbers, the wide connectivity of far-right ideology via the internet makes them an even more concerning issue.[257] At the same time, lone extremists without any explicit group or movement affiliation are considered to be the most dangerous security threat.[258] Reported incidents suggest the persistence of the elevated risk.[259] In March 2019, white supremacist Philip Arps was sentenced to jail for sharing the video of the Christchurch shooting. He was released in January 2020 with a GPS monitor that warns authorities if he gets near a mosque.[260] One of the Dominion Movement's leaders, who happened to be a soldier in the New Zealand army, was charged in December 2019 with "accessing a computer for a dishonest purpose".[261] He was active on neo-Nazi Stormfront site and participated in a rally in Wellington in 2018.[262] A soldier who headed a white nationalist group was charged with espionage in November 2020. He is accused of giving information to another country or foreign organization threatening New Zealand's security.[263] Still, in November 2020, a teenager's confrontational posts drew NZ authorities' attention. The student planned to shoot teachers and fellow pupils at a school. Police found a shotgun and a semi-automatic rifle together with three improvised explosive devices during the search of his house.[264] New Zealand security agencies were on a heightened alert, especially around the anniversary of the March 15 Christchurch attack. Police raided a property in the Christchurch suburb of St Albans, removed computer equipment, and arrested two people on 4

March 2021. Police said an online threat was made earlier against the Al Noor mosque and the Linwood Islamic Centre.[265]

Patterns and trends in far-right terrorism

To identify key trends in the threat associated with far-right terrorism, it is critical to see the nuances in distinctive terrorism patterns. Rigorous and meticulous analyses of national patterns help better understand the broader causes and consequences of far-right terrorism. With this in mind, this concluding section provides facts and figures on far-right terrorist attacks, their modus operandi, and how perpetrators were motivated by far-right extremism. Incidents occurred between 2010 and 2020 in Canada, the United States, the United Kingdom, Sweden, Norway, France, Germany, Australia, and New Zealand are examined in the following analyses. Accordingly, data on the number of completed and thwarted attacks, the lethality of attacks, the diversity of perpetrators, used weapons, and the targets of their operation are processed. Data for the trend and pattern analysis originate from the Global Terrorism Database, EUROPOL TESAT Reports, the ADL Center on Extremism, and open-source incident information.

For the consistency of the analyses, when defining far-right terrorism, it refers to the use of terrorist violence by far-right extremists. Far-right extremism embraces supremacist ideologies that feed on a variety of hateful subcultures. Racist behavior, authoritarianism, xenophobia, misogyny, and hostility towards lesbian, gay, bisexual and transgender as well as immigrant communities characterize their ideologies.[266]

Attack patterns and lethality

Altogether 263 terrorist attacks motivated by far-right ideology took place between 2010 and 2020 in the examined countries. The highest number of these attacks, accounting for 20% of recorded incidents, occurred in 2017, when 57 attacks were carried out. There was a slight decrease starting from 2011 through 2013. Onwards a steady increase characterized the number of far-right terrorist attacks until the peak in frequency in 2017. The number of attacks declined by 2018 and 2019 with an average of about 20 incidents; however, the curve flatted in 2019 and 2020.

Simultaneously, the number of lethal far-right terrorist attacks shows a constantly increasing trend in the examined countries. While before 2017 the lethality of incidents did not exceed 10 lethal attacks per year, in 2020 a record high of 18 fatal attacks motivated by far-right extremism were recorded. It is also informative, however, that nearly 70% of recorded far-right terrorist attacks were not fatal. The percentage of all lethal far-right terrorist attacks ranged from 0% (in 2010) to 85% (in 2020). A clearly increasing trend appears from this ratio. After a moderate rise in the percentage of lethal attacks, the graph peaked in 2014. From that point onwards, slightly fewer fatal attacks occurred. From 2016 the ratio of lethal incidents sharply increased to a concerning 85% value in 2020.

At least 371 people were killed in far-right terrorist attacks in the examined countries between 2010 and 2020. The highest number of deaths, which accounts for 20% of all deaths, was recorded on 22 July 2011 in Norway, when Anders Breivik detonated a van bomb and later shot at the participants of a summer camp. Stephen Paddock came second, who killed 58 people when opening fire at Mandalay Bay Hotel in Las Vegas in 2017. As the third most fatal far-right terrorist incident between 2010 and 2020, Brenton Tarrant was held responsible for shooting 51 people in Christchurch in 2019 (Figure 2.3).

The reported number of far-right terrorist attacks in the European Union appears to have remained largely stable. After a persistent increase in the number of arrests on suspicion of terrorist offences, a record high of 108 detained suspects were registered in 2019. It is yet unclear whether the significant decrease in 2020 indicates a reduced terrorist activity or is a result of operational challenges associated with the novel circumstances generated by COVID-19.[267] It is, however, of great concern that suspects arrested on far-right terrorism charges are increasingly young and have encountered far-right ideologies in online communities.

Altogether 225 terrorist attacks motivated by far-right extremism were recorded in the United States between 2010 and 2020. Until 2015 the annual number of incidents was not higher than 20. After a rising trend, the highest number of attacks occurred in 2017, which accounts for 21% of all reported incidents. Slightly fewer (35) attacks were recorded in 2016 and in 2018 (26) (Figure 2.4).

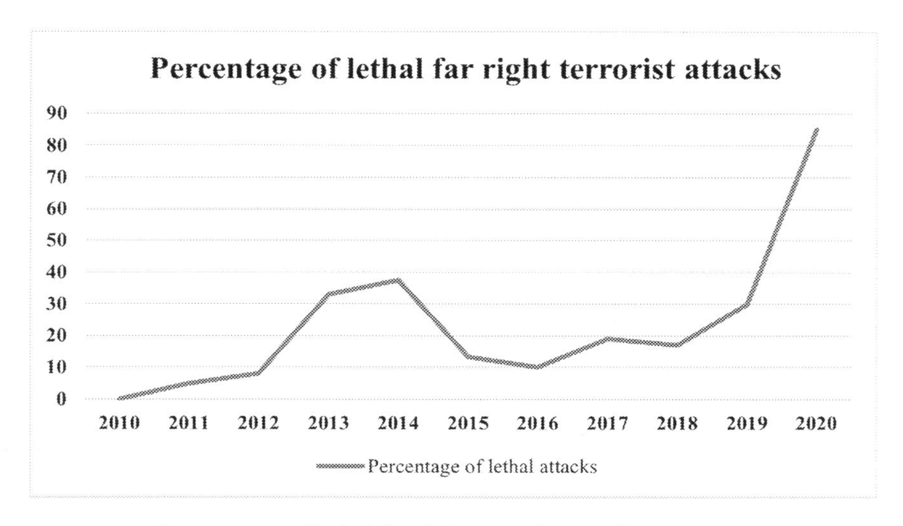

FIGURE 2.3 Percentage of lethal far-right terrorist attacks.

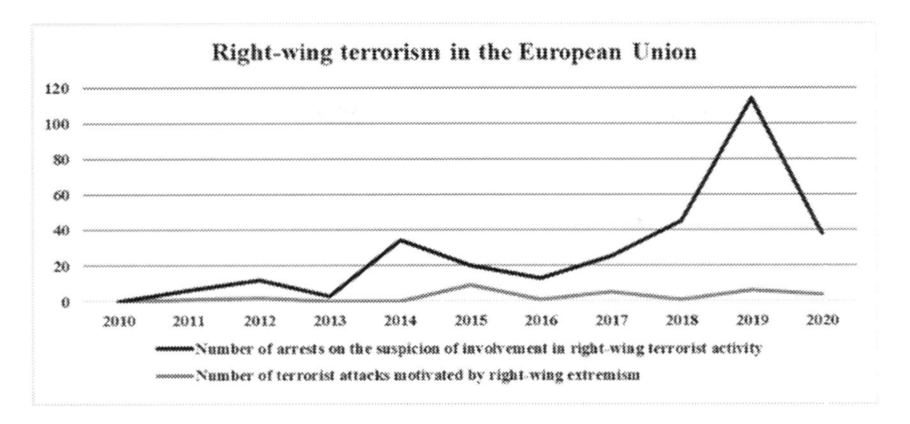

FIGURE 2.4 Right-wing terrorism in the European Union.

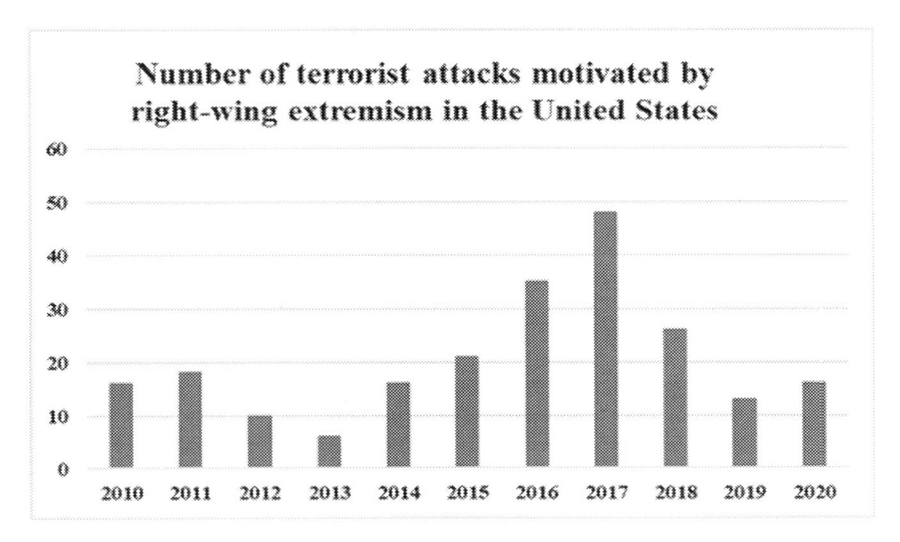

FIGURE 2.5 Number of terrorist attacks motivated by right-wing extremism in the United States.

Interestingly, compared with the trend in the European Union, the pandemic has not diminished but increased the number of US far-right terrorist incidents in 2020 (Figure 2.5).

Perpetrators

Based upon available information on the perpetrators of far-right terrorist incidents, anti-Muslim extremists were attributed to the majority (51%) of reported attacks between 2010 and 2020. White supremacists/nationalists and anti-Semitic extremists were, respectively, held liable for 32% and 24% of recorded incidents. On the other end, specifically named perpetrator organizations (English Defence League, Combat 18, and Nordic Resistance Movement) were held responsible only for a small fraction of committed attacks (Figure 2.6).

Table 2.1 shows the most active perpetrators between 2010 and 2020 in five-year periods. As the data revealed, perpetrators of the same heterogeneity were active but with a differing level of intensity. Anti-Muslim extremists were responsible for the most right-wing terrorist incidents both during 2010–2015 and 2016–2020. Anti-Semitic and anti-immigrant extremists as well as white supremacists/nationalists committed roughly the same number of attacks in both time periods. Interestingly, anti-government extremists were highly active between 2010 and 2015, but accounted only for 2% of all attacks carried out between 2016 and 2020. While anti-police extremist activities more than doubled during 2016–2020, the number of incel extremist attacks considerably decreased. It is also noteworthy that by 2016–2020 the intensity of anti-LGBT and neo-Nazi extremists remarkably increased.

Perpetrators of far-right terrorist incidents continued to embrace a wide heterogeneity of ideologies and political objectives. Far-right extremists operate in organizations such as neo-Nazi and white supremacist groups but online self-radicalized lone actors also pose severe security threats in the examined countries. The following graph illustrates the spatial patterns of the most prevalent perpetrators motivated by far-right ideologies.

Anti-government extremists were charged with attacks exclusively in the United States. Anti-Muslim extremists were highly active in the United

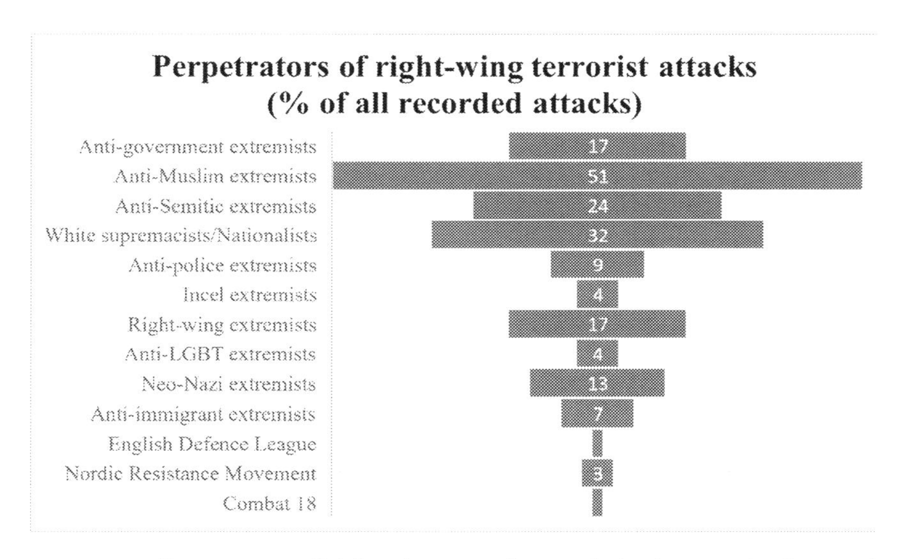

FIGURE 2.6 Perpetrators of right-wing terrorist attacks in the examined countries.

TABLE 2.1 Perpetrators of right-wing terrorist attacks in the examined countries

	2010–2015		*2016–2020*	
	Number of attacks	*Percentage of attacks*	*Number of attacks*	*Percentage of attacks*
Anti-government extremists	13	19%	4	2%
Anti-Muslim extremists	18	26%	33	22%
Anti-Semitic extremists	7	10%	20	13%
White supremacists/Nationalists	11	16%	21	14%
Anti-police extremists	2	2%	7	4%
Incel extremists	3	4%	1	0.6%
Right-wing extremists	9	13%	13	8%
Anti-LGBT extremists	0	0%	4	2%
Neo-Nazi extremists	0	0%	13	8%
Anti-immigrant extremists	4	5%	3	2%
English Defence League	1	0%	0	0%
Nordic Resistance Movement	0	0%	3	2%
Combat 18	1	1%	0	0%

States and in the United Kingdom. Anti-Semitic ideology spurred attacks predominantly in the United States but occurred also in France, Sweden, and the United Kingdom. White supremacists/nationalists were held accountable for attacks mainly in the United States. Among the examined countries, anti-police, anti-LGBT, and incel extremists carried out attacks only in the United States. The vast majority of far-right extremists were held accountable in Germany. Neo-Nazi extremists were charged in Germany, the United States, Sweden, the United Kingdom, and Canada. Anti-immigrant extremists were perpetrators of attacks in Sweden and Germany.

Weapons used in far-right terrorist attacks

Patterns of weapon usage show that perpetrators tended to resort to easily accessible means. The vast majority of attacks involved incendiary (38%) and firearms (32%). Meele weapons were used in 15% of far-right terrorist attacks. Less common was the use of explosives and vehicles, chemicals were reported only in one incident (Figure 2.7).

The frequency of weapon usage varied per the analyzed countries. While in the United States firearms and incendiary were most commonly used in far-right terrorist attacks, in the United Kingdom incendiary were primarily involved. Incendiary was the most common means used in far-right terrorist attacks occurred in Canada and Sweden. Perpetrators of Norwegian terrorist plots used firearms and in one instance explosives. Meele weapons were used in terrorist attacks in the United States, France, and Germany. In both the Australian and New Zealander far-right attacks, firearms were involved (Figure 2.8).

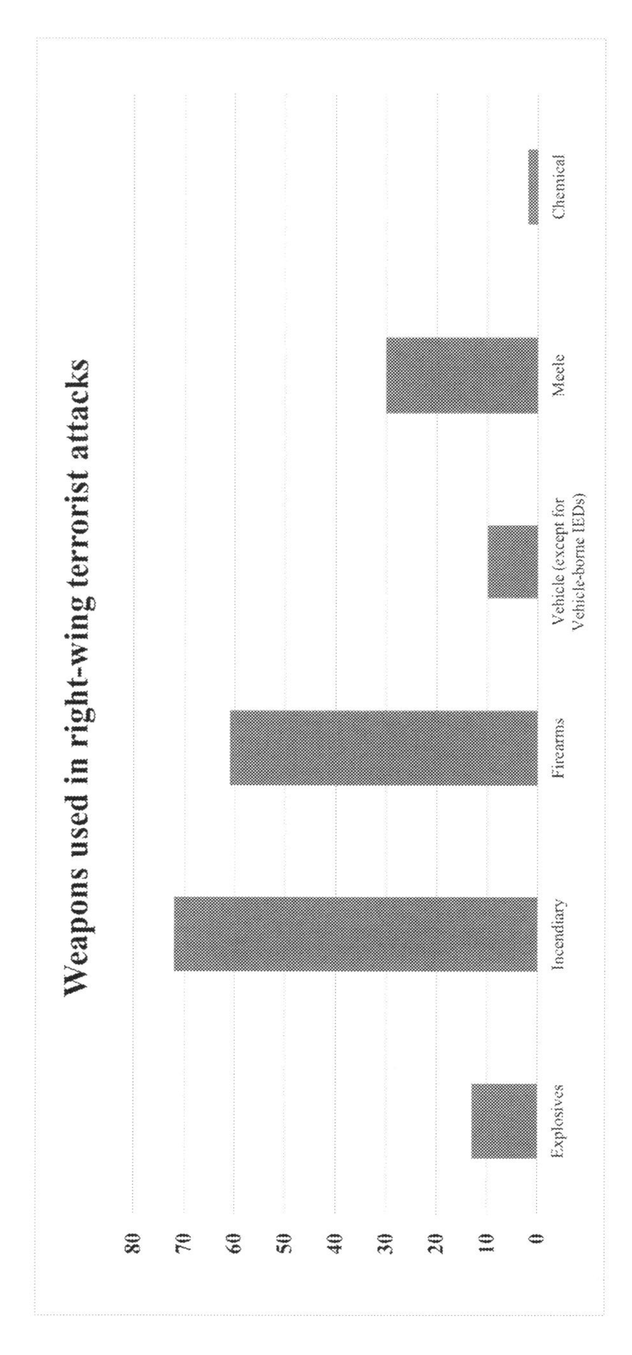

FIGURE 2.7 Weapons used in right-wing terrorist attacks.

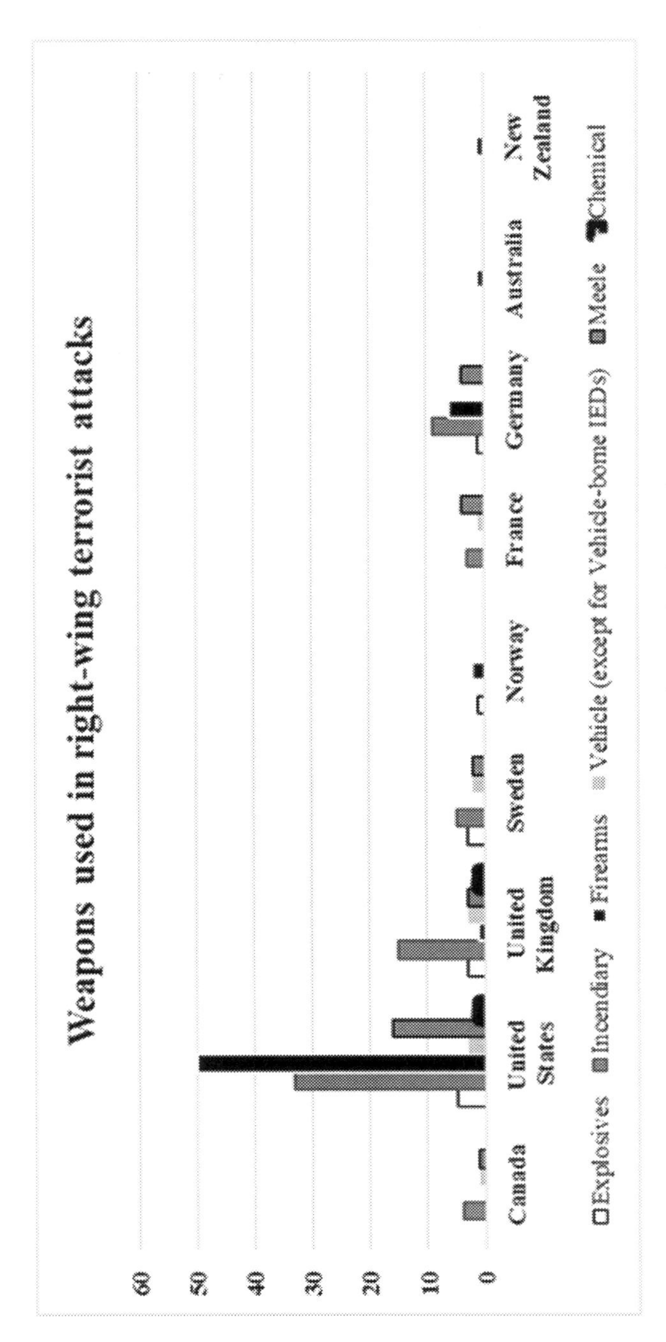

FIGURE 2.8 Weapons used in right-wing terrorist attacks in the examined countries.

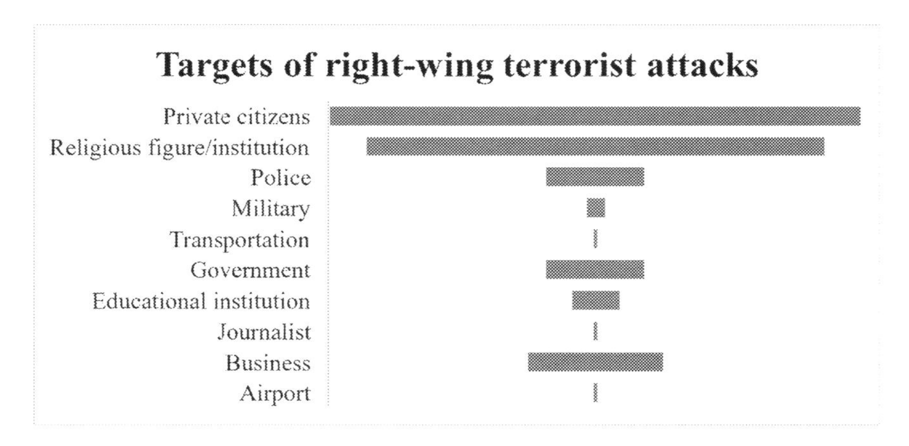

FIGURE 2.9 Targets of right-wing terrorist attacks.

Targets

A wide variety of entities were targeted by far-right terrorist incidents. The most common targets between 2010 and 2020 were private citizens (37%) and religious figures/institutions (32%), which comprise more than half of all targets attacked. Attacks on business, police, and government-related personnel and buildings comprised, respectively, 9%, 7%, and 7% of all attacks. Educational institutions (3%), military (1%), journalists (0.5%), and means of transportation (0.5%) were attacked least frequently (Figure 2.9).

The graph shows religious figures/institutions and private citizens that were targeted by far-right terrorist attacks. Approximately in the same frequency were religious figures/institutions and private citizens attacked in the United States. US police, businesses, government, and educational institutions were targeted in less than 10 instances each. Between 2010 and 2020, US transportation, journalists, and airports were targets of far-right terrorist attacks less frequently. In the United Kingdom, religious figures/institutions were the predominant targets of far-right terrorist attacks. There were only some instances when British citizens, businesses, and the government were targeted. Far-right terrorist attacks primarily attacked Swedish private citizens. Norwegian far-right extremists targeted a religious institute, a private citizen, and a government entity equally in one instance each. Both in Germany and France, private citizens were the most common targets of far-right extremists. In the Australian and New Zealander far-right terrorist attacks, a religious institution was targeted (Figure 2.10).

Conclusion

The patterns of far-right terrorism in the analyzed context illustrate that the threat of far-right terrorism is not uniform. Although the highest number of

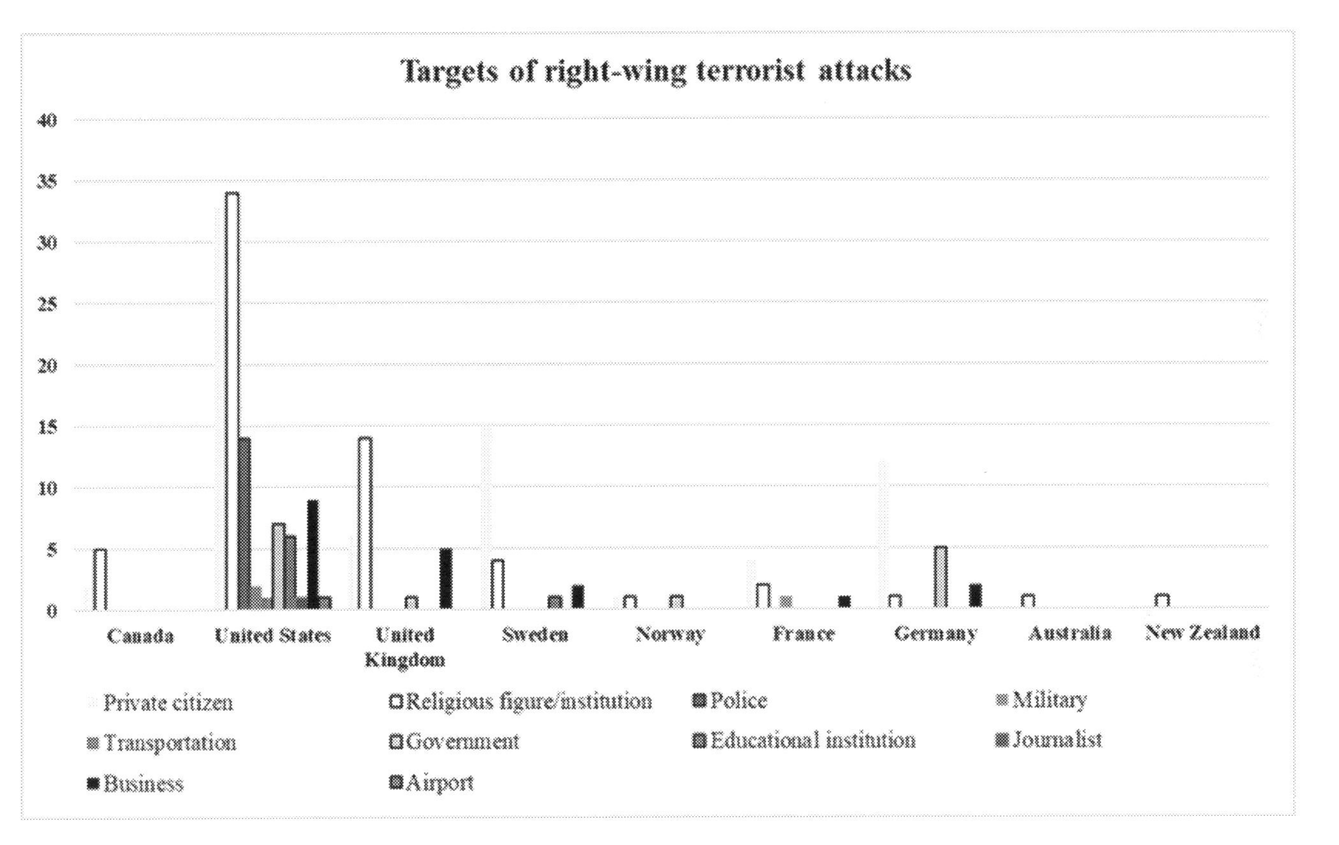

FIGURE 2.10 Targets of right-wing terrorist attacks in the examined countries.

far-right terrorist attacks was recorded in 2017, the growing ratio of lethal attacks and the devastating mass casualty attacks is critical consideration for this trend analysis. The record high number of arrests on the suspicion of involvement in far-right terrorist activities in the European Union clearly justifies the proximity of far-right terrorist threats. Importantly, the mid- and long-term impact of COVID-19 on far-right terrorism requires particular attention to accurately evaluate whether it has brought changes to the operational and ideological environment of far-right extremists.

As the analysis has revealed, perpetrators of the same heterogeneity were active but with a differing level of intensity. The same perpetrators were not continuously active for the entire 2010–2020 time period. It is also highly informative to examine how the dynamics among perpetrators and their prevalence have changed over the years. Patterns of weapon usage indicate a low level of sophistication. In the overwhelming majority of examined incidents, easily accessible types of weapons were involved. This together with the diversity of targets has made the attacks less predictable. Although in more than 50% of examined incidents private citizens and religious figures/institutions were targeted, attacks carried out at businesses, police, and government were in a non-negligible percentage.

Notes

1 Barbara Parry and Ryan Scrivens, "Uneasy alliances: A look at the right-wing extremist movement in Canada". *Studies in Conflict & Terrorism*, 39(9), 823, 2016.
2 Richard B. Parent and James O. Ellis III, "The future of right-wing terrorism in Canada". TSAS Working Paper Series, 16–12, 19–20, July 2016.
3 Terry Haig, "New research points to growth of right-wing extremism in Atlantic Canada", Radio Canada International, 17 December 2020. www.rcinet.ca/en/2020/12/17/new-research-points-to-growth-of-right-wing-extremism-in-atlantic-canada/
4 Craig and Marc Kielburger, "Hate is Canada's national crisis", WE. www.we.org/en-US/we-stories/opinion/hate-crimes-national-crisis-canada
5 D. Quan, "Right-wing extremist groups 'prevalent' across Canada, study warns", *National Post*, 10 February 2016.
6 Parent and Ellis III, "The future of right-wing terrorism in Canada".
7 Ibid.
8 Enzo DiMatteo, "Canada's right-wing extremism problem", Now Toronto, 27 January 2021. https://nowtoronto.com/news/donald-trump-and-the-rise-of-right-wing-extremism-in-canada
9 Jacob Davey, Mackenzie Hart, and Cécile Guerin, "An online environmental scan of right-wing extremism in Canada", ISD, 2020. www.isdglobal.org/wp-content/uploads/2020/06/An-Online-Environmental-Scan-of-Right-wing-Extremism-in-Canada-ISD.pdf
10 Ibid.

11 Yannick Veilleux-Lepage and Emil Archambault, "Soldiers of Odin: The global diffusion of vigilante movements", 2017. www.psa.ac.uk/sites/default/files/conference/papers/2017/Soldiers%20of%20Odin%20-The%20Global%20Diffusion%20of%20Vigilante%20Movements.pdf
12 Ibid.
13 Bih-Ru Lea, Yu Wen-Bin, Nisha Maguluru, and Michael Nichols, "Enhancing business networks using social network based virtual communities". *Industrial Management and Data Systems*, 106, 122, 2006.
14 Bruce Hoffman and Jacob Ware, "Terrorism and counterterrorism challenges for the Biden administration", CTC Sentinel, January 2021. https://ctc.usma.edu/wp-content/uploads/2021/01/CTC-SENTINEL-012021.pdf
15 Vera Bergengruen and W. J. Hennigan, " 'They are fighting blind.' Inside the Biden administration's uphill battle against far right extremism", *Time*, 4 March 2021. https://time.com/5944085/far right-extremism-biden/
16 Southern Poverty Law Center, "Hate groups reach record high", 19 February 2019. www.splcenter.org/news/2019/02/19/hate-groups-reach-record-high
17 Rachel Janik and Keegan Hankes, "The year in hate and extremism 2020", Southern Poverty Law Center, 1 February 2021. www.splcenter.org/news/2021/02/01/year-hate-2020
18 Seth G. Jones, Catrina Doxsee, and Nicholas Harrington, "The escalating terrorism problem in the United States", June 2020. https://csis-website-prod.s3.amazonaws.com/s3fs-public/publication/200612_Jones_DomesticTerrorism_v6.pdf
19 Southern Poverty Law Center, "Flyering remains a recruitment tool for hate groups", 1 February 2021. www.splcenter.org/news/2021/02/01/flyering-remains-recruitment-tool-hate-groups
20 Cynthia Miller-Idriss, "White supremacist extremism and the far right in the U.S.", Gale. www.gale.com/intl/essays/cynthia-miller-idriss-white-supremacist-extremism-far right-us#_edn31
21 Jake Horton and Christopher Giles, "Capitol riots: Are US militia groups becoming more active?", BBC, 21 January 2021. www.bbc.com/news/world-us-canada-55638579
22 Ryan Lucas, "Who are the Oath Keepers? Militia group, founder scrutinized in capitol riot probe", NPR, 10 April 2021. www.nprillinois.org/politics/2021-04-10/who-are-the-oath-keepers-militia-group-founder-scrutinized-in-capitol-riot-probe
23 Christopher Matias, "Amid the pandemic, US militia groups plot 'the Boogaloo' AKA civil war, on Facebook", Huffpost, 24 April 2020. www.huffpost.com/entry/boogaloo-facebook-pages-coronavirus-militia-group-extremists_n_5ea3072bc5b6d376358eba98
24 Vanda Felbab-Brown, "US policing after wave one of COVID-19", Lawfare, 20 May 2020. www.lawfareblog.com/us-policing-after-wave-one-covid-19
25 "White supremacist propaganda spikes in 2020", ADL. www.adl.org/white-supremacist-propaganda-spikes-2020
26 Steve Vockrodt, "FBI: Government's response to virus incited would-be bomber", Stars and Stripes, 15 April 2020. www.stripes.com/news/us/fbi-government-s-response-to-virus-incited-would-be-bomber-1.626141

27 Federal Bureau of Investigation, "White supremacist infiltration of law enforcement", 17 October 2006. https://oversight.house.gov/sites/democrats.oversight.house.gov/files/White_Supremacist_Infiltration_of_Law_Enforcement.pdf
28 Jessica White, "Far right extremism in the US: A threat no longer ignored", RUSI Commentary, 1 February 2021. https://rusi.org/commentary/far right-extremism-us-threat-no-longer-ignored
29 Ibid.
30 Seth G. Jones, Catrina Doxsee, Grace Hwang, and Jared Thompson, "The military, police, and the rise of terrorism in the United States", CSIS Brief, April 2021. https://csis-website-prod.s3.amazonaws.com/s3fs-public/publication/210412_Jones_Military_Police_Rise_of_Terrorism_United_States_1.pdf?
31 US Department of Defense, "Report to armed services committees on screening individuals who seek to enlist in the armed forces", June 2020. https://media.defense.gov/2021/Mar/02/2002592042/-1/-1/0/REPORT-TO-ARMED-SERVICES-COMMITTEES-ON-SCREENING-INDIVIDUALS-WHO-SEEK-TO-ENLIST-IN-THE-ARMED-FORCES.PDF
32 Sarah Slobin and Sam Hart, "When the right wing rallies", Reuters Graphics, 15 April 2021. https://graphics.reuters.com/USA-CAPITOL/SECURITY/xegpbxoadpq/
33 Counter Extremism Project, "Violent right-wing extremism and terrorism – Transnational connectivity, definitions, incidents, structures and countermeasures", November 2020. www.counterextremism.com/sites/default/files/CEP%20Study_Violent%20Right-Wing%20Extremism%20and%20Terrorism_Nov%202020.pdf
34 Blyth Crawford, "Coronavirus and conspiracies: How the far right is exploiting the pandemic", King's College London, 16 September 2020. www.kcl.ac.uk/coronavirus-and-conspiracies-how-the-far right-is-exploiting-the-pandemic
35 ISD, "Far right exploitation of Covid-19", 12 May 2020. www.isdglobal.org/wp-content/uploads/2020/05/20200513-ISDG-Weekly-Briefing-3b.pdf
36 United Nations Security Council CTED, "Member States concerned by the growing and increasingly transnational threat of extreme right-wing terrorism", July 2020. www.un.org/securitycouncil/ctc/sites/www.un.org.securitycouncil.ctc/files/files/documents/2021/Jan/cted_trends_alert_extreme_right-wing_terrorism_july.pdf
37 Jessica White, "Far right extremism steal the show in 2020", RUSI Commentary, 26 November 2020. https://rusi.org/commentary/far right-extremism-steals-show-2020
38 "Anti-racism protesters concerned about increased presence of far right militias at U.S. demonstrations", CBC, 1 September 2020. www.cbc.ca/radio/thecurrent/the-current-for-september-1-2020-1.5707442/anti-racism-protesters-concerned-about-increased-presence-of-far right-militias-at-u-s-demonstrations-1.5707491
39 "Far right US Facebook groups pivot to attacks on Black Lives Matter", VOA News, 5 July 2020. www.voanews.com/usa/race-america/farright-us-facebook-groups-pivot-attacks-black-lives-matter
40 Emily Olson, "Antifa, Boogaloo boys, white nationalists: Which extremists showed up to the US Black Lives Matter protests?", ABC, 27 June 2020. www.abc.net.au/news/2020-06-28/antifa-boogaloo-extremists-at-us-floyd-protests/12388260
41 Horton and Giles, "Capitol riots: Are US militia groups becoming more active?".

42 Garrett M. Graff, "Behind the strategic failure of the capitol police", *Politico*, 8 January 2021. www.politico.com/news/magazine/2021/01/08/capitol-police-failure-456237
43 Del Quentin Wilber, "FBI director says Capitol riot was 'domestic terrorism' ", *Los Angeles Times*, 2 March 2021. www.latimes.com/politics/story/2021-03-02/fbi-wray-testify-congress-capitol-siege
44 "The Capitol Siege: The arrested and their stories", NPR, 5 March 2021. www.npr.org/sections/insurrection-at-the-capitol/2021/01/19/958240531/members-of-right-wing-militias-extremist-groups-are-latest-charged-in-capitol-si
45 Roberto Schmidt, "Members of right-wing militias, extremist groups are latest charged in Capitol Siege", NPR, 19 January 2021. www.npr.org/sections/insurrection-at-the-capitol/2021/01/19/958240531/members-of-right-wing-militias-extremist-groups-are-latest-charged-in-capitol-si
46 Sophie Lewis, "Capitol police warns of 'possible plot to breach the Capitol' by militia group", CBS News, 3 March 2021. www.cbsnews.com/news/capitol-police-increase-security-march-4-qanon-conspiracy-theory/
47 Kevin Rose, "What is QAnon, the viral pro-Trump conspiracy theory?", *The New York Times*, 15 June 2021. www.nytimes.com/article/what-is-qanon.html
48 The George Washington University Program on Extremism, "This is our house! A preliminary assessment of the Capitol Hill Siege participants", March 2021.
49 Andrew Selsky, "Capitol attack reflects US extremist evolution over decades", AP News, 23 January 2021. https://apnews.com/article/capitol-siege-riots-coronavirus-pandemic-b7123f0a223c6ed8098a03b459120c83
50 David Neiwert, "Warning of 'III%' militia plot, fueled by March 4 conspiracy theories, induces House to shut down", Daily Kos, 4 March 2021. www.dailykos.com/stories/2021/3/3/2019262/-Warning-of-III-militia-plot-fueled-by-March-4-conspiracy-theories-induces-House-to-shut-down
51 Cassie Miller and Hannah Gais, "Capitol insurrection shows how trends on the far right's fringe have become mainstream", Southern Poverty Law Center, 22 January 2021. www.splcenter.org/hatewatch/2021/01/22/capitol-insurrection-shows-how-trends-far rights-fringe-have-become-mainstream
52 Jakob Guhl and Jacob Davey, "A safe space to hate: White supremacist mobilisation on Telegram", ISD Briefing, 26 June 2020. www.isdglobal.org/wp-content/uploads/2020/06/A-Safe-Space-to-Hate2.pdf
53 Geneva Sands, "White supremacy is 'most lethal threat' to the US, DHS draft assessment says", CNN, 8 September 2020. https://edition.cnn.com/2020/09/08/politics/white-supremacy-dhs-draft-assessment/index.html
54 Robert O'Harrow, Andrew Ba Tran, and Derek Hawkins, "The rise of domestic extremism in America", *The Washington Post*, 12 April 2021. www.washingtonpost.com/investigations/interactive/2021/domestic-terrorism-data/
55 Jones et al., "The military, police, and the rise of terrorism".
56 Robert O'Harrow, Andrew Ba Tran, and Derek Hawkins, "The rise of domestic extremism in America".
57 Home Office, "Operation of police powers under the Terrorism Act 200 and subsequent legislation: Arrests, outcomes, and stop and search, Great Britain, financial year ending March 2018", 14 June 2018.
58 "Nine years on from the far right terrorist attacks in Norway, and the threat persists", Muslim Engagement and Development, 27 July 2020. www.mend.org.uk/nine-years-on-from-the-far right-terrorist-attacks-in-norway-and-the-threat-persists/

59 Kim Sengupta, "Violent right-wing extremism is a 'major threat' in the UK, MI5 boss says", *Independent*, 15 October 2020. www.independent.co.uk/news/uk/home-news/right-wing-extremism-terrorism-violence-uk-mi5-ken-mccallum-b1039501.html
60 Nick Lowles, "State of hate 2021, backlash, conspiracies and confrontation", 2021. www.hopenothate.org.uk/wp-content/uploads/2021/03/state-of-hate-2021-final-2.pdf
61 Jane's, "Threat from right-wing extremism continues to increase in UK". www.janes.com/docs/default-source/documentation/farrightuk.pdf?sfvrsn=d902087d_0
62 Ibid.
63 Linton Besser and Matt Brown, "Police chief of UK deradicalisation program urges Australia to reinvest in terror prevention as far right referrals rise", ABC, 21 March 2019. www.abc.net.au/news/2019-03-21/top-uk-cop-urges-australia-to-invest-in-terror-prevention/10923654
64 Rhys Martin, "Future trends: Far right terrorism in the UK – A major threat?", Global Risk Insights, 14 April 2021. https://globalriskinsights.com/2021/04/future-trends-far right-terrorism-in-the-uk-a-major-threat/
65 Rhys Martin, "Future trends: Far right terrorism in the UK – A major threat?".
66 "Far right ideas have grown 'exponentially' in the UK", TRT World, 26 March 2021. www.trtworld.com/magazine/far right-ideas-have-grown-exponentially-in-the-uk-45342
67 Nazia Parveen and Harreit Sherwood, "Police log fivefold rise in race-hate complaints since Brexit result", *The Guardian*, 30 June 2016. www.theguardian.com/world/2016/jun/30/police-report-fivefold-increase-race-hate-crimes-since-brexit-result
68 "Labour MP Jo Cox 'murdered for political cause' ", BBC, 14 November 2016. www.bbc.com/news/uk-37978582
69 Melanie Smith and Chloe Colliver, "The impact of Brexit on far right groups in the UK: Research Briefing", Institute for Strategic Dialogue, 2016. www.isdglobal.org/wp-content/uploads/2016/07/Impact-of-Brexit.pdf
70 Ibid.
71 "Far right using COVID conspiracy theories to lure young – UK police", Reuters, 10 May 2021. www.reuters.com/world/uk/far right-using-covid-conspiracy-theories-lure-young-uk-police-2021-05-10/
72 Marc Hudson, "In the UK, a group is using environmentalism to push far right arguments", Scroll.in, 4 April 2020. https://scroll.in/article/957917/in-the-uk-a-group-is-using-environmentalism-to-push-far right-arguments
73 Nick Lowles and Jemma Levene, "A year in lockdown has transformed Britain's far right", *Huffington Post*, 23 March 2021. www.huffingtonpost.co.uk/entry/far right-britain-pandemic_uk_6059b96bc5b6f12839d741b9
74 James McAuley, "France insists it's targeting Islamist extremism. But some foreign observers and French Muslims see a broader agenda", *The Washington Post*, 14 November 2020. www.washingtonpost.com/world/europe/france-terrorism-muslims-confusion/2020/11/13/e40332bc-2042-11eb-ad53-4c1fda49907d_story.html
75 "France teacher attack: Seven charged over Samuel Paty's killing", BBC, 22 October 2020. www.bbc.com/news/world-europe-54632353
76 Angelique Chrisafis, "French police worker killed in knife attack at station near Paris", *The Guardian*, 23 April 2021. www.theguardian.com/world/2021/apr/23/french-police-officer-killed-in-knife-attack-at-police-station-near-paris

77 Kim Willsher, "Samuel Paty murder: How a teenager's lie sparked a tragic chain of events", *The Guardian*, 8 March 2021. www.theguardian.com/world/2021/mar/08/samuel-paty-how-a-teenagers-lie-sparked-a-tragic-chain-of-events
78 Ioana Petrescu, Moritz Hergl, Silvia Fallone, Théo Boucart, and Xesc Mainzer Cardell, "Right-wing terrorism: European perspectives", *The New Federalist*, 12 June 2020. www.thenewfederalist.eu/right-wing-terrorism-european-perspectives?lang=fr
79 Chris Baynes, "Right-wing terrorist plot to kill French president foiled", *Daily Mercury*, 4 July 2017. www.dailymercury.com.au/news/right-wing-terrorist-plot-kill-french-president-fo/3196432/
80 "Six arrested over far right anti-Macron plot", RFI, 6 November 2018. www.rfi.fr/en/20181106-six-arrested-over-far right-anti-macron-plot
81 "French far right plot to attack mosques, migrants, politicians uncovered", RFI, 18 October 2017. www.rfi.fr/en/france/20171018-french-far right-plot-attack-mosques-migrants-politicians-uncovered
82 "Two French women charged over racist stabbing of veiled Muslims", Al-Jazeera, 22 October 2020. www.aljazeera.com/news/2020/10/22/two-french-women-charged-over-racist-stabbing-of-veiled-muslim
83 Raffaello Pantucci and Kyler Ong, "Persistence of right-wing extremism and terrorism in the west". *Counter Terrorist Trends and Analyses*, 13(1), January 2021. www.jstor.org/stable/pdf/26979992.pdf
84 Ibid.
85 "France Far right documentary: Why are many young people turning to Marine Le Pen's National Front?", Channel 4 News, 12 April 2017. www.youtube.com/watch?v=H6cGA8-TH5o
86 "Inside France's young far right", BBC News, 3 April 2017. www.youtube.com/watch?v=QsCLUqWXzcM
87 Petrescu et al., "Right-wing terrorism: European perspectives".
88 Joe Heim and James McAuley, "New Zealand attacks offer the latest evidence of a web of supremacist extremism", *The Washington Post*, 15 March 2019; John Eligon, "The El Paso screed, and the racist doctrine behind it", *The New York Times*, 7 August 2019.
89 Joseph Nasr, "Far right crime hits record high in Germany", Reuters, 4 May 2021. www.reuters.com/world/europe/germany-arrests-suspect-over-hate-mail-using-neo-nazi-acronym-2021-05-04/
90 Kate Connolly, "German society 'brutalised' as far right crimes hit record levels", *The Guardian*, 4 May 2021. www.theguardian.com/world/2021/may/04/rightwing-extremism-germany-stability-interior-minister-says
91 Ibid.
92 Ibid.
93 Frank Jordans and David Rising, "German far right crime rises; police arrest alleged neo-Nazi", AP News, 4 May 2021. https://apnews.com/article/europe-migration-arrests-race-and-ethnicity-immigration-5b12a6caed6103ba3976c6349fe6dee6
94 Kate Connolly, "German society 'brutalised' as far right crimes hit record levels"; Laurenz Gehrke, "Germany records highest level of right-wing extremist crime in 20 years", *Politico*, 4 May 2021. www.politico.eu/article/germany-records-highest-level-of-right-wing-extremist-crimes-in-20-years/
95 Sam Denney, "The German far right doesn't need to win elections to be dangerous", Lawfare, 17 March 2021. www.lawfareblog.com/german-far right-doesnt-need-win-elections-be-dangerous

96 Nasr, "Far right crime hits record high in Germany".
97 Lisa Hänel, "Mass shooting in Hanau: Grief and rage persist one year on", DW, 19 February 2021. www.dw.com/en/mass-shooting-in-hanau-grief-and-rage-persist-one-year-on/a-56612160
98 Jorg Luyken, "Alarming' rise in far right weapons seizures prompts Germany to beef up police power", *Telegraph*, 2019. www.telegraph.co.uk/news/2019/09/29/alarming-rise-far right-weapons-seizures-prompts-germany-beef
99 "IntelBrief: Far right terrorist attack puts Germany on edge", The Soufan Center, 21 February 2020. https://thesoufancenter.org/intelbrief-farright-terrorist-attack-puts-germany-on-edge/
100 Mattia Caniglia, Linda Winkler, and Solène Métais, "The rise of the right-wing violent extremism threat in Germany and its transnational character", 2 March 2020. www.esisc.org/publications/analyses/the-rise-of-the-right-wing-violent-extremism-threat-in-germany-and-its-transnational-character
101 Frank Jordans and David Rising, "German officials say far right crime rising as police arrest alleged neo-Nazi", PBS, 4 May 2021. www.pbs.org/newshour/world/german-officials-say-far right-crime-rising-as-police-arrest-alleged-neo-nazi
102 Joseph Nasr, "Far right crime hits record high in Germany".
103 Kate Connolly, "German society 'brutalised' as far right crimes hit record levels".
104 Jordans and Rising, "German far right crime rises; police arrest alleged neo-Nazi".
105 Julianna Suess, "The budding alliance between lockdown critics and the far right in Germany", RUSI, 2 March 2021. https://rusi.org/commentary/budding-alliance-between-lockdown-critics-and-far right-germany
106 Kyler Ong and Raffaello Pantucci, "From fringe to mainstream: The extreme rightwing in Europe", Observer Research Foundation, 1 July 2020. www.orfonline.org/expert-speak/fringe-mainstream-extreme-rightwing-europe-68848/
107 Christina Gossner, "Anti-lockdown protests in Germany infiltrated by far right extremists", Euractiv, 14 May 2020. www.euractiv.com/section/coronavirus/news/anti-lockdown-protests-in-germany-infiltrated-by-far right-extremists/
108 Paul Peachey, "German far right exploits Covid-19 to rally anti-Muslim fervour", *The National News*, 15 May 2020. www.thenationalnews.com/world/europe/german-far right-exploits-covid-19-to-rally-anti-muslim-fervour-1.1019963
109 Emily Schultheis, "Germany's far right is only getting more radical", *Slate*, 19 April 2021. https://slate.com/news-and-politics/2021/04/germany-far rights-afd-elections.html
110 Denney, "The German far right doesn't need to win elections to be dangerous".
111 Ibid.
112 Katrin Bennhold, "Far right Germans try to storm Reichstag as virus protests escalate", *The New York Times*, 31 August 2020. www.nytimes.com/2020/08/31/world/europe/reichstag-germany-neonazi-coronavirus.html
113 Wolfgang Dick, "What is behind the right-wing 'Reichsbürger' movement?", DW, 24 July 2018. www.dw.com/en/what-is-behind-the-right-wing-reichsb%C3%BCrger-movement/a-36094740
114 Ben Knight, "Germany's far right AfD searching for new momentum ahead of election", DW, 6 April 2021. www.dw.com/en/germany-far right-afd-alternative-for-germany-2021-election-results/a-57054532
115 Ian Bremmer, "These 5 countries show how the European far right is growing in power", *Time*, 13 September 2018. https://time.com/5395444/europe-far right-italy-salvini-sweden-france-germany/

116 Denney, "The German far right doesn't need to win elections to be dangerous".
117 Counter Extremism Project, "Violent right-wing extremism and terrorism – Transnational connectivity, definitions, incidents, structures and countermeasures", November 2020. www.counterextremism.com/sites/default/files/CEP%20Study_Violent%20Right-Wing%20Extremism%20and%20Terrorism_Nov%202020.pdf
118 Denney, "The German far right doesn't need to win elections to be dangerous".
119 Organized Crime and Corruption Reporting Project, "Germany arrests ten in mega operation against neo-Nazi criminal network", 2 March 2021. www.occrp.org/en/daily/13963-germany-arrests-ten-in-mega-operation-against-neo-nazi-criminal-network
120 "German soldier, relative arrested over far right extremism", US News, 1 March 2021. www.usnews.com/news/world/articles/2021-03-01/german-soldier-relative-arrested-over-far right-extremism
121 Gregor Link, "Neo-Nazis in German police issue new threats", World Socialist Web Site, 19 September 2020. www.wsws.org/en/articles/2020/09/19/germ-s19.html
122 Denney, "The German far right doesn't need to win elections to be dangerous".
123 Sindre Bangstad, "Norway is in denial about the threat of far right violence", *The Guardian*, 16 September 2019. www.theguardian.com/commentisfree/2019/sep/16/norway-denial-far right-violence-breivik
124 "Anders Behring Breivik", *The New York Times*. www.nytimes.com/topic/person/anders-behring-breivik
125 "Norway attacks", BBC News. www.bbc.co.uk/news/world-europe-14261716
126 Cato Hemmingby and Tore Bjørgo, "Terrorist target selection: The case of Anders Behring Breivik". *Perspectives on Terrorism*, 12(6), 164–176, 2018.
127 Owen Good and Michael McWhertor, "Oslo terrorist used modern warfare 2 as "training-simulation", world of warcraft as cover", Kotaku, 23 July 2011. https://kotaku.com/oslo-terrorist-used-modern-warfare-2-as-training-simul-5824147
128 Will Englund and Michael Birnbaum, "Suspect in Norway attacks admits involvement, denies responsibility", *The Washington Post*, 24 July 2011.
129 Torgeir Huseby and Synne Sørheim, "Forensic psychiatric statement Breivik, Anders Behring", TV2, 29 November 2011.
130 Paul Ames, "Is Anders Behring Breivik part of a movement?", Global Post, 25 July 2011. www.pri.org/stories/2011-07-25/anders-behring-breivik-part-movement
131 Raffaello Pantucci, "What have we learnt about lone wolves from Anders Behring Breivik?". *Perspectives on Terrorism*, 5, 5–6, 2011.
132 Mark Townsend and Simon Tisdall, "Defiant from the doc, Breivik boasts more will die", *The Guardian*, 25 July 2011. www.theguardian.com/world/2011/jul/25/anders-behring-breivik-terror-cells
133 "Norwegian man gets 21 years for slaying, mosque attack", VOA News, 11 June 2011. www.voanews.com/europe/norwegian-man-gets-21-years-slaying-mosque-attack
134 Asne Seierstad, "Is Norwegian mass murderer Anders Breivik still a threat to Europe?", Newsweek, 13 April 2016. www.newsweek.com/anders-breivik-neo-nazi-suing-norway-asne-seierstad-447247
135 "Vojtěch Mlýnek", The Knights Templar Europe Report, 30 September 2012. https://knightstemplareurope.wordpress.com/2012/09/30/vojtech-mlynek/
136 "Polish professor jailed for plot to bomb parliament building", BBC News, 22 December 2015. www.bbc.com/news/world-europe-35159074

137 Seierstad, "Is Norwegian mass murderer Anders Breivik still a threat to Europe?".
138 "Sandy Hook school shooting", History.com, 14 December 2012. www.history.com/this-day-in-history/gunman-kills-students-and-adults-at-newtown-connecticut-elementary-school
139 Ahmed Shaheed, "Report on Islamophobia or anti-Muslim hatred submitted to the UN Special Rapporteur on Freedom of Religion or Belief", 30 November 2020. www.ohchr.org/Documents/Issues/Religion/Islamophobia-AntiMuslim/Civil%20Society%20or%20Individuals/SindreBangstad.pdf
140 Bangstad, "Norway is in denial about the threat of far right violence".
141 Kiyya Baloch, "Norway's Kristiansand comes together to stand with Muslims in wake of hate crime", *Dawn*, 25 November 2019. www.dawn.com/news/1518605
142 Ibid.
143 Lefteris Karagiannopoulos, "Shooting at Norway mosque investigated as 'possible act of terrorism' – Police", Reuters, 11 August 2019. www.reuters.com/article/uk-norway-attack-idUKKCN1V1099?edition-redirect=uk
144 "Norwegian man gets 21 years for slaying, mosque attack", VOA News, 11 June 2011. www.voanews.com/europe/norwegian-man-gets-21-years-slaying-mosque-attack
145 Ahmed Shaheed, "Report on Islamophobia or anti-Muslim hatred submitted to the UN Special Rapporteur on Freedom of Religion or Belief".
146 Europol, "TE-SAT 2011: EU terrorism situation and trend report".
147 "Radicalisation awareness network". https://icct.nl/project/radicalisation-awareness-network-2021/
148 Ahmed S. Hashim, "Terrorism as an instrument of cultural warfare: the meaning of Anders Breivik". *Counter Terrorist Trends and Analyses*, 3(8), 1–6, August 2011.
149 Ames, "Is Anders Behring Breivik part of a movement?".
150 Praveen Swami, "Anders Breivik and Europe's bling right eye", *The Hindu*, 25 July 2011. www.thehindu.com/opinion/lead/anders-breivik-europes-blind-right-eye/article2290619.ece
151 Ibid.
152 Matthew Tempest, "Commissioner warns of 'growing menace' of right-wing terrorism in EU", Euractiv, 23 March 2017. www.euractiv.com/section/politics/news/commissioner-warns-of-growing-menace-of-right-wing-terrorism-in-eu/
153 Tore Bjørgo and Ingvild Magnæs Gjelsvik, "Right-wing extremists and anti-Islam activists in Norway: Constraints against violence", C-REX Working Paper Series, March 2017. www.sv.uio.no/c-rex/english/publications/c-rex-working-paper-series/constraints-against-right-wing-violence.pdf
154 Ibid.
155 Ibid.
156 Birgitte Prangerød Haanshuus, "Høyreklikk: En studie av norske høyreekstreme bevegelsers aktivisme, ideologi og nettverkstilhørighet i sosiale medier". Oslo: Master thesis, Department of Political Science, University of Oslo, 2015.
157 Tore Bjørgo and Ingvild Magnæs Gjelsvik, "Right-wing extremists and anti-Islam activists in Norway: Constraints against violence".
158 Counter Extremism Project, "Norway: Extremism and terrorism". www.counterextremism.com/countries/norway
159 Mette Wiggen, "As Norway's far right declines in popularity, a new populist force rises", OpenDemocracy, 18 February 2021. www.opendemocracy.net/en/countering-radical-right/as-norways-far right-declines-in-popularity-a-new-populist-force-rises/

160 Ibid.
161 Ida Kvittingen, "Far right groups in Norway instigate more street provocation than before", Science Norway, 29 January 2020. https://sciencenorway.no/political-science-politics-violence/farright-groups-in-norway-instigate-more-street-provocation-than-before/1629662
162 Charlie Duxbury, "Sweden's far right takes a step closer to power", *Politico*, 25 March 2021. www.politico.eu/article/sweden-far right-jimmie-akesson-election-2022-step-closer-to-power/
163 Carlotta Serioli, "Sweden's identity crisis and the rise of the far right", Global Risks Insights, 2 January 2021. https://globalriskinsights.com/2021/01/swed ens-identity-crisis-and-the-rise-of-the-far right/
164 Amy M. Russo, "Sweden steps up deportation", *Foreign Affairs*, 30 June 2017. www.foreignaffairs.com/articles/sweden/2017-06-30/sweden-steps-depo rtation
165 "Sweden's identity crisis and the rise of the far right", Global Risk Insights, 2 January 2021. https://globalriskinsights.com/2021/01/swedens-identity-cri sis-and-the-rise-of-the-far right/
166 Sandro Scocco, "Why did the populist far right in Sweden make gains?", Social Europe, 18 October 2018. https://socialeurope.eu/why-did-the-populist-far right-in-sweden-make-gains
167 "Sweden's identity crisis and the rise of the far right", Global Risk Insights.
168 Simon Johnson and Johan Ahlander, "Sweden's far right eyes election gains as gang violence rises", Reuters, 26 June 2018. www.reuters.com/article/us-swe den-election-crime-insight-idUSKBN1JM0QQ
169 "What's behind the rise in gang violence across Sweden?", *The Local*, 4 July 2019. www.thelocal.se/20190704/in-depth-whats-behind-the-rise-in-gang-violence-across-sweden/
170 "Why Sweden struggles to curb gang violence", *The Economist*, 28 November 2020. www.economist.com/europe/2020/11/28/why-sweden-struggles-to-curb-gang-violence
171 Josh Thomas, "The far right's nationalist response to coronavirus", LSE, 21 January 2021. https://blogs.lse.ac.uk/socialpolicy/2021/01/21/the-far rights-nationalist-response-to-coronavirus/; Hannah Ralph, "Sweden and the radical right", CERS Working Paper, 2012. https://cers.leeds.ac.uk/wp-content/uplo ads/sites/97/2013/05/Sweden_and_the_Radical_Right_Hannah_Ralph.pdf
172 Ralf Melzer and Sebastian Serafin (Eds.), "Right-wing extremism in Europe, country-analyses, counter-strategies and labour-market-oriented exit strategies", Friedrich-Ebert Stiftung, 2014. http://library.fes.de/pdf-files/dialog/10957.pdf
173 Vyacheslav Likhachev, "Far right extremism as a threat to Ukrainian democracy", Freedom House. https://freedomhouse.org/report/analytical-brief/2018/far right-extremism-threat-ukrainian-democracy
174 Huseyn Aliyev, "Is Ukraine a hub for international white supremacist fighters?", Russia Matters, 13 May 2020. www.russiamatters.org/analysis/ukraine-hub-international-white-supremacist-fighters
175 "National Corps: Why Ukraine's far right party is enjoying growing support", Euronews, 3 March 2019. www.euronews.com/2019/03/03/national-corps-why-ukraine-far right-party-is-enjoying-growing-support
176 Mridula Ghosh, "The extreme right in Ukraine", Friedrich Ebert Stiftung, October 2012. https://library.fes.de/pdf-files/id-moe/09407.pdf

177 Aliyev, "Is Ukraine a hub for international white supremacist fighters?".
178 Ibid.
179 "Ukraine's ultra-right increasingly visible as election nears", AP News, 27 March 2019. https://apnews.com/article/ap-top-news-elections-petro-poroshenko-international-news-embezzlement-e971db860c7a4c12a5240fc08ce6c95e
180 OSCE ODIHR Hate Crime Reporting Ukraine, http://hatecrime.osce.org/ukraine
181 Fred Weir, "Militaristic and anti-democratic, Ukraine's far right bides its time", The Christian Science Monitor, 15 April 2019. www.csmonitor.com/World/Europe/2019/0415/Militaristic-and-anti-democratic-Ukraine-s-far right-bides-its-time
182 Vyacheslav Likhachev, "Far right extremism as a threat to Ukrainian democracy".
183 Lev Golinkin, "Neo-Nazis and the far right are on the march in Ukraine", *The Nation*, 22 February 2019. www.thenation.com/article/archive/neo-nazis-far right-ukraine/
184 Weir, "Militaristic and anti-democratic, Ukraine's far right bides its time".
185 April Gordon, "A new Eurasian far right Rising: Reflections on Ukraine, Georgia, and Armenia", Freedom House, January 2020. https://freedomhouse.org/sites/default/files/2020-02/FarRightEurasia_FINAL_.pdf
186 Tim Hume, "Far right extremists have been using Ukraine's war as a training ground. They're returning home", Vice, 31 July 2019. www.vice.com/en/article/vb95ma/far right-extremists-have-been-using-ukraines-civil-war-as-a-training-ground-theyre-returning-home
187 Jack O'Rourke, "Opinion/O'Rourke: U.S. wrong to support Ukraine movement", *The Providence Journal*. https://eu.providencejournal.com/story/opinion/columns/2021/02/17/opinion-orourke-u-s-wrong-support-ukraine-movement/4279815001/
188 Andreas Umland, "Ukraine's far right today continuing electoral impotence and growing uncivil society", Swedish Institute of International Affairs, 2020. www.ui.se/globalassets/ui.se-eng/publications/ui-publications/2020/ui-brief-no.-3-2020.pdf
189 Michael Colborne, "Croatia key to Ukrainian far right's International Ambitions", Balkan Insight, 18 July 2019. https://balkaninsight.com/2019/07/18/croatia-key-to-ukrainian-far rights-international-ambitions/
190 "Ukraine's ultra-right increasingly visible as election nears", AP News, 27 March 2019. https://apnews.com/article/ap-top-news-elections-petro-poroshenko-international-news-embezzlement-e971db860c7a4c12a5240fc08ce6c95e
191 Tali Fraser, "Facebook, Instagram criticised for hosting far right group with 80,000 followers", *Times of Israel*, 24 November 2020. https://jewishnews.timesofisrael.com/facebook-instagram-criticised-for-hosting-far right-group-with-80000-followers/?fbclid=IwAR2EhGlpdkCoq7OxLocsaALXdHXd1TrLx7C8KsouYywBK-V_KB9yXzrtv3s
192 Josh Cohen, "Commentary: Ukraine's neo-Nazi problem", Reuters, 19 March 2018. www.reuters.com/article/us-cohen-ukraine-commentary-idUSKBN1GV2TY
193 Hume, "Far right extremists have been using Ukraine's war as a training ground. They're returning home".
194 Ibid.
195 Alex MacKenzie and Christian Kaunert, "Radicalisation, foreign fighters and the Ukraine conflict: A playground for the far right?". *Social Sciences*, 10, 116, 2021. DOI: https://doi.org/10.3390/socsci10040116

196 Greg Barton, "To shut down far right extremism in Australia, we must confront the ecosystem of hate", The Conversation, 7 February 2021. https://theconversation.com/to-shut-down-farright-extremism-in-australia-we-must-confront-the-ecosystem-of-hate-154269
197 Ben Knight and Josie Taylor, "Why aren't Australian authorities banning more far right extremist groups?", ABC News, 26 March 2021. www.abc.net.au/news/2021-03-27/why-isnt-australia-banning-more-far right-extremist-groups/100032018
198 Paul Karp, "Asio reveals up to 40% of its counter-terrorism cases involve far right violent extremism", *The Guardian*, 22 September 2020. www.theguardian.com/australia-news/2020/sep/22/asio-reveals-up-to-40-of-its-counter-terrorism-cases-involve-far right-violent-extremism
199 Ben Doherty, "Asio boss warns of rising foreign interference and far right extremism in Australia", *The Guardian*, 24 February 2020. www.theguardian.com/australia-news/2020/feb/24/rightwing-extremism-a-real-and-growing-threat-asio-chief-says-in-annual-assessment
200 Australian Government Australian Security Intelligence Organisation, "ASIO annual report 2017–18". www.asio.gov.au/sites/default/files/ASIO%20Annual%20Report%20to%20Parliament%202017-18.pdf
201 Karen Percy, "Phillip Galea found guilty of plotting terrorist attacks on Melbourne 'leftist' centres", ABC News, 5 December 2019. www.abc.net.au/news/2019-12-05/phillip-galea-jury-verdict-plot-to-blow-up-buildings/11755432
202 Clive Williams, "Right-wing extremists were already on spy agencies' radars", *Canberra Times*, 23 March 2019. www.canberratimes.com.au/story/5992498/right-wing-extremists-were-already-on-spy-agencies-radars/
203 Erin Pearson, "Right-wing extremist Phillip Galea jailed for 12 years on terror charges", *The Age*, 20 November 2020. www.theage.com.au/national/victoria/right-wing-extremist-phillip-galea-jailed-for-12-years-on-terror-charges-20201120-p56gzg.html
204 Alexander Darling, Sarah Jane Bell, and Matt Neal, "Calls for cross-burning neo-Nazis camped in The Grampians to be classified as terrorist group", ABC News, 28 January 2021. www.abc.net.au/news/2021-01-28/calls-grampians-far right-group-labelled-terrorist-organisation/13098762
205 "Victoria Police charge man with assault over neo-Nazi video at Channel Nine", ABC News, 3 March 2021. www.abc.net.au/news/2021-03-03/victoria-police-lay-charge-over-channel-nine-nazi-video-incident/13210366
206 "Australia designates far right group as terrorist organisation", Reuters, 22 March 2021. www.reuters.com/article/us-australia-security-idUSKBN2BE0KD
207 Michael McGowan, "Adelaide man arrested for allegedly possessing improvised explosive device in far right raids", *The Guardian*, 8 April 2021. www.theguardian.com/australia-news/2021/apr/08/adelaide-man-arrested-for-allegedly-possessing-improvised-explosive-device-in-far right-raids
208 Cait Kelly, "Who are the neo-Nazi groups threatening Australia's security?", *The New Daily*, 26 February 2020. https://thenewdaily.com.au/news/2020/02/26/australia-neo-nazi/
209 Darling et al., "Calls for cross-burning neo-Nazis camped in The Grampians to be classified as terrorist group".
210 Michael McGowan, "Where 'freedom' meets the far right: The hate messages infiltrating Australian anti-lockdown protests", *The Guardian*, 25 March 2021. www.theguardian.com/australia-news/2021/mar/26/where-freedom-meets-the-far right-the-hate-messages-infiltrating-australian-anti-lockdown-protests

211 Mario Peucker, "Seizing the opportunity: How the Australian far right milieu uses the pandemic to push its nationalist and anti-globalist grand narratives", CRIS Consortium, 2 June 2020. www.crisconsortium.org/cris-commentary/seizing-the-opportunity-how-the-australian-far right-milieu-uses-the-pandemic-to-push-its-nationalist-and-anti-globalist-grand-narratives
212 Mitch Ryan, "Two years after Christchurch shooting, far right haunts Australia", *Nikkei Asia*, 15 March 2021. https://asia.nikkei.com/Politics/Terrorism/Two-years-after-Christchurch-shooting-far right-haunts-Australia
213 John Coyne, "Australia must address the risk of radicalisation posed by recession", *The Strategist*, 25 June 2020. www.aspistrategist.org.au/australia-must-address-the-risk-of-radicalisation-posed-by-recession/
214 Ibid.
215 Geoff Dean, Peter Bell, and Zarina Vakhitova, "Right-wing extremism in Australia: The rise of the new radical right". *Journal of Policing, Intelligence and Counter Terrorism*, 11, 2, 2016.
216 Ibid.
217 Clive Williams, "The shape of far right extremism in Australia", *The Strategist*, 21 March 2019. www.aspistrategist.org.au/the-shape-of-far right-extremism-in-australia/
218 Ibid.
219 Executive Council of Australian Jewry, "Antisemitism in Australia 2020: Incidents and discourse". www.ecaj.org.au/wordpress/wp-content/uploads/Condensed-Antisemitism-Report-Australia-2020.pdf
220 Caitlin Fitzsimmons, "Eight of if 10 Asia-Australians experience discrimination: survey", *The Sydney Morning Herald*, 22 September 2019. www.smh.com.au/business/workplace/eight-out-of-10-asian-australians-experience-discrimination-survey-20190920-p52tfp.html
221 Kristy Campion, "A 'lunatic fringe'? The persistence of right wing extremism in Australia". *Perspectives on Terrorism*, 13, 2, April 2019. https://researchoutput.csu.edu.au/ws/portalfiles/portal/29338723/A_Lunatic_Fringe_POT.pdf
222 Ibid.
223 Gavin Butler, "US neo-Nazi group 'The Base' is recruiting members in Australia", Vice, 26 March 2021. www.vice.com/en/article/7k9gja/neo-nazi-group-the-base-recruiting-in-australia
224 Zeb Holmes and Ugur Nedim, "Right-wing extremists: The real terrorism threat", Sydney Criminal Lawyers, 18 March 2019. www.sydneycriminallawyers.com.au/blog/right-wing-extremists-the-real-terrorism-threat/
225 "Right-wing extremism on rise", SBS News, 2 June 2017. www.sbs.com.au/news/right-wing-extremism-on-rise
226 Australian Government Australian Security Intelligence Organisation, "ASIO annual report 2019–20". www.asio.gov.au/asio-report-parliament.html
227 Ibid.
228 Parliament of Australia, "Terms of reference". www.aph.gov.au/Parliamentary_Business/Committees/Joint/Intelligence_and_Security/ExtremistMovements/Terms_of_Reference
229 Joshua Mcdonald, "Australia: Far right on the rise as intelligence chief warns of terror threat", *The Diplomat*, 28 February 2020. https://thediplomat.com/2020/02/australia-far right-on-the-rise-as-intelligence-chief-warns-of-terror-threat/

230 Information is based upon an interview with an Australian law enforcement officer.

231 Tom Lowrey and David Lipson, "Neo-Nazi Sonnenkrieg Division to become first right-wing terrorist organisation listed in Australia", ABC News, 2 March 2021. www.abc.net.au/news/2021-03-02/sonnenkrieg-division-first-right-wing-terror-group-listed/13206756

232 "Christchurch shootings: How the attacks unfolded", BBC News, 18 March 2019. www.bbc.com/news/world-asia-47582183

233 Helen Regan and Sandi Sidhu, "49 killed in mass shooting at two mosques in Christchurch, New Zealand", CNN, 15 March 2019. https://edition.cnn.com/2019/03/14/asia/christchurch-mosque-shooting-intl/index.html

234 "Christchurch mosque attack livestream", New Zealand Classification Office. www.classificationoffice.govt.nz/news/featured-classification-decisions/christchurch-mosque-attack-livestream/

235 Taylor Lorenz, "The shooter's manifesto was designed to troll", *The Atlantic*, 15 March 2019. www.theatlantic.com/technology/archive/2019/03/the-shooters-manifesto-was-designed-to-troll/585058/

236 Patrick Gower, "Christchurch shooting: Survivors convinced gunman visited mosque to learn layout", Newshub, 12 April 2019. https://web.archive.org/web/20200415113542/www.newshub.co.nz/home/new-zealand/2020/04/christchurch-shooting-survivors-convinced-gunman-visited-mosque-to-learn-layout.html

237 "Christchurch mosque shootings: Bruce Rifle Club closes in wake of terror", *New Zealand Herald*, 17 March 2019. www.nzherald.co.nz/nz/christchurch-mosque-shootings-bruce-rifle-club-closes-in-wake-of-terror/4SOM7W7KD7QAE4X6UC5ZR5SHD4/

238 Nick Perry, "Report finds lapses ahead of New Zealand mosque attack", AP News, 8 December 2020. https://apnews.com/article/intelligence-agencies-shootings-brenton-tarrant-new-zealand-new-zealand-mosque-attacks-d8217fa30fe4ceba45fb001b77857385

239 Kim Sengupta, "Brenton Tarrant: Suspected New Zealand attacker 'met extreme right-wing groups' during Europe visit, according to security sources", *Independent*, 15 March 2019. www.independent.co.uk/news/world/australasia/brenton-tarrant-new-zealand-attacker-far right-europe-gunam-shooting-a8825611.html

240 Brenton Tarrant, "The great replacement", pp. 4–6. www.ilfoglio.it/userUpload/113The_Great_Replacementconvertito.pdf

241 "San Diego synagogue shooting: One person dead in Poway, California", BBC, 28 April 2019. www.bbc.com/news/world-us-canada-48081535

242 Eleanor Dearman, "Racism and the August 3 shooting: One year later, El Paso reflects on the hate behind the attack", *El Paso Times*, 30 July 2020. https://eu.elpasotimes.com/in-depth/news/2020/07/30/el-paso-walmart-shooting-community-reflect-racist-motive-behind-attack/5450331002/

243 Jason Burke, "Norway mosque attack suspect 'inspired by Christchurch and El Paso shootings'", *The Guardian*, 11 August 2019. www.theguardian.com/world/2019/aug/11/norway-mosque-attack-suspect-may-have-been-inspired-by-christchurch-and-el-paso-shootings

244 New Zealand Security Intelligence Service, "Annual report 2018". www.nzsis.govt.nz/assets/Uploads/2018-NZSIS-Annual-Report.pdf

245 Human Rights Commission Te Kahui Tika Tangata, "Reports of race and religious hate crime in New Zealand 2004–2012", June 2019. www.hrc.co.nz/files/1515/6047/9685/It_Happened_Here_Reports_of_race_and_religious_hate_crime_in_New_Zealand_2004-2012.pdf
246 Australian Government Australian Security Intelligence Organisation, "ASIO Annual Report 2016–17". www.asio.gov.au/sites/default/files/Annual%20Report%202016-17.pdf
247 Ibid.
248 Daniel L. Byman, "Reflections on the Christchurch commission report", Brookings, 16 December 2020. www.brookings.edu/blog/order-from-chaos/2020/12/16/reflections-on-the-christchurch-commission-report/
249 "Christchurch shootings: Far right attack 'could happen in UK too' ", BBC News, 18 March 2019. www.bbc.com/news/uk-47618176
250 Alexander Gillespie, "New Zealand was warned a terror attack was possible", Al-Jazeera, 19 March 2019. www.aljazeera.com/opinions/2019/3/19/new-zealand-was-warned-a-terror-attack-was-possible
251 Philip Alpers and Michael Picard, "New Zealand—Gun facts, figures and the law", GunPolicy.org, 17 February 2020.
252 "New Zealand votes to amend gun laws after Christchurch attack", Reuters, 10 April 2019. www.reuters.com/article/us-newzealand-shooting-parliament-idUSKCN1RM0VX
253 "New Zealand tightens gun laws further in response to mass shooting", Reuters, 18 June 2020. www.reuters.com/article/us-newzealand-shooting-idUSKBN23P0TE
254 Daniel Koehler, "The Halle, Germany, synagogue attack and the evolution of the far right terror threat", CTC Sentinel, December 2019.
255 Daniel Koehler, "Right-Wing Terrorism in the 21st Century the 'National Socialist Underground' and the History of Terror from the Far Right in Germany". Routledge, 2018.
256 Paul Spoonley, "Far right extremists still threaten New Zealand, almost one year on from the Christchurch attacks", ABC News, 10 March 2020. www.abc.net.au/news/2020-03-11/christchurch-mosque-attack-far right-extremists-still-threat-nz/12042578
257 Marc Daalder, "The furious world of New Zealand's far right nationalists", The Spinoff, 2 February 2019. https://thespinoff.co.nz/politics/31-12-2019/summer-reissue-the-furious-world-of-new-zealands-far right-nationalists/
258 Hayden Crosby, "Treating NZ's far right groups as terrorist organisations could make monitoring extremists even harder", The Conversation, 16 April 2021. https://theconversation.com/treating-nzs-far right-groups-as-terrorist-organisations-could-make-monitoring-extremists-even-harder-158291
259 Alexander Gillespie, "Two years on from the Christchurch terror attack, how much has really changed?", The Conversation, 14 March 2021. https://theconversation.com/two-years-on-from-the-christchurch-terror-attack-how-much-has-really-changed-156850
260 "Christchurch white supremacist Philip Arps has charge dropped", *NZ Herald*, 11 October 2020. www.nzherald.co.nz/nz/christchurch-white-supremacist-philip-arps-has-charge-dropped/ZEC7BPTE2P4IOA7RXVDR3HQVQQ/

261 Florence Kerr and Thomas Manch, "What's public and what's secret in the case of the soldier arrested for breaching national security", Stuff, 24 February 2020. www.stuff.co.nz/national/crime/119627639/whats-public-and-whats-secret-in-the-case-of-the-soldier-arrested-for-breaching-national-security?m=m
262 Spoonley, "Far right extremists still threaten New Zealand, almost one year on from the Christchurch attacks".
263 Florence Kerr and Thomas Manch, "Linton soldier is the first New Zealander to be charged with espionage", Stuff, 25 November 2020. www.stuff.co.nz/national/300167448/linton-soldier-is-the-first-new-zealander-to-be-charged-with-espionage
264 Jared Savage, " 'Terrorist attack': How police thwarted heavily armed teen's plan to shoot teachers, classmates in South Island school", *NZ Herald*, 13 November 2020. www.nzherald.co.nz/nz/terrorist-attack-how-police-thwarted-heavily-armed-teens-plan-to-shoot-teachers-classmates-in-south-island-school/UIBDQEDPD5OCWPJLYN34DSI53U/
265 "New Zealand police arrest two for threat to Christchurch mosques attacked in 2019", ABC, 4 March 2021. www.abc.net.au/news/2021-03-04/new-zealand-police-arrest-two-plot-christchurch-mosques/13217304
266 EUROPOL, "European union terrorism situation and trend report 2021".
267 Ibid.

3

HOW DO EXTREME RIGHT THREAT GROUPS OPERATE?

It has been argued that far-right extremism and violence are increasingly present in the examined countries. There is an ever-pressing need to better understand the nature of the associated threat. This requires both academics and practitioners to dig deeper into the functioning of far-right threat groups. Analyzing their mode of operation and mindset could take us to those vicious details, which may help us identify ways to detect and counter these malevolent activities. With this in mind, this chapter attempts to scrutinize the functionalities of selected far-right extremist formations. In line with this, first, their ideology and mindset; second, their fundraising methods; third, recruitment; fourth, the structure of these groups; fifth, their communication channels; sixth, their mode of operation, targeting, weaponry; and finally, their transnational network are elaborated.

Ideology and mindset

The radical right movement is far from being homogenous. It embraces a broad spectrum of ideologies.[1] Right-wing extremism is usually defined as a "specific ideology characterized by anti-democratic opposition towards equality".[2] It is generally associated with racism, xenophobia, exclusionary nationalism, conspiracy theories, and authoritarianism.[3] Right-wing ideology inherently embraces anti-Islam, anti-immigration, and anti-government sentiment. This mindset may escalate to white nationalism and identitarianism, which claims an enhanced focus on the importance of the white race (Figure 3.1).[4]

With the intention to map and systematize the prevailing ideological concepts, we sought to break down the analyzed far-right threat groups into subsets. We have chosen to divide these analyzed far-right formations in

DOI: 10.4324/9781032708041-3

FIGURE 3.1 Ideologies of far-right threat groups.

accordance with their primary targets. Breaking them down along with this principle resulted in five subcategories, namely, anti-Muslim, anti-immigration, anti-government, neo-Nazi, and white supremacist threat groups. The following table lists the organizations we studied within each subcategory. Besides these five principal sentiments, we cannot disregard, however, other common narratives, which far-right hate groups frequently espouse. These ideological concepts are summarized at the end of this section.

Anti-Muslim hate groups	*Anti-government hate groups*
La Meute (Canada)	The Boogaloo (USA)
Northern Guard (Canada)	Oath Keepers (USA)
Proud Boys (USA)	Three Percenters (USA)
Britain First (UK)	Reichsbürger (Germany)

Anti-Muslim hate groups	*Anti-government hate groups*
English Defence League (UK)	
PEGIDA (Germany)	
Stop the Islamisation of Norway (Norway)	
Reclaim Australia (Australia)	
Australian Defence League (Australia)	
Wargus Christi (NZ)	
Anti-immigrant hate groups	*Neo-Nazi hate groups*
Soldiers of Odin (Canada)	Atalante (Canada)
Storm Alliance (Canada)	Blood & Honour (UK)
Northern Guard (Canada)	Atomwaffen Division (USA)
Proud Boys (USA)	The Base (USA)
Britain First (UK)	National Action (UK)
Génération Identitaire (France)	Sonnenkrieg Division (UK)
PEGIDA (Germany)	Feuerkrieg Division (UK)
Identitarian Movement (Germany)	Gruppe S (Germany)
National Socialist Underground (Germany)	Reichsbürger (Germany)
Swedish Resistance Movement (Sweden)	Azov Battalion (Ukraine)
Stop the Islamisation of Norway (Norway)	Antipodean Resistance (Australia)
Dominion Movement (NZ)	National Socialist Network (Australia)
White supremacist hate groups	
Feuerkrieg Division (UK)	
The Boogaloo (USA)	
Proud Boys (USA)	
Nordic Resistance Movement (Norway)	
Australian Defence League (Australia)	
Lad's Society (Australia)	
Action Zealandia (NZ)	

Anti-Muslim hate groups

In Canada, La Meute propaganda encourages boycott of halal products, and initiates "petitions against government policies that promote multiculturalism".[5] Meanwhile, Northern Guard patrols in Canada raised concerns among some citizens, especially Muslims.[6] The militant anti-Muslim[7] group's white supremacist beliefs are apparently a threatening factor for non-white members of society.[8]

United States-based Proud Boys members also espouse Islamophobic views.[9] They claim that "they are defending the West from vaguely defined forces that purportedly seek to erode it, often using violence to achieve their goals".[10] Supporters "are staunchly opposed to what they deem political correctness and racial guilt, and call for closed borders, minimal government and maximum protection of free speech and gun rights".[11]

In the United Kingdom, Britain First openly stands against multilateralism and Islamism.[12] They urge a "comprehensive ban on Islam in the UK, including halal slaughter, Sharia courts, religious publications, the operation of mosques and the use of Islamic face coverings, including the burka".[13] The group sees itself "as a Christian 'army' preparing to confront Muslims directly at their homes, mosques and in the streets in order to elicit a violent reaction from the Muslim community".[14] Followers believe that "the apocalyptic end game is near, and that salvation can only be achieved through a war between Christianity and Islam".[15]

English Defence League (EDL) is claimed to be an anti-Islamic and "self-described counter jihad movement".[16] The group stands up for the "white working class"[17] and claims to have "legitimate concerns about radical Islam".[18] Members oppose not only Islamic extremism but the group's actions "deliberately seek to whip up tensions and violence between Muslim and non-Muslim communities".[19] The group

> disavows crude biological determinism and uses a more sophisticated discourse of culture to mark out Islam as a sociological, rather than a biological, impediment to assimilation. [...] It is important, therefore, to emphasize the ideological variance between the movement and its supporters. The group operates as an umbrella organization for anyone who wishes to demonstrate against "Islamic extremism", and those who protest under its banner will surely have additional anxieties.[20]

PEGIDA in Germany opposes what it considers the Islamisation of the "Western world", calling for more restrictive immigration rules, in particular for Muslims.[21] The group "has a nineteen-point manifesto in which it claims to defend 'Judeo-Christian' values and to oppose preachers of hate, regardless of what religion and radicalism, whether religiously or politically motivated. Although it is not against integrated Muslims living here".[22]

Stop the Islamisation of Norway is an anti-Islam[23] formation, which defines Islam as "a totalitarian political ideology that violates the Norwegian Constitution as well as democratic and human values".[24] SIAN leader stated that "most immigrants are not refugees, but rather welfare tourists".[25] Reportedly, Anders Behring Breivik was "heavily influenced"[26] by the anti-Muslim milieu including the Islamisation of Europe.

Reclaim Australia was established in the direct aftermath of the December 2014 Lindt café siege in Sydney. The group openly opposes the practice of Islam in Australia.[27] It strives to ban Shariah Law, the burqa, and Halal certification.[28]

Operating in New Zealand, Wargus Christi claims itself as a "martial-monastic Christian brotherhood"[29] and embraces Islamophobic views.[30] The group's Facebook page, which is no longer available, "regularly threatened Muslims, Jews and homosexuals".[31]

Anti-government hate groups

The Boogaloo Movement is considered to be a "loosely connected anti-government movement that has included some white nationalists who believe in an 'accelerationist' ideology that encourages spurring civil disorder to eventually foment the breakdown of the political system entirely".[32] Accelerationism is best described as "an emerging doctrine that rejects political solutions and seeks to hasten societal collapse through incitement and terrorism".[33] It is the anti-government narrative that may connect the diverse ideologies embraced by the movement's followers.[34] In line with this, the movement "advocates for a violent uprising targeting liberal political opponents and law enforcement".[35] As a Boogaloo explained in a Facebook group in July 2020, "We don't want a civil war, we want the politicians' heads on spikes".[36]

The core idea of the Oath Keepers resembles the ideology of the militia movement, which claims that the United States is "collaborating with a one-world tyrannical conspiracy called the New World Order to strip Americans of their rights. [...] Once Americans are rendered defenseless, they will be enslaved by the New World Order".[37] These beliefs fuel Oath Keepers' anti-government narratives and encourage them to object to this perceived "federal tyranny or continued patterns of violations of fundamental rights of Americans by the American government".[38]

Three Percenters also share a resistance to the US federal government.[39] The group advocates a myth that "only three percent of American colonists took up arms against the British during the American Revolution. Members of the group believe that a small force of well-armed and prepared members with a just cause can overthrow a tyrannical government".[40] "Three Percenters view themselves as modern-day versions of those revolutionaries, fighting against a tyrannical U.S. government rather than the British".[41]

Reichsbürger members acknowledge the 1937 borders of the German Empire and do not "accept the legality of the Federal Republic of Germany nor any of its government authorities".[42] Accordingly, its members

> refuse to pay taxes or fines. [...] They see their personal property, such as their houses, as independent entities outside the authority of the Federal Republic of Germany, and reject the German constitution and other legal texts but also swamp German courts with lawsuits. They produce their own aspirational documents such as passports and driving licenses.[43]

Supporters of the ideology "have declared their own small 'national territories', which they call the 'Second German Empire' the 'Free State of Prussia' or the 'Principality of Germania' ".[44]

Anti-immigration hate groups

Canadian Storm Alliance's "self-described mission is to preserve the rights of the people and Canadian culture".[45] The anti-immigrant group has criticized the federal government for accepting the influx of refugees and has organized numerous protests demonstrating against Canada's immigration policies.[46]

The ultranationalist Canadian Northern Guard has protested together with other far-right groups against illegal immigration. The formation argues that "Canada should simply close the door to any form of immigration until further notice". "There are too many", says Eric Brazeau, a resident of Aylmer, who is the group's spokesperson for Quebec and Ontario. "We are not able to support our veterans and the homeless. We will not pay for the Haitians. In addition, many are criminals. If they do crimes in our community, we will be there to protect and educate our neighbors".[47]

In a similar vein, Proud Boys also espouse anti-immigration ideologies.[48] "Members of the organization assert that they are defending 'the West' from vaguely defined forces that purportedly seek to erode it, often using violence to achieve their goals".[49]

Anti-immigration hate group Britain First "halt any further immigration except in special cases. It rejects and deports asylum seekers who do not originate from countries bordering the United Kingdom".[50] The group bars followers of Islam from public office and urges a "comprehensive ban on Islam in the UK. It also calls for a ban on the use of Islamic face coverings, including the burka".[51]

Génération Identitaire members in France nurture "hostile against migrants and are recognized for inciting discrimination".[52] The group has been hostile to migrants and incited discrimination, hatred, and violence. It has "repeatedly tried to bar migrants from entering the country, conducting high-profile raids in the Alps and the Pyrenees".[53]

Germany-based PEGIDA urges a new immigration law to stop "unregulated, quantitative immigration. Instead of that, new rules for a 'qualitative immigration' shall be established".[54] Followers of the group advocate complementing the constitution with a new passage that would establish the obligation for each immigrant to integrate into German society. "This would eliminate the fear of a disappearing (native) culture and identity".[55]

The Identitarian Movement aims to defend European "white identity and culture from the supposed attack by liberalism, immigration and Islam".[56] "Its supporters subscribe to the 'Great Replacement' conspiracy theory, founded by French philosopher Renaud Camus that a global elite is attempting to replace the white race with others via mass immigration across the western world".[57] As a "pan-European nationalist far-right political ideology asserting the right of Europeans and peoples of European descent to culture and territories claimed to belong exclusively to them".[58] "Identitarians see themselves as the literal defenders of Europe and white European ethnicity".[59] The movement is strongly opposed to the politics and philosophy of Islam, which some critics describe as disguised Islamophobia.[60] Identitarians oppose Europeans who have decided not to have children, they stand against "cultural mixing, non-traditional gender roles, multiculturalism, and the increasing migration of people to Europe, which allegedly increases the so-called Islamization of the continent".[61]

The anti-migrant sentiment was extremely prevalent in the Eastern part of Germany at the beginning of the 1990s. It was also the one that fueled the National Socialist Underground's ideology.[62] Nine of the trio's ten victims who were killed between 2000 and 2007 were immigrants.[63] According to trial documents, Mundlos, Boehnhardt, and Zschaepe intended to "intimidate ethnic minorities and destabilize the German state".[64]

Anti-Islam[65] Swedish Resistance Movement[66] and Stop the Islamisation of Norway define Islam as "a totalitarian political ideology that violates the Norwegian Constitution as well as democratic and human values".[67] Unlike its neighbor Sweden, the Finnish has not welcomed arriving refugees. Soldiers of Odin members patrol in black jackets with a Viking symbol and the Finnish flag to protect native Finns from immigrants.[68] They blame "Islamist intruders" for the elevated level of criminality in Finland.[69]

Dominion Movement believes that "White New Zealanders overrun by multiculturalism and immigrants are 'unworthy imports' ".[70] The group describes itself as a "fraternity of young New Zealand nationalists' united by the belief that Europeans are the defining people of this nation and that they were essential in its creation".[71]

Neo-Nazi hate groups

In Canada, Atalante shares neo-fascist ideology with elements of revolutionary nationalism, anti-capitalism, Islamophobia, and anti-communism.[72] Blood and Honour advocates "white-power ideology"[73] through music festivals and recordings. The group aims to "unite those with legitimate interests in securing the future of European cultural identity".[74] Although Soldiers of Odin refused to espouse neo-Nazi ideologies, its founder Mika Ranta – who was charged with racially motivated assault – is connected with neo-Nazi Nordic Resistance Movement.[75]

Atomwaffen Division embraces "apocalyptic beliefs",[76] the group strives to "accelerate societal collapse, promote chaos, and create a racially-pure white society".[77] The neo-Nazi formation's ideology is based on activist James Mason's 563-page collection, called the *SIEGE*. The document urges "leaderless, cell-structured terrorism and white revolution and implores America's true neo-Nazis to go underground and begin a guerrilla war against what it dubs 'The System' ".[78]

The main essence of The Base's concept is to "inspire a small number of actors to commit themselves wholly to their revolutionary mindset and act on it" – either by forming small, clandestine terror cells or inspiring individuals to carry out "lone actor attacks".[79] The formation adopts "nihilistic and accelerationist rhetoric".[80] Considering that "society should be pushed to collapse so a white ethnostate can arise out of the ruins".[81]

A statement on National Action's website claims "We carry out demonstrations, publicity stunts, and other activities in order to grow and spread our message, that of National Socialism".[82] Their members frequently express their admiration for Hitler, his words are regularly cited in their discussions. In a similar vein, "the Third Reich was a recurrent feature, routinely deployed to justify the group's ultra-nationalism, racism, antisemitism, disablism, homophobia, anti-liberalism and anti-capitalism".[83]

United Kingdom-based Sonnenkrieg Division's white supremacist ideology has been inspired

> both by the historical National Socialist German Worker's Party (Nazi Party) and by the Satanic "Order of Nine Angles" movement. SKD seeks to encourage lone-actor terrorist attacks against its political, racial and ethnic enemies, in order to bring about an apocalyptic "race war" and the creation of a global "white" ethno-state.[84]

Feuerkrieg Division considers the war against society "controlled by Jews as inevitable".[85] They believe it is the only way to "reset cultural and societal norms that have resulted in perceived 'degenerate' values, for which they also blame Jews".[86]

Germany-based Gruppe S embraces the tenets of anti-Semitism, anti-communism, national conservatism, Euroscepticism, German nationalism, neo-Nazism, neo-Fascism, and right-wing populism. Its founding members endeavor to "shake the state and social order of Germany by means of a civil war"[87] in which they would "attack mosques to kill and injure a large number of Muslims"[88] and Jews.[89] Similarly, the Reichsbürger movement openly shares anti-Semitic views.[90]

Azov Battalion adopts principles of Ukrainian nationalism, neo-Nazism, and anti-Semitism.[91]

Likewise, Australian Antipodean Resistance members espouse neo-Nazi and anti-Semitic[92] views. As its followers claim

> we aim to provide an alternative for young Australians to the filth of modern society by setting a good example for people to live up to. This encompasses many areas, but in short, it mainly refers to abstaining from degeneracy such as alcoholism, drugs and race mixing, while encouraging things like physical activity, activism, and comradeship. We are not a political party. Our goals are currently outside of the current political system. We adhere to National Socialism as it is the embodiment of healthy values, it is the best

code to run an organization dedicated to national revival. We are closer to a 21st Century Hitler Youth rather than the NSDAP itself.[93]

National Socialist Network also strives for a "white revolution"[94] and "openly described Indigenous Australians as subhuman and monkeys".[95] They contend "to expand, group members hope to survive as a free and distinct nation".[96]

White supremacist hate groups

Feuerkrieg Division espouses the most "extreme interpretations of white supremacist ideology".[97] Some members of the Boogaloo movement also share white nationalist sentiments and believe in "an accelerationist ideology that encourages spurring civil disorder to eventually foment the breakdown of the political system entirely".[98] Likewise, there are supporters of the Proud Boys, who adopt white supremacist ideologies and/or engage with white supremacist groups.[99]

Similarly, Nordic Resistance Movement strives to "demolish the democratic order and establish a national socialist state for white people".[100] They aim to find "an ethnically pure pan-Nordic nation",[101] "deport most non-ethnic Northern European residents",[102] and "dismantle the global Zionist elite".[103]

In Australia, Australian Defence League gained publicity in 2014 when group members were stalking Muslim women on public transport. They also hung out posters with anti-Islam messages near mosques and threatened to attack an Islamic school.[104] Lads Society's objective is "to build a community of young Australian men to provide job networking, mental and physical health as well as an open space for communication".[105] Their concept is essentially the "reinvigorating Australian culture".[106]

Action Zealandia is considered to be a "radical right ethno-nationalist formation with environment concerns".[107] Their five key principles are "self-improvement, European identity, community building, nationalism and sustainability".[108] The group strives to "build a community for European New Zealanders".[109] They also share identitarian and anti-Maori sentiments. Tenets of the Great Replacement Conspiracy Theory and masculinism are frequently involved in their discussions.[110]

Other ideological concepts adopted by far-right threat groups

Advocating for gun-ownership rights frequently emerges among far-right narratives. When urging for resistance to the US government, Three Percenters calls for a looser protocol to obtain guns.[111] Very similarly, besides its anti-government narratives, the Boogaloo ideology is also pro-gun in nature.[112]

Physical fitness and advanced tactical skills are regularly among the essential requirements imposed on members. Britain First supporters operate as "Britain First Defence Force"[113] and regularly organize so-called activist training camps where they are given self-defence training.[114] Additionally, moral principles are also frequently mentioned as a prerequisite for right-wing activists. Three Percenters, for instance, "must be governed by four principles: moral strength, physical readiness, no first use of force, and no targeting of innocents".[115]

In several instances, far-right extremist groups present themselves as defenders of their communities.[116] According to Canada-based Storm Alliance's Facebook page, "they aim to protect and save the Canadian values that have helped shape Canada into the wonderful country it is today, and to follow a 'no one left behind' motto".[117] They claim to accomplish this through "charitable work, vigilant citizens, and activism in Canadian communities", but do not provide any examples of such work.[118]

Narratives of the Patriot movement frequently emerge among far-right ideologies. Canadian Northern Guard is considered to be an American-style militia movement.[119] Similarly, the Boogaloo ideology "generally share more in common with the Patriot Movement from the 1990s and early 2000s than to contemporary alt-right or white nationalist movements".[120] Likewise, Oath Keepers took the vow to "support and defend the Constitution of the United States against all enemies, foreign and domestic".[121] Foremen of the movement encourage supporters "to disobey orders which they believe would violate the U.S. Constitution".[122] "Broadly speaking, the group started as a response to a perception of what the group would describe as federal tyranny or continued patterns of violations of fundamental rights of Americans by the American government".[123]

In Europe, Generation Identity presents itself as a "patriotic movement",[124] one of its key policies is "remigration – the removal of non-European immigrants to their countries of origin or those of their ancestors".[125] The identitarian movement "has built a culture of violence based on ancient heroes, pantheons, and victorious battles and combined it with the present need for a literal defense".[126] "Identitarians see themselves as the literal defenders of Europe and white European ethnicity".[127]

It has been argued that far-right extremist ideologies advocate anti-women sentiment.[128] The narrative claims that men are deprived in modern societies, while minorities and women are exempted. Therefore, they call for the return to traditional social relations. Proud Boys members, for instance, believe "women are happier when they stay home and have children".[129] Women are "less ambitious" than men, McInnes told a host on Fox News in 2015. "This is sort of God's way – this is nature's way – of saying women should be at home with the kids". Just as he believes women are ill-suited for the workplace, McInnes has argued that the world of politics is best left to men. "When I hear women talk about politics and so often put emotional claptrap over policy", he tweeted in early 2017, "I think, 'Who let these bitches vote?' "[130]

> Women have their own group, the Proud Boys' Girls, who – like all women in the eyes of the Proud Boys – are defined by their relationship to men. Members of the women's contingent, an informal organization, are overwhelmingly the wives and girlfriends of Proud Boys.[131]

Along with Proud Boys, Wargus Christi members also embrace misogynistic views.[132]

Resorting to the use of violence is another common theme in right-wing ideologies. "Violence is firmly entrenched in Proud Boy dogma". McInnes was filmed punching a counter protester outside the DC-based, far-right gathering Deploraball in January 2017. Then, after a speaking engagement at New York University the next month turned violent, he wryly declared, "I cannot recommend violence enough. It's a really effective way to solve problems".[133] Meanwhile Three Percenters oppose the first use of violence.[134]

> The idea of violence is widely accepted within the boogaloo movement; one boogaloo meme uses an image from The Simpsons cartoon to make the point that the purpose of the "boojahideen" is to implement "violently installed Freedom and Liberty" against the federal government.[135]

Feuerkrieg Division, however, embraces violence as a solution to "fix the current political and cultural system, sidestepping concerns about optics and advocating for radical, systemic change".[136] The notion of violence has been "a recurrent feature of British National Action's discourse".[137] For members of the Nordic Resistance Movement, violence has been "necessary to achieve their revolution".[138]

> The group is directly connected to a string of incidents involving members violently confronting minority groups and those who disagree with their ideology. In 2016, a man died after an NMR member kicked him in the chest during a protest in Finland, where he fell and hit his head. Affiliated members planted IEDs outside a far-left cafe and refugee housing in Gothenburg in 2016 and 2017. One of the blasts injured an immigration officer.[139]

LGBT community is a recurring target of far-right extremists. The Atomwaffen Division,[140] the National Action,[141] the Swedish Resistance Movement,[142] and the Antipodean Resistance[143] have all expressed their aversion to homosexuality. National Action was striving to reintroduce a section, which "prohibited the 'promotion of homosexuality' by local councils".[144] Meanwhile, the Antipodean Resistance "took an active stance against the same sex marriage vote".[145]

There are, however, other, idiosyncratic narratives that are also noteworthy in this listing. Let's start with the Boogaloos obsession with pedophiles.[146] Britain First was also arguing for the restoration of capital punishment for pedophiles.[147] Meanwhile, the Dominion Movement advocates the value of the environment, claiming that "the protection of the natural world is one of the greatest inter-generational duties we have".[148] Europe-based far-right entities also took a position with regard to the European Union. The Swedish Resistance Movement has expressed its defiance towards the EU.[149] As "a future vision for Europe",[150] the PEGIDA movement has adopted the concept of the United States of Europe. The idea technically means a "European federation in which every nation retains its distinct identity and culture, but in fact the movement is pursuing Charles de Gaulle's concept of a 'Europe of nation states' ".[151]

Conclusion

Based upon the aforementioned research, the following key findings can be identified.

Anti-immigrant, neo-Nazi, and anti-Muslim sentiments are the most prominent narratives for far-right threat groups operating in Canada. Interestingly, examined Canadian right-wing formations do not embrace either anti-government or white supremacist ideological concepts. Among the analyzed far-right groups in the United States, anti-government, neo-Nazi, and white supremacist narratives are most frequently adopted. Less common are anti-Muslim and anti-immigrant sentiments in US far-right discourses. Right-wing extremists in the United Kingdom embrace neo-Nazi and anti-Muslim ideologies in greater proportion compared with anti-immigrant or white supremacist views. It is noteworthy that none of the examined UK-based far-right threat groups have engaged in anti-government narratives. German right-wing extremists, however, more frequently share anti-immigrant and neo-Nazi ideologies than anti-Muslim or anti-government views. Anti-immigration has been the prominent ideology among both Norwegian and Swedish far-right entities, white supremacism has emerged with regard to Nordic Resistance Movement. Australian right-wing extremists have expressed white supremacist and neo-Nazi – less frequently anti-immigrant – views. Meanwhile far-right groups in New Zealand embrace anti-Muslim, anti-immigrant, as well as white supremacist ideological concepts.

As the following set diagram illustrates (Figure 3.2), there are anti-Muslim hate groups that advocate anti-immigrant narratives. Among the examined far-right threat groups, Proud Boys is the only one, which embraces anti-Muslim, anti-immigrant, and white supremacist sentiments. Another specific example

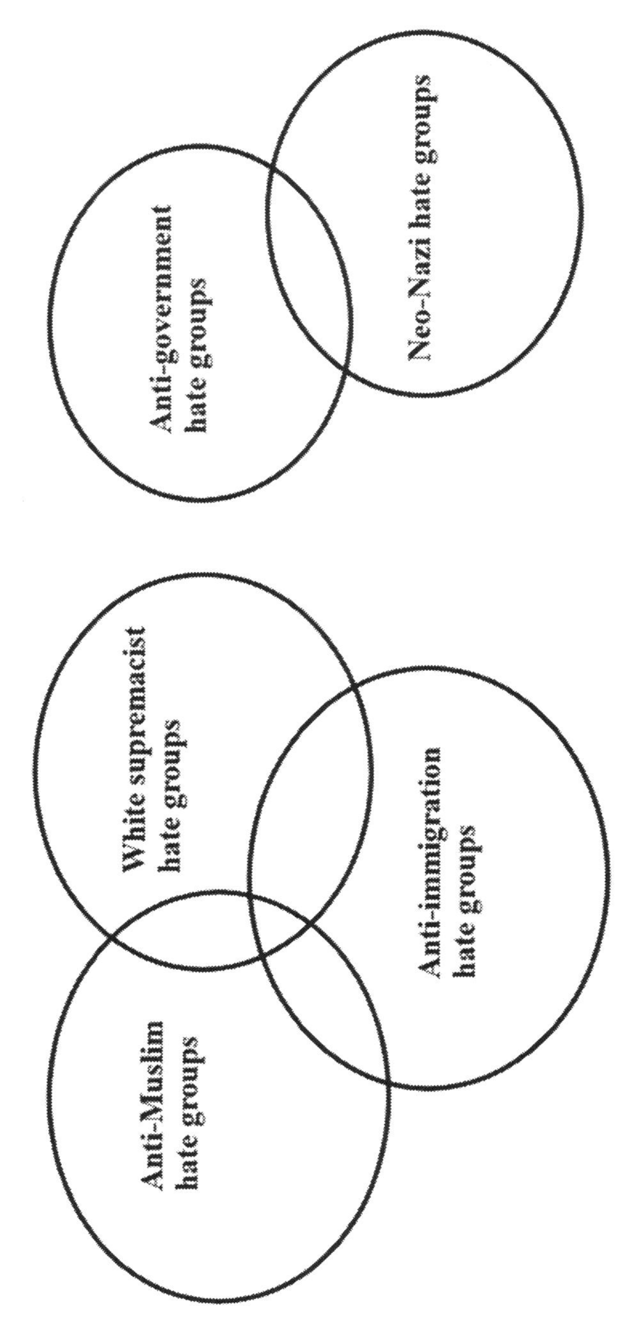

FIGURE 3.2 Ideologies of far-right threat groups – Summary.

is Reischsbürger operating in Germany, which espouses both anti-government and neo-Nazi narratives.

Funding

Finance plays an important role in the successful operation of an extremist movement.[152] It is one of the crucial factors which determines whether the extremist organization can achieve its objectives. On the other end, tracking the finances of hate groups provide excellent insights into their operational practicalities. To effectively tackle the operation of far-right threat groups, we need to limit their ability to raise funds. For this purpose, it is crucial to improve our understanding of their financing and fundraising mechanisms. With this in mind, this chapter aims to map out the forms of selected far-right groups' funding.

For a more nuanced understanding of different fundraising mechanisms, we sought to break down the analyzed far-right groups into subsets. The principle for this categorization is the wide heterogeneity of their primary targets. This process resulted in five subcategories of far-right formations' revenue-generating activities, namely, anti-Muslim, anti-immigration, anti-government, neo-Nazi, and white supremacist. The following table lists the organizations we studied within each subcategory (Table 3.1). These groups were then assessed according to the seven types of fundraising activities identified. Considering that most far-right attacks have been committed by lone actors and small cells, in the last section of this chapter we analyze the forms of their funding.

Membership fees

A common form of raising funds for a political extremist group is collecting fees from members. These mandatory payments can be collected either in cash or by banking transactions. This financing mechanism, however, presumes a more sophisticated level of the extremist organization. It also implies that members of the group have their own income which covers these payments. Obligatory membership fees differ significantly from the financial strategies of, for instance, jihadist terrorist organizations, since some of them pay salaries to their fighters in the conflict zone.[153]

The requirement to pay membership fees occurred with regard to anti-government and neo-Nazi groups. Such financial contributions are Oath Keeper's main source of income. The organization currently charges $50 annually; its lifetime membership, normally $1,200, was recently put "on sale" for $1,000.[154] In a similar vein, Sonnenkrieg Division's activities are likely self-funded by members due to its decentralized structure (Table 3.2).[155]

TABLE 3.1 Subsets of analyzed far-right threat groups

Anti-Muslim hate groups	*Anti-immigration hate groups*
La Meute (Canada)	Soldiers of Odin (Canada)
Northern Guard (Canada)	Storm Alliance (Canada)
Proud Boys (USA)	Northern Guard (Canada)
Britain First (UK)	Proud Boys (USA)
English Defence League (UK)	Britain First (UK)
PEGIDA (Germany)	Génération Identitaire (France)
Stop the Islamisation of Norway (Norway)	PEGIDA (Germany)
Reclaim Australia (Australia)	Identitarian Movement (Germany)
Australian Defence League (Australia)	National Socialist Underground (Germany)
Wargus Christi (New Zealand)	Stop the Islamisation of Norway (Norway)
	Swedish Resistance Movement (Sweden)
	Dominion Movement (New Zealand)
Anti-government hate groups	*Neo-Nazi hate groups*
The Boogaloos (USA)	Atalante (Canada)
Oath Keepers (USA)	Blood and Honour (UK)
Three Percenters (USA)	Atomwaffen Division (USA)
Reichsbürger (Germany)	The Base (USA)
	National Action (UK)
	Sonnenkrieg Division (UK)
	Feuerkrieg Division (UK)
	Reichsbürger (Germany)
	Gruppe S (Germany)
	Azov Battalion (Ukraine)
	Antipodean Resistance (Australia)
	National Socialist Network (Australia)
White supremacist hate groups	
Feuerkrieg Division (UK)	
The Boogaloos (USA)	
Proud Boys (USA)	
Nordic Resistance Movement (Norway)	
Australian Defence League (Australia)	
Lads Society (Australia)	
Action Zealandia (New Zealand)	

Sale of merchandise

Generating revenue through the sale of products is one of the most common fundraising mechanisms among extremist groups. Historically, selling cassette tapes and CDs was a highly lucrative market for hate groups in the late 1990s.

TABLE 3.2 Occurrence of membership fees per examined far-right threat groups

	Membership fees
Anti-Muslim	No instances identified
Anti-immigration	No instances identified
Anti-government	×
Neo-Nazi	×
White supremacist	No instances identified

TABLE 3.3 Occurrence of online market places per examined far-right threat groups

	Sale of merchandise
Anti-Muslim	×
Anti-immigration	No instances identified
Anti-government	×
Neo-Nazi	×
White supremacist	No instances identified

According to a EUROPOL report from those times, it rivaled the hashish trade in Europe.[156] Propaganda pamphlets or music, patches, pins, clothing, or flags are for sale on these formations' webpages or stores.[157]

We identified five far-right hate groups using onsite or online market places (Table 3.3).

In Canada, La Meute co-founder's enterprise produces 24 items of the group branded merchandise.[158] In the United States, the growth of the Boogaloo movement has fueled the creation of Boogaloo-related merchandise. Besides smaller websites offering Boogaloo-related patches, decals, and clothing, a number of businesses sell Boogaloo-related items normally selling firearms, firearms accessories, ammo, or "tactical" gear.[159] The Three Percenter logo was quickly commodified in the form of clothing, patches, stickers, t-shirts, and even gun accessories. Soon one could purchase literally hundreds of products featuring the Three Percenter logo, sold on a myriad of small websites as well as through major online retailers like Amazon.[160] In June 2018, Atomwaffen Division reportedly began selling t-shirts through the online retailer Teespring.[161] The English Defence League (EDL) used its website as a venue through which to sell its branded merchandise, which included hoodies, t-shirts, caps, pin badges, and face masks. Following internal allegations that EDL members were taking the money from this for themselves rather than using it for the organization, the EDL pulled merchandise from its website in September 2010. It has also sold its merchandise items on the auction website eBay.[162] Blood and Honour in the United Kingdom publishes its own magazine, which can be purchased online. According to its website, the price of four issues is £14.[163] Azov Battalion advertises merchandise on its Facebook page.[164] On the ground floor of the group's Cossack House in Kyiv is a shop called Militant Zone, which sells clothes and key chains with stylized swastikas and other neo-Nazi products.[165]

Event fees

White power music events or conferences are highly beneficial for far-right groups. On one hand, they provide opportunities for in-person meetups and function as venues for selling merchandise items. On the other hand, admission fees for these events serve as additional financing sources for certain hate groups (Table 3.4).[166]

Interestingly, only neo-Nazi groups organized such gatherings. Blood and Honour is a musical based resistance network,[167] it organizes music festivals and rallies to spread its propaganda and reach out to new potential members. Concerts are held at a particular property in Lincolnshire, where land is offered by a Blood and Honour member for the event.[168] German right-wing extremists have organized music festivals and martial arts events to which thousands of extremists from a dozen countries have traveled. They recruit and network at martial arts events and music festivals.[169] In December 2019, the fifth neo-Nazi Asgardsrei music festival was held in Kyiv. In the heat of the concerts, participants enthusiastically chanted neo-Nazi slogans and greetings.[170]

Other fundraising activities

Extremist publications or websites may have advertising possibilities. The prevalence of online content, however, substantially lowered these threat groups' income potentials in this regard.

An expert from the Global Disinformation Index noted that 44% of the 73 hate groups he has studied have benefited by securing tax exempt status from the Internal Revenue Service.[171] Among available charity fundraising tools, the most commonly used has been Charity Navigator's "Giving Basket" function. Collecting donations for organizations registered as charitable or social welfare nature help find the loopholes for restrictions. Oath Keeper founder used a

TABLE 3.4 Occurrence of event fees per examined far-right threat groups

	Event fees
Anti-Muslim	No instances identified
Anti-immigration	No instances identified
Anti-government	No instances identified
Neo-Nazi	×
White supremacist	No instances identified

podcast to raise funds for an educational foundation, which operates as a tax-exempt affiliate for the far-right group.[172]

Delivering sessions on martial arts together with tactical and combat training provide additional income sources for extremist groups.[173] This is not least the case in countries like Russia or Ukraine, where paramilitary-like formulations operate.[174] Neo-Nazis also raise money through the sale of self-defence equipment and "doomsday prepping kits".[175]

Crowdfunding and donations

Technological innovations in financing and social media all enriched terrorist capabilities. Social media propaganda offers fruitful financial sources to advance activist goals.[176] Far-right threat groups have been misusing global communication technologies for terrorist financing purposes[177] and established international funding networks via their cross-border linkages.[178] Through donations to campaigns and buying social media advertisements, extremist groups and individuals reportedly cashed in about 1.5 million US dollars through social media platforms and cryptocurrencies.[179] Less formal organizations cannot rely on forms of organizational funding and are highly dependent on occasional donations. Money is sent to them through voluntary financial contributions[180] or targeted fundraising campaigns.[181] Accordingly, forms of donations can be categorized as follows: "internet-based crowdfunding campaigns, sourced openly from deep-pocketed sympathetic donors, and via more discrete peer-to-peer transactions".[182] Unlike crowdfunding, where the sponsor generally does not have trusted relationships with the group or its members, private donations are commonly based upon more personal contact and are gathered in a covered manner.[183]

Crowdfunding offers the potential to build an online fan base, ask for donations, and convert the money into cross-border reach.[184] Right-wing extremists promptly discovered the benefits such crowdsourcing platforms may offer them.[185] Shifts in political extremists' fundraising strategies emerged after two historical turning points. Prior to the "Unite the Right" rally in Charlottesville, crowdfunding websites were prominent financial sources for right-wing political extremists.[186] In the mid-2000s, extremists started to widely use the service provided by Amazon and PayPal. Through these links, they received money back from every dollar their supporters spent on their merchandise.[187] Donations happened either through specific Facebook campaigns. Publicly available hate campaigns however quickly raised concerns among providers of these services and extremists needed to change their strategy. Onwards, they attempted to start projects with misleading purposes, hiding their real motives behind the campaigns. More efficiently, they began to create or find fringe platforms – such as Patreon, GoFundMe, Justgiving, or Kickstarter – explicitly for their occasions.[188]

The August 2017 white nationalist and neo-Nazi march in Charlottesville turned deadly when 20-year-old James Alex Fields rammed his car into a crowd of counter protesters, killing 32-year-old anti-racist protester Heather Heyer and leaving 19 others injured, 5 critically.[189] Reportedly, the organizer of the rally gathered donations for the logistical costs of the event via his PayPal account. He was also active with Patreon campaigns to raise funds as his general income and specifically for the rally.[190] After Charlottesville, mainstream crowdfunding sites shuttered far-right campaigns. GoFundMe communicated that the platform removed several fundraising campaigns associated with James Fields.[191] Crowdfunding site Patreon first banned the account of British conspiracy theorist YouTuber Carl Benjamin. Some weeks later the account of US far-right political commentator James Allsup was removed.[192] Due to hate speech charges, accounts of prominent members of the so-called alt-right movement were banned on Amazon and PayPal.[193] Simultaneously, tech companies like Google, GoDaddy, Airbnb, and Facebook banned white supremacist content.[194] In parallel with this, Apple Pay and PayPal ceased services with white nationalists merchants.[195] In June 2017, PayPal donations account of the Identitarian "Defend Europe" and the English Defence League[196] was locked, and the Identitarian account of the bank "Steiermärkische Sparkasse" was closed.[197]

As a response to PayPal, Stripe, Apple Pay, and Google Pay's refusal to process worrisome online transactions, extremists started to deplatform their fundraising sites. Accordingly, alternative, far-right-specified fundraising websites such as Hatreon,[198] GoyFundMe,[199] MakerSupport,[200] and WeSearchr[201] emerged. For donations Antipodean Resistance set up an account with Hatreon in November 2017, when the page was not functioning anymore, so an account at MakerSupport was established.[202] In the aftermath of the Capitolium siege, a significant surge in the traffic on Gab was reported mostly from new members of Trump supporters.[203] Simultaneously, downloads of the app for Rumble – an alternative to YouTube – doubled and the social media app MeWe became the fifth most popular free application on App Store and Google Play.[204] Britain First was planning a greater collaboration with Russia after being "deplatformed", including financially, in its home country, though he did not respond to questions about any banking arrangements involved.[205]

GiveSendGo, for instance, "offers a Christian cover for violent insurrectionist groups".[206] Several members of the Proud Boys used GiveSendGo to raise money for their court procedures, hiding their projects as "Christian, patriotic cris de Coeur".[207] Arguably, there is a blurred borderline between Christian right and fringe extremist ideologies. An interesting example here is the group, who calls itself Colorado Patriots. They established an initiative on GiveSendGo which urges to "stay well equipped in the event of civilizational breakdown".[208] They claim to "keep innocent families protected against the evil".[209] Their logo, however, contains the iconography of the one Three

Percenters use. MyMilitia on GiveSendGo serves as an organizational hub for militia members including Proud Boys or Three Percenters. These campaigns are relevant factors for fundraising purposes. If no money has been gathered through these sites, they offer handy and cheap opportunities for like-minded individuals to get in touch and keep in contact. GiveSendGo funds are transferred from donors to recipients through the service provided by Stripe. These short-lived and cheap sites were quickly banned by payment service providers.[210] Following the January 6 insurrection, PayPal cut ties with the Christian crowdfunding site[211] and the discussion started with Stripe on finding ways how to tighten existing laissez-faire policies.

Simultaneously, far-right extremist transactions turned into "more discrete, potentially anonymous, peer-to-peer financial activities".[212] To conceal transactions, according to UK-based Blood and Honour and C18 website information, they ask supporters to directly email them for detailed payment information. They also try to avoid cross-border financial transactions and accept only UK bank transfers.[213]

A remarkable amount of the funds used for the insurrection at the Capitolium building was raised through online communication technologies. In a remarkably short period of time, at least 11 crowdfunding campaigns related to Proud Boys and its members raised more than $375,000 "including some facing conspiracy charges related to the Capitol attack".[214] Beneficiaries of the Christian crowdfunding site GiveSendGo were members of far-right groups. Many of the fundraising efforts were directly related to the Capitolium siege.[215] Besides aid projects for a wide range of legitimate charitable purposes, "millions of dollars were raised on the site for far-right causes and groups, many of whom are banned from raising funds on other platforms".[216] More than two dozen fundraisers related to protesting the outcome of the presidential election were identified.[217] Several parallel fundraisers sought to finance the travel and equipment for Proud Boys to attend the January protest. According to a *Washington Post* analysis, some $247,000 was raised on the site for 24 campaigns looking to cover travel costs to DC before the event.[218] Other campaigns raised money for medical assistance for Proud Boys victims following the event.[219]

Campaigns also targeted the fundraising for the legal defense of the participants in the siege. For instance, more than $113,000 were raised for the case of Proud Boys leader Enrique Tarrio on GiveSendGo.com.[220] More than $500,000 was raised through GiveFundGo for Kyle Rittenhouse, who was charged with murdering two protesters at a Black Lives Matter demonstration in Kenosha, Wisconsin.[221] Proud Boys members, Nick Ochs and Nick DeCarlo, who were arrested later in connection with the siege, gathered $300 through the site to help get him to DC.[222] The fundraiser has been shared by the Proud Boys' most popular Telegram channel, which has over 43,000 subscribers at the time of this dispatch. DeCarlo, along with his fundraising manager/fellow

MTM personality Vill Nomerly, is seeking $20,000 for his legal costs with a promise to donate "anything left over ... to a charity supporting similar causes". "Dick needs help, as his media brand is still in a very early stage and can't afford to cover his fees for a federal criminal defense attorney without your assistance", reads the "story" page of DeCarlo's GoGetFunding campaign, which blames the charges against him on a conspiracy between "[t]he mainstream media, leftist Twitter mobs, Antifa, and the FBI". One anonymous donation to DeCarlo's fundraiser included a note from the donor, who claimed to be "a 1Deg from the SATX Chapter", that is, a lowest-level member of the Proud Boys' San Antonio, TX, chapter. The individual further alleged that they were "an attorney licensed in TX and in Federal Courts". The donor then linked to the website of a Texas-based lawyer whose name is prominently displayed on the website. Also among DeCarlo's donors was someone claiming to be Ochs, who donated $100. Ochs has a fundraising goal of $50,000 and provides rewards for high-dollar donors including "Ochs' leather coat" and an "Empty Bottle of Trump Vodka Valued at 800 [dollars]". Like DeCarlo, Ochs is using GoGetFunding as his platform for the fundraiser. "You've already heard about Ochs' legal trouble, but here's the new details: the lawyer costs $50,000 and who knows what other costs might be coming. Unfortunately, with the politicization in America right now it has been hard to raise the money", reads the "story" section of Ochs' fundraiser (Figure 3.3).[223]

A remarkable proportion of the raised money for the Capitolium insurrection came from a number of anonymous high-dollar donors. A Florida-based personal injury lawyer, a Honolulu-based Hawaiian Airlines employee and a former pilot, together with a New York woman whose social media accounts list her as a state-employed special education teacher were among these anonymous donators.[224] More than 80% of the $106,107 raised for medical costs for members of the Proud Boys who were injured during violent clashes in Washington in mid-December was donated by members of the Chinese diaspore. Altogether 1,000 people with Chinese surnames of allegedly conservative Asian Americans gave about $86,000 to a fundraiser on the crowdfunding platform GiveSendGo.[225]

In response to the Capitolium siege, accounts of prominent personalities were shut down. DLive suspended the accounts of "Baked Alaska", "Murder the Media" together with four other accounts, including the one of white nationalist Nick Fuentes, who is the leader of the "Groyper" movement. Accordingly, the DLive balances of these accounts were frozen and future donations are refunded.[226] Airbnb, Amazon, and American Express suspended donations to "all of the legislators who were involved in contesting certification of the electoral results".[227]

As simple and convenient ways to collect funds, crowdfunding campaigns and voluntary donations were mentioned as the main financial resources by 15 hate groups studied.

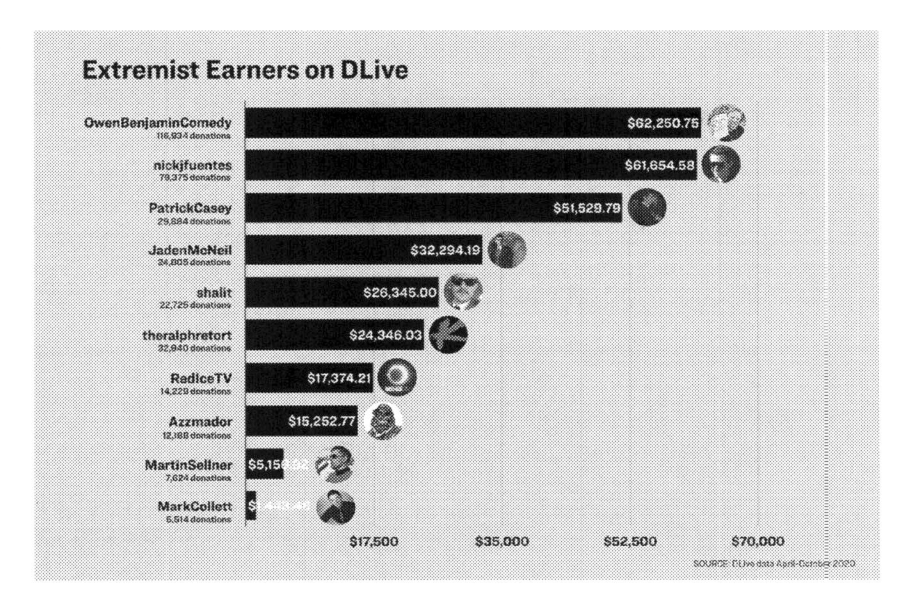

FIGURE 3.3 Extremist earners on DLive.
Source: Illustration by SPLC.

Canadian-based Le Meute was registered as a non-profit organization with the Quebec government in April 2016. Regardless of a banner on the group's social media platforms for donations, in 2017 Le Meute itself confirmed an anonymous donation of $9,000.[228] Additionally, according to former members there are regular monthly donations of up to $100. Annually four or five $25-a-plate fundraising dinners were organized, allegedly with participants of not more than 125 people.[229] Generation Identity in France is not supported by any speculators or governments, it exists solely off of donations[230] from the group's members and supporters.[231] The Norwegian Resistance Movement's funding comes from member donations and sympathetic individuals and organizations. It specifically requests donations through Frihetskamp, the news website owned and operated by the group's Norwegian branch (Table 3.5).[232]

Video streaming

Video streaming platforms like YouTube, Twitch, and DLive offer highly useful opportunities for violent extremists. On one hand, with fewer content moderation policies, clandestine groups can advance their ideologies and interact with their audiences through streaming propagandistic videos. On the other hand, far-right extremists can fundraise via these video streams. Content viewers of video streaming platforms can optionally appreciate videos

TABLE 3.5 Occurrence of crowdfunding and donation per examined far-right threat groups

	Crowdfunding	*Donation*
Anti-Muslim	×	×
Anti-immigration	×	×
Anti-government	×	×
Neo-Nazi	×	×
White supremacist	×	×

through monetary donations. Streamers could monetize their audience by subscriptions to their livestreams or through advertisements.[233]

Twitch is a livestreaming video platform and community for gamers and fans, it is a free streaming service fueled primarily by subscriptions and advertisements. By 2019, gaming platform Twitch viewers live-streamed more than 72% of all live hours watched. On a daily basis, an average of 15 million viewers tune into Twitch to watch, host, and cheer on live streams.[234] According to LifeCourse, 49% of Twitch traffic comes from 18–34-year-olds.[235] QAnon supporters and other far-right influencers earn thousands of dollars broadcasting theories on the streaming site. Besides income stemming from subscriptions, streamers can also raise funds by sending their fans to outside sites to either buy merchandise or donate money.[236]

DLive is an American live streaming service that was founded in 2017. It has become widely popular among violent extremists due to its laissez-faire content policy.[237] According to American website analytics Social Blade, in August 2020 eight of DLive's top-ten earners were far-right extremists or conspiracy theorists.[238] Analysis of DLive's publicly available ledgers of transactions has revealed two important implications. First, the majority of donors use micropayments in varying frequencies. Second, there is a small proportion of donors who spend larger amounts of money on their favorite content creators.[239] Through these mega and smaller donors, far-right extremists can earn more than $100,000 in less than 12 months. Funds are readily available to be cashed out as regular incomes from these platforms.

Social communication technologies played an important role in the storm of the US Capitolium. At least nine DLive streams were online streaming the day's events. One of the most notable among them was alt-right figure Tim Gionet. His account, "Baked Alaska", earned more than $2,000 from tips of the day. On his DLive chat, he was also given tips on where to get into the Capitolium building. Another, Proud Boys-associated account called "Murder the Media" also streamed on that day.[240] Black Lives Matter protests and the storm of the Capitolium building were both livestreamed on Twitch.[241]

Other noteworthy examples are Canada-based Combat 18 and Blood and Honour, which are making use of the video sharing site's automatic addition of adverts to their videos. "Revenue-sharing deals in place under Google's AdSense program allow YouTube members sharing non-copyrighted videos to benefit from adverts which appear in boxes to the right of their uploads".[242]

To avoid censorship, far-right groups form self-branded streaming platforms. Past messages on the GoyimTV Telegram channel indicate the show was hosted on various platforms and domains until arriving at its current streaming site. Prior to acquiring its current GoyimTV domain, the Telegram channel posted links to GoyimTV episodes on alternative streaming services like "DLive" and "JoshWho TV", and was alleged to have been cut off from web services like GoDaddy and Epik. The GoyimTV streaming site describes itself as "a goy-to-goy content sharing platform" where Jews are not welcome. Videos posted to it include ones espousing Holocaust denial, white nationalism, and racial-slur-filled rants against popular media figures, as well as conspiracy theories about COVID-19 and other topics. GoyimTV videos are often posted across other sites. Relatedly, a 24 August 2020 message posted to the GoyimTV Telegram channel claimed that under its previous GoyimTV website "90%" of its content was "being embedded from bitchute". More disguised or innocuously composed content on GoyimTV is also sourced from YouTube, where other users often complain that they've been removed. Other far-right organizations have similarly embraced ventures with their streaming platforms. "Knights Templar", a far-right Christian organization based in Europe, has promoted a platform called "Purged". A post on the Knights Templar Telegram channel describes Purged as suited for "Christian nationalists".[243]

At the same time, political extremists monetize gaming sites such as Twitch's and YouTube's gamers: Streamlabs and StreamElements. These platforms are not only excellent instruments for radicalization and recruitment. Moreover, viewers of these gaming websites are allowed to send monetary donations in addition to their public messages.[244] Another notable example is the Entropy suite of services from Cthonic Software. The program allows extremists whose accounts have been shut down on mainstream services to embed their video streams on its site instead. The software counts a small percentage of donations but in return, it provides a "censorship-free chat service".[245]

We identified anti-Muslim, anti-immigration, and neo-Nazi hate groups, which used video streaming platforms (Table 3.6).

Cryptocurrencies

The relevance of cryptocurrencies offering anonymity for transactions gradually increased with the deplatforming of fundraising websites.[246] Bitcoin as a "decentralized, peer-to-peer, crypto-currency has obvious appeal to hate group leaders and other influential extremists considering that no company and no government can intervene to stop the donations from flowing".[247] Blockchain data and analysis company Chainalysis reported that on 8

TABLE 3.6 Occurrence of video streaming per examined far-right threat groups

	Video streaming
Anti-Muslim	×
Anti-immigration	×
Anti-government	No instances identified
Neo-Nazi	×
White supremacist	No instances identified

December 2020, a person in one single transaction sent 28.15 Bitcoin valued at about $522,000 to 22 separate addresses in a single transaction. Many of these addresses belong to far-right groups and associated individuals.[248] As the biggest beneficiary of the donation, 22-year-old far-right internet personality Nick Fuentes received 13.5 Bitcoin. At the Capitolium siege in January 2021, he was one of the protesters in front of the building. The December 8 donation is by far the largest cryptocurrency donation Fuentes has ever received. "Previously, the most he had ever received in a single month was $2,707 worth of Bitcoin".[249] The extremist donor started the transaction with cryptocurrency from a French exchange. His listed email address belongs to a French computer programmer. The donor later posted a suicide note on his blog and in January 2021 his death was confirmed by media outlets.[250]

The prevalence of the usage of cryptocurrencies also builds upon certain anti-Semitic propaganda. This claims that the Jews own all the banks and therefore, if alt-right supporters do not want to take part in this Jewish-possessed system, they are forced to use cryptocurrencies.[251]

A concerning novelty in violent extremists' financial activities is their shift to Monery. A European alt-right group called Order of Dawn started a cryptocurrency crowdfunding campaign in 2018, specifically for Monero.[252] This cryptocurrency has in-built privacy features which make it less traceable for authorities. It is the entry and exit points of all cryptocurrencies which are informative for law enforcement agencies. The crucial point is when their holders transfer them into flat currencies. Cryptocurrency companies, therefore, are highly recommended to consult with law enforcement agencies when developing their compliance programs which aim to identify potentially malicious actors.[253]

According to our analysis, predominantly anti-Muslim, neo-Nazi, and anti-government hate groups use cryptocurrencies in their financing transactions (Table 3.7).

Self-funding

The threat posed by lone actors and small cells cannot be disregarded here. An individual who is keen to partake in political extremism should consider

TABLE 3.7 Occurrence of cryptocurrencies per examined far-right threat groups

	Cryptocurrencies
Anti-Muslim	×
Anti-immigration	No instances identified
Anti-government	×
Neo-Nazi	×
White supremacist	No instances identified

the following expenses. To stay informed about upcoming events and follow-ups on achievements, a computer and stable internet service are inevitable. An elevated level of engagement requires more significant expenditure. If our activist would like to get into a more personal relationship with his or her like-minded fellows, demonstrations or music festivals organized by the political extremist group offer excellent opportunities for offline meetups. Obviously, this includes travel costs and attendance fees. Potentially merchandise items may be added to this to enhance the uniformity of the movement. For a lone actor, a vehicle and a weapon are elemental to carry out a terrorist attack. Considering that all recorded far-right terrorist attacks included less sophisticated technology, the costs may vary per the chosen mode of operation.

Generally, those political extremists who are not members of any organized groups, fund their expenses from their own financial sources. Their income, savings together with potential family heritage are at their disposal to cover their travel costs or to obtain the necessary weapons or vehicles to carry out the planned attack.[254] This could be completed with self-publish services (e.g., Amazon's CreateSpace) which sell their books, pamphlets, or music of hate.[255] Oklahoma bomber Timothy McVeigh, for instance, sold guns at gun shows to finance their relatively cheap (between $3 and 4,000) fertilizer bomb.[256]

Conclusion

Violent extremists generate revenues through a wide variety of financial mechanisms. This section has attempted to better understand far-right threat groups' fundraising strategies. Implications based upon this analysis can be drawn as follows.

First, charging membership fees suggests that members of more formal far-right groups can afford to pay these obligatory contributions and are not dependent on the movement to make ends meet. Rather, it is their own independent financial decision to devote the amount of a monthly gym pass to supporting extremist ideologies.

Second, as the analysis has revealed predominantly anti-Muslim, neo-Nazi, and anti-government far-right groups sell merchandise products. Besides fundraising purposes, these links with followers enable them to map the circle of their supporters and maintain relations. From a counter-terrorism perspective, tracking these financial transactions may bring significant intelligence to identify worrisome individuals.

Third, music festivals, concerts, and conferences present an important opportunity for far-right threat groups to meet supporters and potential new recruits in person. In addition, fees collected for such gatherings may serve as regular or irregular income. These events are of crucial importance for law enforcement and intelligence authorities, since followers and potential new recruits turn up in person. Such occasions offer the potential for counter efforts to match digital personalities with real life persons.

Fourth, crowdfunding campaigns and voluntary donations make up a remarkable fraction of far-right threat groups' revenues. These fundraising mechanisms were detected with regard to 42% of analyzed hate groups. Measures that aim to counter such entirely legitimate transactions have resulted in the deplatformation of fundraising surfaces, making their tracking even more challenging for authorities. Counter-policing efforts should consider these crucial implications when designing future strategies.

Fifth, cryptocurrencies are yet another methods that extremist groups are using to finance themselves. It is the low cost, easy access, and high speed of these international transfers, which make them attractive for extremist and terrorist use. Financial service providers strive to set up more private and decentralized cryptocurrencies to keep their clients' finances confidential and secure. Unintentionally, they create a constantly safer environment for malicious transactions. It is, therefore, of crucial importance that security agencies and tech companies engage in close collaborations to raise awareness on the security risks of such innovations.

Sixth, tracking the finances of a lone actor or a small cell is a major challenge for authorities. Through the tracking of the other fundraising mechanisms, however, authorities may map out concerning individuals. Therefore, a more comprehensive understanding of threat groups' revenue-generating strategies is of great value.

Recruitment

Constantly increasing the number of members is critical for an organization to survive. Considering that new supporters may join in different ways, multiple strategies are necessary to recruit effectively.[257] It has been argued that recruitment is a gradual and dynamic process,[258] which can occur in various settings and in numerous forms. Individuals are mainly recruited either through family or friends' networks[259] or due to preexisting relationships with current members. Another crucial element is distributing propaganda material[260] and recruit at special events like protests or music festivals.[261] At the same time, extremist groups actively promote joining their causes online.[262] The stigma and the racist message of hate groups may, however, be a dissuasive effect on potential new members.[263] In addition, the movement is "factionalized" and numerous hate groups compete for the same potential recruits.[264]

In order to take account of the most comprehensive avenues for recruitment, after a careful analysis of the selected 35 far-right threat groups, we identified the following 6 categories for recruitment.

Leafleting

Creating signs or slogans and distributing these dissuasive arguments is one of the most common recruiting tactics among political violent extremists.[265] This includes leafleting public areas, schools, or concerts.[266] In most of these cases, the group's objective is informing the public about the groups' political agenda and its "physical presence in the community".[267]

The analysis has revealed that anti-Muslim, anti-immigration, and neo-Nazi threat groups distribute leaflets for recruiting purposes. For instance, anti-Muslim La Meute members are encouraged to recruit in their communities, most frequently by printed pamphlets.[268] In New Zealand, anti-immigration Dominion Movement came to public attention in 2018 when putting up recruitment posters at bus stops in Manawatū[269] and handing out pamphlets on the street.[270] In 2016, neo-Nazi Atomwaffen Division reportedly "posted fliers, buttons, banners, and other propaganda adorned with Nazi imagery on eight college campuses".[271] Neo-Nazi National Action plastered places of education with group propaganda and distributed its material on at least 12 university campuses, including Warwick University and Aston University in Birmingham.[272] Similarly, neo-Nazi Blood and Honor publishes a magazine, moreover several radio programs on its 28 radio networks (Table 3.8).[273]

Personal interactions

Face-to-face interactions provide excellent ways for recruitment.[274] Various forms of such personal interactions were noted in the research.

TABLE 3.8 Occurrence of leafleting per examined far-right threat groups

	Leafleting
Anti-Muslim	×
Anti-immigration	×
Anti-government	No instances identified
Neo-Nazi	×
White supremacist	No instances identified

First, extremists may reach out to potential new members in person at school. Lunch breaks or time spent on the school bus provide handy opportunities to identify vulnerable individuals and enter into discussions with them.[275] Reportedly, Atomwaffen Division targeted college students, teenagers, and other youth – in particular on college campuses – for recruitment.[276] In addition, National Action's recruitment strategy also focused on young university students and initially targeted students, particularly between the ages of 16 and 25.[277] They sought to bring young people directly into National Action, which set itself against far-right political parties, presenting itself as an overtly neo-Nazi street movement that rejected the democratic system.[278]

Second, reaching out to new members through charitable community activities is also a common form of recruitment.

> Groups like the Northern Guard don't always draw people in with white supremacist ideology, but by presenting themselves as performing a service to people in need. This strategy allows them to reach people who wouldn't consider joining an openly racist group. They offer a sense of belonging and purpose.[279]

Third, white power music is considered to be a significant propaganda tool.[280] In accordance with this, white power music events function as occasions to establish contact with potential recruits. These highly frequent recruitment venues enable the undisguised use of group propaganda. In addition, the group can get to know potential new recruits in person and introduce them to the group's subculture. For instance, neo-Nazi Blood and Honour organize music festivals and rallies to spread its propaganda and reach out to new potential members.[281]

Another noteworthy example is the Ukrainian Azov Battalion, which operates a recruitment center at the so-called Cossack House. This four-story brick building stands in the center of Kyiv and is on loan from Ukraine's Defense Ministry. In the courtyard, there is a cinema and a boxing club. "The top floor hosts a lecture hall and a library, full of books by authors who supported German fascism, like Ezra Pound and Martin Heidegger, or whose works were co-opted by Nazi propaganda, like Friedrich Nietzsche and Ernst Jünger".[282]

Undated videos leaked revealed Lads Society Tom Sewell's intention to attract and recruit members from mainstream society under the guise of a men's fitness club.[283] "Amateur promotional videos of the Lads Society show men standing around in groups while others box each other, in scenes seemingly paying homage to cult classic film Fight Club" (Table 3.9).[284]

TABLE 3.9 Occurrence of personal interactions as means of recruitment per examined far-right threat groups

	Personal interactions
Anti-Muslim	No instances identified
Anti-immigration	×
Anti-government	No instances identified
Neo-Nazi	×
White supremacist	×

Interactions through the internet

Social media platforms

Besides threat groups' own websites, organizers have their own profiles on different social media sites. Online forums and far-right pages on social media have become prominent platforms for recruitment. Through internet-based communication technology, they spread hatred against the target of their loathe backed by fake news and distorted facts. Digital platforms provide them with opportunities to broaden their community and maintain contact with like-minded individuals.[285] Tactics to approach the young generation include for instance livestreaming interviews on YouTube with teenagers who are considered rising stars of the far right.[286] The content of far-right threat groups' digital propaganda continues to evolve in accordance with world events. While previously violent far-right narratives strived over the hostility to immigrants and Islam since the pandemic outbreak they have been capitalizing on the rising frustration over pandemic lockdowns in their recruitment efforts.[287]

Instagram has been used to radicalize teenagers and build an international network of mostly teenage members. The application's "focus on visual media aligns well with the content produced by far-right groups, whose messaging usually consists of a few simple words combined with striking imagery".[288] Memes are an effective way to garner attention from young people. They are "easily consumable, funny and they're easy to share. [...] They spread quickly and the humor makes them easier to swallow".[289] It is a slow, rolling process, which gradually

> introduces youngsters to more troubling material. Liking a seemingly innocuous meme can, in turn, present the teenager with more radical content. [...] A kid might like something edgy, Pepe the Frog or something, and that triggers the algorithm and then sends them tumbling down into anti-feminist, racist, Holocaust denial, neo-Nazi type of content.[290]

All five subcategories of far-right formations – namely, anti-Muslim, anti-immigration, anti-government, neo-Nazi, and white supremacist groups – use social media platforms for recruiting purposes. For instance, anti-immigration Soldiers of Odin advertisements are posted on its Facebook page to call for supporters to join their cause.[291] Anti-Muslim and anti-immigration Proud Boys frequently use social media to reach out to possible recruits.[292] "Violence is the group's most effective recruiting tool, and the June 30 rally provided arguably the group's biggest promotional boost".[293] In one of the largest Boogaloo groups on Facebook, members of the group previously shared a bomb-making manual and a manifesto, including a chapter on assassination.[294] Anti-Muslim English Defence League maintained Facebook pages for each of its 17 regional chapters. Facebook suspended the EDL in April 2019. Additionally, it operated a forum on its official website available for registered members.[295]

New members can only join anti-Muslim La Meute's secret Facebook groups if one was recommended by a member. Potential newly recruited are checked and monitored according to their social media posts and actions.[296] Leaders practice an atmosphere of constant mistrust towards the members.[297] Doubtful comments or critical assertions of La Meute result in rejection and refusal of access.[298]

Anti-Muslim and anti-immigration PEGIDA activist Lutz Bachmann posted a video on YouTube on 10 October 2014, showing a rally in Dresden in support of Kurdish fighters against IS. Soon afterward he set up a Facebook group opposing the "Islamisation of the West". This quickly began to attract comments opposing the "advancing Islamisation of our country as well as against the Islamic State, the Kurdish PKK, al-Qaeda and others".[299]

Neo-Nazi German Gruppe S' private Facebook groups were created for "comrades who didn't just want to chat".[300] In these chat groups, group founder Werner S. was looking for men who were willing to make direct attacks. The profile Werner was looking for in applicants was that they had to be "smart, tough, brutal, fast, energetic and trust yourself to do more than participate in demonstrations".[301] Werner recruited the members in very different settings, in Facebook groups, Twitter, Telegram, self-defense groups, rock clubs, and neo-Nazi collectives who were united by their hatred of foreigners, refugees, and Muslims. In the group they showed in the phone calls and intercepted talks a mixture of the imperial bourgeoisie, Germanic mythology, and xenophobia.[302]

Neo-Nazi Feuerkrieg Division specifically targeted teenagers for recruitment and focused its recruitment on social media platforms and encrypted messaging apps. FKD members encouraged the recruitment of high school students for shootings and vandalism. The group required recruits to post propaganda posters and send photos to the group's leader.[303] Similarly, an Azov recruiter was a member of other Facebook groups interested in far-right ideologies. He searched for young men's profiles.[304]

Recruitment for neo-Nazi Antipodean Resistance happens through online posters with Nazi slogans.[305] In January 2018, the group claimed to have 300 members, aged in their late teens and twenties. They aim to provide a nurturing environment for these young white men.[306] Two of the several requirements for membership include: "Race: You must be White to join our organization. No Blacks, Asians, Jews or mixed abominations"; and "No Poofters: We don't allow homosexuals or other sexual deviants in our organization".[307] Videos and pictures taken at a neo-Nazi training camp in the Grampians were also distributed in their online recruitment campaign.[308]

Australian neo-Nazi and National Socialist Network leader Thomas Sewell's social media posts indicate that he appeals to "marginalized, underemployed young Australians in the fringes of society".[309] A leaked 112-page manual reveals how group members manipulate social media communication technologies and journalists (media baiting) to gain publicity, amplify their hate message, and ultimately help them recruit new members.[310]

Alternative tech sites

As a response to major social networking platforms' increased content moderation efforts, right-wing extremist chatter has been deplatformed to alternative tech sites. These surfaces provide services such as networking, video hosting, and crowdfunding. It is their laissez-faire content moderation policy, which makes them favored spaces for the far right. One of the leaders of such free-speech alt-tech social media platforms is Gab, which was launched in 2017.[311] In the aftermath of the Capitolium insurrection, a significant spike in interest and a surge in traffic on Gab, right-wing alternative to Twitter was reported. For instance, after Twitter suspended English Defence League's account in 2017, the group created an account on Gab. As of 13 April 2021, the EDL had 1,000 followers on Gab.[312] Besides Gab, social media platform MeWe, an alternative to Facebook, became the fifth most popular free app on Apple's App Store and Google Play a week after the siege. At the same time, messaging app Telegram was the second most downloaded free application.[313] Other alternative sites such as Wrong Thin (alt-Facebook), PewTube (alt-YouTube), Voat (alt-Reddit), Infogalactic (alt-Wikipedia), and GoyFundMe (alt-Kickstarter) also emerged. WASP.love is another noteworthy site, providing a platform for white nationalist datings (Figure 3.4).[314]

Videogames

It is the interactive format of video games, which makes a more effective and persuasive experience for individuals compared with more traditional forms of media.[315] Extremists disseminate leading social media platforms like YouTube, video platforms, and games like Dlive and Twitch. In the shooting games, they only shoot people of either different religions or different ethnicities. The gamer then becomes a hero with the more people that he or she kill or hurt.[316] White nationalists are Dlive's, the largest live streaming community,

FIGURE 3.4 A screenshot of alt-right provocateur Patrick Casey's "Restoring Order" broadcast on the gaming platform Dlive.

top earners, who while playing video games engage with fans in chatrooms and spread disinformation. Dlive uses childish imagery, "like animated ninjas and ice cream cones, and allows people to play and discuss mainstream video games like The Division 2 and Minecraft".[317] It is these video games' great graphics and good music, which make them attractive to young people. Sonnenkrieg Division members initially communicated through an online gaming forum. The group has posted violent images on social media praising Norwegian terrorist Anders Breivik and calling for violence.[318]

Members of the Boogaloo communities were shut down on Discord, a chat software for online gamers. About 2,258 Boogaloo supporters were among the most active users on the platform. After sharing military experience on its surface, accounts of its members were shut down due to violating Discord policies for threatening and encouraging violence.[319]

Neo-Nazis also use nefarious tactics and recruit vulnerable young people by playing multiplayer games. These platforms are loaded with anti-Semitism, racism, homophobia, and hatred. Once kids are hooked up with these principles, they rank up recruitment.[320] These surfaces offer recruiters platforms for casual conversations about issues of race and identity searching.[321] Neo-Nazi content was identified on Roblox making the popular game among children another frontier for hateful speech (Figure 3.5).[322]

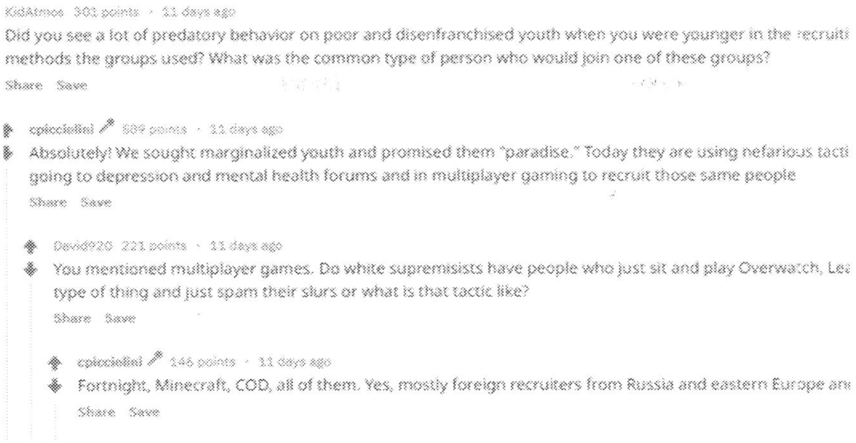

KidAtmos 301 points · 11 days ago
Did you see a lot of predatory behavior on poor and disenfranchised youth when you were younger in the recruiti
methods the groups used? What was the common type of person who would join one of these groups?
Share Save

cpicciolini 509 points · 11 days ago
Absolutely! We sought marginalized youth and promised them "paradise." Today they are using nefarious tacti
going to depression and mental health forums and in multiplayer gaming to recruit those same people
Share Save

David920 221 points · 11 days ago
You mentioned multiplayer games. Do white supremisists have people who just sit and play Overwatch, Lea
type of thing and just spam their slurs or what is that tactic like?
Share Save

cpicciolini 146 points · 11 days ago
Fortnight, Minecraft, COD, all of them. Yes, mostly foreign recruiters from Russia and eastern Europe an
Share Save

FIGURE 3.5 Reformed neo-Nazi Christian Picciolini says children are targeted across an array of multiplayer games.

Source: Reddit.

TABLE 3.10 Digital communication usage for recruitment purposes per examined far-right threat groups

Interactions through the internet				
	Group webpages	*Social media*	*Alternative tech sites*	*Videogames*
Anti-Muslim	×	×	×	×
Anti-immigration	×	×	×	×
Anti-government	×	×	×	×
Neo-Nazi	×	×	×	×
White supremacist	×	×	×	×

As Table 3.10 shows, all five subcategories of far-right threat groups apply digital communication technologies when recruiting new members. Anti-Muslim, anti-immigration, anti-government, neo-Nazi, and white supremacist groups all use their own webpages, social media platforms, alternative tech sites, and videogames to reach out to potential new members.

Other recruitment strategies and specific target groups

Targeting the youth

Right-wing political extremists' propaganda primarily target young people. United Kingdom's Home Office reported a sharp rise in the number of under-18s over concerns about their possible involvement with the far right. While in 2017–2018 a total of 682 children were involved, their number was only 131 in 2014–2015. The total for 2017–2018 includes 24 children under the age of 10. It is also noteworthy that the number of cases linked to the far right and those linked to Islamic radicalization was at an equal ratio.[323]

The Boogaloo tactic

Barriers to entry into the Boogaloo movement are low. The movement is decentralized, and largely organic, and there are no loyalty pledges to a leader. Instead, the beginner's kit for the Boogaloo consists simply of a rudimentary grasp of meme culture, sympathies with America's anti-tyrannical legacy, and the ability to legally purchase a firearm. Though even for those who are lawfully restricted from owning a gun, hardcore firearm enthusiasts have made printing 3D guns and assembling so-called ghost guns easily attainable. Arrest records and social media activity show the Boogaloo movement "holds widespread appeal, recruiting from a broad demographic that spans geography, age, occupation, and level of education".[324]

Targeting the upper classes

Scientists emphasize that anti-Muslim and anti-immigration PEGIDA is not a phenomenon of the lower classes and indeed, the movement mobilizes mostly better-educated men who are also more financially advantaged than the local average.[325]

> The first important observation is that PEGIDA participants are not a socioeconomically marginalized group consisting mainly of unemployed people who have been neglected by the state and society. On the contrary, they have relatively high incomes and are much better educated than average Germans (being three times more likely to be university graduates than members of the general population).[326] Similarly, Swedish Resistance Movement primarily seeks contact with individuals who may constitute a kind of elite and who are prepared to display uncompromising loyalty. Members are strongly pressured to sacrifice time and money for the group.[327]

March as a recruitment tool

A central propaganda and recruitment tool for the white supremacist Nordic Resistance Movement (NRM) has been its public marches. When 60–70 Swedish and Norwegian neo-Nazis from the NRM, including a number of members with violent criminal records, marched through the city center in

Norway's fifth-largest city of Kristiansand on 29 July 2017, the reaction of the very same Norwegian free speech liberals was that "freely permitting them to do so was nothing sort of a litmus test for Norwegian liberal democracy".[328]

Women

While much of the emphasis was on young men, neo-Nazi National Action also sought to appeal to young women – albeit in quite bizarre ways. Possibly the most unusual was the Miss Hitler competition that encouraged female supporters to send in selfies along with answers to a handful of set questions. With names that include A Bus Full of Retards, Eva Bin Gassin, Lady of the Lolocaust, and Galloping Gestapo, some of the young women expressed extremely traditional ideas about women and their perceived role "at home raising children".[329]

Recruiting military and law enforcement members

Both the US and the German Defence Ministry acknowledged that far-right extremists actively recruit among members of the national army. On one hand, skills obtained in the army are highly valuable capabilities for political extremist organizations. On the other hand, military service may "bring legitimacy in their mind to their cause".[330]

One of the largest anti-government Boogaloo groups on Facebook, its members included users "identifying as veterans, active military, retired and active police, supporters and detractors of President Trump, and average citizens with no obvious political ideology".[331] In a similar vein, anti-government Oath Keepers recruits military and law enforcement into its ranks.[332] Neo-Nazi Atomwaffen Division also actively recruits from the military, seeking out servicemen who can provide expertise in firearms and military tactics.[333]

The online application for potential recruits to neo-Nazi The Base specifically asked about applicants' training in the military, science, and engineering. The network specifically seeks to recruit current and former members of the armed forces so that they can share their skills. Military experience and training, together with skills to use weapons or explosives, were regarded as highly valuable competencies for members. Members also set about propagandizing on other platforms such as Twitter and Gab, hoping to lure new recruits.[334] Applicants submit an application form, which includes questions regarding the applicant's current associations with white supremacist organizations; the applicant's military, science, and engineering experiences and training; and the applicant's race and gender.[335] The Base renewed its recruitment campaign in April 2021 and claimed it had instituted new security measures to its vetting process to avoid infiltration. According to its messaging, The Base is focused on networking and practical training, not indoctrination. The group claims it "does not have a radicalization program for recruits and expects potential members to already be radicalized".[336]

The group's social media posts asked for volunteers possessing various skills, including weapons, for this new organization.[337]

Structure

To better understand the threat associated with far-right violence, it is crucial to have a clear picture of the layout and structure of these formations. This will also help determine the extent of the group and estimate the number of its members. Far-right threat groups are organized in different formations. First, more paramilitary-like formations are organized in a top-down leadership with chapters in various regions,[338] then the phenomenon of the so-called leaderless resistance will be elaborated in this section.

More formal structures could be observed with regard to 5 of the examined 35 far-right groups (Figure 3.6).

Canadian La Meute adherents are structured by rank. The top leaders are the Silver Paws, the Red Paws are supervisors of members, regular members are the Black and White Paws.[339] Most of the leaders in the highest ranks are ex-military officers. The milieu is extremely macho tending towards misogyny. Besides the council of chiefs, there are 17 clans representing Québec's 17 administrative districts. Clans are directed by a chief and his deputies. Within each clan, there are separate cells liable for logistics, media, intelligence, counter-intelligence, security, legal and political issues, propaganda, and medical services at protests.[340]

Similarly, the Ukrainian Azov Regiment is structured into specialized units such as reconnaissance, counter-reconnaissance, EOD disposal, interdiction, and special weapons operations.

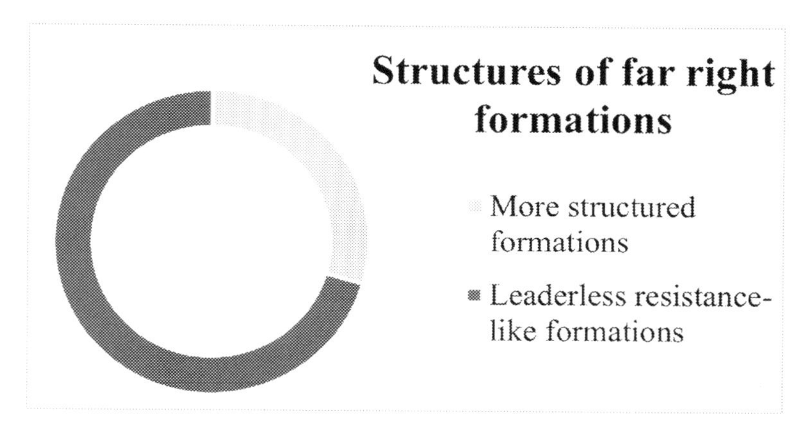

FIGURE 3.6 Structures of far-right formations.

Soldiers of Odin Canada has a decentralized hierarchy. The top leader is called the president. Provinces are run by executive officers and regional divisions which are headed by sgt. majors.[341] The vast majority of its members are former military or police officers together with members of other anti-government organizations.[342]

There are low barriers to entry into the Boogaloo movement, "no loyalty pledges to a leader: a rudimentary grasp of meme culture, sympathies with America's anti-tyrannical legacy, and the ability to legally purchase a firearm".[343] In a similar vein, Oath Keepers is not a rigid, cohesive organization but a loosely knit one.[344] The group states that full membership is open to currently serving military, reserves, National Guard, police, fire-fighters, other first responders and veterans/former members of those services. Others who support the organization's mission can become associate members (Figure 3.7).[345]

Leadership could not be linked to a particular person only in only 6 out of the 35 analyzed threat groups. The name of the leader was not communicated with regard to Canadian Northern Guard, USA-based Boogaloo Movement, French Génération Identitaire, German Identitairan Movement, Australian Antipodean Resistance, and New Zealand-based Action Zealandia.

Another important observation is a constant fluctuation among leaders of far-right organizations. Prominent leading figures compete with each other and as a result of these power struggles, executives of these groups frequently change. For instance, due to ideological arguments, personal grievances, and financial transparency there is an elevated level of rotation among leaders of Canadian far-right groups.[346]

When investigating formations with a traditional structure, membership estimations may also provide insights into the size of far-right groups.[347] The research has established a remarkable difference between the volume of online supporters and the number of followers who actively participate in group

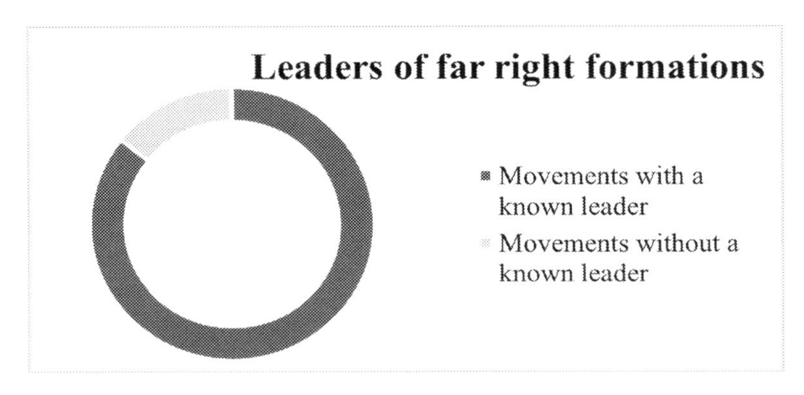

FIGURE 3.7 Leaders of far-right formations.

gatherings. While there are around 45,000 Facebook accounts registered in Canadian La Meute's Facebook group, typically not more than 125–150 members partake in the group's events.[348] Soldiers of Odin Canada's Facebook page reports having 3,000 members, but in reality, an estimated 150 to 200 members are active.[349]

Membership within The Proud Boys is tiered but poorly defined. As such, estimates of membership vary considerably from several hundred to the group's claim of 22,000. Members can also be disavowed, but disavowal does not appear to result in exclusion from Proud Boys events or activities. The degrees of membership range from: (1) outing oneself publicly as a Proud Boy; (2) an initiation ritual in which members beat the initiate until he can name five cereal brands; (3) getting a tattoo with a Proud Boys logo; and (4) fighting members of Antifa to "serve the cause".[350] To become a first degree in the "pro-West fraternal organization" a prospective member simply has to declare, "I am a Western chauvinist, and I refuse to apologize for creating the modern world". To enter the second degree, a Proud Boy has to endure a beating until they can yell out the names of five bowls of breakfast cereals (in order to demonstrate "adrenaline control"). Those who enter the third degree have demonstrated their commitment by getting a Proud Boys tattoo. Any man – no matter his race or sexual orientation – can join the fraternal organization as long as they "recognize that white men are not the problem". The fourth is reserved for those who have gotten in a "fight for the cause". All members are banned from watching pornography or masturbating more than once a month because, in theory, it will leave them more inclined to go out and meet women.[351]

Oath Keepers claims to have tens of thousands of members, although researchers estimate the number is probably no higher than 5,000. The group has local chapters spread across the country, which operate with an enormous amount of independence.[352] The popularity of Oath Keepers' social media accounts illustrates clearly that many more people support the movement without ever officially joining (which requires paying dues).[353] Presumably 6–10% of its members are active-duty police officers and military members, and significantly more are retired or veteran service members.[354]

Around 330 Three Percenter groups were active between 2016 and 2019. At one point they claimed to have 12,000 members in their Facebook group, from all 50 states.[355] Meanwhile, The Base's total membership is unknown as the group has no formal membership, its primary web forum has 45 members.[356]

Reports suggest that UK-based National Action membership has never exceeded 100 individuals.[357] Its online base is wider since it typically attracts no more than 50 supporters to its demonstrations.[358] Britain First has about 1,000 members,[359] with an army of online fans of 6,000.[360]

The English Defence League had a membership of 100–150 in 2016.[361]

Its membership is not homogenous, besides football hooligans, there are supporters got the LGBT wing and has black, Sikh, Hindu and Jewish members. An ordinary EDL member's life has been made exceedingly difficult by structural changes in working class communities (low wages, insecure employment and lack of opportunity) and feel betrayed (abandoned) by conventional Parliamentary politicians.[362]

They are largely white, and male, while initially drawn from the settings of organized football violence and traditional right-wing groups, are now much more frequently from a broader demographic of disaffected, aggrieved, and forgotten white working-class communities.[363] What characterizes supporters is a strong disillusionment with politics. "The experience of being one of many like-minded individuals sharing a common experience elicited solidarity which was amplified through participatory crowding"[364] in the English Defence League. Reportedly, more than 1,200 were present at an EDL's street movement.[365] At its peak in mid-2010, there were around 3,000 members, but around 80% of active members had drifted away. EDL supporters are more likely to be white working class. EDL attracts many more women supporters. Indeed, the organization quotes Islamic attitudes towards women as one of its grievances with Islam.[366]

Sonnenkrieg Division reportedly had 10 to 15 members.[367] According to the Anti-Defamation League, about 30 members joined the Feuerkrieg Division internationally, while the German magazine Spiegel reported 70 members, with the most in the USA (32) and Great Britain (9), along with members in Germany (6) and Canada (6).[368]

French Génération Identitaire has 800–1,000 members[369], according to another source it claims 2,800 members.[370] About 90% of the members are students and have acquired intellectual training that they will certainly continue promoting, either as members of the Rassemblement National or through joint actions with like-minded groups such as la Cocarde étudiante, the New Right think-tank Institut Iliade, and the supporters of Marion Le Pen.[371] In Germany, Pan-European Identitarian Movement has 600 members.[372]

Germany's domestic intelligence agency, the Office for the Protection of the Constitution (BfV), estimated that in 2021 there were around 16,500 Reichsbürger in Germany. Some 3,500 are based in Bavaria, while around 2,500 are living in neighboring Baden-Württemberg. Most are male, on average they are over 50 years old, and they tend to come from socially disadvantaged segments of society.[373] The group has a core membership of just 21 people nationwide, and a further 100 followers. The wider movement counts thousands more members, most of whom are males aged between 40 and 60 years.[374]

Between 100 and 150 further associates were identified who supported the core trio of the National Socialist Underground in their decade-long underground life and provided them with money, false identities, and weapons.[375]

The Swedish Resistance Movement is estimated to have a few hundred members. In 2011, Stop the Islamisation of Norway reportedly had nearly 13,000 members of its Facebook group. It is based in Oslo with immediate access to about 3,000 activists.[376]

Ukrainian Azov Battalion had an estimated 300–600 members in 2014.[377] As of March 2015, their number increased to 900.[378] Azov Media in 2021 had 38,000 subscribers to its YouTube channel.[379]

Australian Antipodean Resistance claims to have around 300 activists.[380] The Australian Defence League has fewer than 30 paid members, but its Facebook page attracted more than 12,000 followers before it was shut down.[381] Australian National Socialist Network has around 438 followers on Gab and 5,002 followers on Telegram.[382] Thirty-eight of its members burnt a cross at the Grampians in Victoria in 2021.[383]

New Zealand-based Dominion Movement's membership is estimated to be under 30. Action Zealandia's membership is approximately 50–100. About 612 on Twitter, 73 on Facebook, and 51 on its Telegram channel. Female members are not permitted.[384]

Individuals supporting a common goal gather around this shared objective without a formal structure.[385] A remarkable amount of extreme right-wing violence is not conducted by members but by sympathizers of far-right narratives.[386] This tactic is known as leaderless resistance defined as "lone wolf operation in which an individual, or a very small, highly cohesive group, engages in acts of anti-state violence independent of any movement, leader, or network of support".[387] Far-right-inspired individuals and groups operate independently of each other and do not report to any central headquarter or a leader.[388] Although lone actors cannot rely on the supply chains operated by a traditional terrorist organization, they are in a better position to evade arrest or detention compared with group-based terrorists.[389] Since lacking this direct contact and collaboration with an organization makes their detection for law enforcement agencies particularly difficult.[390] Such leaderless resistance can be observed with the following far-right threat groups.

Canadian Atalante grew out of the band Légitime Violence, which toured around Europe in 2013 to sell promotional material and create bonds with Europe-based neo-Nazi bands.[391] Blood and Honour Canada chapters do not have other formal leadership.[392] The formation does not have a formal membership. Violent acts are committed by Combat 18, which is closely connected to the group.[393]

Three Percenters' decentralized nature makes it "more of a way of life than a club to join".[394] The godfather of the movement, Michael Brian Vanderboegh, a veteran of the militia movement, advocated the idea that a similarly dedicated group of "patriots" could come together and overthrow a "modern tyrannical government".[395]

> There is no single central authority or definitive group. Instead, there are multiple discrete organizations with a national presence openly associating themselves with the broader movement, such as The Three Percenters – Original, American Patriots The III%, United Patriots 3%, and Three Percent Security Force (also known as IIISF).[396]

It organizes county-level meetings either weekly, biweekly, or monthly and state meetings annually. One does not have to attend the meeting to be a member, but one should be active on the group's Facebook page or forum.[397] With anyone able to declare themselves a Three Percenter, the concept allowed many people to join who were not suited, physically or by inclination, to engage in paramilitary activities.[398]

The Atomwaffen Division is made up of a series of leaderless terror cells.[399] It operates as a cellular-based organization with anywhere from several dozen to 80 members, possibly more, located across the United States.[400] There were between 24 and 36 actively participating in weapons training and hate camps held by the group.[401] Members are particularly young, none of the arrested were over the age of 30 years.[402]

The founder Rinaldo Nazzaro, organized The Base on the "leaderless resistance" concept, pioneered by Ku Klux Klan leader Louis Beam.[403] The Base is a network of small, underground cells, each with a high degree of autonomy.[404] Despite this decentralized model, Nazzaro appeared to adopt a relatively hands-on approach to leading the group. For example, "the BBC obtained recordings of him personally interviewing prospective members over an encrypted messaging app in June 2020".[405]

The English Defence League lacked a central regulatory structure through which to impose a uniform approach to strategy or maintain ideological purity throughout. It operated through a loose network of local divisions, each of which had a good deal of autonomy. The EDL is divided into at least 90 different divisions, some of which are based on locality and others on specialist groups. These have included a women's division, Jewish division, Sikh division, Hindu division, and LGBT division. Branches typically held their meeting in pubs with sympathetic owners, which are referred to as "HQs". Pilkington observed that these meetings always feature alcohol consumption. Such divisional meetings were infrequent and often poorly attended. They were typically unstructured, lacking any formal agenda or the taking of minutes, and were mainly an opportunity for divisional organizers to inform members of their decisions. Sometimes guest speakers were also invited to address the audience. As well as these divisional meetings, the EDL divisions, also held "meet and greet" events to attract new members.[406]

Although Sonnenkrieg Division maintains a decentralized structure, its nominal leader is co-founder Andrew Dymock.[407]

Most of the German Gruppe S members also belonged to other far-right groups, including the Bruderschaft Deutschland (German Brotherhood).[408] Reichsbürger movement is made up of various splinter groups, therefore it is difficult to assess its actual number.[409] It is an umbrella term for individuals and loosely organized groups who deny or question the existence of the Federal Republic and claim to be citizens of the pre-war German Reich.[410] The movement is an amalgamation of right-wing extremists, esoteric, and sovereign citizens and the movement attracts conspiracy theorists, the economically troubled, and people who are a little mentally disordered.[411]

The Swedish Resistance Movement is divided into six geographical zones, dubbed "nests". Each nest has a chief operating officer and is comprised of "battle groups with separate staffs of managers".[412]

Antipodean Resistance claimed that

> We are not a mass movement. We do not want the masses. We want the fanatics, the people who care and who will fight, both during activism and during their day to day lives to bring about the beauty that is National Socialism. We want quality people who mean what they say and will not back down. We are striving for nothing less than the national rebirth of our people. And we will get there only with those fanatics enough to do something about it.[413]

Members are secretive about their identities, concealing both names and face.[414] The formation has developed a specific section for women called the Antipodean Resistance Women's Alliance. According to its webpage, this group offers "the antidote to the poison that has been delivered to our girls and women through the degeneracy of modern society". Activities claimed for this group include gendered roles for women such as sewing, cooking, and gardening, as well as hiking and self-defense, all to help women play their part in "the survival of our race".[415] "Our members have families. Some have wives and children that they seek to protect".[416]

Reclaim Australia is rather a movement than an organization. Accordingly, it does not have a defined or high-profile leadership or a structured organization.[417]

Conclusion

Having a clear picture of the layout and membership of far-right formations enables a more accurate assessment of the associated threat. As the research has revealed the vast majority of the examined groups do not have the traditional top-down structured organization. For those few, which operate as more paramilitary-like formations, a constant rotation in its leaders can be observed. The leaderless resistance concept turned out to be the guiding principle in the structures of the analyzed far-right threat groups. These loosely knit units, however, make the counter efforts extremely demanding. Tracking numerous autonomous cells and individuals require immense resources, and authorities may be distracted in identifying worrisome individuals. On the other end, maintaining a threatening online milieu is highly advantageous for far-right threat formations which may inspire less structured members for violence. As a warning sign, a remarkable difference between the number of online fans and real activists has been observed. Without exception, the volume of followers on social media considerably exceeded the number of members who turn up at in-person group meetings or events.

Communication channels

With the early adoption of modern technologies, right-wing extremists' online and offline domains are in a constant symbiosis.[418] Many of the prominent right-wing extremist strands were born digitally. For instance, supporters of both the Atomwaffen Division and the Nordic Resistance Movement got in contact through the now-defunct online platform Iron March.[419] Following Iron March's removal, the Fascist Forge emerged in 2018 and sought to become the new meeting place for right-wing violent extremists. The platform was founded by a high-ranking member of The Base, which in 2020 decided to remove it, due to its elevated law enforcement scrutiny.[420]

The growing availability of social media and video sharing platforms, as well as messaging services, allow the milieu's actors to spread propaganda and mobilize or coordinate supporters.[421] Right-wing extremists communicate with their followers through various online services. Besides mainstream social media platforms and instant messaging services, they disseminate their messages on their websites, blogs, and alternative news media sites.[422] These platforms provide increased visibility and with strategic framing of content, campaigns aim to enhance engagement.[423] The ambiguity of memes together with the radicalizing role of algorithms may serve as galvanizing factors.[424] User-generated discussion forums such as 4chan, 8kun, Voat, or Gab are important hubs for extremists allowing anonymous participation and little or no content moderation policies.[425]

The 2019 mass shootings in the United States reached a decisive moment when major social media platforms took a number of significant steps to address the misuse of their platforms by far-right extremists. After Facebook, YouTube, Reddit, and Twitter announced a ban on white nationalist content, right-wing extremists migrated to alternative platforms with limited moderation policies.[426] Primarily, the Dubai-based Telegram has become an alternative hub for spreading disinformation, exchanging tactics and orchestrating future attacks.[427] This "cloud-based instant messaging service"[428] was founded by Pavel Durov, who also created the Russian social media platform VKontakte. Telegram is known for its strict privacy standards and independence from government control. The platform allows its users to participate in end-to-end encrypted messaging and communicate en masses via group or individual private messaging channels.[429] Differing strands of the transnational far-right movement interplay on the app and cross-post content to foster online communication with their sympathizers. Politically incorrect jokes and memes, but also manifestos, do-it-yourself weapon guides, and livestream videos of mass shooters are circulated on these platforms.[430]

In the wake of the purge of right-wing extremist content, it is not only Telegram that functions as a stable and secure messaging application for the far-right community. Chat app Signal offers similar anonymity and security for its users. Since the platform allows users to clandestinely communicate en masse, its popularity among anti-government activists exploded after the Black Lives Matter protests and the Capitolium attack.[431]

Another more obscure and harder-to-find forum was Parler prior to Apple banning it. Another Twitter alternative is Gab, the Facebook-similar MeWe, and video-hosting site Rumble.[432] In the aftermath of the Capitolium attack, the download numbers for MeWe tripled while Rumble's more than doubled, Telegram was downloaded more than two times and Signal's downloads grew eightfold.[433] On the walkie-talkie social media app Zello, more than 200 far-right channels were detected ranging from Three Percenters to QAnon groups.[434]

Examined far-right groups' key communication strategies

Through the analysis of the channels and strategies of their communication, this section summarizes the ways in which the examined 35 far-right formations engaged in an exchange of information or ideas.

Social media platforms

Each chapter of Blood and Honour had its own website, however, most of these – together with its Facebook page – have been banned.[435] Twitter banned Proud Boys groups from their platform in August 2018, the Facebook and Instagram acted a bit later, in November of that year.[436] The Boogaloos heavily rely on social media. War and patriot themes have found fertile ground in Facebook's Groups and Pages and encrypted communications platforms like Discord and Telegram.[437] Boogaloo extremists have used social media to "strategize, share instructions for explosives and 3D printed firearms, distribute illegal firearm modifications, and siphon users into encrypted messaging boards en mass".[438]

Atomwaffen Division (AWD) previously posted propaganda videos to YouTube, which led to a February 2018 Daily Beast report on YouTube's refusal to ban AWD for violations of its terms of service. YouTube subsequently suspended AWD's account, citing "multiple or severe violations of YouTube's policy prohibiting hate speech".[439]

Britain First used social media to spread its anti-Muslim and anti-immigrant propaganda on Twitter, Facebook, and YouTube.[440] Facebook banned accounts related to the British National Party, the English Defence League, and Britain First under its "dangerous individuals and organizations" policy.[441] Following this, the group started to post on TikTok.[442]

The French Generation Identity movement is known for its publications on social networks, in which "it defends the idea of a European ethnic identity that would be affected by miscegenation. For its supporters, the cohabitation of diverse cultures is impossible".[443]

Gruppe S members reportedly held regular meetings[444] and communicated using messenger apps.[445] From Facebook, Gruppe S leader Werner S. switched to the Russian network VK, he signed up there with his middle name. In May 2017, he wrote in a "gun lobby" group: "So far, I didn't know anything about VK. I hope for uncensored messages and comments here".[446] Werner S. prefers to deal with weapons here, in a Russian-speaking group he likes photos of knives, pistols, and assault rifles. Of his few visible posts, one is the logo of a "Deutsch-Germanischer Kulturverein eV".[447]

During the pandemic times, PEGIDA mobilized weekly virtual marches livestreamed on YouTube. "The livestreams started with PEGIDA's anthem, featured several speeches, and ended with the performance of the German national anthem".[448]

The Identitarian Movement spreads its messages virally through popular video-sharing platforms.[449] It increases popularity through social media activities and demonstrations.[450] Identitarian Movement Germany had more than 29,500 followers on Twitter before the account was removed and more than 6000 on Telegram; it runs multiple YouTube channels.[451] As the claim, "the internet is their main political space".[452]

The Nordic Resistance Movement YouTube page had 11,444 subscribers as of 19 March 2019. Frihetskamp Media's YouTube page had 685 subscribers as of the same date. Later both accounts were deleted .[453]

Facebook is the main channel for Azov's enhanced social media activities.[454]

Australia-based Antipodean Resistance is active online. It established its website in November 2016. A Twitter account was set up on February 2017 but was later closed by Twitter. In 2017, the group "used its Twitter account to post photos of their vandalism, their distribution of swastika posters and violent stickers at universities and in public places across the nation, as well as radicalization camps in Victoria".[455] Later, Antipodean Resistance installed a Gab account.[456]

Other communication channels

On smaller far-right sites like "Gab" and "Minds", Proud Boys attracted a very small audience of 1,000–2,000 users. The group also maintained a presence on the encrypted messaging app Telegram "with an audience of around 5,000 on their main channel".[457] The group uses jokes, memes, and online trolling for spreading propaganda and for recruiting purposes.[458]

Similarly to the Islamic State, the Boogaloo movement's mythology "attempts to recapture a glorious revolutionary American past in a mythological confrontation".[459] As a "new breed of self-organizing online militias",[460] they use memes to incite violent insurrection and terror against the government and law enforcement. One important subculture that influenced the Boogaloo movement is the "chan" subculture common to forums like 4chan, "with its emphasis on memes, trolling and deliberate irreverence".[461]

Following the Capitolium siege, prosecutors revealed the existence of an Oath Keeper chat group on the encrypted messaging app Signal that they said: "Rhodes and his followers used to conduct surreptitious communications before, during and after the Capitol breach".[462]

Atomwaffen Division posted propaganda videos on the video-sharing service BitChute.[463]

Through encrypted online networks, The Base leader launched chat rooms on Riot, an encrypted messaging app, where members could "meet, discuss ideology and access white supremacist texts".[464] The group previously had an official presence on Gab, Twitter, and Reddit until the respective sites deleted The Base's accounts. The Base has distributed to its members' manuals for lone-wolf terror attacks, bomb-making, counter-surveillance, and guerilla warfare.[465] Followers continue to upload video content to BitChute and the Internet Archive. In January 2021, BitChute banned the account of the Base founder Roman Wolf, a.k.a. Rinaldo Nazzaro. The Base also maintains a channel on Telegram.[466]

English Defence League members created an online radio program on the website BlogTalkRadio. As of June 2020, the show had 286 followers and almost 1,000 episodes. By 13 April 2021, the show "increased to only 292 followers and had 1,066 episodes".[467]

French Generation Identity strives to get people to talk about them. Thus they generally invite journalists to cover their events and at the same time they publicize their actions through their website. They use filming techniques as a PR tool, they

> record in such a way as to portray its members as more numerous than they really are. They also strategically place female members – who are in the minority – at the front of their rallies. Generation Identity is also keen to ensure that their members are relatively well-dressed for the cameras – notably in comparison to the archetypal far right skinheads.[468]

It also operates a website that is now down, but its bimonthly magazine, *La Revue Identitaire*, is unaffected by the ban.[469] The movement has been very careful to ensure that its actions are always fully legal and its messaging is non-violent. "Usually, the only punishable offense of their banner-wielding protests is climbing onto a roof without permission. Even their messaging is nonviolent".[470]

Stop the Islamisation in Norway's largest chapter started a local radio show in Sandnes on the Radio Kos channel in March 2012. The channel's internet radio in turn had to increase its capacity from 25,000 listeners to 200,000 due to high traffic around the same time.[471]

National Socialist Network communicates with potential new members through encrypted online messaging platforms.[472] Reclaim Australia's narratives circulated online to advance their endeavors to establish their political community and construct a collective identity feeling.[473]

Action Zealandia members communicate in encrypted chatrooms.[474] Another instrument to spread its propaganda is the so-called *Voice of Zealandia* magazine.[475]

Modus operandi, tactics, targeting, and weaponry

Far-right extremists engage in multiple types of activities to advance their agenda. This section attempts to take account of their both non-violent and more violent as well as online and offline modus operandi. We have drawn the following implications from our analysis. In the largest numbers, white supremacist far-right formations are engaged in less violent acts. They are closely followed by anti-immigrant and anti-Muslim threat groups. When investigating the nations in which the examined far-right formations operate, primarily British, Australian, and New Zealand-based right-wing extremist organizations participate in less violent acts (Figures 3.8 and 3.9).

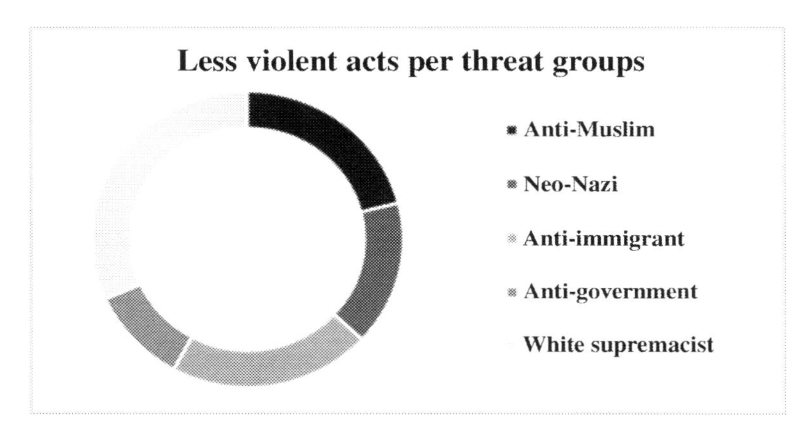

FIGURE 3.8 Ratio of less violent acts per threat group.

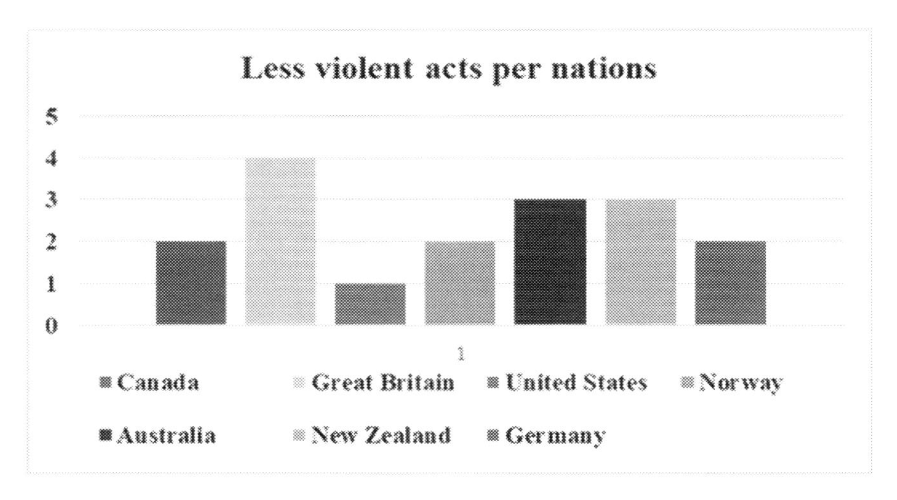

FIGURE 3.9 Ratio of less violent acts per nation.

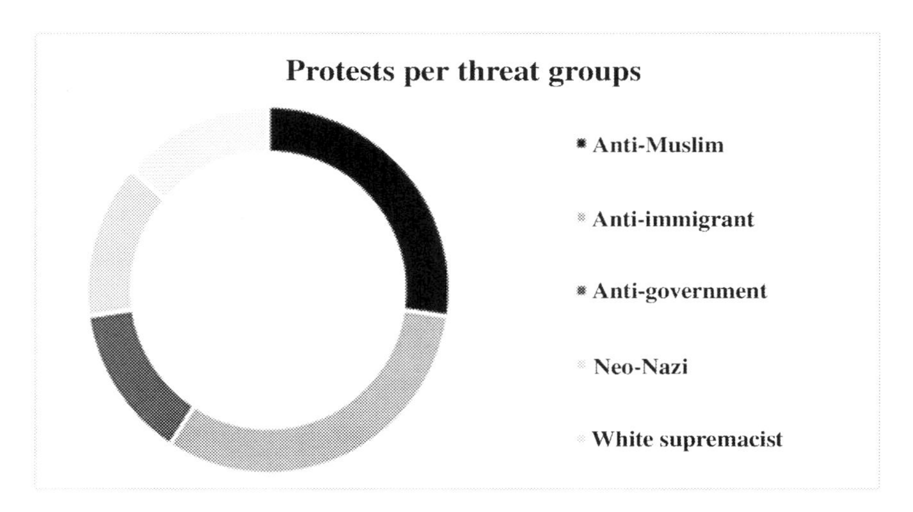

FIGURE 3.10 Ratio of protests per threat group.

Our analysis has revealed that only anti-immigrant threat groups go in for patrolling activities. More interestingly, patrolling occurred only about Canada- and Great Britain-based anti-immigrant entities.

Although protests are important modes of operation for all the five categories of threat groups, predominantly anti-immigrant and anti-Muslim formations organize and participate in demonstrations. It is also noteworthy that far-right groups of all nations engage in protest activities (Figures 3.10 and 3.11).

According to our analysis of more violent acts committed by far-right formations, it is noteworthy that no example of an Australia- or a New Zealand-based group was mentioned in the examined sources. Neo-Nazi and anti-immigrant threat groups are considered to be most active in more violent acts. On the other end, anti-government and white supremacist formations are less engaged in this type of activity. As the analysis has revealed, United States-, Great Britain-, and Germany-based far-right groups more frequently resort to violent acts (Figures 3.12 and 3.13).

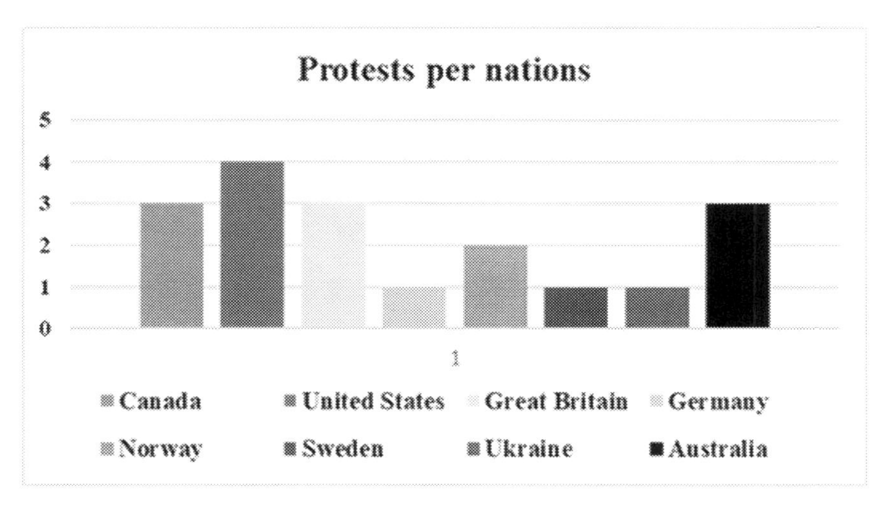

FIGURE 3.11 Ratio of protests per nation.

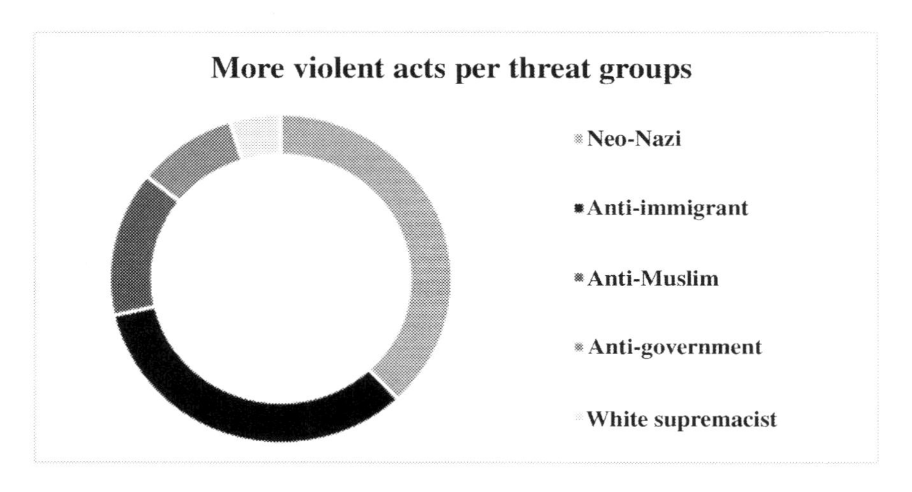

FIGURE 3.12 Ratio of more violent acts per threat group.

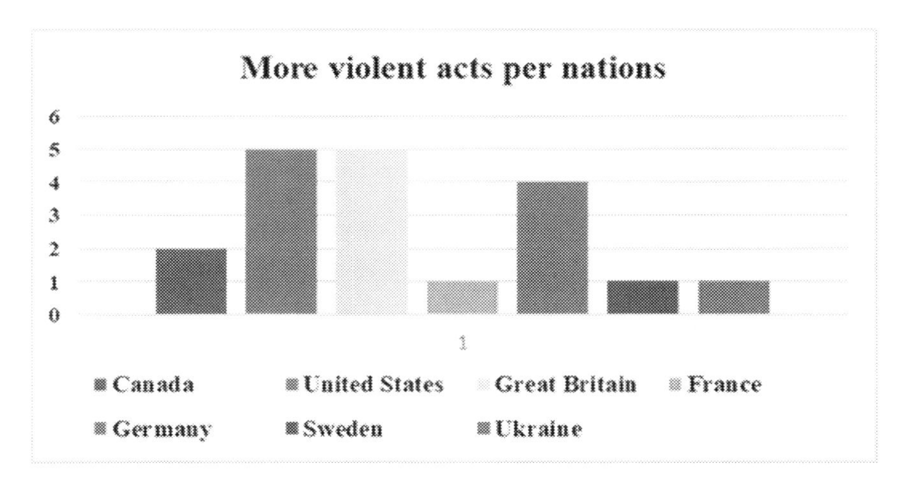

FIGURE 3.13 Ratio of more violent acts per nation.

Less-violent acts

Opportunities offered by the digital sphere are well used by far-right formations. Canadian La Meute, for instance, actively spreads online propaganda.[476] Similarly, British National Action focuses on online intimidation, creating outrage by targeting individuals.[477] National Action follower Garron Helm was sentenced to four weeks in prison for sending anti-Semitic messages to Jewish Member of Parliament, Luciana Berger, on Twitter in October 2014.[478] At the same time, Britain First revel is using patriotic memes shared in its strong social media presence.[479] The Three Percenters have reinforced the political anxiety during the Corona virus crisis by "niche websites, chat boards, and social media accounts that discuss and generate a steady stream of moral outrage over a wide range of issues including anti-fascists ("antifa"), Black Lives Matter, fake news, perceived corrupt politicians, fears of economic collapse, enacting their vision of a constitutionally constrained government".[480] Stop the Islamisation of Norway's online activities has also been accused of promoting stigmatization, exclusion, and discrimination towards Norwegian Muslims.[481]

As a non-violent offline mode of operation, a series of leaflets and banners can spread right-wing propaganda and attest to the groups' presence in the community. In line with this, Atalante members frequently hand out flyers and use banners to disseminate their hateful messages.[482] While the majority of Feuerkrieg Division's activity is online, members have engaged in leafleting efforts.[483] The most common activity by Nordic Resistance Movement has been spreading propaganda through posting stickers and handing out flyers across the region. In general, new members carry out these actions seeking to gain further acceptance and power within the hierarchical organization.[484]

Antipodean Resistance promotes and incites hatred and violence with its anti-Jewish and anti-homosexual posters claiming to "legalize their execution".[485] Their public activity includes putting up posters, stickers, banners, and painting graffiti.[486] For instance, in 2019 stickers with their logos were found at an elderly care facility that homes Holocaust survivors in Melbourne.[487] Action Zealandia members also place stickers in public spaces highlighting their ultra-nationalism.[488] Its Auckland members put up posters espousing anti-Chinese sentiment outside the office of Jian Yang, a Chinese-born New Zealand Parliament member in 2020.[489] English Defence League supporters used sightings of homophobic stickers in 2011 in London to try to stir up hatred of Muslims and divisions between Muslims and LGBT people.[490]

A more violent case study is linked to the Australian Defence League, which came to national attention in 2014 after it was revealed that its followers had been stalking and photographing Muslim women on public transport. They verbally abused Muslims and "displayed anti-Islamic posters outside mosques and threatened to blow up an Islamic school".[491] Meanwhile, the European Identitarian Movement calls for non-violent means of achieving its ends.[492] "Their goal is to win cultural power and use it to advance their ideas and values".[493] In August 2016, members of the Identitarian movement in Germany hung a banner on the iconic Brandenburg Gate in Berlin to protest at European immigration.[494] A year later, its members "helped charter a ship as part of what they said was a campaign to defend Europe and try to stop migrants crossing the Mediterranean from Libya".[495]

Right-wing extremists widely use acts of vandalism to show their presence in their local community. For instance, National Action activists sprayed anti-Semitic graffiti on a menorah in Cannon Hill Park, Birmingham, and hung a Nazi flag on it in June 2015. They recorded the event and publicize this video on YouTube "to encourage and incite antisemitism in others".[496]

A specific example of a mode of operation is the German Reichsbürger movement. Its members print passports and driver's licenses for their supposed states. They simply ignore the fact that such activity is illegal and not recognized by any German authority. They proudly announce their intention to "carry on the fight against the Federal Republic of Germany"[497] on their websites.

Far-right groups frequently offer special opportunities for personal meet-ups. Accordingly, Nordic Resistance Movement regularly organizes martial arts training and paramilitary exercises. Its members also connect through walks in the woods with their brothers in arms and at marches in uniform.[498] For bonding purposes, Antipodean Resistance holds camping, hiking, and martial art training activities, for instance, at their secret radicalization camp that was held in 2017.[499] In a similar vein, the Lads Society claims to hold weekly members-only "fight nights".[500] The clubs include a boxing gym and a library and hold seminars on subjects such as employment in the security industry.[501] National Socialist Network's social media posts are generally about its offline activities, such as camping, burning crosses, graffitiing, and stickering.[502] They regularly congregate at major landmarks to spread their hateful ideology.[503] Meanwhile, New Zealand-based Dominion Movement enthuses community-oriented work.[504] Through a dedication to environmentalism, the group frequently organizes community-work programs.[505] Action Zealandia's monthly report shows young men exercising, hiking, and collecting rubbish.[506] They also organize beach clean-ups, nature walks, and trips to historical landmarks.[507] Through their community service, Oath Keepers has used natural disasters to garner positive press coverage. They assisted vulnerable communities across the United States and Puerto Rico since 2017, this aid includes providing bottled water and food, clearing roads, and helping with rescue missions.[508]

There are a handful of examples when far-right groups offer security services both for communities and for particular personnel. The Oath Keepers frequently solicit volunteers to provide security in a variety of different contexts. For example, following a July 2015 attack on two separate Tennessee military facilities by Mohammad Abdulazeez, the Oath Keepers launched "Operation Protect the Protectors". During the operation, their supporters armed themselves and "stood guard outside various military recruitment centers around the nation under the pretense of guarding unarmed military recruiters".[509] Likewise, Lads Society was hired to provide security for Stefan Molyneux and Lauren Southern during their July tour[510] and were unofficial security for the organizers of the anti-choice "March for Babies".[511]

Patrolling

To portray themselves as defenders of their community, vigilantes of far-right formations are keen to patrol their operational territories. Soldiers of Odin patrol the streets to help the community, they send children to summer camps, helped with restoring a vandalized war monument, and offered volunteer services.[512] The group posts these events on its social media platforms with the purpose to recruit new members. Similarly, through its patrolling Northern Guard strives to recruit new members.[513] Meanwhile, Storm Alliance members patrol the US border crossing.[514] An extraordinary example here is Britain First's so-called Christian Patrols. After two Muslim converts murdered a British soldier, Lee Rigby on the streets of South London in 2013, Britain First launched these patrols in armored vehicles in densely populated Muslim areas of London and walking through similarly populated areas carrying large white crosses.[515] The group also invaded mosques and intimidated Muslims.[516]

Protests

Protests are important operational means for far-right formations. Such in-person meetups provide excellent opportunities for recruitment and at the same time, enable them to maintain their presence in their local community.

Protests are frequent activities of all examined Canada-based far-right organizations. La Meute and Soldiers of Odin demonstrate under heavy police protection.[517] While Atalante members rally against Muslim asylum seekers,[518] Storm Alliance protests with other far-right Canadian entities.[519]

In the United States, Proud Boys supporters were involved in violent demonstrations throughout the country.[520] Arrest and violent instances of Proud Boys members have been linked mostly to street fights. "A favorite tactic of the Proud Boys has been to attend rallies and street protests, often showing up as 'opposition' to anti-fascist rallies and taking part in skirmishes with other protesters".[521] Proud Boys members account for about 8% (28) of all participants federally charged by 12 April 2021 for their involvement in the Capitolium siege. After a prolonged general inactivity following the January 6 events, the Proud Boys returned to street activism in March 2021 in Oregon and Washington states.[522] In 2020, Boogalooers showed up at protests and rallies promoting gun rights or opposing gun control measures.[523] They also demonstrated against pandemic restrictions and the Black Lives Matter protests across the country that followed the killing of George Floyd in May.[524] The Oath Keepers were particularly active in the 2020 anti-lockdown protests, providing vigilante-style "security" for local communities and businesses during the Black Lives Matter demonstrations.[525] Three Percenters have also been active in rallies attempting to pass state-level gun control measures and Black Lives Matter demonstrations. They reacted very negatively to pandemic restrictions "urging defiance and opposition to stay-at-home orders, business closings, and other directives". By April and May 2020, Three Percenters frequently turned up at public protests.[526]

In Great Britain, National Action has held rallies and demonstrations at which supporters have declared that "Hitler was right" and warned against "the disease of international Jewry", which will eventually end "in the chambers" – referring to "Nazi gas chambers".[527] At the same time, Britain First organizes relatively small street demonstrations.[528] One of the group's most noteworthy protests was held in August 2014. After a report revealed that over 1,400 children had been sexually abused in Rotherham, mainly by Pakistani men, Britain First protested inside the headquarters of Rotherham Metropolitan Borough Council with a banner saying "Justice for victims of Muslim grooming".[529] Since its formation at the start of 2009 summer, English Defence League has organized nearly 20 major protests in Britain's cities, including London, Birmingham, Manchester, Leeds, Luton, Nottingham, Glasgow, and Swansea.[530] Demonstrations serve as social events for English Defence League members, helping to forge a sense of solidarity and of the EDL as "one big family".[531] Their protests have been marked by violence, with some bordering on full riots resulting in numerous arrests, property damage, and injuries to law enforcement.[532]

In the wake of the Charlie Hebdo massacre in France, protests were held against the influx of Muslim migrants.[533] PEGIDA group held protests throughout Germany,[534] which attracted around 18,000 supporters.[535] At their weekly rallies and demonstrations, participant numbers consolidate at around 1,500 and 3,000.[536] As the heat of the demonstrations diminished, group members spent time together in sports clubs and private parties.[537]

In August 2020, members of Stop the Islamisation of Norway gathered outside the Norwegian parliament to display their opposition to the Islamic faith.[538] An anti-Islam protester ripped pages from the *Quran*.[539] Similarly, Nordic Resistance Movement regularly marches in shows of force, intimidating journalists, minority groups, and other members of the public.[540] Swedish Resistance Movement occasionally organized rallies together with Svenskarnas Parti, or SvP (Party for the Swedes), to gather around 1,000 activists and extremists from all parts of Sweden together with abroad members' get together.[541]

Ukraine-based Azov's street presence often threatens its adversaries.[542]

Australian Defence League was involved in the Voices of Bendigo and Stop the Mosques Bendigo protests in 2014 and 2015.[543] The group organized public rallies in Melbourne and Sydney.[544] In 2019, Lads Society staged a rally in St Kilda, Victoria, targeting the local African Australian community.[545] Reclaim Australia held street rallies in cities across Australia protesting against Islam.[546]

Due to their extremely violent nature, two of the 2020–2021 demonstrations merit particular attention. First is the Capitolium siege, when a mob of anti-government supporters attacked the United States Capitol on 6 January 2021. Second, after a large-scale protest in the center of Berlin on 29 August 2020, several hundred demonstrators, including Reichsbürger, broke through the security barriers at the Reichstag.[547] As these two instances may suggest, initially relatively peaceful far-right protests have become increasingly violent. It should be noted that demonstrators were ready to attack the symbols of their national legislation to advance their hateful agenda.

More violent acts

While Blood and Honour generally engage in acts of vandalism, allegedly, it is Combat 18 which is responsible for violent activities.[548] Canadian Northern Guard demonstrations frequently resort to vandalism and other forms of violence.[549]

The Proud Boys has been linked to a number of arrests and violent instances, mostly related to street fights.[550] Boogaloo participants have also been involved in several attacks and plots, including "the attempted kidnapping of Michigan's governor, an attempt to sell weapons to Hamas and a deadly attack on a federal security officer in northern California".[551] According to a press release from the US Attorney's Office, in Nevada, federal prosecutors in June 2020 charged three men allegedly affiliated with the Boogaloo movement with possessing a Molotov cocktail explosive and conspiring to cause destruction during protests in Las Vegas.[552] At least nine people associated with the Oath Keepers have been charged with conspiracy in connection with the January 6 attack.[553]

Neo-Nazi Atomwaffen Division's ultimate goal is "to accelerate societal collapse, promote chaos, and create a racially-pure white society".[554] The group seeks to do this by committing violence against racial minorities, the LGBTQ+ community, leftist organizations, government institutions, law enforcement personnel, and infrastructure.[555] In online forums and through its propaganda, AWD idolizes individuals like Timothy McVeigh, Dylan Roof, Anders Breivik, and Brenton Tarrant – all of whom have committed terrorist attacks in the service of a white supremacist ideology.[556] Its propaganda videos have featured members armed with assault weapons. Leaked chat logs of AWD members include discussions of targeting US power facilities and other infrastructure. Although the group specifically has not yet claimed any attack, individual AWD members were held accountable with regard to multiple acts of violence.[557] Atomwaffen was responsible for sporadic violence, including a homophobic and anti-Semitic murder in California in January 2018 and a double murder in Virginia in December 2017 but its members, like its many offshoots and its counterparts in the Base, did not commit any indiscriminate terrorist attacks.[558] Aside from the May 2017 murders, the group had operated covertly for most of its history. In late 2019 and 2020, AWD and its affiliates began to face greater pressure from authorities both in the United States and abroad. In February 2020, US law enforcement authorities executed a nationwide series of arrests of AWD leaders and members. In February 2020, British authorities designated the UK-based AWD affiliate Sonnenkrieg Division as a terrorist organization and followed up in July 2020 with a terrorist designation for the Feuerkrieg Division. Amid the increasing pressure on AWD, the group's advisor and ideological leader, James Mason, announced that the group was disbanding. Two months later, in May 2020, the group publicly revealed a new Russia-based chapter and released Russian translations of its ideological texts. In late July 2020, members of AWD announced that the Atomwaffen Division had reorganized as the National Socialist Order (NSO). An anonymous NSO leader interviewed by VICE News in August 2020 said that the group does not intend to commit violence in the near term. Rather, NSO will focus on propaganda and recruitment, exploiting the COVID-19 pandemic, high unemployment, and political polarization in the United States to cultivate a following. NSO has announced measures to thwart counterterrorism efforts and prevent surveillance and infiltration by authorities, including encrypted communications and in-person interviews of new recruits.[559] Several members of The Base were charged with vandalism and conspiracy to commit murder.[560]

In the aftermath of the killing of British soldier, Lee Rigby, by two Muslim converts in May 2013, the perpetrators had been allegedly radicalized by

Anjem Choudary, founder of the radical Muslim group, Al Muhajiroun. After this incident, Britain First issued a video warrant warning that the group would arrest Choudary if they could find his address. The group also targeted other Muslim radicals in their homes.[561] The English Defence League claims to be committed to non-violence. Nonetheless, its members have been involved in numerous violent clashes with police and other protesters.[562] A National Action activist broke into the grounds of a Manchester synagogue in July 2016 and attached a sticker bearing the slogans "White Zone" and "National Action" to the menorah standing outside the building. A photograph of the desecration was later tweeted by the group.[563] A year later, NA supporter Zack Davies stabbed a Sikh man in Tesco in Wales, while shouting "This is for Lee Rigby", and was consequently found guilty of attempted murder.[564]

An 18-year-old racist, who reportedly posted links to Sonnenkrieg Division's social media, was jailed in 2019. The individual disseminated terrorism manuals including one that gave step-by-step instructions on how to make a working automatic pistol.[565] BBC infiltrated Sonnenkrieg Division's secret chat rooms and discovered the group was threatening Prince Harry for marrying a woman of color. The group also encouraged rape and torture of what they assumed were their political opponents, who included small children and pregnant women.[566]

Although Feuerkrieg Division primarily existed online, in their leaked chat transcripts, members discussed plans for violent attacks and their hopes of a coming civil war. In 2019, in retaliation for the arrest of one of its members in the United Kingdom, the group publicly released a list of police buildings and an image of a senior police officer with a gun to his head. FKD declared the officer to be a race traitor and called for attacks. In the same year, three individuals were charged to possess bomb-making materials and target Jewish and LGBT communities. In January 2020, FKD members discussed online plans to join with other groups in attacking Jewish institutions in Croatia.[567] Since the pandemic outbreak, FKD members incited supporters to spread the virus among Black and Jewish people. In February 2020, the group Eugene Antifa labeled FKD "a pressure cooker for potential terrorists".[568]

France-based Generation Identity published a video titled "A declaration of war" in 2012. A group of young people filmed close-up told the camera they were the generation that had seen an "ethnic divide" and a "bankrupt" experiment in "living together" that included "imposed miscegenation". A month later, they engaged in direct action for the first time by occupying the roof of a mosque under construction in the central French city of Poitiers, using the building to display anti-immigrant banners.[569] The group was also accused of attacking Turkish football supporters attending the Euro 2016 tournament in France.[570] The group repeatedly tried to prevent migrants from entering the country. The organization rented two helicopters and a plane during the spring of 2018 to track down migrants trying to make it into

France by crossing the Alps.[571] The group has carried out high-profile raids against camps or groups of travelers in the Alps and in the Pyrenees, in the south and southeast of the country.[572] In early 2021, Generation Identitaire claimed it was running an anti-migrant operation and conducting its border patrols in the Pyrenees mountains that separate France and Spain. The group's activists traveled to the French border with cars bearing the message "Defend Europe" and deployed drones to enhance their visibility across the frontier in late January 2021.[573] Members of the group deployed a giant banner in a mountain pass, usurping border police functions, and blocking the passage of refugees and migrants from Italy into France.[574]

In Germany, trial documents suggest that a group of 12 reportedly Gruppe S members had 27 unlicensed weapons to prepare for attacks on mosques, asylum centers, and the German parliament.[575] Identitarian Movement members reportedly mistaking the officers for left-wing extremists, attacked two police officers with baseball bats and pepper spray in November 2017.[576] Reichsbürger movement's members frequently engage in assaulting and threatening bailiffs, police officers, and judges; sending hate letters to Muslim and Jewish institutions; boycotting and impeding public institutions; refusing to pay taxes and rejecting administrative rulings.[577] In 2016, a police officer was shot and killed by a member of the Reichsbürger movement during a police raid to seize the man's arsenal of over 30 firearms that he had illegally hoarded. German police detected that at least one of the main suspects in a human-trafficking ring in northern Germany in May 2018 was involved in the Reichsbürger movement.[578] As part of a crackdown on Germany's far right, German Interior Ministry ordered raids on the homes of the groups' leaders in 10 states in 2020. In coordinated raids, 400 police officers searched the dwellings of 21 leading members of the group. Investigators said that they were searching for the homes of various people across Germany, suspected of plotting attacks against Jewish people, asylum seekers, and police.[579] They found weapons, propaganda, and narcotics, but none of the leaders were arrested.[580]

For more than 13 years, National Socialist Underground had been able to live undetected acting under a false identity.[581] The group was held responsible for a series of murders of immigrants and people of foreign origin.[582] NSU was blamed for the killings of eight Turks, a Greek, and a German policewoman between 2000 and 2007.[583] In addition to these murders, the group carried out two bombings in Cologne, Germany, in 2001 and 2004. Twenty-three people were injured in these attacks. Both the murders and the bombing were intended to kill individuals of non-German origin. The three-person terror cell was discovered in 2011 when the bodies of two of the perpetrators, Uwe Mundlos and Uwe Böhnhardt, were found along with evidence of their crimes, including the murder weapon and photographs of the victims and crime scenes. The two men had committed suicide after a failed bank robbery.

Their co-conspirator Beate Zschape turned herself in to the police shortly thereafter.[584] German police arrested a man accused of sending hate mail to public figures using the acronym of a neo-Nazi gang "NSU 2.0", prosecutors said, a reference to the National Socialist Underground.

Swedish Resistance Movement (SRM) members were charged with the possession of weapons and explosives in 2014.[585] Hundreds of masked SRM men rampaged through Stockholm's main train station allegedly targeting refugees in a violent manner in 2016.[586]

A group from Azov's National Militia Units attacked and destroyed a Romany camp in Kyiv on 8 June 2018, after its residents failed to respond to their ultimatum to leave within 24 hours. Police were at the scene but did not intervene, according to witnesses.[587]

Targeting

Based upon the findings of our research, the following implications can be drawn.

The vast majority of anti-Muslim threat groups target not only Muslim communities but also immigrants. White supremacist threat groups disseminate hate messages against Muslims, immigrants, racial minorities, and members of the LGBTQ communities. Anti-immigrant threat groups, however, rarely attack non-immigrant communities. LGBTQ people are victims of only two of them – namely, the Swedish Resistance Movement and the Dominion Movement. Neo-Nazi hate groups have the widest scope of target: Muslims, immigrants, Jews, racial minorities, and LGBTQ communities are all objects of their abuse. Among anti-government threat formations, it is only the Three Percenters that harasses not only government-related targets but also Muslims and immigrants.

When investigating the nations in which threat groups operate, the following results were found. Canada-based hate groups primarily target Muslims and immigrants. It is only the Blood and Honour which taunts Jews and racial minorities. Government is the object of most threat groups operating in the United States. This is followed up by racial minorities and in fewer instances Muslims, immigrants, and – at the least – members of the LGBTQ communities. Muslims and racial minorities are the most common targets of threat groups operating in Great Britain. Immigrants, Jews, and the LGBTQ community are harassed by one hate group each. The only examined French threat group targets only immigrants. Immigrants are most frequently attacked by Germany-based hate groups. Jews, racial minorities, and Muslims are targeted in fewer instances in Germany. While Norwegian threat groups harass Muslims and immigrants, Swedish formations attack immigrants and the LGBTQ community. Ukraine-based Azov's primary objects of abuse are racial minorities and Jews. Threat groups operating in Australia predominantly attack racial minorities, and there are some instances of harassment against LGBTQ, Muslims, and Jews. New Zealand-based threat groups target LGBTQ communities and less frequently Muslims, immigrants, and Jews (Table 3.11).

Weaponry

Paramilitary-styled clothes and conventional weaponry such as explosives and firearms are essential accessories of far-right threat groups. Armored personnel reinforces the presumption that far-right activists are capable of protecting citizens. Nevertheless, right-wing extremists possess various categories of weapons. While members of Canadian Three Percenters wear tactical vests and non-lethal weapons such as shock canes,[588] knuckledusters, a hammer, a chisel, and a bottle of bleach[589] were seized from supporters of the English Defence League. During the house searches at members of the Reichsbürger Movement[590] and the National Socialist Underground,[591] police found large stashes of arms and ammunition. Ukraine-based Azov has at least two training bases and a vast arsenal of weapons, from drones and armored vehicles to artillery pieces.[592] To overcome the ill-equipment of volunteer battalions, the Azov "worked out a barter system with Ukrainian border guards and received weapons and ammunition through those channels".[593] A wide range of explosives, flamethrowers, and incendiary devices were found by US law enforcement agencies at protests during 2020 and 2021. The extent of this weaponry can elucidate the level of violence linked to anti-lockdown protests and right-wing activism.[594]

The proliferation of 3D-printed weapons has been mounting severe concerns. The 2019 Halle attack drew attention to a new phenomenon, the threat posed by homemade weapons. Attacker Stephan Balliet was the first far-right extremist, who manufactured and used 3D-printed elements. Prior to the shootings, the perpetrator, Stephan Balliet, posted on an imageboard called Meguca and wrote that he had manufactured a DIY weapon with a 3D printer. Most of this constructed weapon was made out of steel, aluminum, and wood, but it contained 3D-printed components.[595] He also shared a link to his livestream when testing the newly built firearm.[596] As Balliet summarized, "All you need is a weekend's worth of time and $50 for the materials".[597] Members of the right-wing leaderless resistance can easily obtain handy information on homemade weapons – primarily – on Telegram and in private chats.[598] 3D printers were used also for those functional semi-automatic firearm components, which were seized by one of the leaders of the Atomwaffen Division in 2019. Some months later the FBI apprehended parts kits for milling AR-15s from the Delaware safehouse of The Base.

An increase in the number of convictions for obtaining manuals and attempting to build improvised firearms with 3D elements has been reported in European countries since 2019.

TABLE 3.11 Targets of examined far-right threat groups

Country	*Threat group*	*Muslims*	*Immigrants*	*White supremacist*	*Jews*	*Government*	*Racial minorities*	*LGBTQ communities*
Canada	La Meute	×	×					
Canada	Atalante	×	×					
Canada	Soldiers of Odin		×					
Canada	Three Percenters	×						
Canada	Northern Guard	×	×					
Canada	Blood and Honour			×	×		×	
Canada	Storm Alliance		×					
United States	Proud Boys	×	×	×	×		×	
United States	The Boogaloos					×		
United States	Oath Keepers					×		
United States	Three Percenters	×	×			×		
United States	Atomwaffen Division			×			×	×
United States	The Base			×			×	
Great Britain	National Action			×			×	
Great Britain	Britain First	×	×					
Great Britain	English Defence League	×						
Great Britain	Sonnekrieg Division			×			×	
Great Britain	Feuerkrieg Division	×		×	×		×	×
France	Generation Identity		×					

Germany	Gruppe S			×	×	×	
Germany	PEGIDA	×	×				
Germany	Identitarian Movement		×				
Germany	Reichsbürger Movement				×	×	
Germany	National Socialist Underground		×				
Norway	Stop the Islamisation of Norway	×	×				
Sweden	Swedish Resistance Movement		×				×
Ukraine	Azov			×	×	×	
Australia	Antipodean Resistance				×		×
Australia	Australian Defence League	×		×			
Australia	Lads Society			×			
Australia	National Socialist Network			×			
Australia	Reclaim Australia	×					
New Zealand	Dominion Movement		×				×
New Zealand	Action Zealandia			×			×
New Zealand	Wargus Christi	×			×		×

Reportedly, most of them have close links to far-right formations. Spanish police raided a workshop where 3D-printed weapons were stored in April 2021. Officers found a replica assault rifle and numerous gun barrels at the house search in Santa Cruz de Tenerife. In a raid on right-wing terrorism in Britain, two men and a woman were charged in May 2021 with possessing components of a 3D-printed firearm. A month later, a 15-year-old British girl from Derbyshire was arrested for terror offences including the possession of a manual on building 3D weapons.[599]

Homemade firearms have multiple advantages for violent extremists. They require neither special expertise nor particular ingredients. Moreover, terrorists may circumvent traditional logistics concerns and can minimize the risk of detection by authorities. Another important factor is that manufacturing improvised guns is far less lethal compared with the severe injuries a bomb-maker needs to face.

The 2017, Unite the Right rally in Charlottesville, Virginia, reminds us of the most high-profile vehicle-ramming incident, when a white supremacist drove into the crowd, killing 32-year-old Heather Heyer and injuring several others. Between 27 May 2020 and 7 July 2020, 72 vehicle-ramming attacks were recorded in the United States.[600] Monitoring the ascending trend of ramming incidents, right-wing extremists have turned cars into weapons.[601]

Considering the worrying number of right-wing extremists in law enforcement and in the armed forces of – among others – the United States, Canada, and Germany, particular attention should be paid to radicalized extremists within security services. The links between far-right extremism and members of the army have a long history, which goes back to the 1880s when the Ku Klux Klan was founded by Confederate Civil War veterans. Members of security agencies have access to training, confidential information, as well as weapons. Consistent efforts are necessary to counter the threat posed by weapons and ammunition that were stolen from military or police stockpiles.[602] Reportedly, thousands of US military firearms and explosives have disappeared from army, navy, and air force stockpiles.[603] Grave concerns exist that huge numbers of stolen weapons and explosive materials ended up in the hands of right-wing extremists.[604] German domestic intelligence agency reported more than 1,200 far-right extremists, who have a firearms license. According to the Interior Ministry, 528 of them are members of the so-called Reichsbürger movement. Additionally, between 2019 and 2020, 17 instances of shooting practices attended by right-wing extremists were revealed by German authorities. Reportedly, three-quarters of them took place in other parts of Europe.[605]

As drone technology advances, the potential for the illicit criminal exploitation of these unmanned capabilities has been escalating. There has been an ever-growing concern about the peril posed by non-state actors using an unmanned aerial vehicle (UAV) in an attack. Nevertheless, right-wing extremists have not yet resorted to UAV technologies when carrying out attacks: the Atomwaffen Division, for instance, used UAVs in its propaganda videos.[606] It is also considerable that other militant and jihadist non-state actors have successfully deployed drones in their attacks.[607] It has been argued that due to the fact that terrorist groups observe and learn from each other, right-wing extremist capabilities to develop or use drones may be a credible threat, which requires more focused counter efforts from security agencies.[608]

The transnational network of right-wing extremists

The transnational nature of the far-right extremism and violence-related threat raises the most serious concerns. Regardless of their geographical location, alliances among right-wing extremists exist through multiple interfaces. First, right-wing extremists meet in person on regular occasions. Ties among far-right activists are cemented by joint transnational activities, including participation in hate camps, paramilitary training sessions, protests, and historical commemorations.[609] Their attendance at traditional music festivals and combat training programs facilitates stronger personal bonds. Participants can also exchange experiences and last, but certainly not least, these gatherings are important sources for funding right-wing extremist activities.[610] In addition to networking[611] and fundraising opportunities, these in-person meetups also provide far-right formations with recruitment potential.[612] The 2017 Unite the Right Rally in Charlottesville merits special attention here. As one of the most noteworthy bonding events for far-right ideology supporters, the gathering is undoubtedly recorded as "the largest explicitly extreme right rallies in modern US history".[613]

Second, besides the fact that right-wing extremists travel abroad and within national borders to attend events and meet their fellows, their interaction is also vivid through online platforms.[614] It has been argued that the transnational violent extreme right-wing movement inherently entails a "strong online component".[615] Digital platforms such as the historical example of Iron March offer handy opportunities to spread hate messages and propaganda. At the same time, right-wing extremists historically bond through common narratives.[616] The Great Replacement theory, the 2015 European migration crisis, as well as the COVID-19 pandemic were all exploited along with these old traditional far-right ideologies. Through their transnational networks and ideological bonds, they created a radicalized milieu, which enable them to maintain a stable performance of the associated threat. Once a threat group has been designated as a terrorist entity, the formation dissolves, and re-forms along with very similar ideological principles. Additionally, the transnational dimension of this leaderless movement[617] leaves the possibility for the operation of lone actors open and thereby maintains a steady level of the threat.[618]

North-America-based far-right threat groups

It is an interesting observation that only some of the existing right-wing extremist formations are "solely Canadian creations", but in most cases they are offsprings of other transnational movements.[619] Anti-Muslim La Meute, for instance, is inspired by France's Marine Le Pen and her National Front,[620] but the group also collaborates with Storm Alliance members in Canada.[621]

Mainly via concert tours, neo-Nazi Atalante maintains a vivid relationship with its European counterparts. The formation is considered to be inspired by the Italian anti-immigration far-right group CasaPound and the Bloc Identitaire in France.[622] On the occasion of a seminar, Atalante invited its fellow Italian partners to Canada in 2016, a year later Atalante members visited CasaPound in Rome.[623] Reportedly, Atalante organizer Beauvais-MacDonald was present with other Canadian right-wing extremists at the 2017 Charlottesville "Unite the Right" rally.[624] Atalante is closely connected to other far-right threat groups in Canada. It has direct links to neo-Nazi Federation des Quebecois de Souche, additionally, in Quebec City it frequently organizes street patrols together with members of the anti-immigrant hate group, Soldiers of Odin.[625]

Soldiers of Odin is an offspring of its Finnish parent organization, which was founded by Mika Ranta in 2015.[626] The group has brought its anti-immigrant, anti-Muslim, and refugee-hating ideology[627] first to Sweden and Denmark, then to Germany, the United Kingdom, France, Belgium, the Netherlands, Ireland, Portugal, and Spain.[628] A year later, in 2016 Soldiers of Odin was present in the United States and Canada, moreover, the movement established chapters in Australia (Figure 3.14).[629]

Anti-government Three Percenters are based in the United States, but it also operates units in Canada, and militias are the strongest in Alberta and British Columbia.[630]

Neo-Nazi Blood and Honour chapters are also present in various parts of the globe. Followers of the group are active in the United Kingdom, Germany, Spain, Ukraine, Lithuania, Poland, Belgium, and Serbia.[631] In addition, Blood

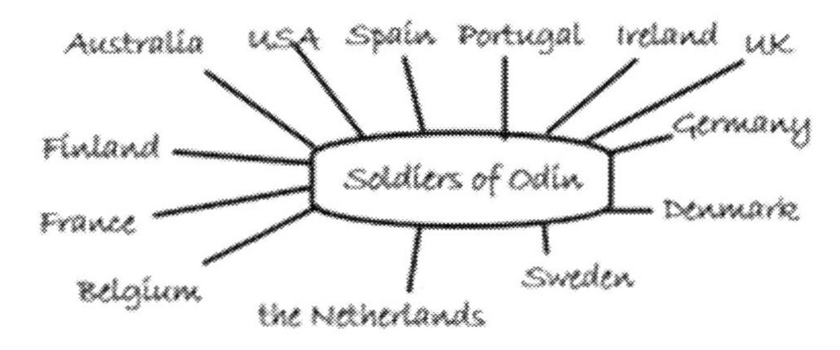

FIGURE 3.14 International linkages of Soldiers of Odin.

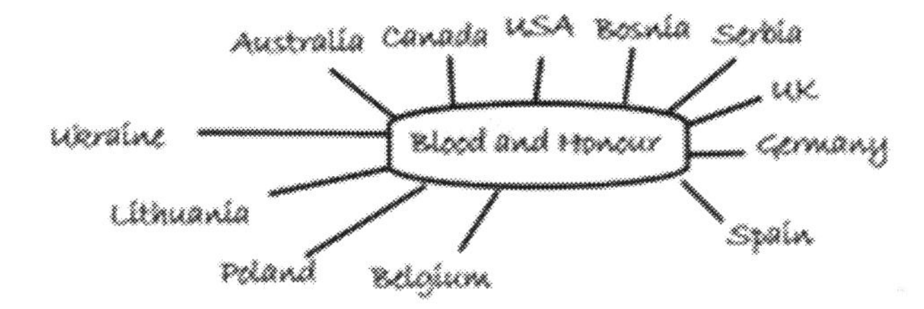

FIGURE 3.15 International linkages of Blood and Honour.

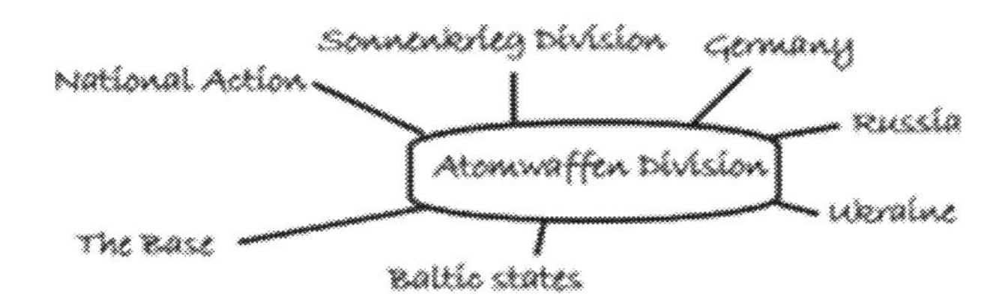

FIGURE 3.16 International linkages of Atomwaffen Division.

and Honour graffiti was discovered in Bosnia in February 2020. Reportedly, the group has spread to Australia, Canada, and the United States (Figure 3.15).[632]

In the United States, together with other white supremacist formations, Proud Boys members were present at the 2017 protests at the University of California-Berkeley[633] and were also involved in the "Unite the Right" rally. The group frequently organizes protests and participates in violent acts around the United States.[634] Referring to its role in the January 6 Capitolium insurrection, the Canadian government designated the group as a terrorist entity.[635] Prior to the Capitol riot, executives of the Oath Keepers allegedly negotiated with Proud Boys on the implementing details of the January 6 attack.[636]

Neo-Nazi Atomwaffen Division has an extensive international footprint and maintains close links with British right-wing extremist groups, including National Action and Sonnenkrieg Division[637] as well as with affiliates in Germany, Russia,[638] Ukraine, and the Baltic States[639]. Allegedly, Atomwaffen Division and The Base members frequently interact on Telegram, they even share members with each other (Figure 3.16).[640]

Europe-based far-right threat groups

Its early handouts suggest that British National Action's ideology has deep roots in Russian neo-Nazis.[641] By 2016, its activists organized street marches and combat training events across Scotland, Yorkshire, Midlands, London, East England, and the north-eastern, north-western, and south-western parts of Britain (Figure 3.17).[642]

FIGURE 3.17 International linkages of National Action.

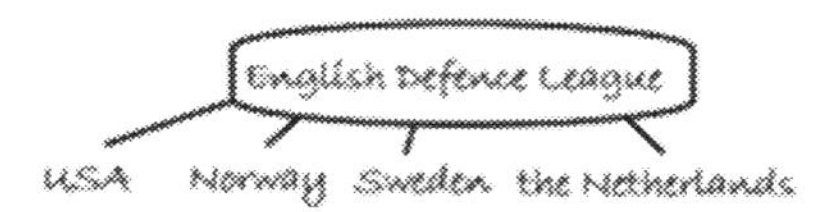

FIGURE 3.18 International linkages of English Defense League.

Anti-Muslim English Defence League established links with other, like-minded anti-Muslim threat groups both in Europe and in the United States. EDL members turned up at affiliated groups' events on various occasions. To mention only some of these instances, in 2010 they participated in the "Ground Zero Mosque" protest in New York[643] and established a working relationship with Stop Islamization of America in the United States.[644] As a result of international expansion, EDL offshoots emerged in Norway, Sweden, and the Netherlands (Figure 3.18).[645]

French Pan-European Génération Identitaire is also present in Canada, they share the common mission: "Homeland, Freedom, Tradition".[646] Through its transnational links with other far-right groups, GI gains advances in its logistical matters.[647] Government reports substantiate that the movement received donations from Christchurch shooter Brenton Tarrant, who reportedly sent "a total of €2,200 ($2,490) to Génération Identaire in late 2017".[648]

German PEGIDA affiliated groups emerged across Germany, "Legida in Leipzig, Bogida in Bonn, Fragida in Frankfurt".[649] The anti-immigrant movement's offspring emerged in Norway, Denmark, Sweden, the United Kingdom, Switzerland but also in Canada and the United States.[650] Executives of 14 fellow right-wing extremist groups including representatives of PEGIDA Austria, PEGIDA Bulgaria, and PEGIDA Netherlands met in 2016 in the Czech Republic to "sign the Prague Declaration, which states their belief that the history of Western civilization could soon come to an end through Islam conquering Europe thus formalizing their membership in the Fortress Europe coalition" (Figure 3.19).[651]

Austrian authorities confirmed that Brenton Tarrant had reached out to anti-immigrant Identitarian Movement leader Martin Sellner[652] and donated €1,500 to the country's chapter of the far-right movement.[653] Beyond its European bases in Austria, Hungary, France, Italy, Denmark, the United

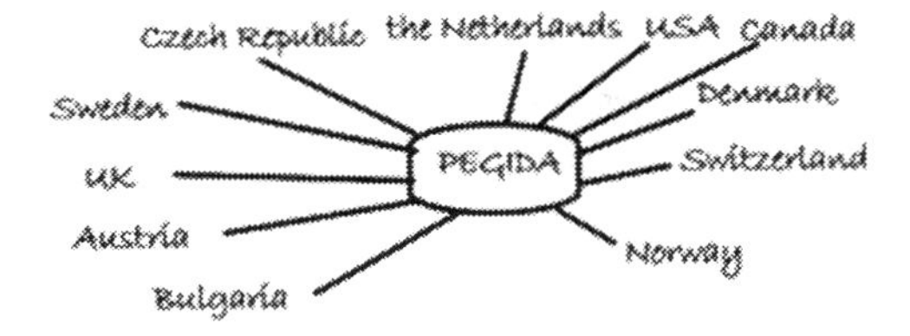

FIGURE 3.19 International linkages of PEGIDA.

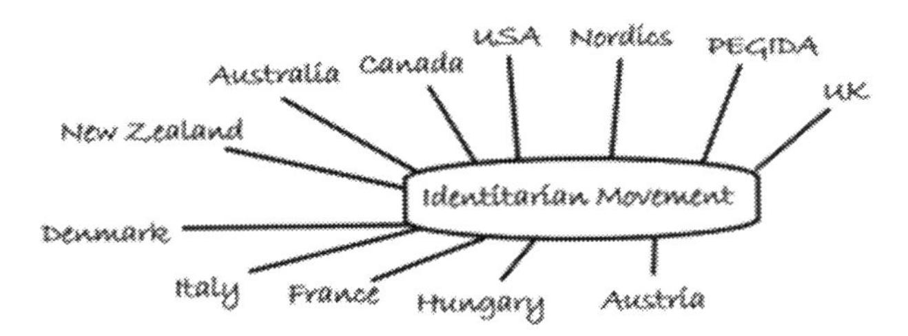

FIGURE 3.20 International linkages of Identitarian Movement.

Kingdom, and the Nordics,[654] white nationalists in North America, Australia, and New Zealand also adhere to its ideology.[655] Besides its transnational linkages, the group has formalized collaborations at a national level. German Identitarians have collaborated with other anti-immigration right-wing extremists in Germany including PEGIDA (Figure 3.20).[656]

Germany-based anti-immigrant National Socialist Underground members were closely connected to British (Blood and Honour and Combat 18) and American (White Knights of the Ku Klux Klan) neo-Nazi activists.[657] Intelligence reports substantiate that members of the trio regularly participated in Blood and Honour concerts,[658] moreover the structure of NSU was constructed according to Combat 18 model.[659]

Stop the Islamisation of Norway as the most powerful anti-Muslim organization in the region is the Norwegian offshoot of "Stop Islamization of Europe (SIOE), which originated in Denmark in 2007".[660] White-supremacist Nordic Resistance Movement is a "transnational, neo-Nazi organization with official chapters operating in Sweden, Finland, and Norway".[661] The movement has activists also in Denmark and Iceland, but no formal chapters have been formed in these countries.

Anti-immigrant Swedish Resistance Movement has been eager to establish "a pan-Nordic resistance movement"[662] including the Finnish resistance movement (Suomen Vastarintaliike), the Norwegian resistance movement (Den norske motstandsbevegelsen), and the Danish resistance movement

(Den Danske Modstandsbevægelse). Reports suggest that while SRM was highly active in this collaboration, other participating movements showed less intensity in engaging.[663]

The armed conflict in Ukraine has attracted more than 2,500 volunteers, "many of whom see their battle as a fight against the extinction of Europe".[664] Experts estimate that "more than 17,000 foreign fighters came to Ukraine since 2015 from 50 countries".[665] A probably even more concerning factor is that "unlike returnees from Syria, the veterans returning home from Ukraine do not undergo deradicalization and resocialization programs in their home states".[666] Although the number of these foreign fighters has considerably declined and counted only a few dozen in 2020, the ideological link between these fighters is still considered to be worrisome.[667]

Purportedly, Azov Battalion organizes paramilitary training sessions through "its own 'Western Outreach Office'".[668] Their mission is "to help recruit and attract foreign fighters that travel to train and connect with people from like-minded violent organizations from across the globe".[669] Americans, Norwegians, Italians, Germans, British, Brazil, Swedish, and Australians were recorded as having traveled get trained with Azov (Figure 3.21). Allegedly, members of The Base and Atomwaffen Division made attempts to reach out to Azov.[670]

> At least one of the members of The Base arrested in January 2020 had expressed a desire to go to Ukraine. According to court documents, William Bilbrough had "repeatedly expressed an interest in traveling to Ukraine to fight with nationalists there" and had tried to recruit two other members of The Base to accompany him.[671]

Besides paramilitary training events, Azov has been striving to offer other grounds for bonding with fellow far-right extremists. Music festivals provide excellent opportunities for these purposes. To mention one of the most noteworthy, the fifth neo-Nazi Asgardsrei music festival was held in Kyiv in December 2019. Videos recorded at the event showed that "in the heat

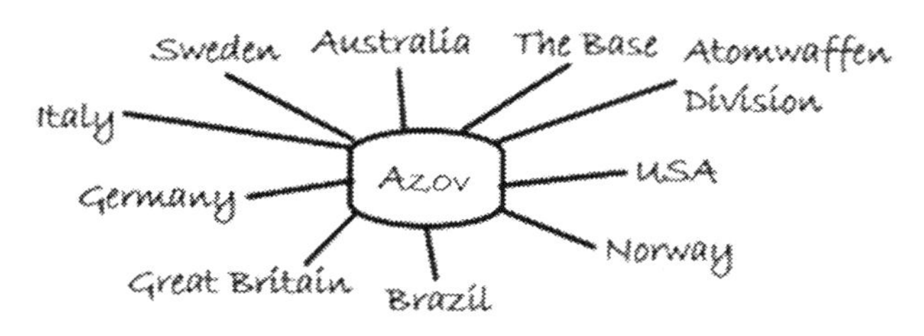

FIGURE 3.21 International linkages of Azov.

of the concerts, participants enthusiastically chanted neo-Nazi slogans and greetings".[672]

Not only do like-minded right-wing extremists visit Azov, members of the battalion also frequently turn up at far-right-inspired events. For instance, Azov members blogged about their participation at the "Young Europe Forum in Dresden in August 2020 alongside far-right sympathizers from groups in Germany, Italy, and Austria".[673] As Azov members reported, they "met with those from groups that Azov considers close allies – for instance, Greece's Golden Dawn, Italy's CasaPound, Poland's Szturmowcy, and Germany's National Democratic Party and Alternative for Germany".[674] On another occasion, Azov members visited their fellows in the Baltic States and Croatia.[675] Videos recorded at these events were then broadly shared on Azov's Facebook and YouTube channels.

Australia- and New Zealand-based far-right threat groups

The web forum of Iron March provided handy opportunities for Australian neo-Nazi Antipodean Resistance members to maintain a vivid connection with their overseas counterparts such as National Action in the United Kingdom, Nordic Resistance Movement in Norway, Sweden, and Finland, as well as with Atomwaffen Division in the United States.[676]

According to New Zealand-based anti-immigrant Dominion Movement's social media content, its members took part in rallies for "Canadian right-wing speakers Stefan Molynuex and Lauren Southern in 2018".[677] They also claimed to have met Identity Australia and the white nationalist National Front.[678] Action Zealandia allegedly maintains a close relationship with Dominion Movement[679] and has published about its linkages to a far-right Scandinavian group, the Nordic Resistance Movement.[680] According to other allegations, a supporter of white supremacist Action Zealandia "participated in chats with members of Atomwaffen Division. They discussed how to establish and operate a terror cell".[681]

Conclusion

Our research in this section has arrived at the following key findings.

First, the examined anti-Muslim threat groups maintain close alliances with fellow counterparts mostly in the Baltic States, the United States, and the Netherlands. Additional linkages exist with followers and chapters in France, the Czech Republic, Bulgaria, Austria, the United Kingdom, Switzerland, and Canada.

Second, anti-government hate groups are typically connected with other threat formations within their national borders. An outstanding example in this regard is the bond between Canada- and US-based anti-government entities.

Third, among the analyzed threat groups, anti-immigrant and neo-Nazi formations obtained and liaised in the greatest number with like-minded entities and individuals. Still, while anti-immigrant clusters maintain close connections with counterparts in the Baltic States, Canada, and Australia, neo-Nazi threat groups are mostly linked with fellows in Germany, the United Kingdom, and the Baltic States.

Fourth, our analysis has revealed that white supremacist threat groups equally interact with their fellows in the Baltic States, the United States, and Canada. As a final observation, the Baltic States, Canada, the United States, and the United Kingdom are home to far-right threat groups of the widest ideological spectrum.

Notes

1 Eitan Azani, Liram Koblenz-Stenzler, Lorena Atiyas-Lvovsky, Dan Ganor, Arie Ben-Am, and Delilah Meshulam, "The far right – Ideology, modus operandi and development trends", 5 January 2021. www.ict.org.il/Article/2643/The_Far_Right_Ideology_Modus_Operandi_and_Development_Trends#gsc.tab=0
2 E. Carter, "Right-wing extremism/radicalism: Reconstructing the concept". *Journal of Political Ideologies*, 23(2), 157–182, 2018; C. Mudde, *Populist Radical Right Parties in Europe*. Cambridge, UK: Cambridge University Press, 2007.
3 Anders Ravik Jupskås and Iris Beau Segers, "What is right-wing extremism?", C-REX, Center for Research on Extremism, www.sv.uio.no/c-rex/english/groups/compendium/what-is-right-wing-extremism.html
4 Jamie Grierson, "Rise of the far right: A disturbing mix of hateful ideologies", *The Guardian*, 19 September 2019. www.theguardian.com/uk-news/2019/sep/19/rise-of-the-far right-a-disturbing-mix-of-hateful-ideologies
5 Jonathan Montpetit, "Inside Quebec's far right: A secretive online group steps into the real world", CBC, 4 December 2016. www.cbc.ca/news/canada/montreal/quebec-far right-la-meute-1.3876225
6 "Right-wing extremist activity on the rise in Atlantic Canada: UNB researchers", NS News, 16 December 2020. www.nsnews.com/national-news/right-wing-extremist-activity-on-the-rise-in-atlantic-canada-unb-researchers-3189677
7 "Non-profit head on defensive after Facebook 'like' of hate group page reported", CBC News, 23 September 2020. www.cbc.ca/news/canada/new-brunswick/humanity-project-northern-guard-1.5734801
8 Alexa MacLean, "Canadian Anti-Hate Network tracking 'hate group' in Halifax", Global News, 5 April 2019. https://globalnews.ca/news/5134538/canadian-anti-hate-network-halifax-northern-guard/
9 "Proud Boys", ADL. www.adl.org/proudboys
10 Aaron Wolfson and Hampton Stall, "Actor Profile: Proud Boys", ACLED. https://acleddata.com/2021/04/22/actor-profile-proud-boys/
11 Blyth Crawford, "The Proud Boys", ICSR Team, 1 October 2020. https://icsr.info/2020/10/01/the-proud-boys/

12 James Rodger, "Who are Britain First and what do they stand for?", Birmingham Mail, 29 November 2017. www.birminghammail.co.uk/news/midlands-news/britain-first-jayda-fransen-who-13231720
13 "The far right: What is Britain First?", Sky News, 30 November 2017. https://news.sky.com/story/the-far right-what-is-britain-first-11149915
14 "Britain First: What you need to know", ADL, 29 November 2017. www.adl.org/blog/britain-first-what-you-need-to-know
15 Chris Allen, "What is Britain First – The far right group retweeted by Donald Trump?", The Conversation, 1 December 2017. https://theconversation.com/what-is-britain-first-the-far right-group-retweeted-by-donald-trump-88407
16 "Radical English Defence League to form political party", ADL, 28 March 2012. www.adl.org/blog/radical-english-defence-league-to-form-political-party
17 Mark Wilding, "The rise and demise of the EDL", Vice, 12 March 2018. www.vice.com/en/article/qve8wm/the-rise-and-demise-of-the-edl
18 Ibid.
19 "English Defence League", Hope not hate. www.hopenothate.org.uk/research/english-defence-league/
20 George Kassimeris and Leonie Jackson, "The ideology and discourse of the English Defence League: 'Not racist, not violent, just no longer silent' ", *The British Journal of Politics and International Relations*, 20 January 2014. https://journals.sagepub.com/doi/10.1111/1467-856X.12036
21 "A European answer to PEGIDA", 31 March 2015. www.thenewfederalist.eu/a-european-answer-to-pegida?lang=fr
22 "Germany PEGIDA protests: Rallies over 'Islamisation' ", BBC, 6 January 2015. www.bbc.com/news/world-europe-30685842
23 Enes Bayrakl and Farid Hafez (Eds.), "European Islamophobia Report 2018". www.islamophobiaeurope.com/wp-content/uploads/2019/09/NORWAY.pdf
24 Atle Andersen, "Advarer mot islamister", *Stavanger Aftenblad*, 9 July 2011.
25 Katrine Fangen and Maria Reite Nilsen, "Variations within the Norwegian far right: From neo-Nazism to anti-Islamism". *Journal of Political Ideologies*, 2020. www.tandfonline.com/doi/pdf/10.1080/13569317.2020.1796347?needAccess=true
26 Matthias Gardell, "Crusader Dreams: Oslo 22/7, Islamophobia, and the quest for a monocultural Europe". *Terrorism and Political Violence*, 26, 2014. www.qub.ac.uk/Research/GRI/mitchell-institute/FileStore/Filetoupload,818003,en.pdf
27 Georgina Connery, "Reclaim Australia Rally drowns out counter protesters", *Canberra Times*, 6 February 2016. www.canberratimes.com.au/story/6054582/reclaim-australia-rally-drowns-out-counter-protesters/
28 "Reclaim Australia", https://web.archive.org/web/20150402175044/ www.reclaim-australia.com/
29 Tom Peters, "New Zealand soldier linked to fascist groups arrested", World Socialist Web Site, 8 January 2020. www.wsws.org/en/articles/2020/01/08/nsmi-j08.html
30 CARR-Hedayah Radical Right Counter Narratives Project, "From gangs to groupuscules: And solo-actor terrorism: New Zealand radical right narratives and counter-narratives in the context of the Christchurch attack", 2021. www.hedayahcenter.org/wp-content/uploads/2021/04/2021APR1_FINAL_NewZealand_Country-Report.pdf

31 Peters, "New Zealand soldier linked to fascist groups arrested".
32 Jane Coaston, "The 'boogaloo,' 'movement,' explained", VOX, 8 June 2020. www.vox.com/2020/6/8/21276911/boogaloo-explained-civil-war-protests
33 Matthew Kriner and Colin P. Clarke, "Eclectic Boogaloo", *Slate*, 19 August 2020. https://slate.com/news-and-politics/2020/08/boogaloos-growth-memes-blm.html
34 Ibid.
35 Brandy Zadrozny, "What is the 'Boogaloo'? How online calls for a violent uprising are hitting the mainstream", NBC News, 19 February 2020. www.nbcnews.com/tech/social-media/what-boogaloo-how-online-calls-violent-uprising-are-getting-organized-n1138461
36 "The Boogaloo movement", ADL. www.adl.org/boogaloo
37 "Oath Keepers", ADL. www.adl.org/resources/backgrounders/oath-keepers
38 Sam Jackson, *Oath Keepers Patriotism and the Edge of Violence in a Right-Wing Antigovernment Group*. New York: Columbia University Press, 2020.
39 Christy Hutter, "Three Percenters are Canada's 'most dangerous' extremist group, say some experts", CBC, 10 May 2018.
40 Jaclyn Diaz and Rachel Treisman, "Members of right-wing militias, extremist groups are latest charged in Capitol Siege", NPR, 19 January 2021.
41 "Three Percenters", ADL. www.adl.org/resources/glossary-terms/three-percenters
42 Wolfgang Dick, "What is behind the right-wing 'Reichsbürger' movement?", DW, 24 July 2018. www.dw.com/en/what-is-behind-the-right-wing-reichsb%C3%BCrger-movement/a-36094740
43 Ibid.
44 Ibid.
45 Annabelle Olivier, "Immigration protesters and counter-protesters rally near Lacolle border", Global News, 19 May 2018. https://globalnews.ca/news/4220246/immigration-protests-lacalle-border-quebec/
46 Jillian Kestler-D'Amours, "Explained: 'Increased legitimacy' of Quebec's far right", Al-Jazeera, 15 November 2017. www.aljazeera.com/news/2017/11/15/explained-increased-legitimacy-of-quebecs-far right
47 Simon Coutu, "Canada's newest ultra-nationalist group plans show of force", Vice, 7 September 2017. www.vice.com/en/article/yww8ab/canadas-newest-ultra-nationalist-group-plans-show-of-force
48 "Proud Boys", ADL.
49 Wolfson and Stall, "Actor Profile: Proud Boys".
50 "The far right: What is Britain First?", Sky News.
51 Ibid.
52 "France vetoes far right group 'Génération Identitaire' ", Archyde, 3 March 2021. www.archyde.com/france-vetoes-far right-group-generation-identitaire/
53 "France bans far right anti-migrant group Generation Identity", France 24, 3 March 2021. www.france24.com/en/france/20210303-france-bans-far right-anti-migrant-group-generation-identity
54 "A European answer to PEGIDA".
55 Ibid.
56 Croucher, "Identitarian movement, linked to Christchurch Mosque shooter, classified as extremist right-wing group by German intelligence agency".

57 Ibid.
58 "Identitarian movement". www.owlapps.net/owlapps_apps/articles?id=40853628&lang=en
59 Christopher J. Adamczyk, "Gods versus titans: Ideological indicators of Identitarian violence", Naval Postgraduate School Thesis, September 2020. www.hsdl.org/?abstract&did=847107
60 "Identitarian movement".
61 Lars Guenther, Georg Ruhrmann, Jenny Bischoff, Tessa Penzel, and Antonia Weber, "Strategic framing and social media engagement: Analyzing memes posted by the German Identitarian Movement on Facebook", *Social Media and Society*, January–March 2020. https://journals.sagepub.com/doi/pdf/10.1177/2056305119898777
62 Frank Jordans, "Neo-Nazi trial puts spotlight on fate of migrants in Germany", AP News, 11 July 2018. https://apnews.com/article/ap-top-news-germany-international-news-crime-munich-2ae82df0e3464317852e4d3bfbb2a709
63 Philip Oltermann, "German neo-Nazi Beate Zschäpe sentenced to life for NSU murders", *The Guardian*, 11 July 2018. www.theguardian.com/world/2018/jul/11/german-neo-nazi-beate-zschape-gets-life-for-nsu-murders
64 Ibid.
65 Bayrakl and Hafez (Eds.), "European Islamophobia Report 2018".
66 "Neo-Nazis, counter-protesters rally in Sweden", VOA, 25 August 2018. www.voanews.com/europe/neo-nazis-counter-protesters-rally-sweden
67 Andersen, "Advarer mot islamister".
68 Jussi Rosendahl and Tuomas Forsell, "Anti-immigrant 'Soldiers of Odin' raise concern in Finland", Reuters, 13 January 2016. www.reuters.com/article/us-europe-migrants-finland-idUSKCN0UR20G20160113
69 Bridge Initiative Team, "Factsheet: Soldiers of Odin", 9 March 2019. https://bridge.georgetown.edu/research/factsheet-soldiers-of-odin/
70 Thomas Manch, "The 'growing' white nationalist group with a 'harmful and violent' ideology", Stuff, 26 March 2019. www.stuff.co.nz/national/christchurch-shooting/111415544/the-growing-white-nationalist-group-with-a-harmful-and-violent-ideology
71 Adam McCleery, "Secretive right-wing group Dominion Movement which described immigrants as 'unworthy imports' goes underground following Christchurch terror attack", *Daily Mail*, 26 March 2019. www.dailymail.co.uk/news/article-6849603/Extreme-right-wing-group-Dominion-Movement-goes-underground-following-Christchurch-terror-attack.html
72 "Mobilisation à Québec contre l'« immigration illégale »", Radio-Canada, 15 August 2017. https://ici.radio-canada.ca/nouvelle/1050424/mobilisation-groupes-extreme-droite-quebec-immigration-illegale-la-meute-atalante
73 Counter Extremism Project, "Blood and Honour". www.counterextremism.com/supremacy/blood-honour-bh
74 The Canadian Centre for Identity-Based Conflict, "Blood and Honour". https://vtsm.org/tools/vtsmdatabase/blood-and-honour/
75 "Police Commissioner: Street patrols have no special rights", Yle, 5 January 2016. https://yle.fi/uutiset/osasto/news/police_commissioner_street_patrols_have_no_special_rights/8573593
76 "Atomwaffen Division/National Socialist Order", Stanford CISAC. https://cisac.fsi.stanford.edu/mappingmilitants/profiles/atomwaffen-division

77 The Soufan Center, "The Atomwaffen Division the evolution of the White Supremacy Threat", August 2020. https://thesoufancenter.org/wp-content/uploads/2020/08/The-Atomwaffen-Division-The-Evolution-of-the-White-Supremacy-Threat-August-2020-.pdf
78 Jacob Ware, "Siege: The Atomwaffen Division and rising far right terrorism in the United States", International Centre for Counter-Terrorism (ICCT) – The Hague, ICCT Policy Brief, July 2019.
79 "The Base", Southern Poverty Law Center. www.splcenter.org/fighting-hate/extremist-files/group/base
80 "The Base", ADL. www.adl.org/resources/backgrounders/the-base
81 "The Base", Southern Poverty Law Center.
82 Sam Christie and Felix Allen, "Who are National Action? Neo-Nazi terror group banned in the UK who praised Jo Cox's killer Thomas Mair", *The Sun*, 3 January 2018. www.thesun.co.uk/news/uknews/2381165/national-action-neo-nazi-terror-group-banned-uk-jo-cox-killer-thomas-mair/
83 Chris Allen, "Commission for Countering Extremism National Action: links between the far right, extremism and terrorism", August 2019. https://assets.publishing.service.gov.uk/government/uploads/system/uploads/attachment_data/file/834342/Chris_Allen_-_National_Action_Post_Publication_Revisions.pdf
84 Australian Government Australian National Security, "Sonnenkrieg Division". www.nationalsecurity.gov.au/Listedterroristorganisations/Pages/sonnenkrieg-division.aspx
85 ADL, "Feuerkrieg Division (FKD)". www.adl.org/resources/backgrounders/feuerkrieg-division-fkd
86 Ibid.
87 "Prozessauftakt Stuttgart: Rechte Terrorgruppe wollte 'demokratisches System abschaffen' ", SWR Aktuell, 14 April 2021. www.swr.de/swraktuell/baden-wuerttemberg/stuttgart/prozess-gegen-rechte-gruppe-s-100.html
88 "Gruppe S: Germany's far right group", Crackit Today Affairs, 15 April 2021. https://crackittoday.com/current-affairs/gruppe-s-germanys-far right-group/
89 Stefan Giese, "Absicht: Moslems und Juden töten, möglichst viele", SWR Aktuell, 13 April 2021. www.swr.de/swraktuell/gruppe-s-vor-gericht-kolumne-100.html
90 Emma Zafari, "Germany's Far Right and Trumpism", International Policy Digest, 11 October 2020. https://intpolicydigest.org/germany-s-far right-and-trumpism/
91 Anton Shekhovtsov, "Why Azov should not be designated a foreign terrorist organization", Atlantic Council, 24 February 2020. www.atlanticcouncil.org/blogs/ukrainealert/why-azov-should-not-be-designated-a-foreign-terrorist-organization/
92 Julie Nathan, "Antipodean resistance: The rise and goals of Australia's new Nazis", ABC, 20 April 2018. www.abc.net.au/religion/antipodean-resistance-the-rise-and-goals-of-australias-new-nazis/10094794
93 "Antipodean Resistance poster", National Library of Australia. https://catalogue.nla.gov.au/Record/7501026
94 Jack Paynter, "Alarm as neo-Nazi group National Socialist Network expands to Adelaide", News, 13 October 2020. www.news.com.au/technology/online/security/alarm-as-neonazi-group-national-socialist-network-expands-to-adelaide/news-story/a68c9d4aa39ce51120c7ab8e3fdf7035
95 Ibid.
96 Ibid.

97 Sten Hankewitz, "The UK is to ban the neo-Nazi group formerly led by a 13-year-old Estonian boy", *Estonian World*, 14 July 2020. https://estonianworld.com/security/the-uk-is-to-ban-the-neo-nazi-group-formerly-led-by-a-13-year-old-estonian-boy/
98 Coaston, "The 'boogaloo,' 'movement,' explained".
99 "Proud Boys", ADL.
100 Daniel Sallamaa and Tommi Kotonen, "The case against the Nordic Resistance Movement in Finland: An overview and some explanations", C-REX, Center for Research on Extremism, 2 November 2020. www.sv.uio.no/c-rex/english/news-and-events/right-now/2020/the-case-against-the-nordic-resistance-movement.html
101 Karis Hustad, "'Most radical organisation': Neo-Nazi group seeks to gain ground in Nordic countries", Euro News, 29 August 2018. www.euronews.com/2018/08/25/-most-radical-organisation-neo-nazi-group-seeks-to-gain-ground-in-nordic-countries
102 Ibid.
103 Ibid.
104 Sean Rubinsztein-Dunlop, "Tensions between Australian Defence League and Muslim community reach violent new heights", Australian Broadcasting Corporation, 21 April 2014. www.abc.net.au/news/2014-04-21/anti-islam-hate-campaign-raises-tensions-to-violent-new-heights/5402526
105 Cait Kelly, "Who are the neo-Nazi groups threatening Australia's security?", *The New Daily*, 26 February 2020. https://thenewdaily.com.au/news/2020/02/26/australia-neo-nazi/
106 Ibid.
107 CARR-Hedayah Radical Right Counter Narratives Project, "From gangs to groupuscules: And solo-actor terrorism".
108 "Action Zealandia: White guilt is a tool that has been used by the financial elite for a century", 12 March 2021. https://tradicijaprotitiraniji.org/2021/03/12/action-zealandia-white-guilt-is-a-tool-that-has-been-used-by-the-financial-elite-for-a-century/
109 Paul Spoonley, "Far right extremists still threaten New Zealand, a year on from the Christchurch attacks", The Conversation, 10 March 2020. https://theconversation.com/far right-extremists-still-threaten-new-zealand-a-year-on-from-the-christchurch-attacks-133050
110 CARR-Hedayah Radical Right Counter Narratives Project, "From gangs to groupuscules: And solo-actor terrorism".
111 Kristy Hutter, "Three Percenters are Canada's most dangerous extremist group, say some experts", CBC News, 10 May 2018. www.cbc.ca/news/canada/three-percenters-canada-1.4647199
112 Coaston, "The 'boogaloo,' 'movement,' explained".
113 Graeme Thomson, "Who are Britain First? Far right group founded by a Scot distances itself from Jo Cox killing", *Daily Record*, 17 June 2016. www.dailyrecord.co.uk/news/politics/who-britain-first-far right-8220189
114 Ibid.
115 Alejandro J. Beutel and Daryl Johnson, "The Three Percenters: A look inside an anti-government militia", Newlines Institute for Strategy and Policy, February 2021. https://newlinesinstitute.org/wp-content/uploads/20210225-Three-Percenter-PR-NISAP-rev051021.pdf

116 "What does Canadian fascism look like? A guide to far right organizations at the Parliament Hill protest", *The Leveller*, 25 October 2017. https://leveller.ca/2017/10/canadian-fascism/
117 Erika Morris, "What far right groups are active in Quebec?", *The Link Newspaper*, 3 April 2018. https://thelinknewspaper.ca/article/what-far right-groups-are-active-in-quebec
118 Morris, "What far right groups are active in Quebec?".
119 "Right-wing extremist activity on the rise in Atlantic Canada: UNB researchers".
120 Robert Evans and Jason Wilson, "The Boogaloo Movement is not what you think", Bellingcat, 27 May 2020. www.bellingcat.com/news/2020/05/27/the-boogaloo-movement-is-not-what-you-think/
121 "Oath Keepers", Southern Poverty Law Center. www.splcenter.org/fighting-hate/extremist-files/group/oath-keepers
122 Terrence McCoy, "The Oath Keepers: The little-known militia now roaming the streets of Ferguson", *The Washington Post*, 28 October 2017.
123 Jackson, *Oath Keepers Patriotism and the Edge of Violence in a Right-Wing Antigovernment Group*.
124 "What is generation identity?", Al-Jazeera, 10 December 2018. www.aljazeera.com/news/2018/12/10/what-is-generation-identity
125 Ibid.
126 Adamczyk, "Gods versus titans: Ideological indicators of Identitarian violence".
127 "What is generation identity?".
128 "Research shows the need to address the root cause of far right extremism", Swinburne University of Technology, 15 April 2021. www.swinburne.edu.au/news/2021/04/research-shows-the-need-to-address-the-root-cause-of-far right-extremism/
129 Paul P. Murphy, "Who are the Proud Boys? Trump's debate callout bolsters far right group", ABC7 News, 1 October 2020. https://abc7.com/proud-boys-trump-presidential-debate-who-are-the/6691389/
130 "Proud Boys", Southern Poverty Law Center. www.splcenter.org/fighting-hate/extremist-files/group/proud-boys
131 Ibid.
132 CARR-Hedayah Radical Right Counter Narratives Project, "From gangs to groupuscules: And solo-actor terrorism".
133 "Proud Boys", Southern Poverty Law Center.
134 Beutel and Johnson, "The Three Percenters: A look inside an anti-government militia".
135 "The Boogaloo Movement".
136 ADL, "Feuerkrieg division (FKD)".
137 Allen, "Commission for Countering Extremism National Action: Links between the far right, extremism and terrorism".
138 Tore Bjørgo, "Right-Wing extremism in Norway: Changes and challenges", C-REX, Center for Research on Extremism, 25 February 2019. www.sv.uio.no/c-rex/english/news-and-events/right-now/2019/right-wing-extremism-in-norway.html
139 Hustad, "'Most radical organisation'".
140 "Atomwaffen Division/National Socialist Order".
141 Centre for Analysis of the Radical Right, "The many faces of neo-Nazism in the UK", Open Democracy, 6 February 2020. www.opendemocracy.net/en/countering-radical-right/many-faces-neo-nazism-uk/

142 "Neo-Nazis, counter-protesters rally in Sweden".
143 Nathan, "Antipodean resistance".
144 Lucy Sheriff, Lucy, "Meet new neo-Nazi Group national action which just wants to 'piss people off' ", *The Huffington Post*, 6 March 2014.
145 Rachel Lang, "Neo-Nazi radicalisation camp held on Sunshine Coast", *Sunshine Coast Daily*, 5 September 2017. www.sunshinecoastdaily.com.au/news/neo-nazi-radicalisation-camp-held-on-sunshine-coas/3220247/
146 "The Boogaloo Movement".
147 "The far right: What is Britain First?", Sky News.
148 "New Zealand 'Identitarian' group shutters after Christchurch massacre", Angry White Men, 16 March 2019. https://angrywhitemen.org/2019/03/16/new-zealand-identitarian-group-shutters-after-christchurch-massacre/#more-47398
149 "Neo-Nazis, counter-protesters rally in Sweden".
150 "A European answer to PEGIDA".
151 Ibid.
152 S.M. Chermak, J.D. Freilich, A. Bringuel, and J.K. Shearer, "Terrorism and counterfeiting: A synopsis of critical issues and research opportunities", in: A.J. Bringuel, J.C. Janowicz, A.C. Valida, E.F. Reid (Eds.). *Terrorism Research & Analysis Project: A Collection of Thoughts, Ideas, & Perspectives*, Volume I. Washington, DC: Government Printing Office, 2011; J.D. Freilich, S.M. Chermak, and J. Simone, Jr., "Surveying American state police agencies about terrorism threats, terrorism sources, and terrorism definitions". *Terrorism and Political Violence*, 21(3), 450–475, 2009; M.C. Horowitz, "Nonstate actors and the diffusion of innovations: The case of suicide terrorism". *International Organization*, 64(1), 33–64, 2010; Siobhan O'Neil, *Terrorist Precursor Crimes: Issues and Options for Congress*. Washington, DC: Congressional Research Service, 2007; T.M. Sanderson, "Transnational terror and organized crime: Blurring the lines". *SAIS Review*, 24(1), 49–61, 2004.
153 FATF, "Ethnically or racially motivated terrorism financing", 2021. www.fatf-gafi.org/publications/methodsandtrends/documents/ethnically-racially-motivatedterrorism-financing.html
154 Ken Bensinger, Jessica Garrison, Jeremy Singer-Vine, and Salvador Hernandez, "The Oath Keepers are facing new membership and money issues following the Capitol Riot", Buzzfeednews, 7 May 2021. www.buzzfeednews.com/article/kenbensinger/finances-membership-for-oath-keepers
155 Australian Government Australian National Security, "Sonnenkrieg Division".
156 Will Carless, "Crowdfunding hate: How white supremacists and other extremists raise money from legions of online followers", *USA Today*, 2 May 2021. https://eu.usatoday.com/story/news/nation/2021/02/05/bitcoin-crowdfunding-used-white-supremacists-far right-extremists/4300688001/
157 Anti-Defamation League, "Funding hate: How white supremacists raise their money". www.adl.org/sites/default/files/documents/adl-report-funding-hate-how-white-supremacists-raise-their-money.pdf
158 Brigitte Noel, "La Meute: The illusions and delusions of Quebec's 'Largest' right-wing group", Vice, 6 January 2017. www.vice.com/en/article/d7pmk7/la-meute-the-illusions-and-delusions-of-quebecs-largest-right-wing-group
159 "The Boogaloo Movement".
160 "Three Percenters", ADL. www.adl.org/resources/backgrounders/three-percenters

161 Counter Extremism Project, "Atomwaffen Division/National Socialist Order". www.counterextremism.com/supremacy/atomwaffen-division-national-socialist-order
162 Paul Jackson, Paul, *The EDL: Britain's "New Far Right" Social Movement*. Northampton: University of Northampton, 2011.
163 Blood & Honour, 'B & H Magazines'. www.bloodandhonourworldwide.co.uk/bhww/magazines
164 Simon Shuster and Billy Perrigo, "Like, share, recruit: How a white-supremacist militia uses Facebook to radicalize and train new members", *Time*, 7 January 2021. https://time.com/5926750/azov-far right-movement-facebook/
165 Ibid.
166 Anti-Defamation League, "Funding hate: How white supremacists raise their money".
167 Counter Extremism Project, "Blood and Honour".
168 Tom Keatinge, Florence Keen, and Kayla Izenman, "Fundraising for right-wing extremist movements". *The RUSI Journal*, 164(2), 10–23, 2019. DOI:10.1080/03071847.2019.1621479
169 "Rechtsextremistische Erlebniswelt: Musik und Kampfsport", Bundesamt für Verfassungschutz. www.verfassungsschutz.de/SharedDocs/hintergruende/DE/Rechtsextremismus/rechtsextremistische-erlebniswelt-musik-und-kampfsp ort.html
170 Sébastien Bourdon, "At Ukraine's Asgardsrei, a French connection", Bellingcat, 1 May 2020. www.bellingcat.com/news/2020/05/01/at-ukraines-asgardsrei-a-french-connection/
171 Peter Stone, "US far right extremists making millions via social media and cryptocurrency", *The Guardian*, 10 March 2021. www.theguardian.com/world/2021/mar/10/us-far right-extremists-millions-social-cryptocurrency
172 Ibid.
173 Kristie Pladson, "German neo-Nazis trained at Russian camps: Report", DW, 5 June 2020; Hans Pfeifer, Mikhail Bushuev, and Vladimir Esipov, "Why are German neo-Nazis training in Russia?", DW, 6 June 2020; *Moscow Times*, "Russian "terrorists" training German neo-Nazi youth in combat – Reports", 9 June 2020.
174 Bethan Johnson, "Financing right-wing extremism and terrorism", Project Craaft Research Briefing no. 5. https://static1.squarespace.com/static/5e399e8c6e9872149fc4a041/t/5fbb892005f44a5f70a75317/1606125861203/CRAAFT+RB5+Final+Version.pdf
175 Katrin Bennhold, "Body bags and enemy lists: How far right police officers and ex-soldiers planned for "day X"", *New York Times*, 4 August 2020; Maik Baumgärtner et al., "Harmless stockpilers or neo-Nazi survivalists?", Spiegel International, 21 November 2019.
176 Mary Fitzgerald and Claire Provost, "The American dark money behind Europe's far right", Open Democracy, 11 July 2019. www.opendemocracy.net/en/5050/the-american-dark-money-behind-europes-far right/
177 Hans-Jakob Schindler, "New technologies: The emerging terrorist financing risk", Acams Today Europe, AML Challenges, May 2020–June 2020. www.acamstoday.org/new-technologies-the-emerging-terrorist-financing-risk/
178 Lizzie Dearden, "British far right extremists being funded by international networks, report reveals", *Independent*, 31 May 2019. www.independent.co.uk/news/uk/home-news/far right-extremism-terrorism-tommy-robinson-funding-international-a8937116.html

179 Stone, "US far right extremists making millions via social media and cryptocurrency".
180 For instance, Christchurch attacker Brenton Tarrant reportedly donated thousands of pounds to international far right groups and websites. Lizzie Dearden, "Christchurch shooter donated thousands to far right groups and websites before attack, report shows", *Independent*, 8 December 2020. www.independent.co.uk/news/world/australasia/brenton-tarrant-christchurch-donations-generation-identity-b1768056.html
181 Anti-Defamation League, "Funding hate: How white supremacists raise their money".
182 Keatinge et al., "Fundraising for right-wing extremist movements".
183 FATF, "Ethnically or racially motivated terrorism financing".
184 Lizzie Dearden, "How crowdfunding helps far right extremism spread round the world", *Independent*, 31 May 2019. www.independent.co.uk/news/uk/home-news/far right-extremism-crowdfunding-tommy-robinson-a8937311.html
185 Anti-Defamation League, "Funding hate: How white supremacists raise their money".
186 Alex Newhouse, "From classifieds to crypto: How white supremacist groups have embraced crowdfunding", Middlebury Institute for International Studies in Monterey, 2019. www.middlebury.edu/institute/sites/www.middlebury.edu.institute/files/2019-06/Alex%20Newhouse%20CTEC%20Paper.pdf?fv=9T_mzirH
187 Carless, "Crowdfunding hate: How white supremacists and other extremists raise money from legions of online followers".
188 Anti-Defamation League, "Funding hate: How white supremacists raise their money".
189 Meghan Keneally, "What to know about the violent Charlottesville protests and anniversary rallies", ABC News, 8 August 2018. https://abcnews.go.com/US/happen-charlottesville-protest-anniversary-weekend/story?id=57107500
190 "Organizers and leaders of Charlottesville's deadly rally raised money with PayPal", Southern Poverty Law Center, 15 August 2017.
191 Adi Robertson, "GoFundMe is banning crowdfunding campaigns for the alleged Charlottesville killer", The Verge, 15 August 2017. www.theverge.com/2017/8/15/16151226/gofundme-james-fields-alt-right-crowdfunding-campaign-ban
192 David Gilbert, "Crowdfunding site Patreon is purging far right figures", Vice, 7 December 2018. www.vice.com/en/article/qvqeev/crowdfunding-site-patreon-is-purging-far right-figures
193 Blake Montgomery, "PayPal, GoFundMe, and Patreon banned a bunch of people associated with the alt-right. Here's why", Buzzfeed News, 2 August 2017. www.buzzfeednews.com/article/blakemontgomery/the-alt-right-has-apayment-processor-problem#.diZvE7ZGp
194 Robertson, "GoFundMe is banning crowdfunding campaigns for the alleged Charlottesville killer".
195 Erin Carson, "Here's where Nazi sympathizers go to raise money", CNET, 4 December 2017. www.cnet.com/news/neo-nazi-sympathizers-crowdfunding/
196 Counter Extremism Project, "English Defence League". www.counterextremism.com/supremacy/english-defence-league-edl
197 Michael Bonvalot, "Weitere Bank kündigt Spendenkonto der Identitären", Die Zeit, 22 June 2017.

198 Hatreon, https://hatreon.net
199 Gab, @Goyfundme, https://gab.com/Goyfundme
200 Twitter, @MakerSupport, https://twitter.com/gomakersupport
201 Gab, @WeSearchr, https://gab.com/WeSearchr
202 Nathan, "Antipodean resistance". https://antipodean-resistance.com/donate/index.html
203 Siladitya Ray, "The far right is flocking to these alternate social media apps — Not all of them are thrilled", *Forbes*, 14 January 2021. www.forbes.com/sites/siladitya ray/2021/01/14/the-far right-is-flocking-to-these-alternate-social-media-apps---not-all-of-them-are-thrilled/?sh=63d8244755a4
204 Ibid.
205 Jane Bradley and Michael Schwirtz, "U.K. far right, lifted by Trump, now turns to Russia", *The New York Times*, 23 April 2021. www.nytimes.com/2021/04/23/world/europe/uk-far right-tommy-robinson-russia.html
206 Talia Lavin, "Crowdfunding hate in the name of Christ", *The Nation*, 5 April 2021. www.thenation.com/article/society/givesendgo-crowdfunding-extremism/
207 Ibid.
208 Ibid.
209 Ibid.
210 Ibid.
211 "PayPal ditches Christian crowdfunding site used by the Proud Boys", Wtop, 12 January 2021. https://wtop.com/business-finance/2021/01/paypal-ditches-christian-crowdfunding-site-used-by-the-proud-boys/
212 Keatinge et al., "Fundraising for right-wing extremist movements".
213 Blood & Honour, "Subscribe". https://bloodandhonourworldwide.co.uk/bhww/28-2/
214 "Proud Boys and other far right groups raise millions through Christian funding sites", *Sydney News Today*, 10 April 2021. https://sydneynewstoday.com/proud-boys-and-other-far right-groups-raise-millions-through-christian-funding-sites-right-end/134371/
215 Jason Wilson, "Proud Boys and other far right groups raise millions via Christian funding site", *The Guardian*, 10 April 2021. www.theguardian.com/world/2021/apr/10/proud-boys-far right-givesendgo-christian-fundraising-site
216 Ibid.
217 Majlie de Puy Kamp and Scott Glover, "Right-wing extremists and their supporters use Christian website to raise funds", CNN, 20 January 2021. https://edition.cnn.com/2021/01/19/us/give-send-go-extremism-invs/index.html
218 Talia Lavin, "Crowdfunding Hate in the Name of Christ".
219 Wilson, "Proud Boys and other far right groups raise millions via Christian funding site".
220 de Puy Kamp and Glover, "Right-wing extremists and their supporters use Christian website to raise funds".
221 Cassie Miller, Hannah Gais, and Megan Squire, "Funding hate: How extremists like the ones who attacked the Capitol are making money off the internet", Southern Poverty Law Center, 1 April 2021. www.splcenter.org/news/2021/04/01/funding-hate-how-extremists-ones-who-attacked-capitol-are-making-money-internet
222 de Puy Kamp and Glover, "Right-wing extremists and their supporters use Christian website to raise funds".

223 SITE Intelligence Group, "Far right media personalities fundraising for legal support after filming themselves inside Capitol building", 25 January 2021.
224 Jason Wilson, "Proud Boys and other far right groups raise millions via Christian funding site".
225 Will Carless, "Proud Boys saw wave of contributions from Chinese diaspora before Capitol attack", *USA Today*, 4 May 2021. https://eu.usatoday.com/story/news/nation/2021/05/04/proud-boys-chinese-americans-community-support-donations/7343111002/
226 Zachary Petrizzo, "Nick Fuentes, 'Baked Alaska' banned from Dlive following Capitol riots", The Daily Dot, 9 January 2021; "Building a safe and welcoming community", DLive, 9 January 2021.
227 "PayPal ditches Christian crowdfunding site used by the Proud Boys".
228 Noel, "La Meute: The illusions and delusions of Quebec's 'Largest' right-wing group".
229 Ibid.
230 "Génération Identitaire: The fight for Europe and against migration", Magyar Nemzet, 10 February 2021. https://magyarnemzet.hu/english/generation-identitaire-the-fight-for-europe-and-against-migration-9354827/
231 Stéphanie Trouillard, "France to ban far right group Generation Identity", France 24, 17 February 2021. www.france24.com/en/france/20210217-france-to-ban-far-right-group-generation-identity
232 Counter Extremism Project, "Nordic Resistance Movement".
233 Cecilia D'Anastasio, "Gaming sites are still letting streamers profit from hate", *Wired*, 2 April 2021. www.wired.com/story/streamlabs-streamelements-far-right-white-supremacy-monetize/
234 Like Fortney, "How Amazon's Twitch Platform Makes Money", 20 October 2019. www.investopedia.com/investing/how-does-twitch-amazons-video-game-streaming-platform-make-money/
235 LifeCourse Associates, "Twitch, Millennials, and the Future of Entertainment", August 2014. www.lifecourse.com/assets/files/reports/Twitch,%20Millennials,%20and%20the%20Future%20of%20Entertainment_August_2014.pdf
236 Kellen Browning, "Extremists find a financial lifeline on Twitch", *The New York Times*, 27 April 2021. www.nytimes.com/2021/04/27/technology/twitch-livestream-extremists.html
237 Gais, Hannah and Edison Hayden, Michael, "Extremists are cashing in on a youth-targeted gaming website", Southern Poverty Law Center, 17 November 2020.
238 Vera Bergengruen, "How far right personalities and conspiracy theorists are cashing in on the pandemic online", *Time*, 20 August 2020.
239 Megan Squire, "Monetizing propaganda: How far right extremists earn money by video streaming". In WebSci'21:13th International ACM Conference on Web Science in 2021, June 21–25, 2021. New York, NY: ACM.
240 Kellen Browning and Lorenz Taylor, "Pro-Trump mob livestreamed its rampage, and made money doing it", *The New York Times*, 8 January 2021.
241 Emily VanDerWerff, "Is the country falling apart? Depends on where you get your news", Vox, 8 January 2021. www.vox.com/culture/22217782/capitol-insurrection-cable-news-twitch-mob-siege
242 "Neo-Nazi hate groups 'make money from British corporations without them knowing' through YouTube ad revenue system", *Daily Mail*, 21 June 2012. www.dailymail.co.uk/news/article-2162526/Neo-Nazi-hate-groups-make-money-British-corporations-knowing-YouTube-ad-revenue-system.html

243 SITE Intelligence Group, "Far right groups forming self-branded streaming platforms to avoid censorship", 18 November 2020.
244 D'Anastasio, "Gaming sites are still letting streamers profit from hate".
245 Miller et al., "Funding hate".
246 Southern Poverty Law Centre, "Bitcoin and the alt-right". www.splcenter.org/bitcoin-and-alt-right
247 Julia Ebner, "The currency of the far right: Why neo-Nazis love bitcoin", *The Guardian*, 24 January 2018; Keatinge et al., "Fundraising for right-wing extremist movements".
248 Chainanysis Team, "Insights", 14 January 2021. https://blog.chainalysis.com/reports/capitol-riot-bitcoin-donation-alt-right-domestic-extremism
249 Ibid.
250 Ibid.
251 Carless, "Crowdfunding hate: How white supremacists and other extremists raise money from legions of online followers".
252 Shahed Warreth, "Crowdfunding and cryptocurrency use by far right and jihadi groups", Voxpol, 21 November 2019. www.voxpol.eu/crowdfunding-and-cryptocurrency-use-by-far right-and-jihadi-groups/
253 Carless, "Crowdfunding hate: How white supremacists and other extremists raise money from legions of online followers".
254 Anti-Defamation League, "Funding Hate: How white supremacists raise their money".
255 Ibid.
256 Edward Helmore, "Oklahoma bomb 'funded by gun sales' ", *The Independent*, 24 July 1995.
257 P. Simi, "Radicalization and Recruitment among Right-Wing Terrorists. An Exploratory Approach". Washington, DC: United States Department of Justice (Final Report to National Institute of Justice), 2009.
258 R. Blazak, "White boys to terrorist men: Target recruitment of Nazi skinheads". *American Behavioral Scientist*, 44(6), 982–100, 2001; T. Bjørgo, "Dreams and disillusionment: Engagement in and disengagement from militant extremist groups". *Crime, Law and Social Change*, 55(4), 277–285, 2011; J. Horgan, "From profiles to pathways and roots to routes: Perspectives from psychology on radicalization into terrorism". *The ANNALS of the American Academy of Political and Social Science*, 618(1), 80–94, 2008; M. Sageman, *Understanding Terror Networks*. Philadelphia, PA: University of Pennsylvania Press, 2004.
259 S.M. Chermak, *Searching for a Demon: The Construction of the Militia Movement*. Boston, MA: Northeastern University Press, 2002; M. Sageman, *Understanding Terror Networks*. Philadelphia, PA: University of Pennsylvania Press, 2004.
260 B. Hoffman, *Inside Terrorism*. New York: Columbia University Press, 2006.
261 M. Sageman, *Understanding Terror Networks*. Philadelphia, PA: University of Pennsylvania Press, 2004; P. Simi, "Radicalization and Recruitment among Right-Wing Terrorists. An Exploratory Approach". Washington, DC: United States Department of Justice (Final Report to National Institute of Justice), 2009.
262 ADL, "Propaganda, extremism and online recruitment tactics". www.adl.org/education/resources/tools-and-strategies/table-talk/propaganda-extremism-online-recruitment

263 B.A. Dobratz and S.L. Shanks-Meile, *White Power, White Pride! The White Separatist Movement in the United States*. New York, NY: Twayne Publishers, 1997; P. Simi and R. Futrell, "Negotiating white power activist stigma". *Social Problems*, 56, 89–110, 2009.
264 J.D. Freilich, S.M. Chermak, and D.J. Caspi, "Critical events in the life trajectories of domestic extremist white supremacist groups: A case study analysis of four violent organizations". *Criminology and Public Policy*, 8(3), 497–530, 2009.
265 Pete Simi, Steven Windisch, and Karyn Sporer, "Recruitment and Radicalization among US Far Right Terrorists". College Park, MD: START, 2016.
266 P. Simi and R. Futrell, "American Swastika: Inside the White Power Movements Hidden Spaces of Hate". Lanham, MD: Rowman & Littlefield, 2010.
267 Ibid.
268 Gappa, "La Meute vue de l'intérieur", 29 January 2016. https://gappasquad.wordpress.com/2016/01/29/la-meute-vue-de-linterieur/
269 Jarrod Gilbert and Ben Elley, "Shaved heads and Sonnenrads: Comparing white supremacist skinheads and the alt-right in New Zealand". *Kōtuitui: New Zealand Journal of Social Sciences Online*, 15(2), 280–294, 2020.
270 Baz Macdonald, "The retreat of NZ white nationalists", Re News, 25 March 2019. www.renews.co.nz/the-retreat-of-nz-white-nationalists/
271 Counter Extremism Project, "Atomwaffen Division/National Socialist Order".
272 Daniel Se Simone, "How neo-Nazi group National Action targeted young people", BBC, 21 March 2020. www.bbc.com/news/uk-48279225
273 Counter Extremism Project, "Blood and Honour".
274 Pete Simi, Steven Windisch, and Karyn Sporer, "Recruitment and radicalization among US far right terrorists".
275 Ibid.
276 Counter Extremism Project, "Atomwaffen Division/National Socialist Order".
277 Counter Extremism Project, "National Action". www.counterextremism.com/supremacy/national-action
278 Se Simone, "How neo-Nazi group National Action targeted young people".
279 El Jones, "Georgie Fagan used to organize with white supremacists. Now he condemns them", *Halifax Examiner*, 7 January 2020. www.halifaxexaminer.ca/featured/georgie-fagan-used-to-organize-with-white-supremacists-now-he-condemns-them/
280 Pete Simi, Steven Windisch, and Karyn Sporer, "Recruitment and radicalization among US far right terrorists".
281 Counter Extremism Project, "Blood and Honour".
282 Shuster and Perrigo, "Like, share, recruit".
283 Michael McGowan, "Australian white nationalists reveal plans to recruit 'disgruntled, white male population' This article is more than 1 year", *The Guardian*, 11 November 2019. www.theguardian.com/australia-news/2019/nov/12/australian-white-nationalists-reveal-plans-to-recruit-disgruntled-white-male-population
284 Rebecca Puddy, "Far right nationalists open private men-only clubs in Melbourne and Sydney", ABC, 7 June 2018. www.abc.net.au/news/2018-06-07/far right-opens-men-only-clubs-in-melbourne-and-sydney/9836458
285 Small Steps, "How does the far right use the internet to recruit?". https://smallstepsconsultants.com/the-far right-threat/how-does-the-far right-use-the-internet-to-recruit/

286 Tom Knowles, "Far right recruiting children on YouTube", The Times, 6 October 2020. www.thetimes.co.uk/article/far right-recruiting-children-on-youtube-0xknjffws
287 Jamie Dettmer, "Violent German far right groups' recruitment aided by lockdown frustrations", VOA News, 19 January 2021. www.voanews.com/europe/violent-german-far right-groups-recruitment-aided-lockdown-frustrations
288 Hebe Campbell, "Far right groups use Instagram to recruit youngsters, report claims", Euronews, 31 March 2021. www.euronews.com/2021/03/22/far right-groups-use-instagram-to-recruit-youngsters-report-claims
289 Joshua Zitzer, "Neo-Nazi groups are using Instagram to recruit young teenagers, experts warn. Memes are being used to entice them", *Insider*, 27 March 2021. www.businessinsider.com/instagram-memes-used-recruit-young-people-to-nazi-groups-experts-2021-3
290 Ibid.
291 "Controversial Soldiers of Odin group recruiting on southeast Avalon", CBC, 15 October 2016. www.cbc.ca/news/canada/newfoundland-labrador/soldiers-of-odin-newfoundland-1.3803680
292 Wolfson and Stall, "Actor profile: Proud Boys".
293 "Proud Boys", Southern Poverty Law Center.
294 Masood Farivar, "Boogaloo boys aim to provoke 2nd US civil war", VOA News, 23 June 2020. www.voanews.com/usa/race-america/boogaloo-boys-aim-provoke-2nd-us-civil-war
295 Counter Extremism Project, "English Defence League".
296 Gappa, "La Meute vue de l'intérieur".
297 Jonathan Montpetit, "How Quebec's largest far right group tries to win friends, influence people", CBC, 21 August 2017. www.cbc.ca/news/canada/montreal/quebec-la-meute-far right-1.4255193
298 Ibid.
299 Anthony Measures, "What is PEGIDA?", Tony Blair Institute for Global Change, 14 January 2015. https://institute.global/policy/what-pegida
300 Florian Flade and Georg Mascolo, "Die Radikalität der "Gruppe S"", Tagesschau, 27 February 2020. www.tagesschau.de/investigativ/ndr-wdr/terrorzelle-gruppe-s-105.html
301 Flade and Mascolo, "Die Radikalität der "Gruppe S"".
302 Ibid.
303 Counter Extremism Project, "Feuerkrieg Division". www.counterextremism.com/supremacy/feuerkrieg-division
304 Shuster and Perrigo, "Like, share, recruit".
305 Bradley Jurd, "Recruitment posters for Antipodean Resistance plastered over Bathurst CSU campus", Western Advocate, 2 January 2018. www.westernadvocate.com.au/story/5147145/recruitment-posters-for-antipodean-resistance-on-bathurst-csu-campus/
306 Paul Gregorie, "The Rise of Australian Neo-Nazis: An Interview with Online Activist Slackbastard", Sydney Criminal Lawyers, 21 April 2018. www.sydneycriminallawyers.com.au/blog/the-rise-of-australian-neo-nazis-an-interview-with-online-activist-slackbastard/
307 Nathan, "Antipodean Resistance"; "The secret radicalisation camp of Aussie 'Hitlers', the Antipodean Resistance", Yahoo News, 7 September 2017. https://au.news.yahoo.com/antipodean-resistance-hitler-nazi-group-radicalisation-camp-36992809.html

308 Rex Martinich, "Neo-Nazi Antipodean Resistance training camp in Grampians National Park used for online recruitment", *The Courier*, 7 October 2017. www.thecourier.com.au/story/4972529/neo-nazi-grampians-camp-used-for-recruitment/
309 Nick McKenzie and Joel Tozer, "'We do not need to wait for a Christchurch': Grampians cross burning spurs call for action", *The Age*, 28 January 2021. www.theage.com.au/politics/federal/we-do-not-need-to-wait-for-a-christchurch-grampians-cross-burning-spurs-call-for-action-20210128-p56xer.html; Jack Paynter, "How extreme right-wing groups have 'weaponised the internet' in Australia", *The Australian*, 8 March 2021. www.theaustralian.com.au/breaking-news/how-extreme-rightwing-groups-have-weaponised-the-internet-in-australia/news-story/ed0950b6bcc9aab54d25280a944f554b
310 Cam Wilson, "Leaked neo-Nazis' manual reveals they're manipulating Australia's media to recruit new members", Crikey, 20 April 2021. www.crikey.com.au/2021/04/20/leaked-neo-nazi-manual-manipulating-media-recruit/
311 Jordan McSwiney, Greta Jasser, and Ed Pertwee, "Gab's gift to the far right", *The Interpreter*, 1 June 2021. www.lowyinstitute.org/the-interpreter/gab-s-gift-far right
312 Counter Extremism Project, "English Defence League".
313 Siladitya Ray, "The far right is flocking to these alternate social media apps — not all of them are thrilled", *Forbes*, 14 January 2021. www.forbes.com/sites/siladitya ray/2021/01/14/the-far right-is-flocking-to-these-alternate-social-media-apps---not-all-of-them-are-thrilled/?sh=d24773155a44
314 Kevin Roose, "The alt-right created a parallel internet. It's an unholy mess", *The New York Times*, 11 December 2017. www.nytimes.com/2017/12/11/technology/alt-right-internet.html
315 Joshua Foust, "Video games are the new contested space for public policy", Stream, 25 March 2021. www.brookings.edu/techstream/video-games-are-the-new-contested-space-for-public-policy/
316 www.facebook.com/VICE/videos/810735666447102/
317 Mark Keierleber, "How white extremists teach kids to hate", The 24 Million, 27 January 2021. www.the74million.org/article/where-hate-is-normalized-how-white-extremists-use-online-gaming-communities-popular-among-teens-to-recruit-culture-warriors/
318 Counter Extremism Project, "Sonnenkrieg Division". www.counterextremism.com/supremacy/sonnenkrieg-division
319 Tess Owen, "The U.S. military has a Boogaloo problem", Vice, 24 June 2020.
320 Andrew Donley, "Neo-Nazis using video games to recruit kids, former member says", ABC3340, 10 July 2018. https://abc3340.com/news/local/neo-nazis-are-using-video-games-to-recruit-your-kids-says-reformed-neo-nazi
321 Zach Beauchamp, "White supremacists are trying to recruit American teens through video games", VOX, 9 April 2019. www.vox.com/policy-and-politics/2019/4/9/18296864/gamer-gaming-white-supremacist-recruit
322 Cyrus Farivar, "Extremists creep into Roblox, an online game popular with children", NBC News, 22 August 2019. www.nbcnews.com/tech/tech-news/extremists-creep-roblox-online-game-popular-children-n1045056
323 Katerina Vittozzi, "Sharp rise in children investigated over far right links - including youngsters under 10", News Sky, 24 November 2020. https://news.sky.com/story/sharp-rise-in-children-investigated-over-far right-links-including-youngsters-under-10-12131565

324 Kriner and Clarke, "Eclectic Boogaloo".
325 Malte Thran and Lukas Boehnke, "The value-based Nationalism of Pegida". *Journal for Deradicalization*, 3, Summer 2015.
326 Piotr Kocyba, "PEGIDA: A movement of right-wing extremists or simply concerned citizens?".
327 Ralph Melzer and Sebastian Serafin (Eds.), *Right-Wing Extremism in Europe Country Analyses, Counter-Strategies and Labor-Market Oriented Exist Strategies Country Analyses Sweden*, Bonn: Friedrich Ebert Stiftung, 2014. http://library.fes.de/pdf-files/dialog/10957.pdf
328 Sindre Bangstad, "The 2019 mosque attack and freedom of speech in Norway", Al-Jazeera, 26 May 2020. www.aljazeera.com/opinions/2020/5/26/the-2019-mosque-attack-and-freedom-of-speech-in-norway
329 Chris Allen, "National Action: what I discovered about the ideology of Britain's violent neo-Nazi youth movement", The Conversation, 6 September 2017. https://theconversation.com/national-action-what-i-discovered-about-the-ideology-of-britains-violent-neo-nazi-youth-movement-83527
330 "Far right extremists recruiting in military: Pentagon", *The Straits Times*, 15 January 2021. www.straitstimes.com/world/united-states/far right-extremists-recruiting-in-military-pentagon
331 Farivar, "Boogaloo boys aim to provoke 2nd US civil war".
332 Ryan Lucas, "Who are the Oath Keepers? Militia group, founder scrutinized in Capitol riot probe", NPR, 10 April 2021. www.nprillinois.org/politics/2021-04-10/who-are-the-oath-keepers-militia-group-founder-scrutinized-in-capitol-riot-probe
333 Jacob Ware, "Siege: The Atomwaffen Division and rising far right terrorism in the United States". International Centre for Counter-Terrorism (ICCT) – The Hague, ICCT Policy Brief, July 2019.
334 "The Base".
335 Alexander Mallin and Luke Barr, "Inside the neo-Nazi hate group 'The Base,' which is the center of an FBI investigation", ABC News, 23 January 2020. https://abcnews.go.com/US/inside-neo-nazi-hate-group-base-center-fbi/story?id=68459758
336 Counter Extremism Project, "The Base". www.counterextremism.com/supremacy/base
337 Daniel De Simone, Andrei Soshnikov, and Ali Winston, "Neo-Nazi Rinaldo Nazzaro running US militant group The Base from Russia", BBC, 24 January 2020. www.bbc.com/news/world-51236915
338 Chermak, Steven M., Joshua D. Freilich, and Michael Suttmoeller, "The Organizational Dynamics of Far-Right Hate Groups in the United States: Comparing Violent to Non-Violent Organizations". Final Report to Human Factors/Behavioral Sciences Division, Science and Technology Directorate, U.S. Department of Homeland Security. College Park, MD: START, December 2011.
339 Noel, "La Meute: The illusions and delusions of Quebec's 'largest' right-wing group".
340 "La Meute", Montréal-Antifasciste.info. https://montreal-antifasciste.info/en/la-meute-2/
341 Montréal-Antifasciste.info, "The Three Percenters". https://montreal-antifasciste.info/en/the-three-percenters-iii/

342 Hutter, "Three Percenters are Canada's most dangerous extremist group, say some experts".
343 Kriner and Clarke, "Eclectic Boogaloo".
344 Lucas, "Who are the Oath Keepers? Militia group, founder scrutinized in Capitol riot probe".
345 "About Oath Keepers", oathkeepers.com.
346 Y. Veilleux-Lepage, "Putting Canada's hate crime data in context", in: E. Leidig (Ed.). *Tracking the Rise of the Radical Right Globally*, Volume 2. Columbia University Press, 193–196, 2020.
347 Benjamin Lee, "Overview of the far right", Centre for Research and Evidence on Security Threats. https://assets.publishing.service.gov.uk/government/uploads/system/uploads/attachment_data/file/834424/Ben_Lee_-_Overview_of_the_far_right.pdf
348 Noel, "La Meute: The illusions and delusions of Quebec's 'largest' right-wing group".
349 Hutter, "Three Percenters are Canada's most dangerous extremist group, say some experts".
350 Wolfson and Stall, "Actor Profile: Proud Boys".
351 "Proud Boys", Southern Poverty Law Center.
352 Lucas, "Who are the Oath Keepers? Militia group, founder scrutinized in Capitol riot probe".
353 "Oath Keepers".
354 Jessica White, "Far right extremism in the US: A threat no longer ignored", RUSI Commentary, 1 February 2021. https://rusi.org/commentary/far right-extremism-us-threat-no-longer-ignored
355 Tess Owen, "This Three Percenter militia group just cancelled itself because of the Capitol riots", Vice, 26 February 2021. www.vice.com/en/article/3anmkv/this-three-percenter-group-just-cancelled-itself-because-of-the-capitol-riots
356 Counter Extremism Project, "The Base".
357 Community Security Trust, " 'White Jihad' Jack Renshaw's journey from far right student to would-be terrorist", 2020. https://cst.org.uk/public/data/file/6/0/Jack%20Renshaw%20-%20White%20Jihad.pdf
358 Chris Allen, "National Action: What I discovered about the ideology of Britain's violent neo-Nazi youth movement", The Conversation, 6 September 2017. https://theconversation.com/national-action-what-i-discovered-about-the-ideology-of-britains-violent-neo-nazi-youth-movement-83527
359 "Britain First: What You Need to Know".
360 Thomson, "Who are Britain First? Far right group founded by a Scot distances itself from Jo Cox killing".
361 "English Defence League".
362 Hilary Pilkington, *Loud and Proud: Passion and Politics in the English Defence League*, New Ethnographics Series. Manchester: Manchester University Press, 2016.
363 James Treadwell and Jon Garland, *More Than Violent Whites? From 'Paki Bashing' to the English Defence League*. London: Routledge, 2016.
364 Elizabeth A. Morrow and John Meadowcroft, "The rise and fall of the English Defence League: self-governance, marginal members and the far right". *Political Studies*, 67(3), 2018. https://journals.sagepub.com/doi/10.1177/0032321718777907

365 Hsiao-Hung Pai, "The English Defence League and the new far right", Open Democracy, 17 February 2015. www.opendemocracy.net/en/english-defence-league-and-new-farright/
366 "Far right extremism: Who are the EDL?", Channel 4, 28 May 2013. www.channel4.com/news/edl-far right-extremism-woolwich-lee-rigby
367 Counter Extremism Project, "Sonnenkrieg Division".
368 Simone Rafael and Miro Dittrich, "What is the 'Feuerkrieg Division'?", Belltower, 24 September 2020. www.belltower.news/farright-terrorism-what-is-the-feuerkrieg-division-104669/
369 Centre for Analysis of the Radical Right, "Génération Identitaire ban could rally supporters of the radical right in France", 11 March 2021. www.opendemocracy.net/en/countering-radical-right/g%C3%A9n%C3%A9ration-identitaire-ban-could-rally-supporters-of-the-radical-right-in-france/
370 "French court confirms ban on anti-migrant group", InfoMigrants, 4 May 2021. www.infomigrants.net/en/post/31971/french-court-confirms-ban-on-anti-migrant-group
371 Ibid.
372 Croucher, "Identitarian movement, linked to Christchurch Mosque shooter, classified as extremist right-wing group by German intelligence agency".
373 Dick, "What is behind the right-wing 'Reichsbürger' movement?".
374 Kate Connolly, "German police arrest members of far right group after state ban", *The Guardian*, 19 March 2020. www.theguardian.com/world/2020/mar/19/german-police-arrest-members-of-far right-group-reichsburger-after-state-ban
375 Daniel Koehler, "The German 'National Socialist Underground (NSU)' and Anglo-American networks. The internationalisation of far right terror", in: Paul Jackson and Anton Shekhovtsov (Eds.). *The Post-War Anglo-American Far Right: A Special Relationship of Hate*. London: Palgrave Macmillan, 122–141, 2014.
376 Andersen, "Advarer mot islamister".
377 Dina Newman, "Ukraine conflict: 'White power' warrior from Sweden", BBC News, 16 July 2014. www.bbc.com/news/world-europe-28329329
378 Oren Dorell, "Volunteer Ukrainian unit includes Nazis", *USA Today*, 10 March 2015.
379 Tim Lister, "The nexus between far right Extremists in the United States and Ukraine", CTC Sentinel, April 2020. https://ctc.usma.edu/wp-content/uploads/2020/04/CTC-SENTINEL-042020.pdf
380 Paul Jackson, "Transnational neo-Nazism in the USA, United Kingdom and Australia", GW Program on Extremism, February 2020. https://extremism.gwu.edu/sites/g/files/zaxdzs2191/f/Jackson%20-%20Transnational%20neo%20Nazism%20in%20the%20USA%2C%20United%20Kingdom%20and%20Australia.pdf
381 Sean Rubinsztein-Dunlop, "Tensions between Australian Defence League and Muslim community reach violent new heights", ABC, 5 January 2015. www.abc.net.au/news/2014-04-21/anti-islam-hate-campaign-raises-tensions-to-violent-new-heights/5402526
382 William Allchorn, "Australian Radical Right Narratives and Counter-Narratives in an age of terror", 13 April 2021. www.hedayahcenter.org/media-center/latest-news/blog-post-australian-radical-right-narratives-and-counter-narratives-in-an-age-of-terror/

383 McKenzie and Tozer, " 'We do not need to wait for a Christchurch' ".
384 CARR-Hedayah Radical Right Counter Narratives Project, "From gangs to groupuscules: And solo-actor terrorism"; Thomas Manch and Florence Kerr, "Leaked 'security guidelines' reveals neo-Nazi plans to avoid detection", Stuff, 10 March 2020. www.stuff.co.nz/national/120135651/leaked-security-guidelines-reveals-neonazi-plans-to-avoid-detection
385 Chermak et al., "The Organizational Dynamics of Far-Right Hate Groups in the United States: Comparing Violent to Non-Violent Organizations".
386 Counter Extremism Project, "Violent right-wing extremism and terrorism – Transnational connectivity, definitions, incidents, structures and countermeasures", November 2020. www.counterextremism.com/sites/default/files/CEP%20Study_Violent%20Right-Wing%20Extremism%20and%20Terrorism_Nov%202020.pdf
387 Jeffrey Kaplan, "Leaderless resistance". *Terrorism and Political Violence*, 9(3), 80–95, 1997.
388 Seth G. Jones, "The rise of far right extremism in the United States", CSIS Briefs, November 2018. www.csis.org/analysis/rise-far right-extremism-united-states
389 R. Spaaij, "The enigma of lone wolf terrorism: An assessment". *Studies in Conflict & Terrorism*, 33, 854–870, 2010.
390 Edwin Bakker and B. de Graaf, "Lone Wolves: How to Prevent this Phenomenon?", The Hague, The Netherlands: International Centre for Counter-Terrorism, 2010. https://openaccess.leidenuniv.nl/bitstream/handle/ 1887/16557/ ICCT%2520EM%2520Lone%2520Wolves%2520Paper.pdf?sequence = 2
391 "Unmasking Atalante", Montréal-Antifasciste.info, 19 December 2018. https://montreal-antifasciste.info/en/2018/12/19/unmasking-atalante/
392 Counter Extremism Project, "Blood and Honour".
393 Ibid.
394 Josh Hafner, "Three Percenters: What is the gun-toting group? And what do its supporters want?", *USA Today*, 1 March 2018. https://eu.usatoday.com/story/news/nation-now/2018/03/01/three-percenters-what-gun-toting-group-and-what-do-its-supporters-want/385463002/
395 Owen, "This Three Percenter militia group just cancelled itself because of the Capitol riots".
396 Beutel and Johnson, "The Three Percenters: A look inside an anti-government militia".
397 Daniel Desrochers, "Who are the Three Percenters, the armed group Kentucky Gov. Andy Beshear called out?", *Lexington Herald*, 27 May 2020. www.kentucky.com/news/politics-government/article243023096.html
398 "Three Percenters".
399 Richard Connor, "What is the Atomwaffen Division?", DW, 11 April 2019. www.dw.com/en/what-is-the-atomwaffen-division/a-51106179
400 Jacob Ware, "Siege: The Atomwaffen Division and rising far right terrorism in the United States", International Centre for Counter-Terrorism (ICCT) – The Hague, ICCT Policy Brief, July 2019.
401 Jonah Engel Bromwich, "What is Atomwaffen? A neo-Nazi group, linked to multiple murders", *The New York Times*, 12 February 2018. www.nytimes.com/2018/02/12/us/what-is-atomwaffen.html

402 Jacob Ware, "Fighting back: The Atomwaffen Division, countering violent extremism, and the evolving crackdown on far right terrorism in America". *Journal for Deradicalization*, Winter 2020/21. https://journals.sfu.ca/jd/index.php/jd/article/view/411/253
403 Stanford CISAC, "The Base". https://cisac.fsi.stanford.edu/mappingmilitants/profiles/the-base#highlight_text_26750
404 Samantha Springer, "Secret tapes show neo-Nazi group The Base recruiting former members of the military", NBC News, 15 October 2020. www.nbcnews.com/news/us-news/secret-tapes-show-neo-nazi-group-base-recruiting-former-members-n1243395
405 De Simone et al., "Neo-Nazi Rinaldo Nazzaro running US militant group The Base from Russia"
406 Pilkington, *Loud and Proud*.
407 Australian Government Australian National Security, "Sonnenkrieg Division".
408 "Gruppe S: German far right group on trial for 'terror plot'", BBC, 13 April 2021. www.bbc.com/news/world-europe-56716712
409 Linda Schlegel, "'Germany does not exist!': Analyzing the Reichsbürger Movement", European Eye on Radicalisation, 17 May 2019. https://eeradicalization.com/germany-does-not-exist-analyzing-the-reichsburger-movement/
410 Sabine Volk, "How the German far Right appropriates ideals of non-violent resistance", Centre for Analysis on the Radical Right, 25 March 2021. www.opendemocracy.net/en/countering-radical-right/how-german-far right-appropriates-ideals-non-violent-resistance/
411 Anthony Faiola and Stephanie Kirchner, "In Germany, right-wing violence flourishing amid surge in online hate", *The Washington Post*, 20 March 2017.
412 Melzer and Serafin (Eds.), *Right-Wing Extremism in Europe Country Analyses, Counter-Strategies and Labor-Market Oriented Exist Strategies Country Analyses Sweden.*
413 Nathan, "Antipodean resistance".
414 Cait Kelly, "'The Hitlers you've been waiting for': Inside Australia's growing Nazi youth movement that wants to eradicate Jews, gays and immigrants while wearing SS death masks to hide their identities", *Daily Mail*, 29 April 2018. www.dailymail.co.uk/news/article-5656387/Australias-neo-Nazi-Hitler-youth-group-Antipodean-Resistance-growing.html
415 "Antipodean Resistance Women's Alliance", Antipodean Resistance. http://web.archive.org/web/20181120174129/http://antipodean-resistance.info/arwa/index.html
416 Kelly, "'The Hitlers you've been waiting for'".
417 Troy Whitford, "Reclaim Australia re-energises radical nationalism", The Conversation, 24 July 2015. https://theconversation.com/reclaim-australia-re-energises-radical-nationalism-45103
418 Heléne Lööw, "Nazismen I Sverige 2000–214", Stockholm:Ordfront förlag, 2015.
419 Michael Edison Hayden, "Mysterious neo-Nazi advocated terrorism for six years before disappearance", Southern Poverty Law Centre, 21 May 2019.
420 Daniel De Simone and Ali Winston, "Neo-Nazi militant group grooms teenagers", BBC, 22 June 2020.
421 Counter Extremism Project, "Violent right-wing extremism and terrorism – Transnational connectivity, definitions, incidents, structures and countermeasures".

422 Karoline Ihlebæk, Tine Figenschou, and Birgitte Haanshuus, "What is the relationship between the far right and the media?", CREX, Center for Research on Extremism. www.sv.uio.no/c-rex/english/groups/compendium/what-is-the-relationship-between-the-far right-and-the-media.html
423 T. Askanius, *Radical Online Video: YouTube, Video Activism and Social Movement Media Practices*. Lund, Sweden: Lund University, 2012.
424 Elise Thomas, "Boogaloo Bois: The birth of a 'movement', from memes to real-world violence", *The Strategist*, 31 March 2021. www.aspistrategist.org.au/boogaloo-bois-the-birth-of-a-movement-from-memes-to-real-world-violence/
425 Karoline Ihlebæk, Tine Figenschou, and Birgitte Haanshuus, "What is the relationship between the far right and the media?".
426 Ayushman Kaul, "Telegram — A free speech Russian platform is a haven for far right terror groups", *The Print*, 24 April 2020. https://theprint.in/opinion/telegram-a-free-speech-russian-platform-is-a-haven-for-far right-terror-groups/407357/
427 Veronika Velch, "Telegram: A growing social media refuge, for good and ill", Just Security, 26 February 2021. www.justsecurity.org/74947/telegram-a-growing-social-media-refuge-for-good-and-ill/
428 Ibid.
429 Caleb, Ecarma, "The far right is relocating online as social media giants try curbing extremism", *Vanity Fair*, 14 January 2021. www.vanityfair.com/news/2021/01/far right-relocating-online-tech-giants-curbing-extremism
430 Siladitya Ray, "The far right is flocking to these alternate social media apps — Not all of them are thrilled", *Forbes*, 14 January 2021. www.forbes.com/sites/siladityaray/2021/01/14/the-far right-is-flocking-to-these-alternate-social-media-apps---not-all-of-them-are-thrilled/?sh=2555c1e255a4
431 Caleb, Ecarma, "The far right is relocating online as social media giants try curbing extremism".
432 Ibid.
433 Ibid.
434 "How Zello became a recruitment & organizing tool for the far right", WNYCStudios, 16 October 2020. www.wnycstudios.org/podcasts/otm/segments/how-zello-became-recruitment-organizing-app-far right
435 Southern Poverty Law Center, "Blood and Honour". www.splcenter.org/fighting-hate/extremist-files/group/blood-honour
436 Crawford, "The Proud Boys".
437 Kriner and Clarke, "Eclectic Boogaloo".
438 Zadrozny, "What is the 'Boogaloo'? How online calls for a violent uprising are hitting the mainstream".
439 Counter Extremism Project, "Atomwaffen Division/national socialist order".
440 "Britain first: What you need to know".
441 Alex Hern, "Facebook bans far right groups including BNP, EDL and Britain First", *The Guardian*, 18 April 2019. www.theguardian.com/technology/2019/apr/18/facebook-bans-far right-groups-including-bnp-edl-and-britain-first?CMP=twt_gu
442 Eoghan Macguire, "Banned from Facebook and Twitter, UK far right turns to TikTok", Al-Jazeera, 16 April 2020. www.aljazeera.com/news/2020/4/16/banned-from-facebook-and-twitter-uk-far right-turns-to-tiktok

443 "France vetoes far right group 'Génération Identitaire' ".

444 "Prozessauftakt Stuttgart: Rechte Terrorgruppe wollte 'demokratisches System abschaffen' ".

445 Tim Stickings, "Gruppe S: German 'far right conspirators' on trial charged with plotting attacks on politicians and Muslims", *The National News*, 13 April 2021. www.thenationalnews.com/world/europe/gruppe-s-german-far right-conspirators-on-trial-charged-with-plotting-attacks-on-politicians-and-muslims-1.1202963

446 Konrad Litschko, Christina Schmidt, and Sebastian Erb, "Großgermanen in U-Haft", TAZ, 16 February 2020. https://taz.de/Rechtsextremistische-Terrorzelle/!5661227/

447 Ibid.

448 Sabine Volk, "Under lockdown, Germany's PEGIDA goes to YouTube", Open Democracy, 7 May 2020. www.opendemocracy.net/en/countering-radical-right/under-lockdown-germanys-pegida-goes-to-youtube/

449 "What is Identitarianism?", *The Week*, 29 March 2019. www.theweek.co.uk/100482/what-is-identitarianism

450 Guenther et al., "Strategic framing and social media engagement".

451 Linda Schlegel, "The cultivated extremist? How the identitarian movement frames its ideology", Global Network on Extremism and Technology, 17 July 2020. https://gnet-research.org/2020/07/17/the-cultivated-extremist-how-the-identitarian-movement-frames-its-ideology/

452 Maresi Starzmann, "Nazi Hipsters: Europe's identitarians are young, fashionable and proto-Fascist", *The Indypendent*, 14 December 2019. https://indypendent.org/2019/12/nazi-hipsters-europes-identitarians-are-young-fashionable-and-proto-fascist/

453 Counter Extremism Project, "Nordic Resistance Movement".

454 Shuster and Perrigo, "Like, share, recruit".

455 Kara Sonter, "Twitter suspends account of Australian neo-Nazi group", Courier Mail, 30 January 2018. www.couriermail.com.au/questnews/twitter-suspends-account-of-australian-neonazi-group/news-story/6d98a5a45f681d54cd84b9b25bda233f

456 Nathan, "Antipodean resistance."

457 Crawford, "The Proud Boys".

458 Wolfson and Stall, "Actor profile: Proud Boys".

459 Alex Goldberg, Joel Finkelstein, and John Farmer Jr., "How the Boogaloo movement is turning memes into violent action", Brookings, 29 June 2020. www.brookings.edu/techstream/how-the-boogaloo-movement-is-turning-memes-into-violent-action/

460 Ibid.

461 "The Boogaloo Movement".

462 Masood Farivar, "Oath Keepers founder feeling the heat from US prosecutors", VOA News, 8 April 2021. www.voanews.com/usa/oath-keepers-founder-feeling-heat-us-prosecutors

463 Counter Extremism Project, "Atomwaffen Division/National Socialist Order".

464 "The Base".

465 Counter Extremism Project, "The Base".

466 Ibid.

467 Counter Extremism Project, "English Defence League".
468 Trouillard, "France to ban far right group Generation Identity".
469 Centre for Analysis of the Radical Right, "Génération Identitaire ban could rally supporters of the radical right in France".
470 "Génération Identitaire: The fight for Europe and against migration".
471 Morten Wiik Larsen, Magne Frafjord, John Skien, and Samina Bruket, "De kan ikke komme her og gjøre Norge islamsk", 9 March 2012.
472 Linton Besser and Roscoe Whalan, "Neo-Nazi groups banned in Canada and Europe set sights on Australia", ABC, 28 March 2021. www.abc.net.au/news/2021-03-28/banned-neo-nazi-groups-set-sights-on-australia/100030072
473 Lella Nouri and Nuria Lorenzo-Dus, "Investigating reclaim Australia and Britain first's use of social media: Developing a new model of imagined political communities online". *Journal for Deradicalization*, Spring 2019. https://journals.sfu.ca/jd/index.php/jd/article/view/183/137
474 Thomas Manch and Florence Kerr, "Leaked 'security guidelines' reveals neo-Nazi plans to avoid detection", Stuff, 10 March 2020. www.stuff.co.nz/national/120135651/leaked-security-guidelines-reveals-neonazi-plans-to-avoid-detection
475 https://action-zealandia.com/category/media
476 "La Meute". Montréal-Antifasciste.info.
477 Hope not Hate, "Briefing: National Action". www.hopenothate.org.uk/research/investigations/briefing-national-action/
478 Community Security Trust, " 'White Jihad' Jack Renshaw's journey from far right student to would-be terrorist".
479 Josh Lowe, " 'Britain First:' What is the British far right group?", Newsweek, 16 June 2016. www.newsweek.com/britain-first-jo-cox-islam-far right-group-471455
480 Beutel and Johnson, "The Three Percenters: A look inside an anti-government militia".
481 Andersen, "Advarer mot islamister".
482 Montpetit, "Inside Quebec's far right: Radical groups push extreme message Social Sharing".
483 Hankewitz, "The UK is to ban the neo-Nazi group formerly led by a 13-year-old Estonian boy".
484 Hustad, " 'Most radical organisation' ".
485 Nathan, "Antipodean resistance."
486 Ibid.
487 "Australian neo-Nazis deface elderly care facility housing Holocaust survivors", *The Times of Israel*, 5 January 2019. www.timesofisrael.com/australian-neo-nazis-deface-elderly-care-facility-housing-holocaust-survivors/
488 Spoonley, "Far right extremists still threaten New Zealand, a year on from the Christchurch attacks".
489 "Far right extremists target Chinese MP Jian Yang", Newshub, 12 January 2020.
490 UNISON, "English Defence League", Conference Notes, 8 August 2011. www.unison.org.uk/motions/2021/conference-type/english-defence-league/
491 Rubinsztein-Dunlop, "Tensions between Australian Defence League and Muslim community reach violent new heights".
492 Croucher, "Identitarian movement, linked to Christchurch Mosque shooter, classified as extremist right-wing group by German intelligence agency".

493 Starzmann, "Nazi Hipsters: Europe's identitarians are young, fashionable and proto-Fascist".
494 "Identitarian movement".
495 "Man charged with New Zealand mosque attacks gave money to Austrian far right, chancellor says", Reuters, 27 March 2019. www.reuters.com/article/us-newzealand-shootout-austria/austrias-kurz-confirms-link-between-christchurch-attacker-and-identitarian-movement-idUSKCN1R80MX
496 Community Security Trust, " 'White Jihad' Jack Renshaw's journey from far right student to would-be terrorist".
497 Dick, "What is behind the right-wing 'Reichsbürger' movement?".
498 Nicholas Potter, "The Pan-European 'IKEA Fascism' of Nordiska MOTSTÅNDSRÖRELSEN", Bell Tower, 6 January 2021. www.belltower.news/nordic-resistance-the-pan-european-ikea-fascism-of-nordiska-motstandsroerelsen-109787/
499 Lang, "Neo-Nazi radicalisation camp held on Sunshine Coast".
500 Puddy, "Far right nationalists open private men-only clubs in Melbourne and Sydney".
501 Ibid.
502 Besser and Whalan, "Neo-Nazi groups banned in Canada and Europe set sights on Australia".
503 Jack Paynter, "How extreme right-wing groups have 'weaponised the internet' in Australia", *The Australian*, 8 March 2021. www.theaustralian.com.au/breaking-news/how-extreme-rightwing-groups-have-weaponised-the-internet-in-australia/news-story/ed0950b6bcc9aab54d25280a944f554b
504 Manch, "The 'growing' white nationalist group with a 'harmful and violent' ideology".
505 Ibid.
506 Gilbert and Elley, "Shaved heads and sonnenrads".
507 "Max Newsome ('Matt') and Action Zealandia", 10 March 2020. https://thewhiterosesociety.writeas.com/max-newsome-matt-and-action-zealandia
508 "Oath Keepers".
509 Ibid.
510 Max Koslowski, "How Australia's far right were divided and conquered – By themselves", *The Sydney Morning Herald*, 11 January 2019. www.smh.com.au/politics/federal/how-australia-s-far right-were-divided-and-conquered-by-themselves-20190108-p50qcb.html
511 Charlie Lewis, "Crikey's updated pocket guide to the far right (yes, there are more)", Crikey, 14 January 2019. www.crikey.com.au/2019/01/14/guide-to-far right-part-four/
512 Kevin Hampson, "Grande Prairie war monument vandalized", *Daily Herald Tribune*, 24 June 2018.
513 Jones, "Georgie Fagan used to organize with white supremacists. Now he condemns them".
514 "Storm Alliance Factsheet", Montréal-Antifasciste.info, 13 September 2017. https://montreal-antifasciste.info/en/2017/09/13/storm-alliance-factsheet/
515 Allen, "What is Britain First – The far right group retweeted by Donald Trump?".
516 "Britain First: What you need to know".
517 Hampson, "Grande Prairie war monument vandalized".

518 Montpetit, "Inside Quebec's far right: Radical groups push extreme message Social Sharing".
519 "Storm Alliance Factsheet".
520 Wolfson and Stall, "Actor profile: Proud Boys".
521 Crawford, "The Proud Boys".
522 Wolfson and Stall, "Actor profile: Proud Boys".
523 "The Boogaloo Movement".
524 Ibid.
525 "Oath Keepers".
526 "Three Percenters".
527 Counter Extremism Project, "National Action".
528 "Britain First: What you need to know".
529 Ewan Palmer, "Rotherham child abuse scandal: EDL and Britain First stage protests following 'appalling' report", *International Business Times*, 28 August 2014.
530 Billy Briggs, "This is England: Masked like terrorists, members of Britain's newest and fastest-growing protest group intimidate a Muslim woman on a train en route to a violent demo", *Daily Mail*, 2 January 2010. www.dailymail.co.uk/home/moslive/article-1238213/This-England-On-trail-English-Defence-League.html
531 Pilkington, *Loud and Proud*.
532 "Radical English Defence League to form political party".
533 Adam Taylor, "German anti-Islamic group Pegida says 'we need a leader' like India's Modi", *The Washington Post*, 15 June 2015. www.washingtonpost.com/news/worldviews/wp/2015/06/15/german-anti-islamic-group-pegida-says-we-need-a-leader-like-indias-modi/
534 Anthony Measures, "What is PEGIDA?".
535 Kate Connolly, "PEGIDA: What does the German far right movement actually stand for?", *The Guardian*, 6 January 2015. www.theguardian.com/world/shortcuts/2015/jan/06/pegida-what-does-german-far right-movement-actually-stand-for
536 Volk, "Under lockdown, Germany's PEGIDA goes to YouTube".
537 Anuradha Sharma, "Germany's PEGIDA anti-Islamisation group says it has a new hero: Narendra Modi", Scroll.in, 15 June 2015. https://scroll.in/article/734263/germanys-pegida-anti-islamisation-group-says-it-has-a-new-hero-narendra-modi
538 Akshay Saraswat, "After being burnt in Sweden, Koran pages torn in Oslo as anti-Islam protests turn violent", *IB Times*, 30 August 2020. www.ibtimes.sg/after-being-burnt-sweden-koran-pages-torn-oslo-anti-islam-protests-turn-violent-video-50873
539 Rebecca Staudenmaier, "Clashes break out in Norway at anti-Islam rally", DW, 29 August 2020. www.dw.com/en/norway-islam-clashes/a-54756338
540 Dominic Hinde, "Far right steps up anti-media campaign ahead of Swedish election", Index on Censorship, 24 August 2018. www.indexoncensorship.org/2018/08/sweden-fraught-election-far right-media/
541 Melzer and Serafin (Eds.), *Right-Wing Extremism in Europe Country Analyses, Counter-Strategies and Labor-Market Oriented Exist Strategies Country Analyses Sweden*.
542 Lister, "The nexus between far right extremists in the United States and Ukraine".
543 Patrick Hatch, "Far right group spreading anti-mosque message in Bendigo", *The Age*, 22 June 2014. www.theage.com.au/national/victoria/farright-group-spreading-antimosque-message-in-bendigo-20140621-zshj4.html

544 New Matilda, "Who are the Australian Defence League?", 29 January 2014. https://newmatilda.com/2014/01/29/who-are-australian-defence-league/
545 Kristy Campion, "A 'lunatic fringe'? The persistence of right wing extremism in Australia". *Perspectives on Terrorism*, 13(2), April 2019. https://researchoutput.csu.edu.au/ws/portalfiles/portal/29338723/A_Lunatic_Fringe_POT.pdf
546 Whitford, "Reclaim Australia re-energises radical nationalism".
547 Volk, "How the German far right appropriates ideals of non-violent resistance".
548 Counter Extremism Project, "Blood and Honour".
549 "The northern guard: Islamophobia, Antisemitism, and QAnon", Anti-Racist Canada. http://anti-racistcanada.blogspot.com/2020/09/the-northern-guard-islamophobia.html
550 Crawford, "The Proud Boys".
551 Angela Ramirez, "American 'Boojahideen': The Boogaloo bois' blueprint for extreme libertarianism and response to the Biden administration". *Terrorism Monitor*, 19(1), 2021. https://jamestown.org/program/american-boojahideen-the-boogaloo-bois-blueprint-for-extreme-libertarianism-and-response-to-the-biden-administration/
552 Robert Kuznia, Drew Griffin, and Curt Devine, "Gun-toting members of the Boogaloo movement are showing up at protests", CNN, 4 June 2020. https://edition.cnn.com/2020/06/03/us/boogaloo-extremist-protests-invs/index.html
553 "Oath Keepers".
554 "The Atomwaffen Division: The Evolution of the White Supremacy Threat", Homeland Security Today, 29 August 2020. www.hstoday.us/subject-matter-areas/counterterrorism/the-atomwaffen-division-the-evolution-of-the-white-supremacy-threat/
555 Ibid.
556 The Soufan Center, "The Atomwaffen Division: The evolution of the white supremacy threat".
557 Counter Extremism Project, "Atomwaffen Division, national socialist order".
558 Ware, "Fighting back".
559 "Atomwaffen Division/National Socialist Order".
560 "The Base".
561 "Britain First: What you need to know".
562 Counter Extremism Project, "English Defence League".
563 Community Security Trust, " 'White Jihad' Jack Renshaw's journey from far right student to would-be terrorist".
564 Ibid.
565 CPS, "Teenage neo-Nazi jailed over 'how to make guns' guides", 20 September 2019. www.cps.gov.uk/cps/news/teenage-neo-nazi-jailed-over-how-make-guns-guides
566 "Were a legacy of National Action", Hope not Hate, 18 June 2019. www.hopenothate.org.uk/2019/06/18/jailed-neo-nazi-satanists-legacy-national-action/
567 Counter Extremism Project, "Feuerkrieg Division".
568 Ibid.
569 Trouillard, "France to ban far right group Generation Identity".
570 "Government bans French far right group Génération Identitaire", RRI, 4 March 2021. www.rfi.fr/en/france/20210304-government-bans-french-far right-group-g%C3%A9n%C3%A9ration-identitaire-anti-immigration-migrants

571 "France seeking to ban far right, anti-migrant group", Reuters, 14 February 2021. www.reuters.com/article/us-france-security-ban-idUSKBN2AE0B6
572 "France vetoes far right group 'Génération Identitaire' ".
573 "Far right anti-migrant group 'Generation Identitaire' outlawed in France", RT News, 3 March 2021. www.rt.com/news/517090-france-bans-rightwing-generation-identitaire/
574 "France: Convictions against peaceful protesters who marched against xenophobic group must be quashed", Amnesty International News, 26 May 2021. www.amnesty.org/en/latest/news/2021/05/france-convictions-against-peaceful-protesters-who-marched-against-xenophobic-group-must-be-quashed/
575 "Gruppe S: Germany's far right group".
576 Peter Hille, "How dangerous is the identitarian movement?", DW, 13 July 2019. www.dw.com/en/how-dangerous-is-the-identitarian-movement/a-49580233
577 "Just harmless lunatics? The "Reichsbürger" movement in Germany", Europe Now, 1 October 2018. www.europenowjournal.org/2018/10/01/just-harmless-lunatics-the-reichsburger-movement-in-germany/
578 Dick, "What is behind the right-wing 'Reichsbürger' movement?".
579 Emma Anderson, "What is Germany's extremist Reichsbürger movement?", The Local, 25 January 2017. www.thelocal.de/20170125/what-is-germanys-extremist-reichsbrger-movement/
580 Christopher F. Schuetze, "Germany Shuts down far right clubs that deny the modern state", *The New York Times*, 19 March 2020. www.nytimes.com/2020/03/19/world/europe/germany-reich-citizens-ban.html
581 "The enemy within: Neo-Nazis and the German state ruptly – Documentary collection". www.c21media.net/screenings/ruptlydocumentarycollection/the-enemy-within-neo-nazis-and-the-german-state/17760/
582 Stanly Johny, "How serious is Germany's far right problem?", *The Hindu*, 1 March 2020. www.thehindu.com/news/international/how-serious-is-germanys-far right-problem/article30952770.ece
583 Joseph Nasr, "Far right crime hits record high in Germany", Reuters, 4 May 2021. www.reuters.com/world/europe/germany-arrests-suspect-over-hate-mail-using-neo-nazi-acronym-2021-05-04/
584 Dora Illei and Zahava Moerdler, "The NSU trial: A case study in structural racism in Germany", 1 November 2016. www.humanrightsfirst.org/blog/nsu-trial-case-study-structural-racism-germany-part-1
585 Melzer and Serafin (Eds.), *Right-Wing Extremism in Europe Country Analyses, Counter-Strategies and Labor-Market Oriented Exist Strategies Country Analyses Sweden*.
586 Jamie Bullen, "Masked mob rampage through Stockholm train station 'looking to attack refugee children' ", *Standard*, 30 January 2016. www.standard.co.uk/news/world/masked-mob-rampage-through-stockholm-train-station-looking-to-attack-refugee-children-a3169061.html
587 "2018 country reports on human rights practices: Ukraine", U.S. State Department, 31 March 2019.
588 Hutter, "Three Percenters are Canada's most dangerous extremist group, say some experts".
589 Briggs, "This is England".
590 Dick, "What is behind the right-wing 'Reichsbürger' movement?".

591 Ben Knight, "Far right terrorism in Germany: Walter Lübcke's murder and the NSU", DW, 21 January 2021. www.dw.com/en/far right-terrorism-in-germany-walter-l%C3%BCbckes-murder-and-the-nsu/a-56304776
592 Shuster and Perrigo, "Like, share, recruit".
593 Michael Cohen and Matthew Green, "Ukraine's Volunteer Battalion", 2016. www.benning.army.mil/infantry/magazine/issues/2016/APR-JUL/pdf/16)%20Cohen_UkraineVolunteers_TXT.pdf
594 Jason Wilson, "Explosives and weaponry found at US far right protests, documents reveal", *The Guardian*, 5 May 2021. www.theguardian.com/us-news/2021/may/05/explosives-incendiary-devices-found-far right-protests
595 Yannick Veilleux-Lepage, "CTRL, HATE, PRINT: Terrorists and the appeal of 3D-printed weapons", ICCT, 13 July 2021. https://icct.nl/publication/ctrl-hate-print-terrorists-and-the-appeal-of-3d-printed-weapons/
596 "Halle (Saale): Stephan Balliet bereitete Tat seit Monaten vor", Der Spiegel, 14 October 2019.
597 Hyder Abbasi, "What's behind far right trend of using 3D tech to make guns?", Al-Jazeera, 31 July 2021. www.aljazeera.com/news/2021/7/31/what-behind-far right-trend-using-3d-tech-make-guns
598 Eric Woods, "Right-wing extremists' new weapon", Lawfare, 15 March 2020. www.lawfareblog.com/right-wing-extremists-new-weapon
599 Hyder Abbasi, "What's behind far right trend of using 3D tech to make guns?".
600 Ari Weil, "Protesters hit by cars recently highlight a dangerous far right trend in America", NBC News, 12 July 2020.
601 Hannah Allam, "Vehicle attacks rise as extremists target protesters", NPR, 21 June 2021. www.npr.org/2020/06/21/880963592/vehicle-attacks-rise-as-extremists-target-protesters
602 Florian Flade, "The insider threat: Far right extremism in the German military and police", CTC Sentinel, June 2021. www.ctc.usma.edu/wp-content/uploads/2021/05/CTC-SENTINEL-052021.pdf
603 Kristin M. Hall, James Laporta, and Justin Pritchard, "US Army has hidden or downplayed loss of firearms for years", AP News, 16 June 2021. https://apnews.com/article/al-state-wire-business-gun-politics-army-government-and-politics-9b85eb5aa443564f5a2bbedd1530dbfe
604 John Wojcik, "Military ties to far right pose clear and present danger", *People's World*, 16 June 2021. https://peoplesworld.org/article/military-ties-to-far right-pose-clear-and-present-danger/
605 "Germany: 1,200 right-wing extremists licensed to own weapons", DW, 2 February 2021. www.dw.com/en/germany-1200-right-wing-extremists-licensed-to-own-weapons/a-56416420
606 Counter Extremism Project, 'Extremist content online: ISIS issues threats in Spain, Iraq', 18 November 2019. www.counterextremism.com/press/extremist-content-online-isis-issues-threats-spain-iraq, accessed 28 August 2020.
607 Håvard Haugstvedt, "The right's time to fly?". *The RUSI Journal*, 166(1), 22–31, 2021. DOI: 10.1080/03071847.2021.1906161
608 Ibid.
609 Daveed Gartenstein-Ross and Samuel Hodgson, "Skinheads, saints, and (national) socialists", Foundation for Defence of Democracies, 14 June 2021. www.fdd.org/analysis/2021/06/14/skinheads-saints-and-national-socialists/

610 Counter Extremism Project, "Violent right-wing extremism and terrorism – Transnational connectivity, definitions, incidents, structures and countermeasures".
611 Jackson, "Transnational neo-Nazism in the USA, United Kingdom and Australia".
612 Gartenstein-Ross and Hodgson, "Skinheads, Saints, and (National) Socialists".
613 Cas Mudde, "The far right hails 'unite the right' a success. Its legacy says otherwise", *The Guardian*, 10 August 2018. www.theguardian.com/commentisfree/2018/aug/10/unite-the-right-rally-alt-right-demise
614 "American White Supremacist Groups Exploiting International Connections", ADL, 16 March 2020. www.adl.org/blog/american-white-supremacist-groups-exploiting-international-connections
615 Counter Extremism Project, "Violent right-wing extremism and terrorism – Transnational connectivity, definitions, incidents, structures and countermeasures".
616 Ibid.
617 Counter Extremism Project, "Violent right-wing extremism and terrorism – Transnational connectivity, definitions, incidents, structures and countermeasures".
618 Robert Lüdecke, "European state of hate: How the far right is organising transnationally", Amadeu Antonio Stiftung, 16 February 2021. www.amadeu-antonio-stiftung.de/en/european-state-of-hate-how-the-far right-is-organising-transnationally-66633/; Sebastian Rotella, "Global right-wing extremism networks are growing. The U.S. is just now catching up", ProPublica, 22 January 2021. www.propublica.org/article/global-right-wing-extremism-networks-are-growing-the-u-s-is-just-now-catching-up
619 "The rise of the Canadian far right", *Political Capital*, 20 June 2018. https://politicalcapital.hu/news.php?article_read=1&article_id=2267
620 Ibid.
621 Ibid.
622 Morris, "What far right groups are active in Quebec?".
623 "Unmasking Atalante".
624 William Allchorn, "From direct action to terrorism: Canadian radical right narratives and counter-narratives at a time of volatility", 2021. www.hedayahcenter.org/wp-content/uploads/2021/02/2021FEB28_Canada_CARR-Hedayah-Report-FINAL.pdf
625 "Atalante", The Canadian Centre for Identity-Based Conflict. https://vtsm.org/tools/vtsmdatabase/atalante/
626 "The rise of the Canadian far right".
627 ADL, "Soldiers of Odin USA". www.adl.org/resources/profiles/soldiers-of-odin-usa
628 https://soldiersofodin.fi/soldiers-of-odin-barcelona/
629 Yannick Veilleux-Lepage and Emil Archambault, "Soldiers of Odin: The global diffusion of vigilante movements", 2017. www.psa.ac.uk/sites/default/files/conference/papers/2017/Soldiers%20of%20Odin%20-The%20Global%20Diffusion%20of%20Vigilante%20Movements.pdf
630 Montréal-Antifasciste Info, "The Three Percenters".
631 Counter Extremism Project, "Blood and Honour".
632 Ibid.
633 "Proud Boys", ADL.
634 "Proud Boys", Southern Poverty Law Center.

635 Emma Jacobs, "Proud Boys named 'terrorist entity' in Canada", NPR, 2 May 2021. www.npr.org/2021/05/02/992846086/proud-boys-named-terrorist-entity-in-canada
636 Alan Feuer, "Justice dept. links Oath Keepers and Proud Boys ahead of Capitol riot", *The New York Times*, 24 March 2021. www.nytimes.com/2021/03/24/us/politics/oath-keepers-proud-boys-capitol-riot.html
637 Lizzie Dearden, "Atomwaffen Division: UK government accused of 'dithering' over ban of neo-Nazi terrorist group", *Independent*, 21 April 2021. www.independent.co.uk/news/uk/home-news/atomwaffen-division-banned-uk-terrorist-group-b1835346.html
638 The Soufan Center, "The Atomwaffen Division the evolution of the white supremacy threat".
639 "The Atomwaffen Division: The evolution of the white supremacy threat".
640 "The Base".
641 Paul Jackson, "#hitlerwasright: National action and national social #hitlerwasright: national action and national socialism for the 21st century". *Journal for Deradicalization*, 1, 97–115, Winter, 2014/15.
642 Paul Jackson, "Transnational neo-Nazism in the USA, United Kingdom and Australia".
643 Catrin Nye, "English Defence League searches for foreign allies", BBC, 6 December 2010. www.bbc.com/news/uk-11923236
644 Nigel Copsey, *The English Defence League: Challenging our Country and our Values of Social Inclusion, Fairness and Equality*. London: Faith Matters, 2010.
645 UNISON, "English Defence League".
646 "The rise of the Canadian far right".
647 "France vetoes far right group 'Génération Identitaire' ".
648 "Suspected Christchurch shooter sent money to French group — Report", DW, 4 April 2019. www.dw.com/en/suspected-christchurch-shooter-sent-money-to-french-group-report/a-48192751
649 Sharma, "Germany's PEGIDA anti-Islamisation group says it has a new hero: Narendra Modi".
650 Anthony Measures, "What is PEGIDA?".
651 Barry Roche, "Anti-Islamic group PEGIDA Ireland to be launched at Dublin rally", *The Irish Times*, 30 January 2016.
652 Croucher, "Identitarian movement, linked to Christchurch mosque shooter, classified as extremist right-wing group by German intelligence agency".
653 "What is Identitarianism?".
654 Anita Nissan, "The trans-European mobilization of 'generation identity' ", Springer Link, 3 June 2020; The Soufan Center, "IntelBrief: The far right seeks to normalize its ideology", 17 April 2019. https://thesoufancenter.org/intelbrief-the-far right-seeks-to-normalize-its-ideology/
655 "American racists work to spread 'identitarian' ideology", Hatewatch, Southern Poverty Law Center, 12 October 2015.
656 Sumi Somaskanda, "Identitarian movement – Germany's 'new right' hipsters", DW, 23 June 2017. www.dw.com/en/identitarian-movement-germanys-new-right-hipsters/a-39383124
657 Koehler, "The German 'National Socialist Underground (NSU)' and Anglo-American networks. The internationalisation of far right terror".

658 Daniel Koehler, "Right-Wing Terrorism in the 21st Century". Routledge, 2014.
659 "NSU-Prozess: Die Rolle der 'Combat-18'-Zelle", Der Spiegel, 11 June 2014, www.spiegel.de/panorama/justiz/nsu-prozess-in-muenchen-zu-mord-in-dortmund-a-1001474.html.
660 L. E. Berntzen, *Liberal Roots of Far Right Activism: The Anti-Islamic Movement in the 21st Century*. London: Routledge, 2019.
661 Counter Extremism Project, "Nordic Resistance Movement".
662 Melzer and Serafin (Eds.), *Right-Wing Extremism in Europe Country Analyses, Counter-Strategies and Labor-Market Oriented Exist Strategies Country Analyses Sweden*.
663 Ibid.
664 Simon Purdue, "Foreign fighters and the global war for white supremacy", *Fair Observer*, 18 February 2020. www.fairobserver.com/more/international_security/far right-foreign-fighters-white-supremacy-history-azov-battalion-international-security-news-88711/
665 Shuster and Perrigo, "Like, share, recruit".
666 Hikmet Karcic, "The Balkan connection: Foreign fighters and the far right in Ukraine", Newlines Institute, 1 May 2020. https://newlinesinstitute.org/eurasia/the-balkan-connection-foreign-fighters-and-the-far right-in-ukraine/
667 Lister, "The nexus between far right extremists in the United States and Ukraine"; The Soufan Center, "White supremacy extremism: The transnational rise of the violent white supremacist movement", September 2019. https://thesoufancenter.org/wp-content/uploads/2019/09/Report-by-The-Soufan-Center-White-Supremacy-Extremism-The-Transnational-Rise-of-The-Violent-White-Supremacist-Movement.pdf
668 "IntelBrief: The transnational network that nobody is talking about", The Soufan Center, 22 March 2019. https://thesoufancenter.org/intelbrief-the-transnational-network-that-nobody-is-talking-about/
669 "IntelBrief: The transnational network that nobody is talking about".
670 Huseyn Aliyev, "Is Ukraine a hub for international white supremacist fighters?", Russia Matters, 13 May 2020. www.russiamatters.org/analysis/ukraine-hub-international-white-supremacist-fighters
671 "USA v Brian Mark Lemley, Patrik Jordan Mathews and William Garfield Bilbrough", p. 10.
672 Bourdon, "At Ukraine's Asgardsrei, A French connection".
673 Christopher Miller, "This neo-Nazi group is organizing on Facebook despite a year-old ban", BuzzFeed News, 16 November 2020. www.buzzfeednews.com/article/christopherm51/neo-nazi-group-facebook
674 Ibid.
675 Ibid.
676 Nathan, "Antipodean resistance."
677 Manch, "The 'growing' white nationalist group with a 'harmful and violent' ideology".
678 Florence Kerr and Thomas Manch, "Soldier alleged to have traded military information was leader of white nationalist group", Stuff, 22 January 2020. www.stuff.co.nz/national/118952222/soldier-alleged-to-have-traded-military-information-was-leader-of-white-nationalist-group

679 Marc Daalder, "Action Zealandia linked to Dominion Movement", Newsroom, 13 March 2020. www.newsroom.co.nz/action-zealandia-linked-to-dominion-movement

680 Ibid.

681 Ibid.

4

HOW HAVE GOVERNMENTS REACTED TO THE RISE

Elaborating national counter-policy practices

The phenomenon of far-right extremism and violence is not a new one for most of the examined national legal regimes. The complex threat posed by contemporary far-right terrorism, however, has urged national legislation to keep up with the evolving threat and reconsider existing practices. This chapter attempts to better understand the concepts of how the analyzed countries aim to prevent and counter malicious right-wing extremists. First, the most relevant pillars of each national counter-strategy are scrutinized. Then, in the concluding section, our findings based upon this analysis are summarized.

Azov is worth special mention here. Compared with the other examined far-right threat groups, the Azov Movement is a "broader socio-political organization".[1] This "multi-faceted entity"[2] comprises the Azov Regiment, which operates within Ukraine's National Guard, "firmly within the command and control structures of the Ukrainian ministry of interior, with its backers in the government in Kyiv".[3] Considering this unique legal entity of Azov, Ukrainian countermeasures will not be elaborated here.

Canada

Building resilience against terrorism across the four strands of *prevent*, *detect*, *deny*, and *respond* is one of the core principles in the Canadian counter-terrorism strategy.[4] Acknowledging that "terrorism is a complex phenomenon and requires a multi-faceted response",[5] a multi-agency approach aims to foster social cohesion which indirectly supports the prevention of radicalization to violence.[6] As researchers Parent and Ellis suggest, Canada should delve into anti-immigrant narratives and build a more cohesive and resilient milieu in these communities. Detected signals for increasing violence in these circles

DOI: 10.4324/9781032708041-4

may serve as excellent early warning signs for an elevated level of extremist violent acts.[7] The government effort to counter radicalization is led by the Canada Centre for Community Engagement and Prevention of Violence. The center, which was launched in 2017, provides policy, guidance, plans, and coordinates research to better understand radicalization, promotes coordination and collaboration to build and share knowledge together with financial support to initiatives.[8] A national expert committee was established in 2019 to advance the work of the center.[9]

Community engagement and partnership provide the elemental pillar in Canadian law enforcement agencies' counter-terrorism strategy. The countering violent extremism (CVE) work lies upon extensive community-based relationships. A series of prevention and early intervention-type activities characterize the CVE work, where the operational focus is on vulnerable individuals prone to engage in extremist ideologies.[10] It is one of the key challenges in counter-terrorism policing to build an effective relationship with the right communities, while not further alienating them by devoting more suspicious attention to their activities.[11] Academic–practitioner collaborations in the field substantially enrich on-field officers' understanding of crucial aspects of radicalization.

In 2018, the House of Commons Heritage Committee articulated 30 recommendations as part of a national strategy against racism and hate crimes. These included "training for media pundits and politicians about how their portrayals of certain religious or racial groups could contribute to a climate of hate",[12] better enforcement of laws to prevent racist fake news, and more resources for police to tackle hate crimes. In 2019, a $1.33 million pilot project was initiated to "provide at-risk persons with individualized intervention plans"[13] and a $279,329 grant was allocated to analyze the media coverage and online content on ideologically motivated violent extremism. Moreover, a digital repository was created to assist smaller companies to detect and remove worrisome online terrorist content.[14] The Canadian government added four far-right extremist groups – the Russian Imperial Movement (RIM), the Atomwaffen Division (AWD), The Base, and the Proud Boys – to their list of proscribed terrorist entities in February 2021.[15] Onwards active participation in the group's activities can constitute a terrorist offence.[16]

The United States

Since 9/11 the US counter-terrorism machinery has overwhelmingly focused on jihadists and put a considerably lower emphasis on white supremacists.[17] As researcher Jacob Ware has summarized the Achilles heel of US counter-terrorism strategy is that it "lacks a comprehensive approach, the efforts are short-term, piecemeal, and targeted at groups".[18] The most concerning in this regard is the threat posed by lone actors, which cannot be detected or eliminated without a consistent and solid framework for the fight against domestic terrorism. A noteworthy example is the case of AWD, which quickly morphed into a new formation called the National Socialist Order when rumors started to go around about considerations to designate it as a terrorist entity.[19] AWD requires specific attention for another reason. It has been the first far-right threat group that induced a targeted law enforcement operation and shed light on the challenges associated with combatting domestic terrorism.[20] Individuals affiliated with AWD could only be prosecuted for gun or drug possession charges. When comparing this with convicted Muslims who were sentenced to a decade in prison for attempting to provide material support for a designated Islamist terrorist group, the impact of these countermeasures can be regarded as marginal.[21] April 2020 marked another breakthrough, when the RIM has become the first far-right terrorist formation that was designated as a terrorist organization in the United States.[22]

The White House announced the first-ever US domestic counter-terrorism strategy in June 2021.[23] The concept was "formulated as a direct response to the January 6, 2021 insurrection at the Capitol".[24] The document urges "better information-sharing among law enforcement agencies and efforts to prevent extremist groups from recruiting online".[25] In parallel, the United States has joined the Christchurch Call to Action to Eliminate Terrorist and Violent Extremist Content Online, "an international partnership between governments and technology companies that works to develop new multilateral solutions to eliminating terrorist content online while safeguarding the freedom of online expression".[26] The need for an enhanced screening protocol for military and law enforcement officers has been articulated to eliminate the threat posed by insiders.[27] A particular emphasis has been put on the "importance of understanding and sharing domestic terrorism-related research and analysis".[28] Besides traditional counter-terrorism instruments, the strategy entails "a broader approach to combat the root causes of violence in local communities and online".[29] Contrasted with the previous countering violent extremism model, this new concept relies upon a public-health-based approach and involves non-traditional counter-terrorism agencies, such as local authorities, non-government organizations (NGOs), and the private sector.[30]

Regrettably, handling right-wing extremists and enabling their restoration and reintegration into US society has been left open. However, as researcher, John Horgan underlined

> deradicalization efforts to address the increasingly diverse population of homegrown terrorists could include psychological counseling and restorative justice. The benefits could extend beyond the decreased risk of future extremism, to rebuilding trust in government agencies and communities torn apart by political and cultural discord.[31]

United Kingdom

United Kingdom counter-strategy, called CONTEST, addresses all forms of terrorism. Its *prevent* strand "seeks to tackle the influences of radicalization and respond to the ideological challenge of terrorism. It also seeks to encourage debate and provide a credible counter narrative to terrorist ideologies".[32] It aims to "prevent people from being drawn into terrorism while ensuring they are given appropriate advice and support",[33] for these purposes it "works with sectors and institutions where there are risks of radicalization".[34]

A specific national agenda has been set for countering violent extremist efforts in the United Kingdom. This "multi-agency safeguarding program"[35] has been accomplished through the counter-extremism strategy. As a critical milestone in the fight against right-wing extremism, the document declared first that "Islamist extremism is not the only threat, as seen by the vicious actions of a number of extreme right-wing and neo-Nazi groups".[36] A significant novelty is that the responsibility for detecting extreme right-wing terrorist offences has been transferred from the police to the UK intelligence agency MI5.[37] This reprioritization requires additional efforts for the necessary proactive and multi-layered counter-response to the growing threat of right-wing extremism.[38] Arguably, important steps have been taken towards "an increasingly active, coordinated, and indeed multi-layered response to right-wing extremism".[39] Acknowledging the threat posed by the far right, since July 2019 right-wing extremism has been included in the national assessment for the terrorism threat level.[40] Another significant advancement is that after the Finsbury Park attack in 2017, MI5 started to work closely with the Joint Terrorism Analysis Centre (JTAC) to detect and counter right-wing terrorism in a duly manner.[41]

Five far-right extremist groups have been banned in the United Kingdom. National Action was the first right-wing extremist group, which the UK government designated as a terrorist group in December 2016.[42] This means that being a member or inviting support for this organization is a criminal offence. As the recital states, "National Action is a racist, anti-Semitic and homophobic organization which stirs up hatred, glorifies violence and promotes a vile ideology".[43] The ban could "physically degrade and dismantle the group"[44] but authorities struggle to undermine its online propaganda. Despite the shutdown of its webpage, adherents continued to communicate through encrypted apps.[45] Some years later, in 2020 first Sonnenkrieg Division then Feuerkrieg Division, Atomwaffen Division, and The Base were banned in the United Kingdom.[46]

France

Undoubtedly, the devastating 2015 terror attacks introduced a new basis for French anti-terrorism legislation. In the direct aftermath of the incidents, a state of emergency was declared in the country. This irregular regime expired but the extraordinary countermeasures remained in force due to a newly adopted anti-terror law. Consequently, emergency measures turned into the "normal criminal and administrative practice".[47]

The horrific beheading of French schoolteacher, Samuel Paty, in October 2020 added new flames to the counter-terrorism legislation. French government adopted a new regulation aiming to fight Islamic radicalism. These novel provisions targeted online hate speech and authorized closer oversight of NGOs and religious associations. Critics argued that this highly controversial law may be an infringement of religious freedom.[48] The French president has been eager to further tighten counter-terrorism actions and has been considering permitting the use of algorithms to detect online extremist activity.[49] Another problem concerns that roughly 250 sentenced prisoners will be released by the end of 2022. Reflecting on this, new legislation obliges "convicted terrorists to two years of administrative follow-ups after their release from prison".[50]

As the French interior minister said, Génération Identitaire (GI) "incites discrimination, hatred and violence and has ties to white supremacist groups",[51] the organization was banned by a decree in March 2021. The decree also accused GI of being open about its stated aim of "entering into war against all those who want to tear us from our roots and make us forget who we are" and that it ran a boxing club next to its headquarters to "train members in combat and self-defence".[52] In December 2020, a former leading figure of GI was convicted of incitement to terrorism and violence.[53]

Germany

In the aftermath of NSU discovery in 2011, the murder of Lübcke in 2019, the Halle (2019) and Hanau (2020) attack, the German government adopted a new strategy to combat far-right extremism and hate speech on the internet.[54] In accordance with these new measures, social media companies are not only required to delete hate speech within a certain period of time but are obliged to report acts of hate speech to German authorities and provide the IP address of concerned users. Each weapon permit will be checked by the Federal Office for the Protection of the Constitution. Funding for the development of prevention programs tackling right-wing extremism, anti-Semitism and racism has been allocated. In parallel, police and intelligence agencies will establish new mechanisms for enhanced cooperation on right-wing extremism.[55] Germany has outlawed several far-right groups, in 2020 it banned the German chapter of Combat 18 and neo-Nazi group Phalanz 18, and in June 2020, the neo-Nazi Nordadler group.[56] In May 2021, German intelligence services announced that they would widen their surveillance of PEGIDA movement in its home state of Saxony.[57]

The harm caused by online extremist content has been a persistent issue. Government and tech company initiatives have been put in place to remove worrisome communications. As a response to the countermeasures against major online platforms, extremists started to migrate to fringe platforms. This has generated a particularly "complex and multi-pronged web of platforms and applications the far right use as an online ecosystem".[58] In 2020, the digital analysis unit of Institute for Strategic Dialogue monitored 379 far-right and right-wing populist channels. As their study asserted most of the content on the analyzed alternative platforms was non-violent and not obviously racist. Nevertheless, "the disproportionate amount of content focusing only on the negative aspects of immigration, which frames entire parts of the population as a threat, creates a sense of urgency to act in order to defend one's in-group".[59] In articulating ways how to respond to illegal online content, they recommended that "mainstream platforms, international initiatives, and research organizations should strengthen partnerships with smaller alternative platforms to improve their ability to counter illegal terrorist or violent extremist content".[60] At the same time when determining which far-right online platforms meet the requirements for content removal, the decentralized nature of far-right terrorism should be taken into account.

Germany is considered to be a model for education-based counter-extremism work. Having historical accounts of rebuilding democracy after the Holocaust, education operates across all levels of society, including arts and sports programs, religious groups, and local advisors.[61] In November 2020, the cabinet committee for the fight against racism and right-wing extremism presented its extensive list of measures on how to fight right-wing extremism. One of the central pillars of the concept is to better understand the root causes of racism and right-wing extremism. Additionally, the support base for victims has been extended and the value of a diverse society will be strengthened. With this in mind, cooperation has been enhanced among security authorities, the judiciary, and relevant state civil society bodies. In line with this, for the 2021–2024 period, a budget of over 1 billion euros has been allocated for these purposes.[62]

Norway

The 2011 Oslo and Utøya attacks fundamentally changed the Norwegian counter-terrorism legal regime. The receipt of terrorist training, preparing for a terrorist attack, as well as providing support to a terrorist organization were criminalized by the 2013 provisions.[63] In November 2016, Norway adopted the 2016–2020 strategy against hate speech. The concept "aims to create arenas for dialogue and raise awareness of the consequences of hate speech, as well as facilitating the identification, investigation, and conviction of those who incite hatred".[64] Police's close monitoring of right-wing extremist activities together with the severity of settable punishments seems to serve as effective deterrence for extremists.[65] In line with this, the preventative dialogue approach of security services reportedly managed to make young activists disengage from far-right entities.[66]

The ratio of the Muslim population in Norway is estimated to be 4.2%.[67] According to a 2017 survey, "34% of Norwegian bear anti-Muslim sentiments",[68] 28% are markedly hostile,[69] and roughly 40% engage with the idea that Muslims "pose a threat to the Norwegian culture".[70] A new national action plan was presented in 2020 to address the growing hatred towards Muslims in Norway. The document will apply between 2020 and 2023 and aims to promote dialogue and bridge existing gaps.[71] Interestingly, the far-right terrorist attack against the al-Noor Mosque in Bærum on 10 August 2019 was thwarted by two elderly Norwegian-Pakistani members of the mosque congregation.[72] In January 2019, the National Criminal Investigation Service established a center responsible for active digital policing. Despite the growing number of convictions, there is a noteworthy number of cases that remain in "the grey area of legality".[73]

Researcher Tore Bjørgo draws attention to an interesting novelty in the threat landscape, namely the disappearance of racist youth cultures. They are only adults who operate and partake in right-wing extremist movements and organizations. As he explains, xenophobia has gradually decreased among young people who were born into a multicultural society, and it is the older generation that worries more of foreign influence.[74] This needs to be taken into account when designing effective countermeasures. While preventative strategies were heavily based upon youngsters,[75] a new approach with new collaborative stakeholders and agencies is necessary to target the elder activists.[76]

Sweden

The Swedish counter-terrorism concept puts prevention and accordingly intelligence work into its operational center. The Swedish Security Service has the principal responsibility for countering terrorism. Considering the transnational nature of terrorism, collaboration among government agencies, other stakeholders, and international partners plays a crucial role in the work.[77] The Counter-Terrorism Cooperation Council pools all relevant national authorities, its convenor is the security service. In 2005, the National Center for Terrorist Threat Assessment was established as a working group within the Counter-Terrorism Cooperation Council. National Centre for Terrorist Threat Assessment (NCT) is tasked with "producing long and short-term strategic assessments of the terrorist threat against Sweden and Swedish interests".[78]

Recruiting and encouraging people to commit acts of terrorism has been criminalized since 2010. Traveling abroad to partake in military training and financing these trips became illegal by the 2016 legislation. In the wake of the 2017 Stockholm terrorist attacks, new provisions were adopted to further tighten Swedish anti-terrorism laws. Accordingly, security arrangements for potential soft targets were strengthened and information-sharing practices among security agencies were enhanced.[79]

A national plan to combat racism and hate crime is in place since 2016. Future initiatives include the establishment of special hate crime groups in police, registering hate speech to enable the collection of data and increased police monitoring.[80] The National Center for Preventing Violent Extremism under the Ministry of Justice is responsible for the coordination among government ministries, local municipalities, and civil society organizations.[81] Additionally, there is a consistent and close working relationship "between various governmental agencies and ministries with their counterparts in other Nordic countries".[82] A pedagogical program tailored for public schools and civil society organizations provided the central element for the Swedish strategy. The concept is centrally coordinated and monitored, its main tenets have been set in the so-called *Conversation Compass*, which is a guidebook for teachers and social workers involved in countering violent extremism.[83]

Australia

Australian national counter-terrorism strategy (prepare for, prevent, respond to, and recover from a terrorist act) implies "a multi-layered and collaborative approach based on strong relationships between governments, private industry, members of the community and international partners".[84] Additionally, partnerships with other countries and companies aim to "ensure terrorists cannot operate with impunity in ungoverned digital spaces".[85] By "challenging terrorist propaganda and recruitment techniques as well as via early intervention and community engagement the drivers of violent extremism"[86] are contested. At the same time, citizens and businesses "play a critical role in reporting suspicious activity and putting plans and infrastructure in place to keep everyone safe".[87]

Preventing and countering radicalization to violent extremism lies in a community policy aspect.[88] In particular, the social conditions are to be investigated and changed "to reduce the propensity for violence".[89] To build community resilience to violent extremist ideologies, Australian Government initiative "Living Safe Together" explains what violent extremism is, how to recognize the signs, and what residents can do about it.[90] The August 2014 Australian CVE strategy aims "to combat the threat posed by home-grown terrorism and to discourage or deter Australians from traveling offshore to participate in conflicts. It indicates that the emphasis of the program is on prevention and early intervention through tailored support".[91] CVE efforts aim to "reduce the risk of homegrown terrorism by strengthening Australians' resilience to radicalization and assisting individuals in disengaging from violent extremist influences and beliefs".[92] Additionally, the Community Awareness Training Manual – Building Resilience in the Community program (CAT) was delivered. By providing information to community members and service providers, this initiative aims to help identify and counter behaviors that may lead to violent extremism. Awareness of community members and service providers is increased by both general informational and train-the-trainer sessions.[93]

Victorian State P/CVE measures can be classified into three categories: primary prevention, secondary intervention, and tertiary intervention. Primary prevention programs aim to build resilience in communities by educating them about the risk of violent extremism. Secondary interventions address vulnerable individuals. Through social and mental support, such programs target the underlying problems leading to radicalization (family violence, drug or alcohol abuse). Tertiary interventions are aimed to disengage those individuals from violent actions who are already engaged in violent extremist networks.[94]

The *Point Magazine*, an online publication administered by the New South Wales state government body Multicultural NSW, is a noteworthy CVE instrument. Its specific focus lies on the impact overseas conflict can have on the young members of local communities in Australia. Directly addressing the most contentious issues help sustain social cohesion.[95]

For a realistic understanding of the underlying factors, rigorous empirical research and analysis are advisable on the complexity of causes resorting to violent extremism.[96] To counter violent extremist narratives, the target audience's values should be assessed. It should be investigated what community members await from Australia to be provided. Once in the possession of this information, opportunities should be offered accordingly.[97] Frustrations should be given chances to be heard, and the government should design measures in accordance with these articulated concerns.[98]

Extensive and consistent legislation characterizes the fight against counter terrorism in Australia. Even though, it has been argued that instead of "continually reworking existing strategies",[99] a more creative approach would be required to combat the threat of terrorism. Through structured conversations, topics such as religion and diversity should be comprehensively addressed. Countering extremist narratives could effectively immunize citizens against radical ideologies and could debunk extremist myths. Community Action for Preventing Extremism's (CAPE) "Exit White Power" project is a noteworthy example that attempted to spread radical right counter narratives.[100]

New Zealand

The report of the Royal Commission of Inquiry into the Terrorist Attacks on Christchurch mosques on 15 March 2019 recommended that "fundamental to New Zealand's future wellbeing and security is social cohesion".[101] In the wake of the Christchurch shootings, the New Zealand government adopted its counter-terrorism strategy on 10 September 2019 and released the Christchurch Call to Action.[102] This letter seeks to establish international cooperation among online platforms and national security agencies "to monitor and act against extreme racist content and violence in the cyberspace".[103]

With amendments to the Terrorism Suppression Act 2002 and Search and Surveillance Act 2012, New Zealand government is planning to introduce novel counter-terrorism provisions which will criminalize terrorist weapons and combat training. It will also create a new criminal offence for traveling overseas to engage in terrorism. Planning and preparation of terror attacks will constitute a criminal offence accordingly.[104] Critics argue, however, that this may result in further complicating the task for police and intelligence services. In the meantime, calls have been circulated to expand New Zealand's terror lists. It is important to consider, however, that membership in a banned group may "add extraordinary glam for the groups' followers, making the involvement of their activities even more attractive for committed individuals".[105]

The balance has shifted to the digital sphere, which means that geographical differences do not count anymore.[106] With this in mind, New Zealand cannot be regarded as an isolated area from the terrorist threat. The core element in the New Zealand counter-terrorism strategy lies in "leveraging our high level of trust, our tolerant and inclusive society, and strong connections in and between communities".[107] "The Government should focus on creating and implementing policies and programs that address the social causes behind particularly young white men being radicalized into fascism".[108] The National Security Investigations Team is striving to establish close and direct relationships with communities.[109] New Zealand Security Intelligence Service adopted new terminologies for threats from its Canadian counterparts. To avoid people may affiliate previous categories with certain communities, "faith-motivated extremism" and "identity-motivated violent extremism" have been applied.[110]

Conclusion

Findings of our analysis can be summarized in Table 4.1.

All the eight examined national legal regimes have in place specific counter-terrorism strategies, however, in most cases, these concepts were primarily tailored for jihadist terrorism and have been modified in accordance with the evolving threat posed by domestic extremists. Traditional countermeasures are the essential pillars of all these strategies. It is worth mentioning here that

TABLE 4.1 Counter-strategies in the examined countries

	Canada	*USA*	*UK*	*France*	*Germany*	*Norway*	*Sweden*	*Australia*	*New Zealand*
Is there a specific strategy involved?									
Traditional counter-terrorism instruments									
A broader approach									
Traditional counter-terrorism agencies involved									
Local authorities involved									
Non-government organizations involved									
Long-term solutions									
Short-term solutions									
Is online radicalization involved in the counter-terrorism strategy?									
Is deradicalization involved in the counter-terrorism strategy?									

Canada designated Atomwaffen Division, National Socialist Order, The Base, The Proud Boys, the Russian Imperial Movement (RIM), Blood and Honour as well as Combat 18 as terrorist entities. Australia proscribed Sonnenkrieg Division and the United States has labeled RIM a "Specially Designated Global Terrorist entity".[111] Besides traditional counter-terrorism instruments, the need for a broader approach to fighting far-right extremism and violence has been articulated in each of the analyzed national policies. Acknowledging the comprehensive nature of radicalization and the lone actor-related threat, collaboration among national agencies, civil society organizations, and international partners has been given priority status. It is a striking factor, though, that well-working national best practices have been taken over and have been embedded into other countries' legal contexts, presuming an already successful interaction and communication among the relevant stakeholders.

One of the most frequent criticism addresses the overwhelmingly reactive nature of counter-policies. It is particularly important that the request for a proactive approach has already been formulated. Such a concept could ensure proportionate and appropriate responses to domestic terrorism not only in the short term but also in the long term. Widely shared concerns over online radicalization have been addressed in all the examined national legislations, deradicalization and exit programs, however, have not yet been so widespread. Practices in Australia or the Nordic countries could set excellent examples for future policy trajectories in this regard.

Notes

1 Kacper Rekawek, "Don't designate Azov why the U.S. should not include the Azov movement on the foreign terrorist organizations (FTO) list", Counter Extremism Project, 14 April 2021. www.counterextremism.com/blog/dont-designate-azov
2 Ibid.
3 Ibid.
4 Government of Canada, "Building resilience against terrorism Canada's counter terrorism strategy", 2013. www.publicsafety.gc.ca/cnt/rsrcs/pblctns/rslnc-gnst-trrrsm/rslnc-gnst-trrrsm-eng.pdf
5 "The views of Canadian scholars on the impact of the anti-terrorism act". www.justice.gc.ca/eng/rp-pr/cj-jp/antiter/rr05_1/p5_1.html#start
6 Government of Canada, "National strategy on countering radicalization to violence", 2018. www.publicsafety.gc.ca/cnt/rsrcs/pblctns/ntnl-strtg-cntrng-rdclztn-vlnc/ntnl-strtg-cntrng-rdclztn-vlnc-en.pdf
7 Richard B. Parent and James O. Ellis, "The future of right-wing terrorism in Canada", Canadian Network for Research on Terrorism, Security and Society, July 2016. www.tsas.ca/wp-content/uploads/2018/03/TSASWP16-12_Parent-Ellis.pdf
8 "Canada Centre for Community Engagement and Prevention of Violence". www.publicsafety.gc.ca/cnt/bt/cc/index-en.aspx
9 United States Department of State, "Canada country reports on terrorism 2019". www.state.gov/reports/country-reports-on-terrorism-2019/canada/

10 Sara K. Thompson, Feras Ismail, Mathew Murray, and Lorna Ferguson, "An Examination of Competencies for and the Evaluation of CVE in Policing". Canadian Network for Research on Terrorism, Security and Society, 2021. www.tsas.ca/wp-content/uploads/2021/03/Thompson-et-al-TSAS-CVE-Research-Brief-FINAL_Revised3_11_2021.pdf
11 H. Qadir, *Preventing and Countering Extremism and Terrorist Recruitment: A Best Practice Guide*. United Kingdom: John Catt Educational, 2016.
12 House of Commons Chambre des Communes, CHCP Committee Report. www.ourcommons.ca/DocumentViewer/en/42-1/CHPC/report-10/page-18
13 United States Department of State, "Canada country reports on terrorism 2019".
14 Ibid.
15 Amarnath Amarasingam and Michael Nesbitt, "Understanding Canada's recent ban of far right extremist groups", Global Network on Extremism and Technology, 8 February 2021. https://gnet-research.org/2021/02/08/understanding-canadas-recent-ban-of-far right-extremist-groups/
16 "About the listing process", Public Safety Canada. www.publicsafety.gc.ca/cnt/ntnl-scrt/cntr-trrrsm/lstd-ntts/bt-lstng-prcss-en.aspx
17 Adam Gabbatt, "Close to home: how US far right terror flourished in post-9/11 focus on Islam", *The Guardian*, 6 September 2021. www.theguardian.com/us-news/2021/sep/06/terrorism-far right-white-supremacists-911-us
18 Jacob Ware, "Fighting back: The Atomwaffen Division, countering violent extremism, and the evolving crackdown on far right terrorism in America". *Journal for Deradicalization*, Winter 2020/21. https://journals.sfu.ca/jd/index.php/jd/article/view/411/253
19 Ben Makuch, "Audio recording claims neo-Nazi terror group is disbanding", Vice, 15 March 2020. www.vice.com/amp/en_us/article/qjdnam/audio-recording-claims-neo-nazi-terror-group-is-disbanding.
20 Ware, "Fighting back".
21 Ibid.
22 Charlie Savage, Adam Goldman, and Eric Schmitt, "U.S. will give terrorist label to white supremacist group for first time", *New York Times*, 6 April 2020. www.nytimes.com/2020/04/06/us/politics/terrorist-label-white-supremacy-Russian-Imperial-Movement.html.8Frontline
23 "FACT SHEET: National Strategy for Countering Domestic Terrorism", 15 June 2021. www.whitehouse.gov/briefing-room/statements-releases/2021/06/15/fact-sheet-national-strategy-for-countering-domestic-terrorism/
24 Eviane Leidig and Charlie van Mieghem, "The US National Strategy on Countering Domestic Terrorism as a model for the EU", ICCT, September 2021. https://icct.nl/app/uploads/2021/10/EU-US-Counter-Terrorism-Leidig_VanMieghem.pdf
25 Mikkel Dack, Colleen Murphy, Gary LaFree, John Horgan, Kurt Braddock, and Monica Nalepa, "Why is it so difficult to fight domestic terrorism? 6 experts share their thoughts", The Conversation, 30 August 2021. https://theconversation.com/why-is-it-so-difficult-to-fight-domestic-terrorism-6-experts-share-their-thoughts-165054
26 "FACT SHEET: National Strategy for Countering Domestic Terrorism".
27 Ibid.
28 Colin Clarke and Mollie Saltskog, "Assessing the national strategy for countering domestic terrorism", War on the Rocks, 22 June 2021. https://warontherocks.com/2021/06/assessing-the-national-strategy-for-countering-domestic-terrorism/

29 Catrina Doxsee and Jake Harrington, "The first U.S. national strategy for countering domestic terrorism", CSIS, 17 June 2021. www.csis.org/analysis/first-us-national-strategy-countering-domestic-terrorism
30 Ibid.
31 Dack et al., "Why is it so difficult to fight domestic terrorism? 6 experts share their thoughts".
32 Home Office, "Fact sheet: Right-wing terrorism", 20 September 2019. https://homeofficemedia.blog.gov.uk/2019/09/20/fact-sheet-right-wing-terrorism/
33 Chris Allen, Arshad Isakjee, and Özlem Ögtem-Young, "Counter extremism PREVENT, and the extreme right-wing: Lessons learned and future challenges", LIAS Working Paper Series, Volume 2, 2019. https://journals.le.ac.uk/ojs1/index.php/lias/article/view/3074/2792
34 Ibid.
35 "United Kingdom National Submission: Best practice and lessons learned on how protecting and promoting human rights contributes to preventing and countering violent extremisms". www.ohchr.org/Documents/Issues/RuleOfLaw/PCVE/UK.pdf
36 Lucia Zedner, "Countering terrorism or criminalizing curiosity? The troubled history of UK responses to right-wing and other extremism". *Common Law World Review*, 50(1), 2021. https://journals.sagepub.com/doi/full/10.1177/1473779521989349
37 Ibid.
38 Graham Macklin, "The evolution of extreme-right terrorism and efforts to counter it in the United Kingdom", CTC Sentinel, January 2019. https://ctc.usma.edu/wp-content/uploads/2019/01/CTC-SENTINEL-012019.pdf
39 Ibid.
40 Jane's, "Threat from right-wing extremism continues to increase in UK". www.janes.com/docs/default-source/documentation/farrightuk.pdf?sfvrsn=d902087d_0
41 Home Office, "Fact sheet: Right-wing terrorism".
42 UK Home Office, "National Action becomes first extreme right-wing group to be banned in UK", 16 December 2016. www.gov.uk/government/news/national-action-becomes-first-extreme-right-wing-group-to-be-banned-in-uk
43 Ibid.
44 Graham Macklin, " 'Only bullets will stop us!' – The banning of National Action in Britain". *Perspectives on Terrorism*, 12(6), December 2018. www.jstor.org/stable/pdf/26544646.pdf?refreqid=excelsior%3Af10d6ba2d37f444e9991de6969de242f
45 Ed Ceasar, "The undercover Fascist", *The New Yorker*, 20 May 2019. www.newyorker.com/magazine/2019/05/27/the-undercover-fascist
46 The Soufan Center, "IntelBrief: UK to proscribe neo-Nazi group the Base in continued crackdown on far right extremism", 15 July 2021. https://thesoufancenter.org/intelbrief-2021-july-15/
47 Aude Mazoue, "How the November 2015 attacks marked a turning point in French terror laws", France24, 5 September 2021. www.france24.com/en/france/20210905-how-the-november-2015-attacks-marked-a-turning-point-in-french-terror-laws
48 "French MPs to vote on 'anti-separatism' bill to battle Islamist radicalism", France 24, 1 February 2021. www.france24.com/en/france/20210216-french-mps-vote-on-anti-separatism-bill-to-battle-islamist-radicalism

49 Angelique Chrisafis, "France planning to allow use of algorithms to detect extremism online", *The Guardian*, 28 April 2021. www.theguardian.com/world/2021/apr/28/france-planning-allow-use-algorithms-detect-extremist-activity
50 Mazoue, "How the November 2015 attacks marked a turning point in French terror laws".
51 "Government bans French far right group Génération Identitaire", RRI, 4 March 2021. www.rfi.fr/en/france/20210304-government-bans-french-far right-group-g%C3%A9n%C3%A9ration-identitaire-anti-immigration-migrants
52 Kim Willsher, "France bans far right 'paramilitary' group Génération Identitaire", *The Guardian*, 3 March 2021. www.theguardian.com/world/2021/mar/03/fra nce-bans-far right-paramilitary-group-generation-identitaire
53 James Kleinfeld, "Generation identity: France begins shutting down far right group", Al Jazeera, 22 February 2021. www.aljazeera.com/news/2021/2/22/fra nce-shuts-down-far right-group-after-of-al-jazee-investigation
54 Kate Brady, "Germany announces plans to combat far right extremism and online hate speech", DW, 30 October 2019. www.dw.com/en/germany-announces-plans-to-combat-far right-extremism-and-online-hate-speech/a-51049129
55 Brady, "Germany announces plans to combat far right extremism and online hate speech".
56 Counter Extremism Project, "Germany: Extremism and terrorism". www.count erextremism.com/countries/germany
57 "German spy agency calls anti-Islam PEGIDA protest group 'anti-constitutional' ", The Local, 7 May 2021. www.thelocal.de/20210507/german-spy-agency-calls-anti-islam-pegida-protest-group-anti-constitutional/
58 Jakob Guhl, Julia Ebner, and Jan Rau, "The online eco-system of the German far right", Institute for Strategic Dialogue, 2020. www.isdglobal.org/wp-content/uploads/2020/02/ISD-The-Online-Ecosystem-of-the-German-Far right-English-Draft-11.pdf
59 Ibid.
60 Ibid.
61 Cynthia Miller-Idriss, "How to counter far right extremism? Germany shows the way", *The Guardian*, 17 May 2019. www.theguardian.com/commentisfree/2019/may/17/counter-far right-extremism-germany-uk-teachers
62 Cabinet Committee, "A clear signal in the fight against right-wing extremism and racism", 25 November 2020. www.bundesregierung.de/breg-en/news/cabinet-right-wing-extremism-1820094
63 US Department of State, "Country reports on terrorism 2013". https://2009-2017.state.gov/j/ct/rls/crt/2013/index.htm
64 Norwegian Ministry of Children and Equality, "The government's strategy against hate speech 2016–2020". www.regjeringen.no/contentassets/72293ca519564 2249029bf6905ff08be/hatefulleytringer_eng_uu.pdf
65 Tore Bjørgo and Ingvild Magnæs Gjelsvik, "Right-wing extremists and anti-Islam activists in Norway: Constraints against violence", C-REX Working Paper Series, March 2017. www.sv.uio.no/c-rex/english/publications/c-rex-working-paper-ser ies/constraints-against-right-wing-violence.pdf
66 Ibid.
67 Sindre Bangstad, "Report on Islamophobia or anti-Muslim hatred submitted to the UN Special Rapporteur on freedom of religion or belief", 30 November 2020. www.ohchr.org/Documents/Issues/Religion/Islamophobia-AntiMuslim/Civil%20Society%20or%20Individuals/SindreBangstad.pdf

68 "Norway launches National Action Plan against Islamophobia", The Nation, 25 September 2020. https://nation.com.pk/25-Sep-2020/norway-launches-national-action-plan-against-islamophobia
69 Bangstad, "Report on Islamophobia or anti-Muslim hatred submitted to the UN Special Rapporteur on freedom of religion or belief".
70 "Norway launches National Action Plan against Islamophobia".
71 Ibid.
72 Bangstad, "Report on Islamophobia or anti-Muslim hatred submitted to the UN Special Rapporteur on freedom of religion or belief".
73 Tore Bjørgo, "Right-Wing extremism in Norway: Changes and challenges", C-REX – Center for Research on Extremism, 25 February 2019. www.sv.uio.no/c-rex/english/news-and-events/right-now/2019/right-wing-extremism-in-norway.html
74 Ibid.
75 Casie Elizabeth Daugherty, "Deradicalization and disengagement: Exit programs in Norway and Sweden and addressing neo-Nazi extremism", *Journal for Deradicalization*, Winter 2019/20. https://core.ac.uk/download/pdf/276532683.pdf
76 Tore Bjørgo, "Right-Wing extremism in Norway: Changes and challenges", l.
77 Swedish Security Service, "Counter terrorism". www.sakerhetspolisen.se/en/swedish-security-service/counter-terrorism.html
78 Ibid.
79 "Sweden says to tighten laws to fight terrorism", US News, 7 June 2017. www.usnews.com/news/world/articles/2017-06-07/sweden-says-to-tighten-laws-to-fight-terrorism
80 European Commission, Migration and Home Affairs, "Report on right-wing extremism: A study visit in Sweden", 2019. https://ec.europa.eu/home-affairs/sites/default/files/docs/pages/2019_right_wing.pdf
81 US Department of Sweden, "Country reports on terrorism 2019: Sweden". www.state.gov/reports/country-reports-on-terrorism-2019/sweden/
82 Nima Khorrami, "Swedish counter-radicalization strategies: An overview", European Eye on Radicalization, 3 April 2019. https://eeradicalization.com/swedish-counter-radicalization-strategies-an-overview/
83 Ibid.
84 Australian Federal Police, "Fighting terrorism". www.afp.gov.au/what-we-do/crime-types/fighting-terrorism
85 Australian Government, "2017 Foreign policy white paper". www.dfat.gov.au/sites/default/files/minisite/static/4ca0813c-585e-4fe1-86eb-de665e65001a/fpwhitepaper/foreign-policy-white-paper/chapter-five-keeping-australia-and-australians-safe-secure-and-free-4.html
86 Ibid.
87 Government of South Australia, "Keeping South Australians safe: A focus on counter-terrorism". www.asial.com.au/documents/item/1277
88 C. Agius, K. Cook, L. Nicholas, A. Ahmed, H. bin Jehangir, N. Safa, T. Hardwick, and S. Clark, "Mapping Right-Wing Extremism in Victoria. Applying a Gender Lens to Develop Prevention and Deradicalisation Approaches". Melbourne: Victorian Government, Department of Justice and Community Safety: Countering Violent Extremism Unit and Swinburne University of Technology, 2020. https://apo.org.au/sites/default/files/resource-files/2020-12/apo-nid307612.pdf

89 J. True and S. Eddyono, "Preventing violent extremism: gender perspectives and women's roles", Monash GPS, 2017. www.monash. edu/__data/assets/pdf_file/0011/1779068/Policybrief-PVE-2017.pdf
90 "Living Safe Together". www.livingsafetogether.gov.au/pages/home.aspx
91 Cat Barker, "Update on Australian Government measures to counter violent extremism: A quick guide", 18 August 2017. https://parlinfo.aph.gov.au/parlInfo/download/library/prspub/5461291/upload_binary/5461291.pdf;fileType=application%2Fpdf#search=%22library/prspub/5461291%22
92 Andrew Lauland, Jennifer D. P. Moroney, John G. Rivers, Jacopo Bellasio, and Kate Cameron, "Countering violent extremism in Australia and abroad", RAND Corporation, 2019. www.rand.org/content/dam/rand/pubs/research_reports/RR2100/RR2168/RAND_RR2168.pdf
93 Ibid.
94 Agius et al., "Mapping Right-Wing Extremism in Victoria. Applying a Gender Lens to Develop Prevention and Deradicalisation Approaches".
95 Andrew Lauland, Jennifer D. P. Moroney, John G. Rivers, Jacopo Bellasio, and Kate Cameron, "Countering violent extremism in Australia and abroad".
96 Nell Bennett, "One man's radical the radicalisation debate and Australian counterterrorism policy". *Security Challenges*, 15(1), 47–62, 2019. https://research-management.mq.edu.au/ws/portalfiles/portal/121574597/Publisher_version.pdf
97 Sharyn Rundle-Thiele and Renata Anibaldi, "Countering violent extremism: From defence to attack". *Security Challenges*, 12(2), 53–64, 2016. www.jstor.org/stable/26465607?seq=1#metadata_info_tab_contents
98 John Coyne, "Australia must address the risk of radicalisation posed by recession", *The Strategist*, 25 June 2020. www.aspistrategist.org.au/australia-must-address-the-risk-of-radicalisation-posed-by-recession/
99 Nicola McGarrity and Jessie Blackbourn, "Australia has enacted 82 anti-terror laws since 2001. But tough laws alone can't eliminate terrorism", The Conversation, 29 September 2019. https://theconversation.com/australia-has-enacted-82-anti-terror-laws-since-2001-but-tough-laws-alone-cant-eliminate-terrorism-123521
100 William Allchorn, "Australian radical right narratives in an age of terrorism", 13 April 2021. www.hedayahcenter.org/media-center/latest-news/blog-post-australian-radical-right-narratives-and-counter-narratives-in-an-age-of-terror/
101 "Royal Commission of inquiry into the terrorist attacks on Christchurch mosques on 15 March 2019". https://christchurchattack.royalcommission.nz/assets/Publications/Report-summary.pdf
102 Sheridan Webb, "From hijackings to right-wing extremism: The drivers of New Zealand's counter-terrorism legislation 1977–2020", *National Security Journal*, 9 April 2021. https://nationalsecurityjournal.nz/wp-content/uploads/sites/13/2021/04/NSJ-2021-WaS-April-Webb.pdf
103 Paul Spoonley, "Opinion: Will the "Christchurch call" be enough?", 17 October 2019. www.massey.ac.nz/massey/about-massey/news/article.cfm?mnarticle_uuid=E9A26A0B-F437-44F3-A100-5763985834FD
104 Thomas Manch, "Government to 'close gap' in counter-terrorism laws, criminalising terror attack planning and preparation", Stuff, 13 April 2021. www.stuff.co.nz/national/politics/124820505/government-to-close-gap-in-counterterrorism-laws-criminalising-terror-attack-planning-and-preparation

105 Hayden Crosby, "Treating NZ's far right groups as terrorist organisations could make monitoring extremists even harder", The Conversation, 16 April 2021. https://theconversation.com/treating-nzs-far right-groups-as-terrorist-organisations-could-make-monitoring-extremists-even-harder-158291
106 Jarrod Gilbert and Ben Elley, "Shaved heads and sonnenrads: Comparing white supremacist skinheads and the alt-right in New Zealand". *Kōtuitui: New Zealand Journal of Social Sciences Online*, 15, 280–294, 2020.
107 "Extract from Cabinet Paper ERS-19-SUB-0026: Looking forward: Strengthening New Zealand against terrorism and violent extremism". https://dpmc.govt.nz/publications/cabinet-decision-ers-19-sub-0026-looking-forward-strengthen ing-nz
108 Hugh Collins, "Anti-fascist researchers' tipped off police after detecting Christchurch mosque threat", *NZ Herald*, 7 March 2021. www.nzherald.co.nz/nz/anti-fascist-researchers-tipped-off-police-after-detecting-christchurch-mos que-threat/HUY7IMMWEESXAJUDHLGVCKVUJY/
109 Royal Commission of Inquiry into the Terrorist Attacks on Christchurch mosques in 15 March 2019, "The role of New Zealand Police in the counter-terrorism effort". https://christchurchattack.royalcommission.nz/the-report/part-8-assess ing-the-counter-terrorism-effort/new-zealand-police/
110 Phil Pennington, "Balance lacking in surveillance trends – Security expert", RNZ, 9 April 2021. www.rnz.co.nz/news/national/440129/balance-lacking-in-surve illance-trends-security-expert
111 The Soufan Center, "IntelBrief: UK to proscribe neo-Nazi group the Base in continued crackdown on far right extremism".

5

FUTURE IMPLICATIONS

How to address the rising threat of the far right?

The presence of far-right-inspired political violence is not a novel phenomenon in the so-called Western world. Noteworthy novelties can be detected, however, in these groups' modus operandi and in the functionalities of their fundraising, recruitment, and communication. Building upon our findings in the previous parts of the research, this chapter attempts to put forward implications on future counter-terrorism policies. With this in mind, first, developments in these threat groups' funding, recruitment, and communication practices as well as their operational tactics, targeting, and weaponry are established. Second, in line with these advancements we try to identify legislative and operational gaps in counter-policies and accordingly design the most effective countermeasures.

Funding practices

Ethnically or racially motivated terrorism[1] employs fundraising activities of a particularly wide array. This section first aims to identify the challenges in tackling these terrorist financing methods. Second, where possible the most effective corresponding countermeasures are designed.

Historically, counter-terrorist financing has overwhelmingly focused on Islamist-inspired terrorism. There are, however, considerable differences when investigating the financial activities of jihadist terrorist organizations and right-wing extremists. One of the most noteworthy differences is the size of their funding structure. While a complex terrorist organization requires regular and well-structured financial mechanisms, violent extremist attacks carried out by lone actors or small cells with low sophisticated means have only limited prerequisites.[2] It is more likely, that legitimate sources such as salary or personal savings cover these expenses, which are all beyond traditional countering

DOI: 10.4324/9781032708041-5

terrorism financing intervention.[3] Another challenge is that there is no single determined group, but the far-right movement is of a highly diffuse nature with various small cells and worrisome individuals.

This leads us to the next obstacle. It is obvious that taking legal measures against designated terrorist entities is much easier. Nevertheless, only a very few far-right threat groups have been designated as terrorist groups.[4] The essential pillar of international counter-terrorist financing has been the application of targeted sanctions to freeze and block assets associated with individuals linked to designated terrorist groups. Novel forms of terrorism, however, are outside formal financial systems as well as formal terrorist organizations.[5] It is a burning issue that no United Nations or other international designation regime exists for targeting ethnically or racially motivated terrorism. Restrictive measures based upon counter-terrorism designations, however, play a crucial role in countering terrorist financing efforts.[6]

- Still, very similar laws to countering foreign terrorist financing will be required to curb the money flows of domestic terrorists.[7] Already existing international counter-strategies to prevent and disrupt al-Qaeda and the Islamic State's actions can provide the framework for how to step up against the ascending far-right-related threat.
- Existing policy tools should be applied to far-right terrorist financing.[8] Instruments and the regulatory system of the United Nations could be used to inform policy-makers, the private sector, and civil society about the fundamental guidelines. UN Security Council Resolution 1373 and the Counter-Terrorism Committee focus on preventing and disrupting terrorist activities in a general scope. In addition, legally binding Security Council resolutions exist that apply to all forms of terrorism.[9]
- These international bodies (UN, Financial Action Task Force (FATF)) should ensure that adequate operational guidelines are available on violent far-right extremist groups.[10] The United Nations should step up as a main coordinator for the necessary multiagency cooperation and establish a platform for the regular encounter of governments, private sector representatives, and civil society organizations. This common instrument could enable a standardized surface for sharing best practices and challenges.[11]
- The FTAF has a crucial role in global efforts to combat terrorist financing. It is responsible for setting global standards and assists jurisdictions in implementing financial provisions of the United Nations Security Council resolutions on terrorism. Additionally, it puts forward evaluations on countries' ability to prevent, detect, investigate, and prosecute the financing of terrorism.[12] With this in mind, guidance from the FATF on how to counter far-right entities' fundraising efforts would be highly informative for banks on extremists' mode of operation and tactics.[13]

- Considerably less is known about far-right extremists' fundraising capabilities and actions, therefore there is a need for a more nuanced understanding of their practices. To do so, through the UN's Global Research Network (the RESOLVE) academics and the private sector should be involved to identify contradictions or failures and accordingly alert authorities about these potential loopholes.[14]
- There is a stressed need for effective cooperation and communication with all competent actors from the judiciary, the police, and intelligence services. It is also important to build upon the expertise of actors from civil society working on the analysis of the right-wing extremist threat.[15]
- A noteworthy example here is the Italian approach. Italian authorities have noted the difficulties in defining right-wing-related acts as terrorism and prosecuting them under the counter-terrorism legislation. Therefore, incidents caused by right-wing extremism via social media are prosecuted under anti-discrimination and hate crime legislation. A new article concerning propaganda and the instigation of crimes for the purposes of discrimination was added to the Italian Criminal Code in 2018.[16]
- To facilitate interregional and international collaboration among national authorities, Interpol's notice and diffusion system enables member countries to reach out to each other in specific matters.[17]

The United Nations CTED has noted[18] the growing transnational nature of right-wing extremism as of particular concern. Despite this growing internationalization of ethnically or racially motivated extremism and terrorism, attacks are carried out by lone actors. Most of these plots are low-tech incidents that typically do not rely on special operational networks. Detecting the mode of operations is challenging for law enforcement authorities as no financial trails are left behind.[19]

- Risk indicators with regard to each fundraising mode should be identified.[20] To ensure the reporting of worrisome acts, channels for prompt communications should be established. It is also important that reporting entities also receive feedback on the information they have provided. This bilateral communication may ensure development of a smooth reporting mechanism among the relevant stakeholders.[21]
- Existing legislation on suspicious activity reporting, financial intelligence practices, as well as tax policies should be reviewed in accordance with the threat posed by right-wing terrorism-related extremism and terrorism.[22]
- Similar to social media companies, financial service providers have a significant role in tackling terrorist financing. Besides raising their awareness of trends and modus operandi, they should be involved in the flow of information on novel research findings and best practices aiming to disrupt malicious financial activities.[23]

- Public–private partnerships and information sharing among these domains are crucial in combating terrorist financing and money laundering. Such collaborations are yet to be established to identify ethnically or racially motivated extremism and terrorism-related financing.[24]
- Keatinge et al. draw on an interesting idiosyncrasy of far-right mode of operation which may help trace worrisome money flows. Together with symbols, specific numbers have prominent meanings for these violent extremists. Compiling repositories of numbers with symbolic relevance and tracking them in message fields concerning transactions may also help detect malicious vendors.[25]

Neither the dissemination of extremist content nor the respective financial flows stop at national borders. The system of instruments and institutions for countering the financing of hateful group activities varies per national legal regimes. This makes the internationalization and harmonization of counter-efforts, particularly, challenging.[26]

- To better understand the alternative online ecosystem of the alt-right,[27] there is a need for a rigorous dataset on recorded instances when right-wing actors or groups have misused certain financial streams. This rigorously compiled database would be a highly informative asset to develop evidence-based counter-terrorist financing strategies. Thereby, key patterns and trends, the resourcing of terrorist organizations together with the financing of terrorist acts can be identified, and lessons from previous malevolent acts can be learned.[28] Financial intelligence is a necessary component of all counter-terrorism activities.[29] Information on the financial flows of threat groups or lone actors should be put into context with other, non-financial aspects of terrorism investigation.[30]
- Sharing these implications with financial service providers would enable the development of industry best practices or protocols.[31] Relevant companies thereby do not need to set idiosyncratic guidelines but should follow the steps of a sector-specific handbook of instructions.
- Online payment processors should be encouraged to broaden their resources with the purpose to have enough capacities for detecting and preventing the exploitation of their services.[32]
- This multi-agency collaboration should assist financial companies in drafting and drawing up terms of use policies.[33] This would ensure a standard, sector-wide counter-policy.

Technological innovations have undoubtedly enriched terrorist capabilities including novel digital fundraising options. As a response to that, mainstream financial services, as well as social media sites, have adopted provisions to restrict or bar extremists from their services or sites.[34] The emergence of novel technical capabilities, however, does not mean that extremists have indeed decided to terminate using traditional avenues for raising funds. Therefore, it is highly advisable that counter-efforts should pay particular attention parallel to old-school and new digital options.[35]

- Roughly half of the most commonly used financial technological platforms have in place restrictions on their use by hate groups. For instance, GiveSendGo terms and conditions "prohibit any abusive or hateful language on its platform, as well as campaigns for items that promote hate, violence and racial intolerance".[36] What is more concerning is that 38% of them do not have "any terms of service governing their use by hate groups".[37] In reality, the enforcement of these policies is very occasional. Service-providers should be urged to be more proactive in enforcement of these rules and should not wait until hateful acts have already been carried out. At the same time, tech companies should closely collaborate to see the impact of one company's decisions. They should anticipate what will happen to a worrisome user if his or her content or activity has been banned on Platform A and therefore will migrate to Platform B. This collaboration should be among several sectors, including banks, social media companies, and infrastructure providers. It is also important to involve smaller companies in this communication and not apply only to mega service-providers.[38]
- Tech companies should also acknowledge their unique position in having first-hand data on terrorist funding attempts. Governments should encourage them to appreciate this and reward them once this information is used for good purposes.[39] At the same time, mechanisms for mandatory reporting of instances of the abuse of their systems are to be installed. In these abuse cases, service-providers should be required to investigate and report the details of such incidents.[40]
- The use of cryptocurrencies has come to the fore in parallel with the deplatforming of fundraising websites.[41] It is their presumed anonymity which may make them beneficial for violent extremists. These considerations, however, turned out to be incorrect since every transaction can be viewed by anyone. Information from Bitcoin blockchains is readily retrievable, there may be, however, difficulties in tracing transaction-related records in the case of a Monero blockchain. When referring to donations, far-right formations frequently ask for donations through their Bitcoin wallets. For these transactions, they are required to send the ID of their Bitcoin wallets to the donators.[42] These traces provide excellent opportunities for the identification of concerning partners.
- Another worthwhile consideration is that, as specialists argue, law enforcement agencies can limit extremist trade in cryptocurrencies by monitoring the "entry and exit points" for Bitcoin, Monero, and others. Due to the inherent transparency of cryptocurrency blockchains, law

enforcement agencies can track these transactions in real time and should collaborate with cryptocurrency businesses to identify extremist payments and activity.[43] Similarly, considering that cryptocurrencies are to be exchanged into fiat currencies when purchasing a product or a service. Such payment processors are crucial elements to detect transactions for malicious purposes or by malevolent actors.[44] An important step forward is that in line with the Fifth AML Directive (5AMLD), the EU has included custodial wallets and custodial exchange service providers with the entities obliged to adhere to the reporting requirements of financial institutions.[45] In practice, this means that both online service providers as well as regulators have installed appropriate mechanisms for customer identification and verification.[46]

- This incredible volume of cryptocurrency data, however, requires new technical capabilities and monitoring capacities from the regulatory authorities.[47] Meanwhile, there is a stressed need for specialized research and training programs in technologies that are essential to prevent and disrupt online financial harm.[48] Currently, available resources, therefore, need to be remarkably enhanced posing extraordinary challenges for the respective realms.

Recruitment and communication channel

Internet technology enables that individuals can engage with potentially violent ideologies without being members of a particular threat group. This resulted in a more loosely affiliated alt-right movement and their narratives are widely available to the online community.[49] Extremists were banned from major tech platforms after the Charlottesville rally and migrated to so-called alt-tech platforms to advance their agendas. These decentralized technologies operate under minimalist terms of service agreements and provide the basic digital surface for extremist ideologies. Besides these decentralized services, violent actors use encrypted and peer-to-peer applications for communication and recruitment purposes. Banning extremist hateful content from mainstream social media channels turned out to be counterproductive, as activists started to deplatform their communication and got outside the reach of authorities. It is more difficult to monitor and curb chatter which may manifest in real violence on private platforms compared with more public forums.[50] It is "dangerous that they don't appear to have any infrastructure in place to police these platforms".[51]

- Due to the COVID-19 pandemic, vulnerable young people spend most of their time online. They can become easy targets for extremists who may exploit their grievances. Youngsters need a stable social support system so as not to become the victims of radicalization. Responsible adults on the frontline for detecting concerning indications of radicalization require specialized help to identify these warning signs. There is an urgent need for a guide similar to the one titled *Building Resilience and Confronting Risk in the COVID-19 Era*[52] compiled by the Southern Poverty Law Center and the American University's Polarization and Extremism Research and Innovation Lab (PERIL). The number of people considered extreme Islamist in Germany increased from 100 to at least 1,600 between 2013 and 2017. As a response to the dramatic rise in young people radicalized online, the Turkish community in Germany has installed a service primarily for Turkish- and Arabic-speaking parents. Funded by the European Union and German Ministry for Families, the service called "emel" provides parents help via email or by making an appointment for a live chat.[53] Similarly, via a multi-layered network of dedicated professionals, PREVENT in the United Kingdom plays "a fundamental role in tackling radicalization up and down in the country".[54]

- The threat posed by lone actors or small cells obviously complicates law enforcement efforts to detect the warning signs of a violent attack. Threat groups are well aware of this beneficial situation and strive to enhance their digital radicalization-related activities which may fortify the chance for a lone terrorist plot.[55] Considering that since the Corona virus outbreak extremists are overwhelmingly active in the digital sphere, law enforcement and intelligence authorities are participating in clandestine far-right communications online to be able to intercept concerning individuals.
- Extremists capitalize on concerning topical issues in a timely manner. Uncertainties around the pandemic as well as potential Islamist terrorist attacks may add extra flames to their misguiding narratives. Government should devote resources to communicate these threatening topics promptly to eliminate the general frustration in people. Responsible media practices should also be established to avoid sensational and alarmist reporting of worrisome events.[56]
- Countering extremist narratives may be even more effective once persuasive influencers are former "believers or defectors".[57]
- The EU Counter-Terrorism Coordinator called attention to the threat of right-wing extremism and terrorism. His discussion paper proposed the development and sharing of good practices through the Radicalization Awareness Network, which was established by the European Commission.[58]
- UN Security Council Resolution 1624 (2005) called on states to prohibit incitement to terrorism and the glorification of terrorist acts. This legally binding provision applies to all types of terrorism, including far-right-inspired violence.[59]
- The so-called Aarhus model in Denmark represents a particularly remarkable approach. The concept is based upon municipality-level cooperation with

the police via community engagement and family support to prevent radicalization.[60]

Multifaceted approaches characterize the fight against right-wing extremism and terrorism in the United Kingdom and more recently in Germany. In both of these instances, countermeasures embrace the prosecution of violent attacks and the proscribing of worrisome organizations.[61]

Norway is another noteworthy example here, which has built up a society-wide approach to combat all forms of violent extremism. Nine government industries and several civil society organizations are involved in its action plan against radicalization.[62]

- To enhance the effectiveness of countering violent extremism programs, it is crucial to involve all relevant stakeholders.[63] It is also important to act proactively once early indications of violence or intent for committing such acts are noted.[64]
- Although these online platforms have in place policies that prohibit behavior that is motivated by hatred, prejudice, or intolerance, their actions to counter such malicious acts are mainly reactive and never proactive.[65]
- Young people are widely targeted by extremists through online gaming platforms. These alt-right groups use such online teenager gaming communities "to recruit culture warriors".[66] Parental responsibility should be enhanced to detect the warning signs of radicalization. Guides compiled by radicalization experts should be distributed through schools to raise awareness and provide advice for families on what to search for and how to respond.
- The quest for significance[67] is an important common factor in individuals who are prone to engage in extremism. This paired with enthusiasm towards weapons, military lifestyle, and patriotic ideologies may be all valuable assets and considerable potential for security forces. Recruitment programs, community-level events, and specialized law enforcement or military secondary schools should reach out to these young people and offer a narrative, a pathway, and a good purpose to fight for. It would be important to get in touch with these juveniles during those years when they are seeking self-identity and social bonds. A meticulous vetting screening process would ensure that individuals with psychological disorders are filtered out. Nurturing with great care a new generation for the military and law enforcement community can help these youngsters manage their grievances and find the meaning of their lives while pursuing something that is of their interest.

Instagram's, Facebook's, and YouTube's recommended video function plays a major role in users' viewing habits, which often begin automatically after the video they are watching has finished playing. These algorithms may divert users to malicious online content. What is more concerning is that these algorithms do not create new content. These channels exist and through these recommendations, users may be connected and interact with each other. Thereby the fragmented units of the far right may unite via such instruments.[68] To counter this, it needs to be acknowledged that recommending content is not the act of a neutral platform, and therefore specific legal liabilities are to be set for such actions.[69]

Previous case studies show that recruitment regularly happened through posters with Nazi slogans.[70] This may suggest that threat groups target individuals who are not laics but are already familiar with far-right ideologies. Considering that these recruiting posters were placed on campuses, educational institutions should draw attention to concerning students who may have expressed their extremist views and may be more vulnerable to these recruiting attempts.

Law enforcement and military members are key targets for far-right threat groups' radicalization efforts. In the German Parliamentary Oversight Panel's 2020 December report, the committee concluded: "in the Bundeswehr and in several other security services on federal and state level (police and intelligence agencies) – despite a security screening – there are a number of public servants with an extreme far right and violence-oriented mindset".[71] Having an extremist presence in the law enforcement and military can truly undermine public trust in these institutions especially among "marginalized and persecuted communities".[72]

- Meticulous insider threat programs and their oversight mechanisms should be established to counter armed-group infiltration into security forces. Vulnerable individuals in the security forces should be scrutinized in all stages of their service. Vetting procedures should be revised and counter extremism education should be given a particular emphasis.[73] At the same time, law enforcement and military officers who have been engaged in extremist movements should be held responsible for their acts.[74] Reforms should address necessary changes in the training and education of the staff.[75]
- German Federal Office for Military Counterintelligence Service (Bundesamt für den Militärischen Abschirmdienst, BAMAD) introduced a new comprehensive concept for tackling extremism in the ranks of military forces. German domestic intelligence services maintain a database on criminal acts of extremism, together with worrisome individuals considered high risk for violence. In accordance with the novel provisions, through an early background check, applicants' data are cross-checked with this database on extremists.[76] Meanwhile, specialized commissioners operate at local police headquarters explicitly tackling extremism and anti-Semitism in the ranks of security forces.[77]
- Veterans with psychological or physical problems may be more vulnerable to these attempts. Therefore, specified programs should be developed and

> delivered to provide rehabilitation and reintegration assistance for these former militants.[78]

Consistent prosecution and sentencing of far-right individuals en masse may generate new platforms for radicalization in prisons.

> White supremacist groups, such as the Aryan Brotherhood, long thrived in U.S. prisons; recall that dangerous criminal groups such as the Mara Salvatrucha (MS-13), Calle 18, and the Mexican Mafia were born in or fostered by prisons in the United States and abroad.[79]

Right-wing extremists' imprisonment should be diligently monitored to counter such radicalization efforts.

It has been argued that there is no such thing as a "typical extremist", these individuals come from a range of backgrounds and experiences. Influencing factors are complex, multifaceted, and compound, this is the complexity and diversity[80] that should be better understood. As a response to the intertwined nature of the root causes for radicalization, countermeasures should be organized across the prevailing domains. Simultaneously, each individual has his or her own pathway towards radicalization, therefore each story should be assessed on a case-by-case basis. Four essential pillars should be included in an effective countering violent extremism strategy, namely, "breaking down deeply-entrenched conspiracy theories both online and offline, developing social media-based counter-radicalization tools, embracing a whole-of-society approach, and expanding exit paths".[81]

Acknowledging that radicalization is a multidimensional phenomenon, its dynamics could be better grasped via locally based counterstrategies. The ultimate goal of these bottom-up approaches is building resilient communities.[82] In parallel, consistent efforts are necessary to educate people on identifying the first indications of radical behavior. Searching for purpose and bonds is one of the most frequently identified reasons for engaging in radicalization. Seeking self-identity and meaning, however, can be taught and can be learnt.[83] Mental health programs should embrace these practices to develop the skills for "meaning-making".[84] Such comprehensive prevention strategies presume a multi-agency approach in which police, social and healthcare services, educational institutions, as well as civil society should be involved.[85] Best practices should be regularly exchanged among the participating partners. This balanced collaboration may eliminate instances of excessive detection, which may give rise to contra-productiveness.[86]

The complexity of individual circumstances should be taken into account when assessing the risk. Similarly, the progress in each individual case is to be closely monitored.[87] At the same time, through established responsible and trustful collaboration, reporting mechanisms of vulnerable individuals should be set to enable communication in a timely manner. While novel social and economic consequences of the COVID-19 pandemic considerably increased the vulnerability to radicalization, spending more time at home office or due to digital schooling may enhance the chances for early intervention in the radicalization process. Focused communication campaigns should raise citizens' attention to keep their watchful eyes on members of their communities who may be exposed to radicalization.

Modus operandi

Designating a threat group as a terrorist entity is one of the instruments which enables the most effective prosecution of a terrorist threat. By proscribing an extremist formation, their property can be frozen or seized. Considering the loosely connected far-right terrorist milieu, it may be an even more severe consequence of proscription that participating in or contributing to an activity of a terrorist group is against the law, too. This means that not only active engagement but recruitment and fundraising for these formations are also illegal.[88] Designation, however, is not an appropriate tool to counter so-called soft extremist violence which is a serious predictor of future physical violence. Soft violent activities such as wearing specific clothing, using memes and symbols do not constitute a terrorist offence, additionally, members of these right-wing movements can freely join other, non-designated formations.[89] Disbanding and reforming far-right threat groups is not an unprecedented phenomenon. "In the UK, proscribed National Action reformed as Sonnenkrieg Division, while in the US an affiliated group, Atomwaffen Division (AWD), disbanded after the arrests of prominent members and rebranded as the National Socialist Order (NSO) in mid-2020".[90] It is not the physical group but the existence of hateful online propaganda which is more concerning in these instances. Proscription from this perspective could not cease either the followers' enthusiasm or their access to ideology. It is a more credible scenario that right-wing groups continue to operate in a more decentralized operational environment.[91]

Fundamentally, countering international terrorism is a top-down concept in which local agencies mostly rely on central agencies with nationwide jurisdiction. In the case of domestic terrorism, however, a bottom-up approach should be adopted. Suspicious transactions and worrisome individuals could be best detected by local authorities. In parallel, single local points should be designated to ensure a smooth flow of intelligence.[92] Proactive communication should be encouraged among relevant authorities and representatives of local communities to ensure a consistent exchange of information.[93] At the same time, authorities should maximize the utilization of existing partnership working arrangements. Authorities' deterrence capacity should be enhanced by effective prosecutions of unlawful activities. As a consequence, the increasing number of right-wing extremists in prisons and their rehabilitation back to society should be given particular attention.[94]

It has been articulated that a better understanding of far-right extremism-inspired political violence is necessary to effectively counter the associated threat. Far-right ideology and violence is not novel phenomena. Both the concepts and the conspiracy theories are well known by authorities. This historical knowledgebase should be further deepened by recent trends to fortify counter-efforts in dismantling the fractioned far right.[95] With this in mind, a comprehensive and rigorously compiled database on right-wing attacks and seized weapons as well as explosives could provide highly informative insights into the details of threat groups' operations. Building upon the information in the constructed database, a series of trend analyses can be provided. This detailed set of incident data allows for delineating the broad characteristics of trends, measuring the metrics of the criminal trafficking/smuggling/theft/sale/attempted or completed plots and also serves to identify non-random spatial and temporal patterns. Trend analysis – as a powerful tool for strategic planning – would provide a reliable basis for threat assessment and forecasting of hot trafficking spots; moreover, it could contribute to the identification and development of channels of smuggling or trafficking. The consistent analyses of the above-indicated perspectives could delve into the practical attributes of the perpetration and ensure a widespread, empirical examination of these incidents' characteristics and thus formulate an insightful understanding of the phenomenon. Furthermore, the outcome of the research would enrich our understanding of the terrorists' operational environment and could offer deeper insights into their modus operandi, technical/tactical capabilities and practices, and links to organized crime. Finally, this analysis will allow for more accurate forecasting of far-right threats, and thereby overcome both exaggerated speculations and downplayed risks.

This information repository would be highly informative for counter-efforts in numerous ways.

- First, analysts should draw the implications of all relevant house search records and then share these findings with law enforcement and intelligence authorities in the widest possible scope. This may help these agencies better understand threat groups' modus operandi and more practically, anticipate what kind of firearms or explosive devices may emerge at upcoming scheduled demonstrations. A very similar document was produced by the US National Explosives Task Force, which is responsible for coordinating data and information sharing about explosive incidents between the Bureau of Alcohol, Tobacco and Firearms (ATF) and local, state, and federal agencies. The report outlined the use of various explosive devices which were confiscated from protesters around the country or found at the scene of attempted and successful bombing attacks since May 2020.

The document was circulated in January 2021 in the United States "in preparation for potential violent activity in connection with upcoming presidential inauguration events and to enhance first responder and bomb technician awareness by highlighting examples of devices and their tactical employment".[96] Such bailouts are even more valuable once considering the difficulties in detecting worrisome transactions. The major difficulty resides, however, in the fact that right-wing extremists operate in their own homeland, and logistics are easier to be arranged considering their familiarity with local opportunities.

- Second, based upon the tactics of far-right extremists, stricter legislation to ban some types of guns and strengthening background checks could prevent easy access to these frequently used firearms.[97] Mapping national legislative regimes on gun control could shed light on loopholes, where legislation could be strengthened.[98] In the preparation of legislative proposals law enforcement and intelligence agencies' representatives should be actively involved to ensure that the requirements are in line with prevailing criminal trends.
- Third, with such a meticulous dataset the origin of seized weapons by extremists could be identified. For these purposes, from previous house search reports investigators should try to establish the origin of weapons and with forensic examinations determine whether they have been used in crimes.[99]
- Fourth, based upon the target selection of far-right threat groups, operators of the most worrisome venues should be encouraged to enhance security arrangements to deter and prevent potential terrorist attacks.[100]
- Fifth, by learning the lessons of recorded right-wing extremist attacks, local communities should be better educated on potential warning signs and stable points for reporting, and communications should be established. These measures can considerably mitigate the harmful effect of a future terrorist attack.
- It is a recurring phenomenon that prosecuted right-wing extremists proved to have previous criminal records. To enhance the effectiveness of counter-efforts, authorities should establish and meticulously apply a mechanism to index racial or ethnic-related hate crime offenders and allocate resources to maintain a rolling file on them. Monitoring the types of criminal activities these individuals have been prosecuted for could also provide useful information for authorities.

Without a solid regulative framework for right-wing-inspired extremism and violence, authorities are unable to charge offenders with a dedicated criminal offence. Until a threat group is designated as a terrorist entity, law enforcement agencies can only apply charges such as illegal possession or carrying of weapons, drug-related criminal activities, or rioting offences.[101] For more effective combat against far-right terrorism, these competencies should be reconsidered and expanded.[102] With this in mind, specific attention should be paid to hate crimes, which may be important indications of extremism.[103] Investigating and prosecuting hate crimes as well as advancing reporting mechanisms may develop better transparency relating to these criminal activities. Targeted anti-hate crime programs should introduce another focus and challenge hate speech, especially online.[104]

Serious concerns exist regarding the threat posed by extreme right-wing groups' access to unregistered firearms. Guides on how to manufacture homemade pistols were seized by law enforcement officials after the assassination of British parliament member Jo Cox in 2016. An 18-year-old man was arrested for stockpiling manuals on creating automatic weapons. Later in February 2020, German police seized "a slam-fire shotgun during a raid on a terrorist cell planning attacks on mosques and assassinations of politicians".[105] Arguably, 3D-printed guns made completely from plastics are not resistant enough for firing live rounds and therefore are generally strengthened by original metal parts. To avoid detection, The Base for instance manufactured the so-called Tec-9 firearm, where the metal barrel was assembled with a 3D-printed receiver. Compared with Europe, such firearms may more likely remain undetected by US authorities, considering that most gun components are not regulated in the United States.[106]

- To be able to more accurately evaluate the risks associated with novel technologies, Veilleux-Lepage emphasizes that analyses of these threats are required to "consider the existing limitation of these technologies along with alternative (and often easier) means by which terrorists can obtain firearms. However, this need to also be balanced by an understanding and recognition that the appeal of 3D-printed weapons far exceeds their effectiveness".[107] Homemade firearms have obvious limitations, which needs to be taken into consideration. The technical skill of the manufacturer, 3D-printed weapons' lower level of professionality, as well as the unreliability of available manuals are all important factors that may determine whether extremists will resort to these novel technologies compared with other, more familiar traditional means.[108] In the case of countries, however, where it is challenging for criminals to acquire real guns, it is more likely that threat groups will apply novel technologies and by risking to use reliable weapons they can fill in these operational loopholes.[109]
- Nevertheless, isolated case studies like Anders Behring Breivik, who spent months experimenting with bomb supplies demonstrate that there is a small subset of terrorists who are dedicated enough to improve the reliability of these weapons.[110] Veilleux-Lepage remembers us that "one of the most striking lessons from the Report of the 9/11 Commission was the suggestion that the failure to prevent the attack was partly a failure

of imagination – a situation wherein something seemingly predictable and undesirable was not properly planned for".[111]

- Similarly, although the "likelihood of right-wing extremists using armed UAVs in attacks is considered low",[112] this may change as knowhow on exploiting these technologies will grow. For these reasons, extremists' interests, capabilities, and transnational networks should be consistently monitored.

Conclusion

We have been thrilled to interpret our research findings in policy terms and enrich existing counter-strategies and legislative regimes with our implications. Therefore, this chapter has attempted to first identify the development of right-wing extremists' operational practices in fundraising, recruitment, communication techniques, as well as their mode of operation. Second, based upon these detected functionalities recommendations on future counter-policies have been put forward.

Notes

1 FATF, "Ethnically or racially motivated terrorism financing, FATF", Paris, France, 2021. www.fatf-gafi.org/publications/methodsandtrends/documents/ethnically-racially-motivatedterrorism-financing.html
2 Tom Keatinge, Florence Keen, and Kayla Izenman, "Fundraising for right-wing extremist movements". The RUSI Journal, 164(2), 10–23, 2019. DOI: 10.1080/03071847.2019.1621479
3 Ibid.
4 Jason M. Blazakis and Naureen Chowdhury Fink, "The international far right terrorist threat requires a multilateral response", Lawfare, 4 April 2021. www.lawfareblog.com/international-far right-terrorist-threat-requires-multilateral-response
5 The Soufan Center, "Countering terrorist financing and strategic communications: Lessons learned for tackling far right terrorism", June 2021. https://thesoufancenter.org/wp-content/uploads/2021/06/TSC-Issue-Brief_June-2021_COUNTERING-TERRORIST-FINANCING.pdf
6 FATF, "Ethnically or racially motivated terrorism financing, FATF".
7 Peter Stone, "US far right extremists making millions via social media and cryptocurrency", *The Guardian*, 10 March 2021. www.theguardian.com/world/2021/mar/10/us-far right-extremists-millions-social-cryptocurrency
8 The Soufan Center, "Countering Terrorist financing and strategic communications".
9 Blazakis and Fink, "The international far right terrorist threat requires a multilateral response".
10 The Soufan Center, "Countering terrorist financing and strategic communications".
11 Ibid.
12 Financial Action Task Force, "Operational reports on fighting terrorist financing". https://graces.community/faft-terrorist-financing/

13 Jason M. Blazakis and Naureen Chowdhury Fink, "The international far right terrorist threat requires a multilateral response".
14 Ibid.
15 "Eurojust expert workshops on violent right-wing extremism and terrorism summary of the discussions", April 2021. www.eurojust.europa.eu/eurojust-expert-workshops-violent-right-wing-extremism-and-terrorism
16 Ibid.
17 Ibid.
18 UN CTED, "Member states concerned by the growing and increasingly transnational threat of extreme right-wing terrorism", CTED Trend Alert, July 2020. www.un.org/securitycouncil/ctc/sites/www.un.org.securitycouncil.ctc/files/files/documents/2021/Jan/cted_trends_alert_extreme_right-wing_terrorism_july.pdf
19 FATF, "Ethnically or racially motivated terrorism financing, FATF".
20 Similar to Gibraltar Financial Intelligence Unit, "Counter terrorist financing guidance notes", February 2021. www.gfiu.gov.gi/uploads/docs/publications/Counter-Terrorist-Financing-Guidance-v1.0.pdf
21 Gibraltar Financial Intelligence Unit, "Counter terrorist financing guidance notes", February 2021. www.gfiu.gov.gi/uploads/docs/publications/Counter-Terrorist-Financing-Guidance-v1.0.pdf
22 George Selim, "A persistent and evolving threat: An examination of the financing of domestic terrorism and extremism", 15 January 2020. www.adl.org/media/13945/download
23 Ibid.
24 FATF, "Ethnically or racially motivated terrorism financing, FATF".
25 Tom Keatinge, Florence Keen, and Kayla Izenman, "Fundraising for right-wing extremist movements".
26 FATF, "Ethnically or racially motivated terrorism financing, FATF".
27 "New technologies: The emerging terrorist financing risk", ACAM's Today Europe, 3 June 2020. www.acamstoday.org/new-technologies-the-emerging-terrorist-financing-risk/; Selim, "A persistent and evolving threat".
28 Tom Keatinge, "A sharper image: Advancing a risk-based response to terrorist financing", RUSI, 9 March 2020. https://rusi.org/explore-our-research/publications/occasional-papers/sharper-image-advancing-risk-based-response-terrorist-financing
29 FATF Report, "Financing of recruitment for terrorist purposes", January 2018. www.fatf-gafi.org/media/fatf/documents/reports/Financing-Recruitment-for-Terrorism.pdf
30 Tom Keatinge, "A sharper image: Advancing a risk-based response to terrorist financing".
31 Selim, "A persistent and evolving threat".
32 Ibid.
33 Ibid.
34 Bethan Johnson, "Financing right-wing extremism and terrorism", Project Craaft, Research Briefing no. 5, 2020. https://static1.squarespace.com/static/5e399e8c6e9872149fc4a041/t/5fbb892005f44a5f70a75317/1606125861203/CRAAFT+RB5+Final+Version.pdf
35 Bethan Johnson, "Financing right-wing extremism and terrorism".

36 Majlie de Puy Kamp and Scott Glover, "Right-wing extremists and their supporters use Christian website to raise funds", CNN, 20 January 2021. https://edition.cnn.com/2021/01/19/us/give-send-go-extremism-invs/index.html
37 Institute for Strategic Dialogue, "Bankrolling bigotry: An overview of the online funding strategies of American hate groups", 2020. www.isdglobal.org/wp-content/uploads/2020/10/bankrolling-bigotry-3.pdf
38 "Testimony of Lecia Brooks Chief of Staff, Southern Poverty Law Center before the Subcommittee on National Security, International Development and Monetary Policy Committee on Financial Services United States House of Representatives", 25 February 2021. www.splcenter.org/sites/default/files/splc_statement_for_house_financial_services_subcommittee_hearings_on_domestic_terrorism_financing.pdf
39 Ibid.
40 Ibid.
41 Southern Poverty Law Centre, "Bitcoin and the alt-right". www.splcenter.org/bitcoin-and-alt-right
42 Eric Carson, "Here's where Nazi sympathizers go to raise money", CNET, 4 December 2017. www.cnet.com/news/neo-nazi-sympathizers-crowdfunding/
43 Chainanalysis Team, "Alt-right groups and personalities involved in the January 2021 Capitol riot received over $500K in bitcoin from French donor one month prior", Insights, 14 January 2021. https://blog.chainalysis.com/reports/capitol-riot-bitcoin-donation-alt-right-domestic-extremism
44 Will Carless, "Crowdfunding hate: How white supremacists and other extremists raise money from legions of online followers", *USA Today*, 5 February 2021. https://eu.usatoday.com/story/news/nation/2021/02/05/bitcoin-crowdfunding-used-white-supremacists-far right-extremists/4300688001/
45 "Directive (EU) 2018/843 of the European Parliament and of the Council of 30 May 2018 amending Directive (EU) 2015/849 on the prevention of the use of the financial system for the purposes of money laundering or terrorist financing, and amending Directives 2009/138/EC and 2013/36/EU", Official Journal of the European Union, 30 May 2018. https://eur-lex.europa.eu/legal-content/EN/TXT/PDF/?uri=CELEX:32018L0843&from=EN
46 "New technologies: The emerging terrorist financing risk", ACAM's Today Europe.
47 "Testimony of Lecia Brooks Chief of Staff, Southern Poverty Law Center before the Subcommittee on National Security, International Development and Monetary Policy Committee on Financial Services United States House of Representatives".
48 Ibid.
49 Ibid.
50 Kyle Daly and Sara Fischer, "The online far right is moving underground", Axios, 12 January 2021. www.axios.com/the-online-far right-is-moving-underground-e429d45d-1b30-46e0-82a3-6e240bf44fef.html
51 Siladitya Ray, "The far right is flocking to these alternate social media apps — Not all of them are thrilled", *Forbes*, 14 January 2021. www.forbes.com/sites/siladityaray/2021/01/14/the-far right-is-flocking-to-these-alternate-social-media-apps---not-all-of-them-are-thrilled/?sh=2555c1e255a4
52 "Building Resilience & Confronting Risk in the COVID-19 Era: A Parents & Caregivers Guide to Online Radicalization", Southern Poverty Law Center/American University's Polarization and Extremism Research and Innovation Lab (PERIL). www.splcenter.org/sites/default/files/splc_peril_covid_parents_guide_jan_2021_1.pdf

53 "Germany introduces extremism counseling service", DW, 9 January 2019. www.dw.com/en/germany-introduces-extremism-counseling-service/a-47005422
54 "Government acts to overhaul Prevent in the fight against radicalization", 8 February 2023. www.gov.uk/government/news/government-acts-to-overhaul-prevent-in-the-fight-against-radicalisation
55 Daniel Koehler, "Right-wing extremism and terrorism in Europe current developments and issues for the future", *PRISM*, 6(2), 84–105, 2016. https://cco.ndu.edu/PRISM/PRISM-Volume-6-no-2/Article/839011/right-wing-extremism-and-terrorism-in-europe-current-developments-and-issues-fo/
56 "Far right groups to continue successful radicalization and recruitment campaigns in 2021; raising the potential for attacks and unrest", Max Security. www.max-security.com/security-blog/far right-groups-to-continue-successful-radicalization-and-recruitment-campaigns-in-2021-raising-the-potential-for-attacks-and-unrest/
57 Vanda Felbab-Brown, "How to counter right-wing armed groups in the United States", Brookings, 21 January 2021. www.brookings.edu/blog/order-from-chaos/2021/01/21/how-to-counter-right-wing-armed-groups-in-the-united-states/
58 "Right-wing extremism and terrorism in the European Union: Discussion paper", EU Counter-Terrorism Coordinator, 30 August 2019. www.statewatch.org/media/documents/news/2019/sep/eu-council-ctc-right-wing-11756-19.pdf
59 "UN Security Council Resolution 1624", United Nations Security Council, 2005, https://undocs.org/S/RES/, 311624(2005).
60 European Commission, "Aarhus model: Prevention of radicalisation and discrimination in Aarhus". https://ec.europa.eu/home-affairs/node/7423_en
61 Counter Extremism Project, "Violent right-wing extremism and terrorism transnational connectivity, definitions, incidents, structures and countermeasures", November 2020. www.counterextremism.com/sites/default/files/CEP%20Study_Violent%20Right-Wing%20Extremism%20and%20Terrorism_Nov%202020.pdf
62 The Soufan Center, "Countering terrorist narratives and strategic communications: Lessons learned for tackling far right terrorism".
63 Ibid.
64 Ibid.
65 Mark Keierleber, "How white extremists teach kids to hate", The 74 Million, 29 January 2021. www.the74million.org/article/where-hate-is-normalized-how-white-extremists-use-online-gaming-communities-popular-among-teens-to-recruit-culture-warriors/
66 Ibid.
67 Arie Kruglanski, "How the quest for significance and respect underlies the white supremacist movement, conspiracy theories and a range of other problems", The Conversation, 11 March 2021. https://theconversation.com/how-the-quest-for-significance-and-respect-underlies-the-white-supremacist-movement-conspiracy-theories-and-a-range-of-other-problems-156027
68 Jonas Kaiser and Adrian Rauchfleisch, "Unite the right? How YouTube's recommendation algorithm connects the U.S. far right", Medium, 11 April 2018. https://medium.com/@MediaManipulation/unite-the-right-how-youtubes-recommendation-algorithm-connects-the-u-s-far right-9f1387ccfabd
69 Center for Countering Digital Hate: Briefing Note, "Malgorithm". https://252f2edd-1c8b-49f5-9bb2-cb57bb47e4ba.filesusr.com/ugd/f4d9b9_9877528dd81b402b948044ab10a989d9.pdf

70 Bradley Jurd, "Recruitment posters for Antipodean Resistance plastered over Bathurst CSU campus", Western Advocate, 2 January 2018. www.westernadvocate.com.au/story/5147145/recruitment-posters-for-antipodean-resistance-on-bathurst-csu-campus/

71 "Erkenntnisse, Beiträge und Maßnahmen von Bundesamt für den Militärischen Abschirmdienst, Bundesamt für Verfassungsschutz und Bundesnachrichtendienst zur Aufklärung möglicher rechtsextremistischer Netzwerke mit Bezügen zur Bundeswehr", PKGr Report, 11 December 2020.

72 Jessica White, "Far right extremism in the US: A threat no longer ignored", RUSI Commentary, 1 February 2021. https://rusi.org/commentary/far right-extremism-us-threat-no-longer-ignored

73 Seth G. Jones, Catrine Doxsee, and Grace Hwang, "The military, police, and the rise of terrorism in the United States", CSIS Brief, 12 April 2021. www.csis.org/analysis/military-police-and-rise-terrorism-united-states

74 Felbab-Brown, "How to counter right-wing armed groups in the United States".

75 Florian Flade, "The insider threat: Far right extremism in the German military and police", CTC Sentinel, June 2021. www.ctc.usma.edu/wp-content/uploads/2021/05/CTC-SENTINEL-052021.pdf

76 Ibid.

77 Cynthia Miller-Idriss, "When the far right penetrates law enforcement", Foreign Affairs, 15 December 2020. www.foreignaffairs.com/articles/united-states/2020-12-15/when-far right-penetrates-law-enforcement?utm_medium=social&utm_campaign=fb_daily_soc&utm_source=facebook_posts

78 Felbab-Brown, "How to counter right-wing armed groups in the United States".

79 Ibid.

80 Ömer Ta¸spınar, "Fighting radicalism, not 'terrorism': Root causes of an international actor redefined". *SAIS Review*, XXIX(2), 76, 2009. www.brookings.edu/wp-content/uploads/2016/06/summer_fall_radicalism_taspinar.pdf

81 Jacob Ware, "Fighting back: The Atomwaffen Division, countering violent extremism, and the evolving crackdown on far right terrorism in America". *Journal for Deradicalization*, Winter 2021, https://journals.sfu.ca/jd/index.php/jd/article/view/411/253

82 Search for Common Ground, "Bottom-up approach to countering violent extremism in Tunisia, final evaluation report". www.sfcg.org/tag/violent-extremism/

83 Radicalisation Awareness Network, "A mental health approach to understanding violent extremism", Ex Post Paper RAN Policy and Practice, 3 June 2019, p. 7. https://ec.europa.eu/home-affairs/sites/homeaffairs/files/what-we-do/networks/radicalisation_awareness_network/about-ran/ran-h-and-sc/docs/ran_hsc_prac_mental_health_03062019_en.pdf

84 C. S. Lloyd, B. af Klinteberg, and V. DeMarinis, "An assessment of existential worldview function among young women at risk for depression and anxiety—A multi-method study". *Archive for the Psychology of Religion*, 39(2), 165–203, 2017.

85 City of Copenhagen Employment and Integration Administration, "Less radicalization through an effective and coherent effort", August 2015, p. 23. www.kk.dk/sites/default/files/uploaded-files/Recommendations%20of%20the%20Expert%20Group%20-%20Municipality%20of%20Copenh...pdf

86 Pomme Woltman and Wessel Haanstra, "Ex post paper on a holistic local approach to preventing radicalization in Helsinki", 2017, p. 9. https://ec.europa.eu/home-affairs/sites/homeaffairs/files/what-we-do/networks/radicalisation_awareness_network/ran-papers/docs/ran_paper_holistic_local_approach_to_preventing_radicalisation_8-9_06_en.pdf
87 Ibid.
88 Garth Davies and Edith Wu, "Proud Boys terrorist group designation may deter new recruits and fundraising", The Conversation, 11 February 2021. https://theconversation.com/proud-boys-terrorist-group-designation-may-deter-new-recruits-and-fundraising-154718
89 Candyce Kelshall, "Designating the Proud Boys a terrorist organization won't stop hate-fuelled violence", The Conversation, 9 February 2021. https://theconversation.com/designating-the-proud-boys-a-terrorist-organization-wont-stop-hate-fuelled-violence-154709; Graham Macklin, "'Only bullets will stop us!' – The banning of National Action in Britain". Perspectives on Terrorism, 12(6), 104–122, 2018. www.jstor.org/stable/26544646.
90 Jennifer Percival, "An endless game of whack-a-mole?", The Interpreter, 4 March 2021. www.lowyinstitute.org/the-interpreter/endless-game-whack-mole
91 Daniel Sallamaa and Tommi Kotonen, "The case against the Nordic Resistance Movement in Finland: An overview and some explanations", Science Norway, 3 November 2020. https://sciencenorway.no/blog-extremists-researchers-zone/the-case-against-the-nordic-resistance-movement-in-finland-an-overview-and-some-explanations/1765952
92 Seth G. Jones, Catrina Doxsee, and Nicholas Harrington, "The tactics and targets of domestic terrorists", CSIS Briefs, July 2020. https://csis-website-prod.s3.amazonaws.com/s3fs-public/publication/200729_Jones_TacticsandTargets_v4_FINAL.pdf
93 "Managing far right activity toolkit". https://preventforfeandtraining.org.uk/wp-content/uploads/2017/09/Managing-Far right-Activity-Toolkit.pdf
94 Vanda Felbab-Brown, "How to counter right-wing armed groups in the United States".
95 Bruce Hoffman and Jacob Ware, "The terrorist threat from the fractured far right", Lawfare, 1 November 2020. www.lawfareblog.com/terrorist-threat-fractured-far right
96 Jason Wilson, "Explosives and weaponry found at US far right protests, documents reveal", *The Guardian*, 5 May 2021. www.theguardian.com/us-news/2021/may/05/explosives-incendiary-devices-found-far right-protests
97 Seth G. Jones, Catrina Doxsee, and Nicholas Harrington, "The tactics and targets of domestic terrorists".
98 "Germany: 1,200 right-wing extremists licensed to own weapons", DW, 2 February 2021. www.dw.com/en/germany-1200-right-wing-extremists-licensed-to-own-weapons/a-56416420
99 "Austrian police seize haul of weapons intended for German extremists", Reuters, 12 December 2020. www.reuters.com/article/austria-arms-idUSKBN28M0O5
100 Seth G. Jones, Catrina Doxsee, and Nicholas Harrington, "The tactics and targets of domestic terrorists".
101 Ware, "Fighting back".

102 Jon Lewis and Seamus Hughes, "Our laws have a problem calling domestic terrorism what it is", *The Hill*, 6 February 2020. https://thehill.com/opinion/national-security/481166-our-laws-have-a-problem-calling-domestic-terrorism-what-it-is
103 Jon Lewis and Seamus Hughes, "White supremacist terror: Modernizing our approach to today's threat", April 2020. https://extremism.gwu.edu/sites/g/files/zaxdzs2191/f/White%20Supremacist%20Terror%20final.pdf
104 John Coyne, "ASIO sounds the alarm", Asia and the Pacific Policy Society. www.policyforum.net/asio-sounds-the-alarm/
105 Eric Woods, "Right-wing extremists' new weapon", Lawfare, 15 March 2020. www.lawfareblog.com/right-wing-extremists-new-weapon
106 Eric Woods, "Right-wing extremists' new weapon".
107 Yannick Veilleux-Lepage, "CTRL, HATE, PRINT: Terrorists and the appeal of 3D-printed weapons", ICCT Publications, 13 July 2021. https://icct.nl/publication/ctrl-hate-print-terrorists-and-the-appeal-of-3d-printed-weapons/
108 Eric Woods, "Right-wing extremists' new weapon".
109 Hyder Abbasi, "What's behind far right trend of using 3D tech to make guns?", Al-Jazeera, 31 July 2021. www.aljazeera.com/news/2021/7/31/what-behind-far right-trend-using-3d-tech-make-guns
110 Eric Woods, "Right-wing extremists' new weapon".
111 Yannick Veilleux-Lepage, "CTRL, HATE, PRINT: Terrorists and the appeal of 3D-printed weapons".
112 Håvard Haugstvedt, "The right's time to fly?". *The RUSI Journal*, 166(1), 22–31, 2021. DOI: 10.1080/03071847.2021.1906161

APPENDIX: TEN FAR-RIGHT ATTACKS

1. Christchurch Mosque shootings

Date: 15 March 2019
Australian national Brenton Tarrant shot and killed 51 people and wounded 40 others during Friday prayer on 15 March 2019.[1] The 28-year-old gunman entered two mosques, first the Al Noor and 12 minutes later drove to the Linwood Islamic Centre.[2] White supremacist attacker livestreamed the first shooting on Facebook[3] and prior to the attack posted an online manifesto.[4] He meticulously prepared for the attack, visited the Al Noor mosque several times,[5] and practiced shooting in the range of a South Otago gun club.[6] He was a frequent member of right-wing discussions on 4chan and 8chan,[7] and also came into contact with far right organizations during his trips to Europe.[8] In his manifesto, titled The Great Replacement, he claimed to have been inspired by Anders Breivik and white supremacist Dylan Roof, who killed nine African Americans at a church in Charleston, South Carolina.[9]

Before the Christchurch attack, both Australia and New Zealand reported that their main security risk was from Islamist terrorism. The latest annual report of New Zealand's Security Intelligence Service made no reference to right-wing extremism.[10] Meanwhile, the New Zealand Human Right Commission reported about 100 race- and religion-related hate crimes during the period of 2004–2012. These collected media reports included incidents ranging from murder and kidnapping to serious assault, abuse, deliberate damage to property, and desecration of sacred sites.[11] According to the Australian Security Intelligence Organisation's 2017 report the country "experiences low levels of communal violence [...] one person was charged with far-right terrorism in 2016".[12] The document did not dismiss the possibility of a far-right attack but claimed that "far right extremist attacks would probably target the Muslim and left-wing community, be low-capability, and be more likely to be perpetrated by a lone actor or small group on the periphery of organized groups".[13] Two days prior to the attack Tarrant tweeted images about the weapons he was about to use, 30 minutes before the shootings he detailed his plans in an online forum. A few minutes before the attack he emailed a manifesto explaining the reasons for his actions. The fact that Tarrant had no close friends and was financially independent considerably diminished the chances for warning signs.[14]

Prior to the attack, the Global Peace Index had New Zealand as the second most peaceful country on the planet.[15] The terror rating was "low" (meaning attacks were believed to be unlikely). The national homicide rate by firearms (about 10 a year for the whole country) was insignificant by international standards.[16] When assessing the right-wing threat in New Zealand, two important factors should be considered. First, the far-right followers – of a couple of hundred – were nurtured online. Tutorials and guides teach people how to obtain, manufacture, and use weapons. At the same time, these virtual communities reinforce individual extremist ideologies.[17] Second, weapons are easily accessible in New Zealand. "Its rate of gun ownership is one of the highest in the world and civilians are able to legally obtain semiautomatic guns".[18] About 4.6 million New Zealanders own 1.5 million guns.[19] Only six days after the attack, the New Zealand Parliament passed the gun reform bill and banned the sale of all military-style semi-automatics and assault rifles.[20] In its second set of gun reforms, a new firearms registry was introduced. License holders will be required to update this repository as they buy or sell guns.[21]

The last two years of 2010s decade witnessed a surge in far-right terror attacks. The October 2018 synagogue shooting in Pittsburgh, PA; the March 2019 gun attacks on mosques in Christchurch, New Zealand; the April 2019 Poway, CA, synagogue shooting; the August 2019 attack targeting the Hispanic community at a Walmart in El Paso, TX; and the October 2019 Halle, Germany, shootings, in which a synagogue was targeted. Poway, El Paso, and Halle attackers all referred to Tarrant and his "Great Replacement" in their online manifestos.[22] Considering these copycat attacks, Tarrant has further internationalized right-wing terrorism. Far-right entities historically had widespread international connections with like-minded groups, but their target audience was the nation of their origin. His manifesto and the livestreaming of his acts have designed the far right's own weapons.[23] Posting these outlets in English facilitates reaching out to followers on a global scale. This elevated level of publicity about an attack is also a novelty. Previously, publicity was considered as a risky potential to be detected by authorities.[24]

Reported incidents suggest the persistence of the elevated risk in New Zealand.[25] A soldier who headed a white nationalist group was charged with espionage in November 2020. He is accused of giving information to another country or foreign organization threatening New Zealand's security.[26] Still, in November 2020, a teenager's confrontational posts drew NZ authorities' attention. The student planned to shoot teachers and fellow pupils at a school. Police found a shotgun and a semi-automatic rifle together with three improvised explosive devices during the search of his house.[27] New Zealand has been on a heightened alert, especially around the anniversary of the 15 March Christchurch attack. Police raided a property in the Christchurch suburb of St Albans, removed computer equipment, and arrested two people on 4 March 2021. Police said an online threat was made earlier against the Al Noor mosque and the Linwood Islamic Centre.[28]

2. Bombing of the Alfred P. Murrah Federal Building in Oklahoma City

Date: 19 April 1995
The deadliest act of domestic terrorism in US history happened on 19 April 1995. The explosion killed at least 186 people, injured more than 680 others, and destroyed or damaged 324 other buildings and 86 cars.[29] Ex-soldiers and anti-government extremists Timothy McVeigh and Terry Nichols were charged with the act.[30] McVeigh, a veteran of the Gulf War, sympathizing with the so-called US militia movement detonated a rented Ryder truck loaded with 2,200 kg of explosives[31] in front of the building.[32] He was motivated by his dislike for the US federal government and his disillusion over its handling of the Waco Massacre in 1993.[33] The timing of the plot was the second anniversary of the fire that ended the Waco siege on the Branch Davidians sect in Waco, TX.[34] Nichols had assisted him in manufacturing the bomb.[35] During the meticulous planning of the assassination,[36] McVeigh and Nichols obtained and then stored the hazardous chemicals in rented sheds.[37] McVeigh's intentions were to improve Ramzi Yousef's attack, who planted a fertilizer bomb under the World Trade Center two years earlier.[38] Investigators started to track the rented vehicle and found McVeigh in prison, who was arrested by an Oklahoma State Trooper 90 minutes after the blast for driving in a car with a missing license plate.[39] In the aftermath of the attack, the US Congress passed the Antiterrorism and Effective Death Penalty Act of 1996 and legislation to strengthen security around federal buildings.

The Oklahoma Bombing was not the beginning of the extreme right wing's surge in the United States, but rather its culmination. There was a rise in violent far-right extremism in the 1980s as a result of the fact that far-right movements recruited from the US military, especially after the Vietnam war.[40] The Southern Poverty Law Center alerted Janet Reno, the United States Attorney General, to "the growing danger posed by unauthorized militias that have recently sprung up in at least eighteen states".[41] Inter alia he drew attention to the conviction of 22 members of Order, an armed and fanatical white racist group in 1984. The charged people had robbed armored cars, possessed military weapons, and killed a prominent figure in Denver.[42]

Anti-government extremism in the United States in the early 1990s was fueled by numerous triggering events. This includes the election of Bill Clinton after 12 years of a conservative administration, the North American Free Trade Agreement, and gun-control-related legislation.[43] Two incidents further accelerated separatist ideologies. First, at Ruby Ridge, FBI agents and US marshals engaged in an 11-day standoff with Randy Weaver and his family in a remote cabin in Idaho. Weaver shared the Aryan Nation's white supremacist and anti-government views. After he refused to become an ATF informant, federal agents issued weapon charges against him. He did not turn up at trial and the US Marshal Service was responsible to arrest him on 21 August 1992. The situation turned violent and Weaver's wife, his 14-year-old son, as well as a US marshal were killed in the siege.[44] At the Waco siege starting in early 1993, federal agents raided a compound of a millennial Christian sect called the Branch Davidians near Waco, TX. The siege ended on 19 April 1993, and caused the death of 75 people including 25 children.[45] The government handling of both incidents is considered to have fueled the anti-government voices of US homegrown militias.

After the deadliest domestic terror attack on US soil, the Clinton Administration approved the Omnibus Counterterrorist Act to bolster US deterrence of terrorism. In line with this, the need to improve the gathering and sharing of intelligence has been articulated. President Clinton proposed the establishment of a domestic counter-terrorism center under the aegis of the FBI. To help improve coordination among intelligence and law enforcement agencies, the center should collect, analyze, and disseminate timely information on domestic terrorist groups.[46]

Echoing the Oklahoma bombing, in 2017, 23-year-old Jerry Varnell was taken in custody by FBI charges that he had planned to blow up an Oklahoma City bank building with a van loaded with explosives. An undercover agent posed as a co-conspirator and supervised Varnell's actions who intended to build a 454 kg explosive device. He also prepared a message that would have been circulated on social media after the explosion.[47] Marking the 25th anniversary of the Oklahoma bombing, US law enforcement agencies argued that the threat posed by violent white supremacists and anti-government extremists remains persistent and evolving. "Significant drivers have remained constant, for instance, perceptions of government overreach, reactions to immigration policies together with the argument for the superiority of the white race".[48]

3. Anders Behring Breivik

Date: 22 July 2011

A 32-year-old Norwegian right-wing extremist held accountable for the two sequential domestic terrorist attacks on 22 July 2011.[49] The first explosion was plotted inside a van in the government quarter of Oslo. The blast killed 8 people and injured at least 209 people.[50] Less than two hours later occurred the second attack at a summer camp organized by the youth division of the ruling Norwegian Labour Party. In a homemade police uniform, Breivik took a ferry to the island and opened fire at the participants killing 69 and injuring at least 110.[51] He was meticulously preparing for the attacks, mastered his shooting skills, and as a training aid used the Call of Duty video game.[52] In his 1,518-page compendium, he expressed his militant far-right ideology and xenophobic worldview.[53] Breivik was diagnosed criminally insane with paranoid schizophrenia and was psychotic at the time of offending.[54]

Breivik claimed to be a modern-day Templar Knight, a Christian crusader fighting to chase Islam from Europe and rid the world of "Marxists".[55] In his manifesto, he argued that he had operated as an online ideological guide for others in forum discussions. He also established contact with online communities, which "had a considerable influence on him".[56] He used the internet not only for ideological but also for operational purposes. He obtained weapons, purchased chemicals and tools but also raised money for their own actions online. Breivik was placed on Norway's intelligence watch list as buying chemical fertilizer from a Polish company that was under scrutiny. The transaction was regarded as legal, therefore there was no reason for further investigation.[57]

His manifesto titled "2083 – A European Declaration of Independence" was cited by right-wing blogs as valuable reading material. Russian far-right entities chanted "Glory to Anders Breivik" in the national movement's annual Russian March in Moscow, and his assertions were shared extensively on right-wing forums.[58] Admiration for Breivik was on the rise until early 2015. Important contacts of Breivik's circles were detected via about 4,000 letters sent and received during his detainment. After the first 12 months in detention, the Norwegian Ministry of Justice ordered to isolate Breivik and started to censor his incoming and outgoing letters. This was a milestone in losing sympathizers, Breivik fans shut down their forums and turned to other national heroes.[59]

Prior to the Norway attacks, Europol had noticed an elevated level of sophistication and a surge in far-right propaganda. Even though the threat of a large-scale attack was considered to be on the decline. As the 2010 Europol report concluded, there is a "lack of cohesion, a lower degree of overall coordination of right-wing terrorist and extremist groups, little public support and effective law enforcement operations [...] had gone a long way towards accounting for the diminished impact of right-wing terrorism".[60] In parallel with this, European interior ministers agreed to revisit the threat posed by far-right extremists, and the EU Radicalisation Awareness Network was established to operate in September 2011.[61] Breivik's case drew authorities' attention to the fact that right-wing extremists substantially differ from those neo-Nazi fanatics who carried out violent acts in 1980s Europe. This new far right has a more considerable support base.[62]

In 2012, Czech and Polish authorities foiled two Breivik copycat attacks. Breivik-sympathizer, Vojtěch Mlýnek, was stockpiling weapons and manufacturing a remotely operated explosive device when police arrested him.[63] Meanwhile, Brunon Kwiecień, a 45-year-old lecturer in chemical engineering at the Agricultural University of Cracow, was preparing a similar attack against the lower house of the Polish parliament.[64] With charges to carry out violent extremist attacks, four people were arrested in the United Kingdom between January 2013 and June 2015.[65] Twenty-year-old Adam Lanza – allegedly obsessed with Breivik – opened fire at an elementary school in Newtown, CT, on 14 December 2012. He shot and killed 26 people including 20 young people before shooting himself.

Terrorist acts in modern Norwegian history were predominantly perpetrated by right-wing extremists.[66] Populist right-wing Progress Party of which Breivik was a member got into the Norwegian parliament in 2013 in alliance with the Conservative Party. While the Conservative Party gained control over economic policies, Progress settled down the principles for the national immigration and integration policy. In its 2019 annual threat assessment, the Norwegian Police Security Service placed the threat from radical Islamists on top of the list and declared the threat posed by right-wing extremism as "very unlikely".[67] A 21-year-old white nationalist Norwegian national, Philip Manshaus, opened fire inside Al-Noor Islamic Centre on 10 August 2019. Earlier on the same day, Manshaus shot to death his stepsister, who was adopted from China as a 2-year-old, her mother married Manshaus' father later.[68]

Capitalizing on the economic recession and immigration, there has been an increasing support base of nationalist political parties in Europe. For instance, the National Front in France, the Dutch Freedom Party, together with the Norwegian Progress Party, all entered the national political mainstream. There are only estimations of how many Europeans are involved in far-right parties. According to German intelligence sources, the number of ultra-rightists is around 25,000 including those 5,000 who are of great security concern. The Swedish far-right internet forum Nordisk.nu has 22,000 followers.[69] A 2008 report of collaboration among Dutch organizations claimed that

> right-wing terrorism is not always labeled as such because right-wing movements use the local traditions, values, and characteristics to define their own identity, the report argued, many non-rightist citizens recognize and even sympathize with some of the organization's political opinions – a formulation which will be familiar to Indians, where communal violence is almost never referred to as a form of mass terrorism.[70]

The European Union Security Commissioner, Sir Julian King, asserted, "I'm not aware of a single EU member state that is not affected in some way by right-wing violent extremism. I think we also need to keep in mind the growing menace of right-wing violent extremism".[71] He cited the Breivik massacre in Oslo, the assassination of British MP Jo Cox, and attacks on asylum centers in Sweden. On the ninth anniversary of the Oslo attack, the threat posed by the far right remained persistent. Data emerging from the UK Home Office asserted that the number of far-right prisoners is record high, with 44 people serving their sentence for terror offences.[72]

4. Thwarted Singapore attack

Date: 27 January 2021

A 16-year-old boy was the first detainee on 27 January 2021, inspired by far-right extremist ideology in Singapore. He was arrested for allegedly planning to knife Muslims in two nearby mosques on the Christchurch attacks anniversary. Inspired by Brenton Tarrant, the detained boy intended to livestream his attack. Due to the strict gun-control rules in Singapore, he decided to use a machete instead of a rifle like Tarrant.[73] The boy intended to steal his father's credit card and arrive at the scene driving a rented car without a driving license. The ministry of home affairs claimed that he is a Protestant Christian of Indian ethnicity and has been motivated by a strong antipathy towards Islam and a fascination with violence. "He was watching Islamic State propaganda videos and falsely believing that IS represents Islam. He prepared a manifesto for dissemination prior to the attack".[74] While in detention, he will receive a comprehensive program of religious, psychological, and social rehabilitation.[75]

Singapore has not suffered any terrorist attacks since the mid-1990s.[76] Nevertheless, the state-country regards the threat of a terrorist attack as potential and attempts to proactively react to the ever-changing trends in terrorism.[77] Considering its multi-ethnic and multi-religious population, social resilience is the bastion of its counter-terrorism strategy. It believes that "reducing racial and religious tension in this multi-ethnic and multi-religious country is critical in preventing future acts of terrorist violence in Singapore".[78] Aligning with this, first the Inter-Racial Confidence Circles were established for the country's 84 constituencies.[79] Later so-called Harmony Circles were organized for schools and work places,[80] the government launched the Community Engagement Program in 2006[81] and the Religious Rehabilitation Group was formed with Islamic scholars and teachers.[82] In 2009 security arrangements around soft targets in the country were upgraded. At the same time, a new standard for hotel security was set.[83] The 2017 new Infrastructure Protection Act increased businesses' responsibility for high-risk events with a large crowd.[84] To enhance the protection of critical IT infrastructure against cyber-espionage and cyber-terrorism, the Singapore Infocomm Technology Security Authority was founded.[85] To test the country's multi-agency response plan, the largest counter-terrorism exercise with the participation of the Singapore Civil Defence Force, the Immigration and Checkpoint Authority, the Singapore Armed Forces, and the People's Association took place between 17 and 18 October 2016.[86]

Singaporean security services successfully thwarted numerous attempts to carry out violent extremist acts prior to detaining the teenager boy. Since 2015, about 32 self-radicalized individuals were arrested because of indications of violent behaviors. The Internal Security Department announced that it had arrested a former full-time national serviceman, Amirull Ali who had been self-radicalized and was sympathetic to Palestinians in Israel. A 33-year-old Malaysian was deported in February 2021 and intended to join the Islamic state.[87] Singapore Law and Home Affairs minister declared that "since 2015, seven people under the age of 20 have been detained or given restriction orders under the International Security Department".[88] An increase in Anti-Muslim sentiments had been recorded prior to the incident. The Centre for Research in Islamic and Malay Issues noted a growing number of instances for microaggression towards the Muslim community.[89]

5. El Paso shooting

Date: 3 August 2019
Patrick Wood Crusius, a 21-year-old from Allen, TX, shot and killed 23 people and injured 23 others at a Walmart store in El Paso, TX, on 3 August 2019. The gunman drove 11 hours through Texas, walked into the store, and opened fire with a semi-automatic WASR-10 rifle. Later he surrendered to police as he was driving away from the scene. The incident has been recorded as the deadliest attack on Latinos in modern US history. Crusius allegedly posted a manifesto with white nationalist and anti-immigrant themes on 8chan prior to the attack. He cited the Christchurch mosque shootings and the right-wing conspiracy theory known as the Great Replacement as inspiration for the attack. Seven weeks after the El Paso shooting, the acting homeland security secretary announced a roadmap plan for how the Department of Homeland Security will switch to homegrown terrorist threats from foreign ones.[90]

Although Crusius acts were affected by preceding high-profile far-right attacks, there are noteworthy differences compared with Anders Breivik or Brenton Tarrant. Crusius' manifesto was compiled in a rush – according to his words in the document – and he spent "maybe a month or less"[91] preparing for the attack. His mother had concerns over his son possessing an AK-type firearm and called the City of Allen Police Department roughly five weeks prior to the massacre. Her anonym call did not raise any suspicion as she did not claim any threat posed by his son to himself or others.[92] As Professor Kathleen

Belew at the University of Chicago asserts, El Paso was not a single act of violence, a generations-old social movement is behind it. The most worrisome is that these attacks are not meant to be the end point of this organizing, but are ideological and political actions that may recruit new members into the movement.[93]

Numerous violent right-wing incidents preceded Crusius' mass shooting. White supremacist John T. Ernest opened fire inside a synagogue in Poway, CA, in April 2019.[94] Some months before, in November 2018, Scott Beierle killed two people and wounded four others when opening fire inside a yoga studio in Tallahassee, FL. The virulently racist former high school teacher and army veteran was associated with online misogynists.[95] Only days earlier, in October 2018, white supremacist Robert Bowers massacred 11 people and injured 7 more at the Tree of Life synagogue in Pittsburg, PA.[96] There has been an upsurge in the frequency of far-right attacks in the United States. Between 2007 and 2011, there were 5 or fewer incidents per year, in 2012 this rose to 14, and then in 2017 up to 31.[97] According to the Anti-Defamation League in 2018, right-wing extremists were responsible for at least 50 killings, which is higher than in any year since the Oklahoma City Bombing in 1995 when again a far-right extremist killed 186 people. In the 2010s decade, right-wing extremists committed 73.3% of extremist killings compared with 23.4% by Islamic jihadists.[98] In 2018 and 2019, at least four major attacks occurred in the United States (including one in Texas) conducted by racially motivated actors, and at least four other incidents were thwarted. This activity outnumbered other types of domestic terrorism.[99]

There was only one right-wing attack in the 12 months after the El Paso shooting where people were injured. In this case, incel-fed Armando Hernandez Jr. opened fire at a shopping mall and wounded three people.[100] Nevertheless, thwarted and foiled far-right attacks in this time frame depict the elevated level of the right-wing-related terror threat. The alleged plots in these instances varied from synagogues, mosques, a hospital, an African-American church, and a local LGBTQ-friendly bar.[101] White supremacists continued to inflict the Hispanic community via propaganda and online narratives. Hate crimes rose by 9% in the major US cities in 2018 for a fifth consecutive increase.[102] As the FBI said, in 2019 the agency had 5,000 open terrorism cases and 850 of these are domestic.[103] The Center on Extremism recorded nearly as much white supremacist rhetoric in the first seven months of 2020 as for the whole year in 2019.[104] The Texas-based Patriot Front, the New Jersey European Heritage Association, and the American Identity Movement circulated anti-immigration propaganda.[105] Twenty-nine-year-old Alex Barron of Horizon City was arrested on 9 May 2021, by the El Paso Federal Bureau of Investigation. The man was charged with alleged active shooter threats against El Paso Walmart stores.[106] A 43-year-old El Paso man was detained after he had posted a video online threatening to kill Black Lives Matter protesters. In the video, Manuel Flores showed an AR-15-style rifle and said “it was his dream to kill Black protesters”.[107]

6. Hanau shootings

Date: 19 February 2020
Tobias Rathjen (43-year-old), a far right extremist shot and killed nine people and wounded five others targeting two shisha bars in Hanau on 19 February 2020.[108] After the attacks, the gunman returned to his apartment, where he killed his mother and then committed suicide.[109] The attacker legally possessed a hunting license and weapons since 2002, despite the fact that German authorities were aware of the perpetrator’s paranoid delusions.[110] He left behind a letter of confession in which he expressed extreme right-wing views.[111] Through his own YouTube account and his personal website, Rathjen shared English- and German-language content with the clear intention to reach out to not only German-speaking but a broader audience.

The evolving threat posed by the far right raised concerns prior to the Hanau attack. A week beforehand German police raided a neo-Nazi cell, whose members were planning to carry out attacks on mosques, politicians, and asylum-seekers.[112] In Halle, in October 2019, Stephan Balliet shot two people and wounded two others. He livestreamed his acts as trying to storm a synagogue. Walter Lübcke, a pro-migrant politician was shot and found dead in his garden in June 2019. The attacker was linked with far-right connections. A 38-year-old right-wing extremist was arrested in Neuhausen, Munich, on 15 October 2019, for an anti-Semitic attack on teenagers. A wheelchair-bound Libyan migrant was assaulted by a group of people in Chemnitz on 14 September 2019. One of the attackers yelled anti-immigrant slogans at him. A 26-year-old Eritrean man was shot on 22 July 2019, in a small town near Frankfurt in an alleged racist attack. A 27-year-old man stabbed a 16-year-old traveler in a tram in Bremen after shouting anti-Muslim narratives.[113] An 18-year-old, Iranian-German David Ali Sonboly opened fire at fellow teenagers at a McDonald’s restaurant on 22 July 2016.[114] In 2018, altogether 1,091 firearms were confiscated from right-wing extremists, which shows a 61% increase compared with the previous year.[115]

The German government issued an 89-point policy paper in the aftermath of the Hanau attacks. The document addressed the threat posed by right-wing extremism and racism and put forward recommendations on strengthening the cooperation of security agencies, raising the funds for civil society organization, and enhancing the prevention work.[116] For the period of 2021–2024, the German government allocated more than 1 billion euros to fight racism and right-wing terrorism. More specifically, they articulated the need for a better understanding of the root causes of racism and right-wing extremism.[117]

7. Eric Rudolph

Date: 27 July 1996
The Centennial Olympic Park bombing was Eric Rudolph's first violent attack on 27 July 1996.[118] He planted a backpack with an explosive device during a free concert in Atlanta, GA, where thousands gathered to celebrate the Olympics. The blast killed a woman and injured 100 others.[119] Police had received a warning call prior to the attack, but the bomb exploded earlier than the anonymous caller said.[120] Shortly after, Rudolph plotted three more explosions, one at an Atlanta abortion clinic and another at a gay bar in suburban Atlanta. Two of the Atlanta attacks included secondary devices, timed to detonate after law enforcement officers had arrived to the scene.[121] A fourth bombing rocked an abortion clinic in Birmingham, killing a police officer and severely wounding a nurse.[122] After a five-year manhunt, Rudolph was arrested in 2003.[123] Certain media outlets portrayed him as being a supporter of the white supremacist Christian Identity movement.[124] Rudolph denied these allegations and offered religious motives for his militant opposition to abortion.[125] His social environment made him develop personal grievances that drove him to commit violent acts. His views were greatly influenced by the Patriot movement, and his anti-government rhetoric was instilled by his mother from his early age.[126]

Right-wing movements heavily relied on former members of the Army in the 1990s. Like Timothy McVeigh, Rudolph was also a former military member and a part of a growing violent far-right extremism in the 1980s and 1990s. According to 2013 statistics, 3.5% of the surveyed 17,080 soldiers were contacted by extremist organizations for recruitment purposes.[127] As he said in a statement, he bombed the Olympics "to embarrass the United States on the world stage for legalizing abortion".[128] This was the first attack in the United States that drew authorities' attention to abortion clinics and major sporting events as potential soft targets for terrorists.

According to the Southern Poverty Law Center, white radicals were responsible for attempted terrorist attacks in 2018. Only one of them was considered Islamic terrorism in which a former white supremacist started to engage in Islamic beliefs prior to the attack.[129] Between 2007 and 2017, there was a 1,450% increase in far-right terrorist attacks.[130] In 2009, the US Department of Homeland Security issued a report titled "Right-wing Extremism: Current Economic and Political Climate Fuelling Resurgence in Radicalisation and Recruitment" warning that small cells as members of "leaderless resistance"[131] together with "white supremacist lone wolves"[132] are the most pertaining threat to the homeland. The document raised serious concerns over far-right extremists' endeavor to recruit veterans in order to "boost their violent capabilities".[133] This echoed a very similar violent extremist trend that was predominant in the 1990s in the United States.[134]

8. Ted Kaczynski, The Unabomber

Date: 1978 to 1995
The former Mathematics professor killed 3 and wounded 23 others in a nationwide bombing campaign between 1978 and 1995.[135] He argued that his violent acts were necessary to draw attention to the erosion of industrialization.[136] He targeted people who advance modern technologies and thereby destruct the environment.[137] He mailed or hand-delivered highly sophisticated explosive devices that varied widely through the years.[138] Kaczynski left false clues in most of the bombs and involved the theme of nature or wood.[139] His manifesto was published in *The Washington Post* on 19 September 1995. Its linguistic idiosyncrasies helped authorities identify Kaczynski as the author of the manuscript.[140]

As global warming and its climate impacts are getting more extreme, right-wing extremists have reinterpreted eco-fascism and attempted to capitalize on environmentalism to accelerate hatred.[141] White supremacist rhetoric with ecological narratives started to gain ground in the far-right community.[142] Kaczynski is still a prominent figure for these eco-fascists. This ideology has been thriving in the online subculture since the release of the Netflix show titled "Manhunt: Unabomber in 2017". Supporters of the eco-fascist Pine Tree Party movement embrace ideologies that promote infrastructure damage and violence. The subscribers of the Pine Tree Party's public channel on Telegram have been increasing rapidly and due to the fact that they are present on various social media platforms, communication among followers is well-connected. It is of great concern that according to the manifestos of El Paso shooter Patrick Crusius as well as Brenton Tarrant and Anders Breivik, all of them shared eco-fascist ideologies.[143] As Crusius wrote, "if we can get rid of enough people then our way of life can become more sustainable".[144] Finnish ecologist writer Pentti Linkola also plays a prominent role in contemporary eco-fascism. He clearly "calls for an end in immigration, the reversion to pre-industrial life ways and authoritarian measures to keep human life within strict limits".[145] Through this dictatorship, killing people en masse could eliminate overpopulation which he claims to be the main reason for the degradation of the planet.[146]

Restrictions due to the COVID-19 pandemic provided a new perspective for eco-fascists. They argue that coronavirus is the vaccine for nature as in times of lockdowns the earth can recover. Claiming that we humans are the virus and we need to die to protect the planet is the core idea of the rising tide of eco-fascism.[147] Considering that we need to cope with the climate crisis and live together with coronavirus, obscure discussions in the digital sphere warn about the rising threat of eco-fascism.[148]

9. Michael Holt

Date: 2017
White supremacist, 27-year-old, Michael James Holt was sentenced to 4.5 years for stockpiling an arsenal of weapons and child pornography offences in 2017.[149] He threatened to carry out a mass shooting in a shopping center on the NSW Central Coast. He expressed his neo-Nazi views on his online profiles. Australian authorities confirmed that he is not affiliated with any far-right groups, but is rather a loner with developmental difficulties.[150] Holt has Asperger's syndrome and low intelligence capabilities, but his homemade weapons prove his sophisticated skills.[151]

As the director general of the Australian Security Intelligence Organization (ASIO) said in 2020, the threat of right-wing terrorism was real and growing, and the number of terror-related investigations doubled compared with the previous year.[152] In its 2017–2018 annual report ASIO noted "While the threat of terrorist attacks conducted by lone actors continues, these threats are not isolated to Islamic extremists. Individuals motivated by other ideologies – such as extreme left or right-wing ideology – may consider conducting an act of terrorism".[153] There was only one closely preceded far-right incident recorded by ASIO. Thirty-one-year-old Phillip Michael Galea in Melbourne was charged with preparations for an alleged terrorist attack. According to the prosecution, Galea intended to overcome "the perceived Islamisation of Australia".[154] He allegedly had affiliations with the UK Combat 18 and the United Patriots Front in Australia.

A significant shift has been observed in the Australian right-wing extremists' narratives towards a more far-right and violent ideology.[155] Anti-immigrant rhetoric is a "strategic tool"[156] for far-right entities. They strive to capitalize on the ambiguity and fear associated with immigration. These narratives lack factual bases. "The overwhelmingly productive and law-abiding 2% of the Australian nation is blamed for the country's economic and social problems".[157] Compared with the situation in Europe and the United States, the Jewish diaspora is less frequently attacked in Australia. Nevertheless, the Executive Council of Australian Jewry reported a year-by-year 30% increase in the number of verbal harassment and intimidation towards Jews.[158] According to a 2019 national survey, 82% of Asian Australians, 81% of Australian of Middle East descent, and 71% of Indigenous Australians had experienced forms of discrimination.[159]

The ASIO 2019–2020 Annual Report asserted "right-wing extremists are more organized, sophisticated, ideological and active than previous years [...] these individuals compromised around one-third of our counter-terrorism investigative subjects".[160] Director General of ASIO Mike Burgess added that the number of terrorist cases leads under investigation doubled in 2019. "While we expect any right-wing extremist-inspired attack in Australia to be low capability, i.e. a knife, gun or vehicle attack, more sophisticated attacks are possible".[161] The document went on to say that these groups and individuals promptly seized on the COVID-19 pandemic and see it "as proof of the failure of globalization, multiculturalism and democracy, and confirmation that societal collapse and a 'race war' is inevitable".[162] Considering the elevated level of isolation among young people due to the epidemiological restrictions, the Parliamentary Joint Committee on Intelligence and Security inquired into extremism and radicalization in Australia.[163]

Meanwhile, in March 2021, neo-Nazi Sonnenkrieg Division was formally listed in Australia. This United Kingdom-based terrorist organization is the first right-wing entity to be banned on the Australian continent. Consequently, it became an offence to be a member of the group, fund, or in any other ways associate with its members.[164] Although Australian security agencies reported no Australian directly involved with Sonnenkrieg Division, concerns are growing to list other worrisome right-wing groups. In a Western Victorian national park, a group of 30 men practiced Nazi salutes and chanted Nazi slogans in January 2021. Local residents stated that the participants posted stickers with emblems of the National Socialist Network.[165]

10. Capitolium Siege

Date: 6 January 2021
The Department of Homeland Security reported in 2020 that white supremacists remain the "most persistent and lethal threat in the homeland".[166] A mob of protesters rioted the United States Capitol on 6 January 2021. In the unrest, five individuals were killed and over 100 people were injured.[167] Federal authorities arrested almost 300 individuals[168] who participated in the 6 January riot. Members of various extremist groups throughout the country coalesced in the storm of the US Capitol. They are allegedly affiliated with organizations such as The Three Percenters, The Oath Keepers, Proud Boys, and Texas Freedom Force.[169] Several followers of the QAnon online conspiracy theory were also arrested.[170] Charged persons arrived at the siege from over 180 counties throughout the United States.[171] It was an unprecedented event when previously concurring and disparate extremist groups mobilized themselves together. It is of great concern whether these violent extremists have established links with each other and will mobilize themselves together in the future.[172]

The Anti-Defamation League reported that right-wing domestic extremists were responsible for 75% of 435 violent terrorist attacks in the United States between 2010 and 2019. The year 2019 was the deadliest year for right-wing extremist violence since the Oklahoma bombing in 1995.[173] An internal 2009 DHS report warned the administration that the economic recession together with the election of the first Black President "could create a fertile recruiting environment for right-wing extremists".[174] There has been a steady growth in the far-right-related threat. According to the Southern Poverty Law Center, the number of home-grown extremist groups increased by 250% in the first year of Barack Obama's presidency. The number of hate groups operating across the United States increased to a record high – 1,020 – in 2018.[175] Right-wing extremists were liable for two-thirds of the attacks on US soil in 2019. Between 1 January and 8 May 2020, this ratio increased to 90%.[176]

The 2020 Homeland Security Threat Assessment warned of "ideologically motivated lone offenders and small groups, who will pose the greatest terrorist threat to the Homeland, with domestic violent extremists presenting the most persistent and lethal threat".[177] In practice, the threat may have been "downplayed".[178] The bulletin issued by the FBI, the Department of Homeland Security, and the National Counter-terrorism Centre concluded that in 2021 the "anti-government specifically militia violent extremists will likely pose the greatest domestic terrorism threats".[179] The United States Capitol Police Department issued a statement on 3 March 2021, about potential threats towards the members of Congress and the Capitol complex. Security arrangements have been accordingly upgraded on the venue.[180] The FBI sent a memo to law enforcement agencies on 11 January 2021, alerting them of potential armed protests at all 50 state Capitols. Accordingly, capital cities and their police department reported increased security and monitoring of the events.[181] In April 2020, armed protesters attempted to storm the legislative chambers of the state capitol in Lansing.[182] In October 2020, members of a right-wing militant group were arrested who tried to kidnap and kill the state's democratic governor, Gretchen Whitmer.[183]

Some days after the inauguration of President Joe Biden, the National Terrorism Advisory Bulletin claimed that "information suggests that some ideologically-motivated violent extremists with objections to the exercise of governmental authority and the presidential transition, as well as other perceived grievances fueled by false narratives, could continue to mobilize to incite or commit violence".[184] Due to the associated threat, Biden's director of national intelligence works together with the FBI and the DHS. The National Security Council's new four-person office set a 100-day deadline to look into the problem and identify ways how to effectively counter it.[185] As the FBI director advised Congress on 2 March 2021, the agency is working on about 2,000 domestic terrorism cases, which is more than double as it was in September.[186]

Far-right online propaganda and the militia subculture ideology have been thriving since the COVID-19 lockdowns. By mid-April 2020, at least 125

Boogaloo-promoting groups were identified on Facebook, 60% of these were founded within three months with an online membership of 73,000.[187] The YouTube video titled "Top 5 Boogaloo Guns" was watched 340,000 times.[188] In 2020, white supremacist propaganda efforts doubled compared with the previous year according to the Anti-Defamation League's Center on Extremism. While in 2019, about 2,724 incidents were reported, in 2020 a total of 5,125 cases were recorded.[189] In a COVID-19-related thwarted attack, Timothy Wilson died in a shooting with FBI agents, who tried to arrest him. He was suspected to attack a hospital with an explosive-loaded vehicle in its parking lot. He was also considering a nuclear plant and Islamic centers and the Walmart headquarters as potential plots.[190]

Another worrisome circumstance that the FBI also acknowledged is the white supremacist infiltration of law enforcement. These violent extremist groups not only recruit from law enforcement communities, but law enforcement officers in ranks volunteer their professional resources for white supremacist purposes.[191] About 6–10% of Oath Keepers members are active-duty police officers and military officials. Even more followers are veterans or retired officers.[192] Likewise, ranks of police and the army make up a considerable number of Three Percenters' members.[193]

Notes

1 "Christchurch shootings: How the attacks unfolded", BBC News, 18 March 2019. www.bbc.com/news/world-asia-47582183
2 Helen Regan and Sandi Sidhu, "49 killed in mass shooting at two mosques in Christchurch, New Zealand", CNN, 15 March 2019. https://edition.cnn.com/2019/03/14/asia/christchurch-mosque-shooting-intl/index.html
3 "Christchurch mosque attack livestream" New Zealand Classification Office. www.classificationoffice.govt.nz/news/featured-classification-decisions/christchurch-mosque-attack-livestream/
4 Taylor Lorenz, "The shooter's manifesto was designed to troll", The Atlantic, 15 March 2019. www.theatlantic.com/technology/archive/2019/03/the-shooters-manifesto-was-designed-to-troll/585058/
5 Patrick Gower, "Christchurch shooting: Survivors convinced gunman visited mosque to learn layout", Newshub, 12 April 2019. https://web.archive.org/web/20200415113542/www.newshub.co.nz/home/new-zealand/2020/04/christchurch-shooting-survivors-convinced-gunman-visited-mosque-to-learn-layout.html
6 "Christchurch mosque shootings: Bruce Rifle Club closes in wake of terror", New Zealand Herald, 17 March 2019. www.nzherald.co.nz/nz/christchurch-mosque-shootings-bruce-rifle-club-closes-in-wake-of-terror/4SOM7W7KD7QAE4X6UC5ZR5SHD4/
7 Nick Perry, "Report finds lapses ahead of New Zealand mosque attack", AP News, 8 December 2020. https://apnews.com/article/intelligence-agencies-shootings-brenton-tarrant-new-zealand-new-zealand-mosque-attacks-d8217fa30fe4eeba45fb001b77857385

8 Kim Sengupta, "Brenton Tarrant: Suspected New Zealand attacker 'met extreme right-wing groups' during Europe visit, according to security sources", Independent, 15 March 2019. www.independent.co.uk/news/world/australasia/brenton-tarrant-new-zealand-attacker-far-right-europe-gunam-shooting-a8825611.html
9 Tarrant, Brenton, "The great replacement", pp. 4–6. www.ilfoglio.it/userUpload/113 The_Great_Replacementconvertito.pdf
10 New Zealand Security Intelligence Service, "Annual report 2018". www.nzsis.govt.nz/assets/Uploads/2018-NZSIS-Annual-Report.pdf
11 Human Rights Commission Te Kahui Tika Tangata, "Reports of race and religious hate crime in New Zealand 2004–2012", June 2019. www.hrc.co.nz/files/1515/6047/9685/It_Happened_Here_Reports_of_race_and_religious_hate_crime_in_New_Zealand_2004-2012.pdf
12 Australian Government Australian Security Intelligence Organisation, "ASIO annual report 2016–17". www.asio.gov.au/sites/default/files/Annual%20Report%202016-17.pdf
13 Australian Government Australian Security Intelligence Organisation, "ASIO annual report 2016–17". www.asio.gov.au/sites/default/files/Annual%20Report%202016-17.pdf
14 Daniel L. Byman, "Reflections on the Christchurch commission report", Brookings, 16 December 2020. www.brookings.edu/blog/order-from-chaos/2020/12/16/reflections-on-the-christchurch-commission-report/
15 "New Zealand ranked the second most peaceful country in the world", NZ Herald, 19 June 2019. www.nzherald.co.nz/travel/new-zealand-ranked-the-second-most-peaceful-country-in-the-world/DU2ZNGX2I34TRLJLB36P6Y4LPQ/
16 Merrit Kennedy, "In New Zealand, mass shootings are very rare", NPR, 15 March 2019. www.npr.org/2019/03/15/703737499/in-new-zealand-mass-shootings-are-very-rare
17 "Christchurch shootings: Far-right attack 'could happen in UK too' ", BBC News, 18 March 2019. www.bbc.com/news/uk-47618176
18 Alexander Gillespie, "New Zealand was warned a terror attack was possible", Al Jazeera, 19 March 2019. www.aljazeera.com/opinions/2019/3/19/new-zealand-was-warned-a-terror-attack-was-possible
19 Philip Alpers and Michael Picard, "New Zealand—Gun facts, figures and the law", GunPolicy.org, 17 February 2020.
20 "New Zealand votes to amend gun laws after Christchurch attack", Reuters, 10 April 2019. www.reuters.com/article/us-newzealand-shooting-parliament-idUSKCN1RM0VX
21 "New Zealand tightens gun laws further in response to mass shooting", Reuters, 18 June 2020. www.reuters.com/article/us-newzealand-shooting-idUSKBN23P0TE
22 Friderike Wegener, "The globalisation of right-wing copycat attacks", Global Network on Extremism and Technology, 16 March 2020. https://gnet-research.org/2020/03/16/the-globalisation-of-right-wing-copycat-attacks/
23 Daniel Koehler, "The Halle, Germany, synagogue attack and the evolution of the far-right terror threat", CTC Sentinel, December 2019.
24 Daniel Koehler, "Right-Wing Terrorism in the 21st Century the 'National Socialist Underground' and the History of Terror from the Far-Right in Germany". Routledge, 2018.

25 Alexander Gillespie, "Two years on from the Christchurch terror attack, how much has really changed?", The Conversation, 14 March 2021. https://theconversation.com/two-years-on-from-the-christchurch-terror-attack-how-much-has-really-changed-156850
26 Florence Kerr and Thomas Manch, "Linton soldier is the first New Zealander to be charged with espionage", Stuff, 25 November 2020. www.stuff.co.nz/national/300167448/linton-soldier-is-the-first-new-zealander-to-be-charged-with-espionage
27 Jared Savage, " 'Terrorist attack': How police thwarted heavily armed teen's plan to shoot teachers, classmates in South Island school", NZ Herald, 13 November 2020. www.nzherald.co.nz/nz/terrorist-attack-how-police-thwarted-heavily-armed-teens-plan-to-shoot-teachers-classmates-in-south-island-school/UIBDQEDPD5OCWPJLYN34DSI53U/
28 "New Zealand police arrest two for threat to Christchurch mosques attacked in 2019", ABC, 4 March 2021. www.abc.net.au/news/2021-03-04/new-zealand-police-arrest-two-plot-christchurch-mosques/13217304
29 History.com Editors, "Oklahoma City Bombing", 16 December 2009. www.history.com/topics/1990s/oklahoma-city-bombing
30 "Oklahoma City Bombing", FBI History. www.fbi.gov/history/famous-cases/oklahoma-city-bombing
31 Lou Michel and Dan Herbeck, "American terrorist", Scientific American, 2001. https://archive.org/details/americanterroris00loum/page/217
32 "Timothy McVeigh", Britannica. www.britannica.com/biography/Timothy-McVeigh
33 Douglas O. Linder, "The Oklahoma City Bombing and the trial of Timothy McVeigh", 2006. http://law2.umkc.edu/faculty/projects/ftrials/mcveigh/mcveighaccount.html
34 Andrew Gumbel, "Oklahoma City bombing: 20 years later, key questions remain unanswered", The Guardian, 13 April 2015. www.theguardian.com/us-news/2015/apr/13/oklahoma-city-bombing-20-years-later-key-questions-remain-unanswered; Kelly-Leigh Cooper, "Oklahoma City bombing: The day domestic terror shook America", BBC News, 19 April 2020. www.bbc.com/news/world-us-canada-51735115
35 "The Oklahoma Bombing Conspirators". http://law2.umkc.edu/faculty/projects/ftrials/mcveigh/conspirators.html
36 Andrew Gumbel, "Oklahoma City bombing: 20 years later, key questions remain unanswered", The Guardian, 13 April 2015. www.theguardian.com/us-news/2015/apr/13/oklahoma-city-bombing-20-years-later-key-questions-remain-unanswered
37 "A study of the Oklahoma City Bombing", Homeland Security Television, 2006.
38 David C. Teague, "Mass casualties in the Oklahoma City bombing", National Library of Medicine, 2004. https://pubmed.ncbi.nlm.nih.gov/15187837/
39 "Library Factfiles: The Oklahoma City Bombing", The Indianapolis Star, 9 August 2004.
40 Kathleen Belew, "Bring the War Home: The White Power Movement and Paramilitary America". Harvard University Press, 2018.
41 "Letter to honorable Janet Reno", 25 October 1994. www.splcenter.org/sites/default/files/d6_legacy_files/media/splc_letterjanetreno_okc.pdf

42 Ibid.
43 "Then and now, right-wing extremism in 1995 and 2015", Anti-Defamation League. www.adl.org/sites/default/files/documents/assets/pdf/combating-hate/Right-Wing-Extremism-in-1995-and-2015.pdf
44 "Ruby Ridge", Britannica. www.britannica.com/event/Ruby-Ridge
45 "Waco siege", History. www.history.com/topics/1990s/waco-siege
46 James Phillips, "Combatting terrorism in the wake of the Oklahoma City Bombing", The Heritage Foundation, 26 April 1995. www.heritage.org/homeland-security/report/combatting-terrorism-the-wake-the-oklahoma-city-bombing
47 "Man arrested in Oklahoma bomb plot that echoed 1995 attack", Reuters, 14 August 2017. www.reuters.com/article/us-oklahoma-crime-idUSKCN1AU1T6
48 Mike Levine, "Feds issue warning ahead of Oklahoma City bombing's 25th anniversary", ABC News, 16 April 2020. https://abcnews.go.com/Politics/feds-issue-warning-ahead-oklahoma-city-bombings-25th/story?id=70191809
49 "Anders Behring Breivik", The New York Times. www.nytimes.com/topic/person/anders-behring-breivik
50 "Norway attacks", BBC News. www.bbc.co.uk/news/world-europe-14261716
51 Cato Hemmingby and Tore Bjørgo, "Terrorist target selection: The case of Anders Behring Breivik". Perspectives on Terrorism, 12(6), 2018.
52 Owen Good and Michael McWhertor, "Oslo terrorist used Modern Warfare 2 as 'training-simulation', World of Warcraft as Cover", Kotaku, 23 July 2011. https://kotaku.com/oslo-terrorist-used-modern-warfare-2-as-training-simul-5824147
53 Will Englund and Michael Birnbaum, "Suspect in Norway attacks admits involvement, denies responsibility", The Washington Post, 24 July 2011.
54 Torgeir Huseby and Synne Sørheim, "Forensic psychiatric statement Breivik, Anders Behring", TV2, 29 November 2011.
55 Paul Ames, "Is Anders Behring Breivik part of a movement?", Global Post, 25 July 2011. www.pri.org/stories/2011-07-25/anders-behring-breivik-part-movement
56 Raffaello Pantucci, "What have we learnt about lone wolves from Anders Behring Breivik?". Perspectives on Terrorism, 5(5–6), 2011.
57 Mark Townsend and Simon Tisdall, "Defiant from the doc, Breivik boasts more will die", The Guardian, 25 July 2011. www.theguardian.com/world/2011/jul/25/anders-behring-breivik-terror-cells
58 "Norwegian man gets 21 years for slaying, mosque attack", VOA News, 11 June 2011. www.voanews.com/europe/norwegian-man-gets-21-years-slaying-mosque-attack
59 Asne Seierstad, "Is Norwegian mass murderer Anders Breivik still a threat to Europe?", Newsweek, 13 April 2016. www.newsweek.com/anders-breivik-neo-nazi-suing-norway-asne-seierstad-447247
60 Europol, "TE-SAT 2011: EU terrorism situation and trend report".
61 "Radicalisation awareness network". https://icct.nl/project/radicalisation-awareness-network-2021/
62 Ahmed S. Hashim, "Terrorism as an instrument of cultural warfare: The meaning of Anders Breivik". Counter Terrorist Trends and Analyses, 3(8), August 2011.
63 "Vojtěch Mlýnek", The Knights Templar Europe Report, 30 September 2012. https://knightstemplareurope.wordpress.com/2012/09/30/vojtech-mlynek/
64 "Polish professor jailed for plot to bomb parliament building", BBC News, 22 December 2015. www.bbc.com/news/world-europe-35159074

65 Asne Seierstad, "Is Norwegian mass murderer Anders Breivik still a threat to Europe?".
66 Singre Bangstad, "Norway is in denial about the threat of far-right violence", The Guardian, 16 September 2019. www.theguardian.com/commentisfree/2019/sep/16/norway-denial-far-right-violence-breivik
67 "Threat assessment 2019", Norwegian Police Security Service. https://pst.no/alle-artikler/trusselvurderinger/trusselvurdering-2019/#h5sectionTitleAnchor3
68 "Norwegian man gets 21 years for slaying, mosque attack", VOA News, 11 June 2011. www.voanews.com/europe/norwegian-man-gets-21-years-slaying-mosque-attack
69 Paul Ames, "Is Anders Behring Breivik part of a movement?", Global Post, 25 July 2011. www.pri.org/stories/2011-07-25/anders-behring-breivik-part-movement
70 Praveen Swami, "Anders Breivik and Europe's bling right eye", The Hindu, 25 July 2011. www.thehindu.com/opinion/lead/anders-breivik-europes-blind-right-eye/article2290619.ece
71 Matthew Tempest, "Commissioner warns of 'growing menace' of right-wing terrorism in EU", Euractiv, 23 March 2017. www.euractiv.com/section/politics/news/commissioner-warns-of-growing-menace-of-right-wing-terrorism-in-eu/
72 "Nine years on from the far-right terrorist attacks in Norway, and the threat persists", Muslim Engagement and Development, 27 July 2020. www.mend.org.uk/nine-years-on-from-the-far-right-terrorist-attacks-in-norway-and-the-threat-persists/
73 Aquil Haziq Mahmud, "16-year-old Singaporean detained under ISA after planning to attack Muslims at 2 mosques", CNA, 27 January 2021. www.channelnewsasia.com/news/singapore/16-year-old-singaporean-detained-isa-planned-attack-2-mosques-14052400
74 "Singapore boy held for Christchurch-inspired mosque attack plot", BBC News, 28 January 2021. www.bbc.com/news/world-asia-55836774
75 Aquil Haziq Mahmud, "16-year-old Singaporean detained under ISA after planning to attack Muslims at 2 mosques".
76 Hans Mathias Moeller, "Terrorism in Southeast Asia: Singapore in the crosshairs?", Global Risk Insights, 20 April 2017. https://globalriskinsights.com/2017/04/singapore-crosshairs/
77 "The Fight Against Terror", National Security Coordination Centre (NSCC), Singapore, 2004.
78 Gavin Chua Hearn Yuit, "Singapore's approach to counterterrorism". CTC Sentinel, 2(12), 2009. https://ctc.usma.edu/wp-content/uploads/2010/08/CTCSentinel-Vol2Iss12-art7.pdf
79 "Challenges for IRCCs", Straits Times, 14 January 2007.
80 "Community development: Promote racial harmony & community bonding", Government of Singapore's eCitizen portal, 28 February 2007.
81 "Community engagement programme". www.mom.gov.sg/~/media/mom/documents/employment-practices/cep/cep%20pamphlet.pdf?la=en
82 Kumar Ramakrishna, "A holistic critique of Singapore's counter ideological program". CTC Sentinel, 2(1), 2009.
83 "Launch of SS 545 Singapore standard for hotel security", SPRING Singapore, 27 August 2009.

84 Hans Mathias Moeller, "Terrorism in Southeast Asia: Singapore in the crosshairs?", Global Risk Insights, 20 April 2017. https://globalriskinsights.com/2017/04/singapore-crosshairs/
85 "Singapore infocomm technology security authority set up to safeguard Singapore against IT security threats", Singapore Ministry of Home Affairs, 1 October 2009.
86 Prashanth Parameswaran, "Singapore launches biggest anti-terror drill", The Diplomat, 18 October 2016. https://thediplomat.com/2016/10/singapore-launches-biggest-anti-terror-drill/
87 Ng Jun Sen, "Mounting challenge to identify radicalised persons who plot in secret: Shanmugam", Today, 10 March 2021. www.todayonline.com/singapore/isd-faces-mounting-challenge-identifying-radicalised-persons-who-plot-secret-shanmugam
88 "Singapore teenager arrested for plotting attack on Muslims", Al-Jazeera, 27 January 2021. www.aljazeera.com/news/2021/1/27/singapore-arrests-teenager-for-plotting-attacks-against-muslims
89 Linette Lai, "Islamophobia: Singapore not exempt from global climate", The Straits Times, 24 March 2019. www.straitstimes.com/singapore/singapore-not-exempt-from-global-climate
90 Nick Miroff, "The agency founded because 9/11 is shifting to face the threat of domestic terrorism", The Washington Post, 14 February 2021. www.washingtonpost.com/national/dhs-domestic-extremism-threat/2021/02/14/41693dd0-672f-11eb-bf81-c618c88ed605_story.html
91 Graham Macklin, "The El Paso terrorist attack: The chain reaction of global right-wing terror", CTC Sentinel, December 2019. https://ctc.usma.edu/el-paso-terrorist-attack-chain-reaction-global-right-wing-terror/
92 Scott Glover and Majlie de Puy Kamp, "Exclusive: El Paso suspect's mother called police concerned about gun", CNN, 9 August 2019.
93 "Why domestic terrorism is an underestimated national threat", PBS, 5 August 2019. www.pbs.org/newshour/show/why-domestic-terrorism-is-an-underestimated-national-threat
94 "Poway attack illustrates danger right-wing extremists pose to Jews, Muslims", ADL, 2 May 2019. www.adl.org/blog/poway-attack-illustrates-danger-right-wing-extremists-pose-to-jews-muslims
95 "Tallahassee Shooter Appears to Have Been Racist Incel", ADL, 4 November 2018. www.adl.org/blog/tallahassee-shooter-appears-to-have-been-racist-incel
96 "Deadly shooting at Pittsburgh synagogue", ADL, 27 October 2018. www.adl.org/blog/deadly-shooting-at-pittsburgh-synagogue
97 Global Terrorism Database, START.
98 "Murder and extremism in the United States in 2018", ADL Center on Extremism, January 2019.
99 Texas Department of Public Safety, "Assessing the mass attacks threat to Texas", January 2020. www.dps.texas.gov/sites/default/files/documents/director_staff/media_and_communications/2020/txmassattackassessment.pdf
100 Eliott C. Mclaughlin, Andy Rose, and Konstantin Toropin, "Prosecutors: Arizona shooting suspect says he targeted couples", The Mercury News, 21 May 2020. www.mercurynews.com/2020/05/21/prosecutors-arizona-shooting-suspect-says-he-targeted-couples/
101 "The El Paso attack, one year later: Extremist threat remains high", ADL, 31 July 2020. www.adl.org/blog/the-el-paso-attack-one-year-later-extremist-threat-remains-high

102 "Report to the nation: 2019 Factbook on hate and extremism in the US and internationally", Center for the Study of Hate and Extremism. www.csusb.edu/sites/default/files/CSHE%202019%20Report%20to%20the%20Nation%20FINAL%207.29.19%2011%20PM.pdf
103 Jeff Pegues, "FBI warns of the 'continued threat' of violent extremists and hate crimes", CBS, 5 August 2019. www.cbsnews.com/news/fbi-warns-of-continued-threat-violent-extremists-hate-crimes-2019-08-05/
104 2,600 incidents were recorded for the first seven months of 2020, 2,724 for the entire 2019. "The El Paso attack, one year later: Extremist threat remains high", ADL, 31 July 2020. www.adl.org/blog/the-el-paso-attack-one-year-later-extremist-threat-remains-high
105 "The El Paso attack, one year later: Extremist threat remains high", ADL, 31 July 2020. www.adl.org/blog/the-el-paso-attack-one-year-later-extremist-threat-remains-high
106 Codell Rodriguez, "FBI arrests Horizon City man alleged active shooter threats against El Paso Walmart stores", El Paso Times, 9 May 2020. https://eu.elpasotimes.com/story/news/2020/05/09/fbi-arrests-individual-active-shooter-threat-against-el-paso-walmarts/3102742001/
107 "Texas man who posted threatening video sentenced to prison", The Associated Press, 31 January 2021. www.nbcdfw.com/news/local/texas-news/texas-man-who-posted-threatening-video-sentenced-to-prison/2527907/
108 "Germany shooting: What we know about the Hanau attack", BBC News, 20 February 2020. www.bbc.com/news/world-europe-51571649
109 Lisa Hänel, "Mass shooting in Hanau: Grief and rage persist one year on", DW, 19 February 2021. www.dw.com/en/mass-shooting-in-hanau-grief-and-rage-persist-one-year-on/a-56612160
110 Mithu Sanyal, "The Hanau terror attack shows the need for honesty about racism in Germany", The Guardian, 3 March 2020. www.theguardian.com/world/commentisfree/2020/mar/03/hanau-terror-attack-germany-racism-angela-merkel
111 Philip Oltermann and Kate Connolly, "Germany shooting: far-right gunman kills 10 in Hanau", The Guardian, 20 February 2021. www.theguardian.com/world/2020/feb/19/shooting-germany-hanau-dead-several-people-shisha-near-frankfurt
112 "IntelBrief: Far-right terrorist attack puts Germany on edge", The Soufan Center, 21 February 2020. https://thesoufancenter.org/intelbrief-far-right-terrorist-attack-puts-germany-on-edge/
113 Mattia Caniglia, Linda Winkler, and Solène Métais, "The rise of the right-wing violent extremism threat in Germany and its transnational character", 2 March 2020. www.esisc.org/publications/analyses/the-rise-of-the-right-wing-violent-extremism-threat-in-germany-and-its-transnational-character
114 "Hanau: Germany boosts security amid far-right threat", BBC, 21 February 2020. www.bbc.com/news/world-europe-51586283
115 Jorg Luyken, "'Alarming' rise in far-Right weapons seizures prompts Germany to beef up police power", Telegraph, 2019. www.telegraph.co.uk/news/2019/09/29/alarming-rise-far-right-weapons-seizures-prompts-germany-beef
116 The Federal Government, "A clear signal in the fight against right-wing extremism and racism", 25 November 2020. www.bundesregierung.de/breg-en/news/cabinet-right-wing-extremism-1820094

117 Cabinet Committee, “A clear signal in the fight against right-wing extremism and racism”. www.bundesregierung.de/breg-en/news/cabinet-right-wing-extremism-1820094
118 “Bomb at the Olympics; heart ailment kills war survivor in Atlanta”, The New York Times, 28 July 1996.
119 Jeffrey Gettleman and David M. Halbfinger, “Suspect in ‘96 Olympic Bombing and 3 other attacks is caught”, The New York Times, 1 June 2003.
120 “Bombing at Centennial Olympic Park”, History. www.history.com/this-day-in-history/bombing-at-centennial-olympic-park
121 “Eric Rudolph”, Bureau of Alcohol, Tobacco, Firearms and Explosives. www.atf.gov/our-history/eric-rudolph
122 “Olympic Bomb suspect Rudolph caught”, ABC News, 7 January 2006. https://abcnews.go.com/WNT/story?id=129666&page=1
123 “Eric Rudolph”, FBI History. www.fbi.gov/history/famous-cases/eric-rudolph
124 “Arrest of accused Olympic Park Bomber sparks debate on ‘Christian Terrorism’ ”, VOA News, 5 June 2003.
125 Crystal Bonvillian, “Serial bomber Eric Rudolph targeted Olympics, gay club, abortion clinics”, Atlanta Journal-Constitution, 19 March 2018.
126 Lars Endal, “Radicalization and lone wolf terrorism: A case study of right wing terrorists”, M.Sc. Thesis, Noragric, 2018. https://nmbu.brage.unit.no/nmbu-xmlui/bitstream/handle/11250/2503433/Endal%202018.pdf?sequence=5&isAllowed=y
127 David Sterman, “The greater danger: Military-trained right-wing extremists”, The Atlantic, 24 April 2013. www.theatlantic.com/national/archive/2013/04/the-greater-danger-military-trained-right-wing-extremists/275277/
128 Becky Little, “Why the hunt for the Real Atlanta Bomber took nearly 7 years”, History.com., 13 December 2019. www.history.com/news/atlanta-bombing-richard-jewell-domestic-terror-investigation
129 “Centennial Olympic Park Bombing: A warning shot from the alt-right we never knew”, The Shadow League, 31 January 2019. https://theshadowleague.com/centennial-olympic-park-bombing-a-warning-shot-from-the-alt-right-we-never-knew/
130 Seth Jones, “The rise of far-right extremism in the United States”, CSIS, 7 November 2018.
131 US Department of Homeland Security, “Right-wing extremism: Current economic and political climate fuelling resurgence in radicalization and recruitment”, 7 April 2009. https://fas.org/irp/eprint/rightwing.pdf
132 Ibid.
133 Ibid.
134 Charles P. Blair, “Looking clearly at right-win terrorism”, Bulletin of the Atomic Scientists, 9 June 2014. https://thebulletin.org/2014/06/looking-clearly-at-right-wing-terrorism/
135 Jean Marbella, “Berkeley recalls little about bomb suspect: Assistant professor left few traces in 1969 when he abruptly quit TTC”, Baltimore Sun, 7 April 1996.
136 William Glaberson, “The unabomber case: The overview, Kaczynski avoids a death sentence with guilty plea”, The New York Times, 23 January 1998. www.nytimes.com/1998/01/23/us/unabomber-case-overview-kaczynski-avoids-death-sentence-with-guilty-plea.html
137 “Excerpts from letter by ‘terrorist group’, FC, which says it sent bombs”, The New York Times, 26 April 1995.

138 Ken Frazier, "Disabling the unabomber's final bomb: Objective was not just to defuse it, but to surgically defuse it, says Christ Cherry", Sandia Lab News, 13 February 1998.
139 "Affidavit of Assistant Special Agent in Charge", Court TV, 18 December 2008.
140 Caleb Crain, "The Bard's fingerprints". Lingua Franca, 29–39, 1998.
141 Louise Boyle, "The rising threat of eco-fascism: Far right co-opting environmentalism to justify anti-immigration and anti-Semitic views", Independent, 20 March 2021. www.independent.co.uk/climate-change/news/ecofascism-immigration-anti-semitism-b1819718.html
142 Alexander C. Kaufman, "Eco-fascism featured in El Paso terrorism suspect's alleged manifesto", HCN, 6 August 2019. www.hcn.org/articles/climate-desk-eco-fascism-featured-in-el-paso-terrorism-suspects-alleged-manifesto
143 Ardian Shajkovci, Allison McDowell-Smith, and Mohamed Ahmed, "Eco-Fascist 'Pine Tree Party' growing as a violent extremism threat", Homeland Security Today.US, 27 September 2020. www.hstoday.us/subject-matter-areas/counterterrorism/eco-fascist-pine-tree-party-growing-as-a-violent-extremism-threat/
144 Alex Chitty, "COVID-19: The return of eco-fascism", The Gryphon, 8 April 2020. www.thegryphon.co.uk/2020/04/08/covid-19-the-return-of-eco-fascism/
145 Jason Wilson, "Eco-fascism is undergoing a revival in the fetid culture of the extreme right", The Guardian, 19 March 2019. www.theguardian.com/world/commentisfree/2019/mar/20/eco-fascism-is-undergoing-a-revival-in-the-fetid-culture-of-the-extreme-right
146 Evangelos D. Protopapadakis, "Environmental ethics and Linkola's ecofascism: An ethics behind humanism". Frontiers of Philosophy in China, 9(4), 2014. www.jstor.org/stable/44156920?seq=1
147 Alex Chitty, "COVID-19: The return of eco-fascism", The Gryphon, 8 April 2020. www.thegryphon.co.uk/2020/04/08/covid-19-the-return-of-eco-fascism/
148 Alexander Morgan, "Are the COVID-19 lockdowns sparking a rise on eco-fascism?", Euronews, 5 August 2020. www.euronews.com/2020/05/08/are-the-covid-19-lockdowns-sparking-a-rise-in-eco-fascism-culture-clash
149 Harriet Alexander, "White supremacist Michael Holt sentenced to 4.5 years for weapons, child porn offences", The Sydney Morning Herald, 29 September 2017. www.smh.com.au/national/nsw/white-supremacist-michael-holt-sentenced-to-45-years-for-weapons-child-porn-offences-20170929-gyrmuf.html
150 Rachel Olding, "White supremacist threatened to shoot up Central Coast shopping centre", The Sydney Morning Herald, 28 January 2017. www.smh.com.au/national/nsw/white-supremacist-threatened-to-shoot-up-sydney-shopping-centre-20170120-gtvod0.html
151 "Alleged neo-Nazi reportedly plotted shooting at New South Wales mall", The Guardian, 28 January 2017. www.theguardian.com/australia-news/2017/jan/29/alleged-neo-nazi-reportedly-plotted-shooting-at-new-south-wales-mall
152 Ben Doherty, "Asio boss warns of rising foreign interference and far-right extremism in Australia", The Guardian, 24 February 2020. www.theguardian.com/australia-news/2020/feb/24/rightwing-extremism-a-real-and-growing-threat-asio-chief-says-in-annual-assessment
153 Australian Government Australian Security Intelligence Organisation, "ASIO Annual Report 2017–18". www.asio.gov.au/sites/default/files/ASIO%20Annual%20Report%20to%20Parliament%202017-18.pdf

154 Clive Williams, "Right-wing extremists were already on spy agencies' radars", Canberra Times, 23 March 2019. www.canberratimes.com.au/story/5992498/right-wing-extremists-were-already-on-spy-agencies-radars/
155 "Right-wing extremism on rise", SBS News, 2 June 2017. www.sbs.com.au/news/right-wing-extremism-on-rise
156 Zeb Holmes and Ugur Nedim, "Right-wing extremists: The real terrorism threat", Sydney Criminal Lawyers, 18 March 2019. www.sydneycriminallawyers.com.au/blog/right-wing-extremists-the-real-terrorism-threat/
157 "Right-wing extremism on rise", SBS News, 2 June 2017. www.sbs.com.au/news/right-wing-extremism-on-rise
158 Executive Council of Australian Jewry, "Antisemitism in Australia 2020: Incidents and discourse". www.ecaj.org.au/wordpress/wp-content/uploads/Condensed-Antisemitism-Report-Australia-2020.pdf
159 Caitlin Fitzsimmons, "Eight of if 10 Asia-Australians experience discrimination: Survey". The Sydney Morning Herald, 22 September 2019. www.smh.com.au/business/workplace/eight-out-of-10-asian-australians-experience-discrimination-survey-20190920-p52tfp.html
160 Australian Government Australian Security Intelligence Organisation, "ASIO Annual Report 2019–20". www.asio.gov.au/asio-report-parliament.html
161 Joshua Mcdonald, "Australia: Far-right on the rise as intelligence chief warns of terror threat", The Diplomat, 28 February 2020. https://thediplomat.com/2020/02/australia-far-right-on-the-rise-as-intelligence-chief-warns-of-terror-threat/
162 Australian Government Australian Security Intelligence Organisation, "ASIO Annual Report 2019–20". www.asio.gov.au/asio-report-parliament.html
163 Parliament of Australia, "Terms of reference". www.aph.gov.au/Parliamentary_Business/Committees/Joint/Intelligence_and_Security/ExtremistMovements/Terms_of_Reference
164 Tom Lowrey and David Lipson, "Neo-Nazi Sonnenkrieg Division to become first right-wing terrorist organisation listed in Australia", ABC News, 2 March 2021. www.abc.net.au/news/2021-03-02/sonnenkrieg-division-first-right-wing-terror-group-listed/13206756
165 Alexander Darling, Sarah Jane Bell, and Matt Neal, "Calls for cross-burning neo-Nazis camped in The Grampians to be classified as terrorist group", ABC News, 28 January 2021. www.abc.net.au/news/2021-01-28/calls-grampians-far-right-group-labelled-terrorist-organisation/13098762
166 US Department of Homeland Security, "Homeland threat assessment October 2020".
167 Del Quentin Wilber, "FBI director says Capitol riot was 'domestic terrorism'", Los Angeles Times, 2 March 2021. www.latimes.com/politics/story/2021-03-02/fbi-wray-testify-congress-capitol-siege
168 "The Capitol Siege: The arrested and their stories", NPR, 5 March 2021. www.npr.org/sections/insurrection-at-the-capitol/2021/01/19/958240531/members-of-right-wing-militias-extremist-groups-are-latest-charged-in-capitol-si
169 Roberto Schmidt, "Members of right-wing militias, extremist groups are latest charged in Capitol Siege", NPR, 19 January 2021. www.npr.org/sections/insurrection-at-the-capitol/2021/01/19/958240531/members-of-right-wing-militias-extremist-groups-are-latest-charged-in-capitol-si
170 Sophie Lewis, "Capitol Police warns of 'possible plot to breach the Capitol' by militia group", CBS News, 3 March 2021. www.cbsnews.com/news/capitol-police-increase-security-march-4-qanon-conspiracy-theory/

171 The George Washington University Program on Extremism, "This is our house! A preliminary assessment of the Capitol Hill siege participants", March 2021.
172 Andrew Selsky, "Capitol attack reflects US extremist evolution over decades", AP News, 23 January 2021. https://apnews.com/article/capitol-siege-riots-coronavirus-pandemic-b7123f0a223c6ed8098a03b459120c83
173 Bruce Hoffman and Jacob Ware, "Terrorism and counterterrorism challenges for the Biden administration", CTC Sentinel, January 2021. https://ctc.usma.edu/wp-content/uploads/2021/01/CTC-SENTINEL-012021.pdf
174 Vera Bergengruen and W. J. Hennigan, "'They are fighting blind.' Inside the Biden administration's uphill battle against far-right extremism", Time, 4 March 2021. https://time.com/5944085/far-right-extremism-biden/
175 Southern Poverty Law Center, "Hate groups reach record high", 19 February 2019. www.splcenter.org/news/2019/02/19/hate-groups-reach-record-high
176 Seth G. Jones, Catrina Doxsee, and Nicholas Harrington, "The escalating terrorism problem in the United States", June 2020. https://csis-website-prod.s3.amazonaws.com/s3fs-public/publication/200612_Jones_DomesticTerrorism_v6.pdf
177 US Department of Homeland Security, "Homeland threat assessment", October 2020. www.dhs.gov/sites/default/files/publications/2020_10_06_homeland-threat-assessment.pdf
178 Zolan Kanno-Youngs and Nicholas Fandos, "DHS downplayed threats from Russia and white supremacists, whistle blower says", The New York Times, 9 September 2020. www.nytimes.com/2020/09/09/us/politics/homeland-security-russia-trump.html
179 Farrah Tomazin, "Inspired by the Capitol siege, extremists remain top of terror list", The Sydney Morning Herald, 20 January 2021. www.smh.com.au/world/north-america/inspired-by-the-capitol-siege-extremists-remain-top-of-terror-list-20210120-p56vj8.html
180 United States Capitol Police, "Capitol police increase security following threat", 3 March 2021. www.uscp.gov/media-center/press-releases/capitol-police-increase-security-following-threat
181 Vera Bergengruen, "'A real nightmare.' State capitols are racing to catch up to the far-right threat", Time, 13 January 2021. https://time.com/5929296/far-right-extremism-state-capitols/
182 Lois Beckett, "Armed protesters demonstrate against Covid-19 lockdown at Michigan capitol", The Guardian, 30 April 2020. www.theguardian.com/us-news/2020/apr/30/michigan-protests-coronavirus-lockdown-armed-capitol
183 Andrew Prokop, "Charges announced in plot to kidnap the governor of Michigan", VOX, 8 October 2020. www.vox.com/2020/10/8/21507895/michigan-governor-whitmer-kidnapping-militia
184 US Department of Homeland Security, "National terrorism advisory system bulletin", 27 January 2021. www.dhs.gov/ntas/advisory/national-terrorism-advisory-system-bulletin-january-27-2021
185 Vera Bergengruen and W. J. Hennigan, "'They are fighting blind.' Inside the Biden Administration's uphill battle against far-right extremism", Time, 4 March 2021. https://time.com/5944085/far-right-extremism-biden/
186 Ibid.
187 Christopher Matias, "Amid the pandemic, US militia groups plot 'The Boogaloo' AKA civil war, on Facebook", Huffpost, 24 April 2020. www.huffpost.com/entry/boogaloo-facebook-pages-coronavirus-militia-group-extremists_n_5ea3072bc5b6d376358eba98

188 Vanda Felbab-Brown, "US policing after wave one of COVID-19", Lawfare, 20 May 2020. www.lawfareblog.com/us-policing-after-wave-one-covid-19
189 "White supremacist propaganda spikes in 2020", ADL. www.adl.org/white-supremacist-propaganda-spikes-2020
190 Steve Vockrodt, "FBI: Government's response to virus incited would-be bomber", Stars and Stripes, 15 April 2020. www.stripes.com/news/us/fbi-government-s-response-to-virus-incited-would-be-bomber-1.626141
191 Federal Bureau of Investigation, "White supremacist infiltration of law enforcement", 17 October 2006. https://oversight.house.gov/sites/democrats.oversight.house.gov/files/White_Supremacist_Infiltration_of_Law_Enforcement.pdf
192 Jessica White, "Far-right extremism in the US: A threat no longer ignored", RUSI Commentary, 1 February 2021. https://rusi.org/commentary/far-right-extremism-us-threat-no-longer-ignored
193 Ibid.

INDEX

Printed in the United States
by Baker & Taylor Publisher Services